Giorgio Piola
formula1
technical analysis 2000

2 The season 2000

6 Chassis history

14 Table of cars

16 Table of engines

18 Engines 2000

22 The new regulations

26 Controversy in 2000

29 New features and trends

33 Cockpits, pedals and steering wheels

Talking about brakes and tyres **36**

Talking about suspension **42**

Talking about downforce **46**

Talking about underbodies **54**

Talking about noses **58**

The two rivals **64**

The secrets of 2000 F1 **66**

Teams' technical development **70**

GIORGIO NADA EDITORE

THE SEASON 2000

The 2000 Formula One season saw little in the way of new technical developments, on which this publication is based, but assumed almost historic proportions due to Michael Schumacher winning the world drivers' title in his Ferrari. A victory that almost relegates to a second level the fact that no other team was able to win a single race, except the two title contenders Ferrari and McLaren: a sign of a certain technological delay, compared to the two leaders. The ambitions of Jaguar and Jordan, based on the potential they showed in the '99 season, sank without trace in a year to be forgotten by both teams. The interest created by the great competitiveness of the Rosse or red cars from Maranello, made up for the technical alignment that characterised the year. It should be remembered that it was the last season in a cycle that began in '98, with the reduction of the track and the introduction of grooved tyres, both measures that enlivened the technical side. A situation that should repeat itself in 2001, due to the aerodynamic limitations introduced by the Federation, and the competitive climate created between Bridgestone and the return of Michelin. So there remains the fact that the world drivers' title had not been won by Ferrari since the distant 1979 triumph of Jody Scheckter and the famous T4. The 2000 success came a year after the team had won the constructors' cup, which it did in spite of Schumacher's dramatic accident in the Gp of Great Britain: a mishap that pushed Eddie Irvine into the role of duellist with the McLaren drivers. But the 1999 constructors' championship satisfied a hunger which had existed at Maranello since it last won that title in 1983. Winning both championships in 2000, the drivers' a race before the season ended, no less, is due

Ferrari F1 2000

THE LAST WORLD CHAMPION

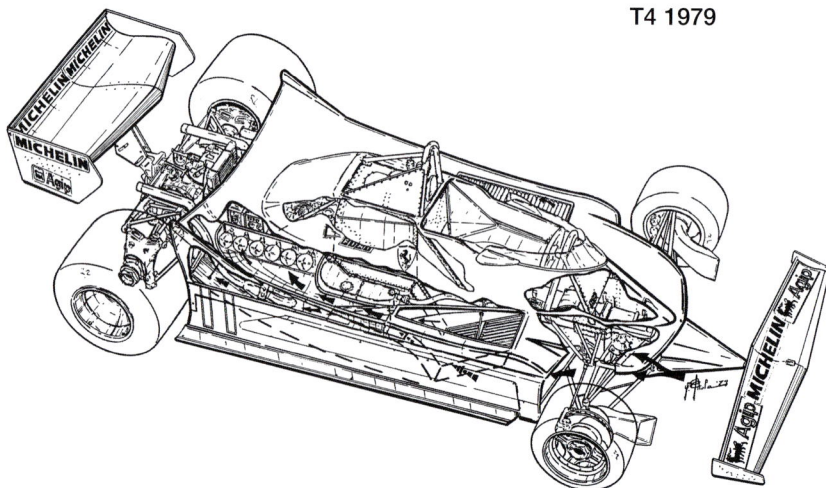

T4 1979

It was back in 1979 that Ferrari won its last F1 world drivers' championship. The driver was Jody Scheckter and the car was the T4. A car in every respect light years behind the F1 2000 that enabled Michael Schumacher to beat the McLaren Mercedes of Mika Hakkinen. Designed by Mauro Forghieri, it was one of the last cars with a semi-tubular chassis in aluminium, before the advent of sandwich panels, introduced by Harvey Postlethwaite with the C2 of 1982, followed in 1983 by the first carbon fibre chassis of the C3. Light years away, starting with the engine, the legendary 12- cylinder boxer, a car with mini-skirts along the sides and winged profiles, the suspension with springs and shock absorbers, to conclude with the tyres, Michelin of France in place of Bridgestone of

McLaren MP4/15

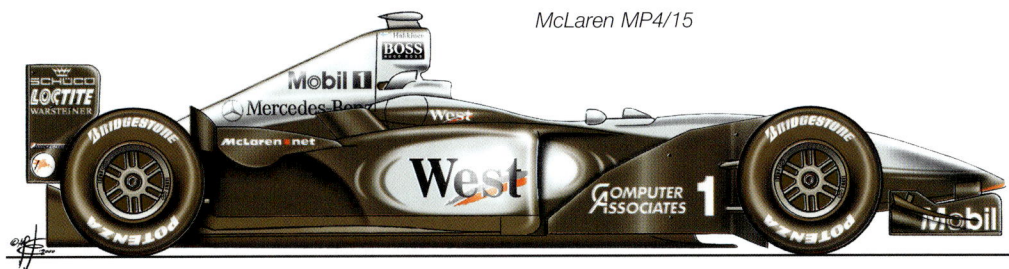

Williams FW22

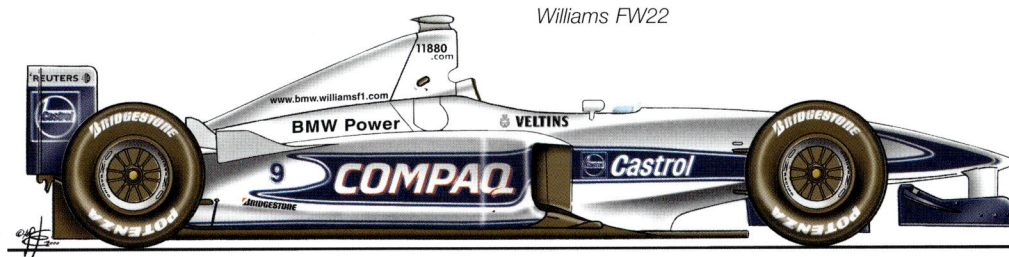

T4 Monaco

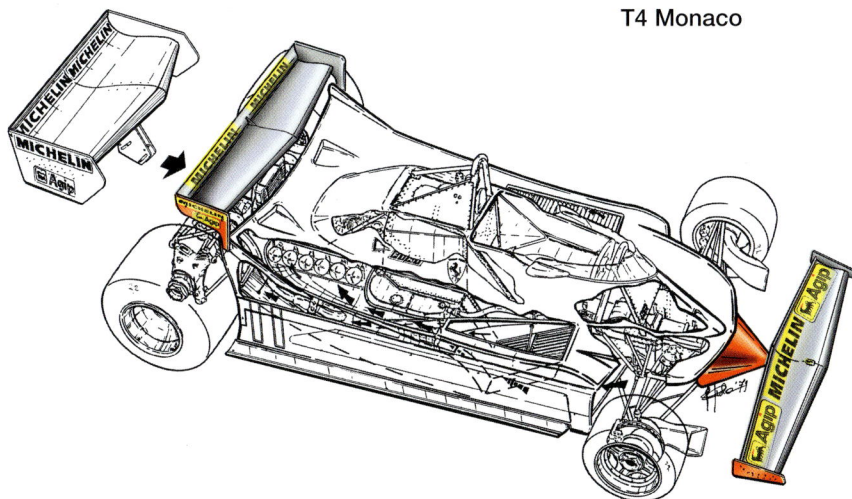

Japan. The enormous engine air intake shows the different regulation limits, also noticeable from the dimensions of the big wings. Next to the basic version, the T4 is shown on the grid at Monaco, with the front wing close to the body of the car and the rear wing in front of the axle, so as to utilise the whole 140 cm length of the plane.

TECHNICAL OUTLINE FERRARI T4

wheelbase	2700 mm
front track	1700 mm
rear track	1600 mm
engine	12 cylinder boxer
gearbox	five speed Ferrari
weight	584 kg
tyres	Michelin

not only to the bravura of Schumacher, but also to the F1 2000, a car that showed it was competitive against its rival Mp4/15 from the first race of the season in Australia, shattering the tradition that had consolidated itself in recent years, which saw Ferrari always chasing, first Williams and in the last two seasons McLaren. Schumacher's three consecutive victories at the beginning of the championship laid serious claim to the title, with the German at the head of the drivers' table. A leadership that he lost at the Gp of Belgium, due to a negative period during the summer Grands Prix. Designed by Rory Byrne under the direction of Ross Brawn, the two architects of Schumacher's first two world championships at Benetton, the F1-2000 was, perhaps, the most innovative Ferrari of recent years. A successful car from the start, it needed further mainly detailed development, with great attention paid to aerodynamics, which revealed themselves once again to be slightly below the level of their rival, McLaren. Almost like a film script repeated many times, the evolution started at the Gp of France, but not with the major changes of previous seasons. Two important new developments were introduced at Magny Cours, both inspired by McLaren: a "wooden" plank in Stellite adopted by the rival MP4/15 at the Gp of Canada, that permitted a reduction in chafing when in contact with the ground, and chimneys for the hot air side vents. At first, the chimneys were only tried in testing and remained unused in racing until the Gp of Hungary, where they were brought in to combat the torrid heat radiating from the Hungaroring track surface. At the Gp of Great Britain, there was an important adjustment to the position of the ballast, moved further forward to improve

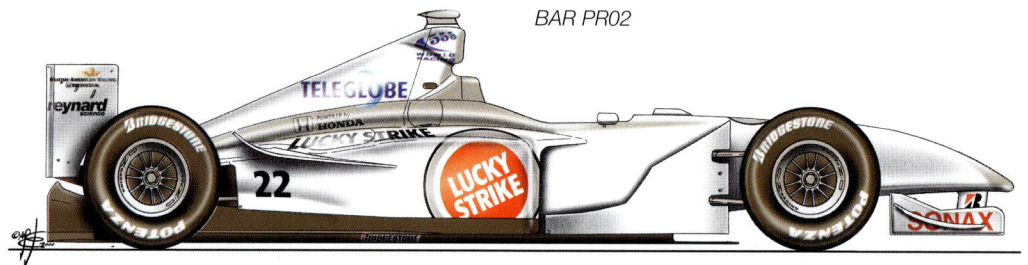
BAR PR02

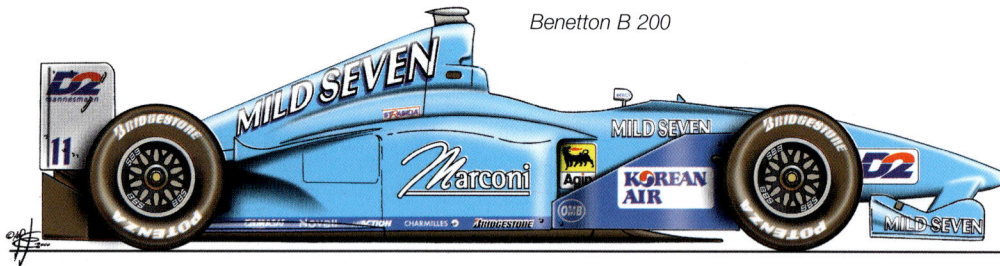
Benetton B 200

exploitation of the front tyres. The latter a sector that created difficulty for rivals McLaren, comfortable with the softer tyres supplied by Bridgestone. From that point, there was a two-phased introduction of a total of seven sensors to monitor the temperature of the rear tyres on the track. The desire to forge ahead in an attempt to recoup the disadvantage accumulated at the Gp of Hungary against the MP4/15 prompted the simultaneous introduction in Belgium of too many new developments, which ended up reducing the competitiveness of the Rosse. But that situation had already been corrected by the next race at Monza, where Ferrari went back to being slightly superior to the McLarens. And the reason for the success was the renewed 10-cylinder engine, designed in line with the global needs of the project, which meant a notable reduction in centre of gravity and weight of the last version, the 049C, which was introduced at the Gp of Belgium, but used only for qualifying until the Gp of Japan. An engine, however, that was worth pole position in the race at which Ferrari won the world drivers' championship, one grand prix before the season ended. A contribution also came from the aerodynamics, wisely tested at Mugello and characterised by the disappearance of the delta-type front wing, which was substituted by a rectangular plan. The greater reliability of the 10-cylinder Ferrari, compared to the rival Mercedes, was one of the strong points in Michael Schumacher's battle for the title: he only retired once with engine failure, at the Gp of France. As in previous seasons, Ferrari was able to count on a technical advantage in the brake area with the use, even if no longer exclusive, of CCR discs supplied by Brembo, and the introduction at the second race of the season, of a qualifying system composed first of 21 mm thick discs against the 28 mm maximum allowed by the regulations, then successively smaller, lighter calipers. Developments that were used by McLaren only in the last three races.

Winning the world drivers' title at Suzuka with a race in hand was the result not only of the great driving ability of Michael Schumacher and the validity of the F1-2000, but also of a wise and inspired race strategy, which revealed itself to be a winner on more than one occasion, against that of the rivals McLaren: race tactics that are discussed in the chapter "The Secrets of the F1-2000" and do not regard any specific car development. McLaren seemed inferior to Ferrari in strategy, even considering Ron Dennis' team had its two drivers fighting for the title for much of the season. The MP4/15, from the "pencil" of Adrian Newey, appeared to be slightly

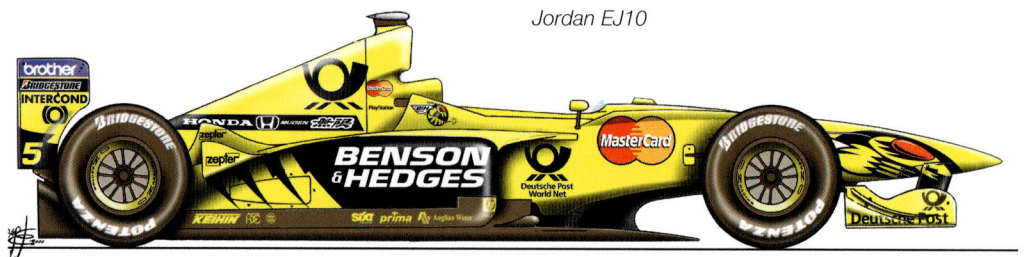
Jordan EJ10

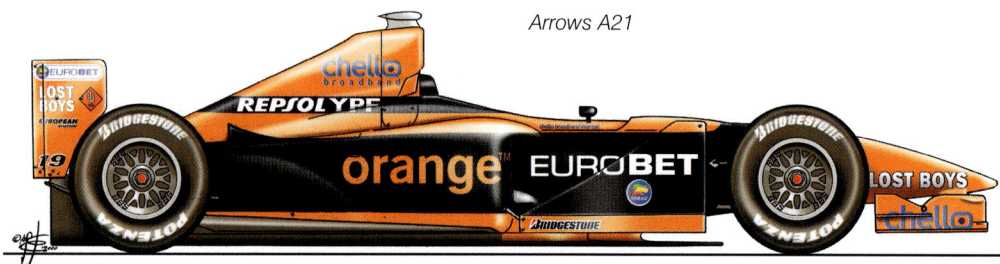
Arrows A21

inferior to the rival F1 2000 and, above all, at the beginning of the season, also seemed less reliable. While following the design of the previous year's car, the MP4/15 was rich in technical content and new developments, even though the most evident, the chimneys in front of the rear wheels to expel hot air from the sides, had already been seen way back in 1979 – by coincidence, the year of Ferrari's last dri-

Sauber C19

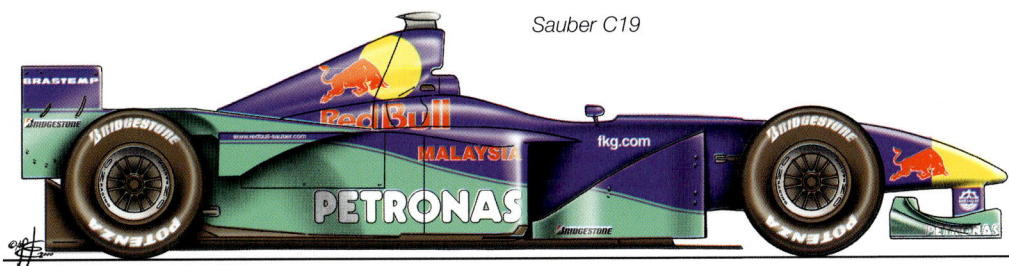

vers' title – on the Shadow DN9. At that time, the chimneys were considered an isolated experiment, but the idea brought back by Newey last season was copied by Ferrari and Williams, who used it in races in which there was a great need for thermal dissipation.

It was the season of the return to the top three of Williams, whose merit it was to bring BMW back to the world of Formula One for the first time since 1988. The team, directed by Patrick Head, produced a car which was unconventional in many ways, but which revealed itself very effective, achieving results that went well beyond those expected of it during a test season, particularly when considering that in '99 Williams, world champions with Jacques Villeneuve in '97, had slipped to fifth place in the constructors table. For their part, BMW produced an engine without great inventiveness but which revealed itself, particularly for a debutante, reliable and "sufficiently powerful" as Patrick Head described it. BAR made a big comeback, jumping from last place to fourth in the championship, thanks to the

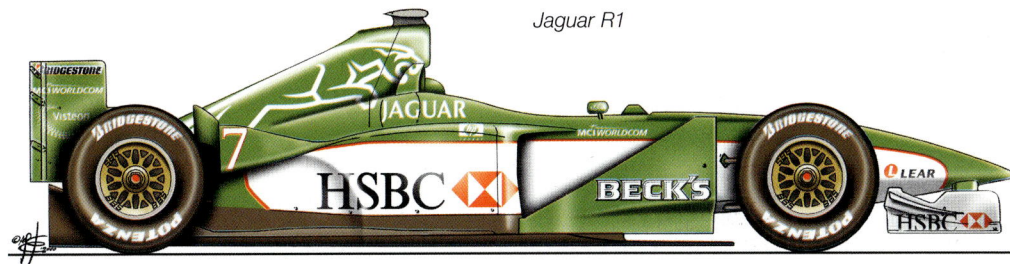

Jaguar R1

tors' championship, while Jordan dropped to sixth position.

The 2000 season was Bridgestone's goodbye to its two-year F1 monopoly, with the return of the French company Michelin in 2001. A return that will bring with it a notable escalation in performance, due to an intensification in tyre development as a result of open competition. For this reason, the Federation has introduced aerodynamic limitations for 2001 to try to reduce performance. From the safety point of view, 2000 was a positive season as far as drivers were concerned, the only negative being the acci-

dent that involved a CEA marshal at Monza, who was hit by a wheel from Frentzen's Jordan. An episode that convinced the Federation to double wheel retention cables, even if, in this case, the answer should be sought more in the standards of safety that should be guaranteed by the circuits, under certain circumstances, than at the level of progress made by the cars that race on them.

As with previous editions, it remains the sub-division by topic that highlights the developments that have taken place in the individual sectors of F1, even if this format may sometimes clash a little with the chapters regarding the single teams.

Although produced at the end of the season to avoid them containing only the approximate values of the official presentations, the compilation of the "car" and "engine" tables has, regardless, increasingly produced pigeon holes containing estimated values, as in the case of the "engines" table, compiled in collaboration with Engineer Enrico Benzing.

Prost AP03

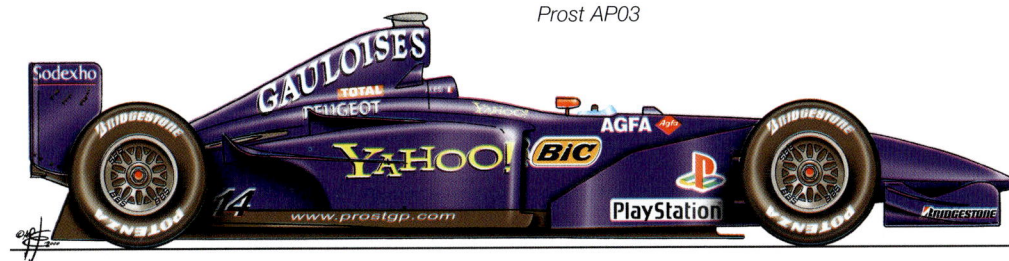

power of the 10 cylinder Honda in a car which was, however, very traditional. Failed ambitions after the promise of '99 for Jordan and Jaguar, respectively third and fourth (when Jaguar was Stewart) in the '99 season. The British car manufacturer, making its return to the world of F1 in pomp and circumstance by acquiring Stewart, completely failed to achieve its objective, coming ninth in the construc-

Minardi M02

CHASSIS
HISTORY

It has almost become a tradition to open the technical analysis of a Formula One season with graphs of the chassis, used during the year by the different teams. From their examination, it is possible to arrive at an initial understanding of the development of the various F1 cars, and of the teams' efforts to provide their drivers with continually updated material. In this third year after the introduction of grooved tyres and a narrower track, trends took shape that, in practice, slowed the creativity of the designers. Modified versions of the different models did not appear and neither did variations on the theme at mid-season, as was the case in 1998, when almost all the teams modified the two fundamental parameters of wheelbase and weight distribution. The number of destroyed chassis diminished: from eight in '98 to six in '99 down to three in 2000. A good result if the tragedy of Monza, which involved one of the many heroes of

the CEA safety service, had not negatively affected the safety factor and caused the death of Paolo Gislimberti. A tyre struck him in the spectacular and dramatic multi-car pile up during the opening stages of the Grand Prix of Italy. A tragedy that marred the celebration of Michael Schumacher's victory, in front of a sea of Prancing Horse fans. A harsh outcome of an accident that seemed like it had caused no injury to the drivers, and the loss of just one chassis, that of Pedro De La Rosa's Arrows which flew dangerously through the air over other cars to end up in the Roggia sand. There was criticism, once again, of the tyre retention cable, considered insufficient to stop a tyre and wheel unit in the case of a serious accident, so much so that the Federation opted to double the system for 2001. The Monza pile-up was a weekend late in happening: it followed the by now traditional appointment with such calamities at the Grand Prix of Belgium, which was the preceding GP. In 1998, Spa claimed no fewer than 13 cars, with four chassis destroyed and five damaged. The destruction of the first 2000 season monocoque took place in the narrow streets of the Principality of Monaco: it was Sauber number 03 of Pedro Paolo Diniz. The second chassis to be thrown away was the Arrows 05 of De La Rosa, while the last serious accident took place at the final race in Malaysia: it was Johnny Herbert's farewell GP, during

which the Englishman's Jaguar chassis number 06 was destroyed following a rear suspension break. It was necessary to carry out demanding repairs to chassis that were damaged in accidents, or which wandered onto the shoulder, no less than 25 times. As with the last two seasons, the number of teams remained at 11, the only variation being the change of name from Stewart to the glorious Jaguar.

The average maximum number of chassis built for the season further decreased by one. In 1998, Ferrari constructed nine monocoques, in 1999 eight, the same as its archrival McLaren and the debutant BAR. In 2000, the limit of eight units was reached only by Ferrari, followed by seven for McLaren, Williams, Benetton and Sauber. Four teams built six chassis: Jordan, Jaguar, Arrows and BAR. Prost also built five and Minardi four.

The "award" for the most successful chassis goes to the Ferrari 205, with four Schumacher victories out of a total of 10 scored by Maranello during the season; that is followed by three wins for Schumacher's 198 and Hakkinen's McLaren 06. There was one victory each for the Ferrari 200 and 203 with Schumacher driving, and one for the 202 driven by Barrichello, the McLaren 02 with Coulthard and the 04 with Hakkinen. Victory in the 2000 Grands Prix was monopolised by Ferrari and McLaren, with 10 and seven respectively.

The chassis that competed in most races was Minardi's 03, which took part in 16 races out of a possible 17, driven by Marc Gené, followed

MC LAREN • MP4/15 • N° 1-2

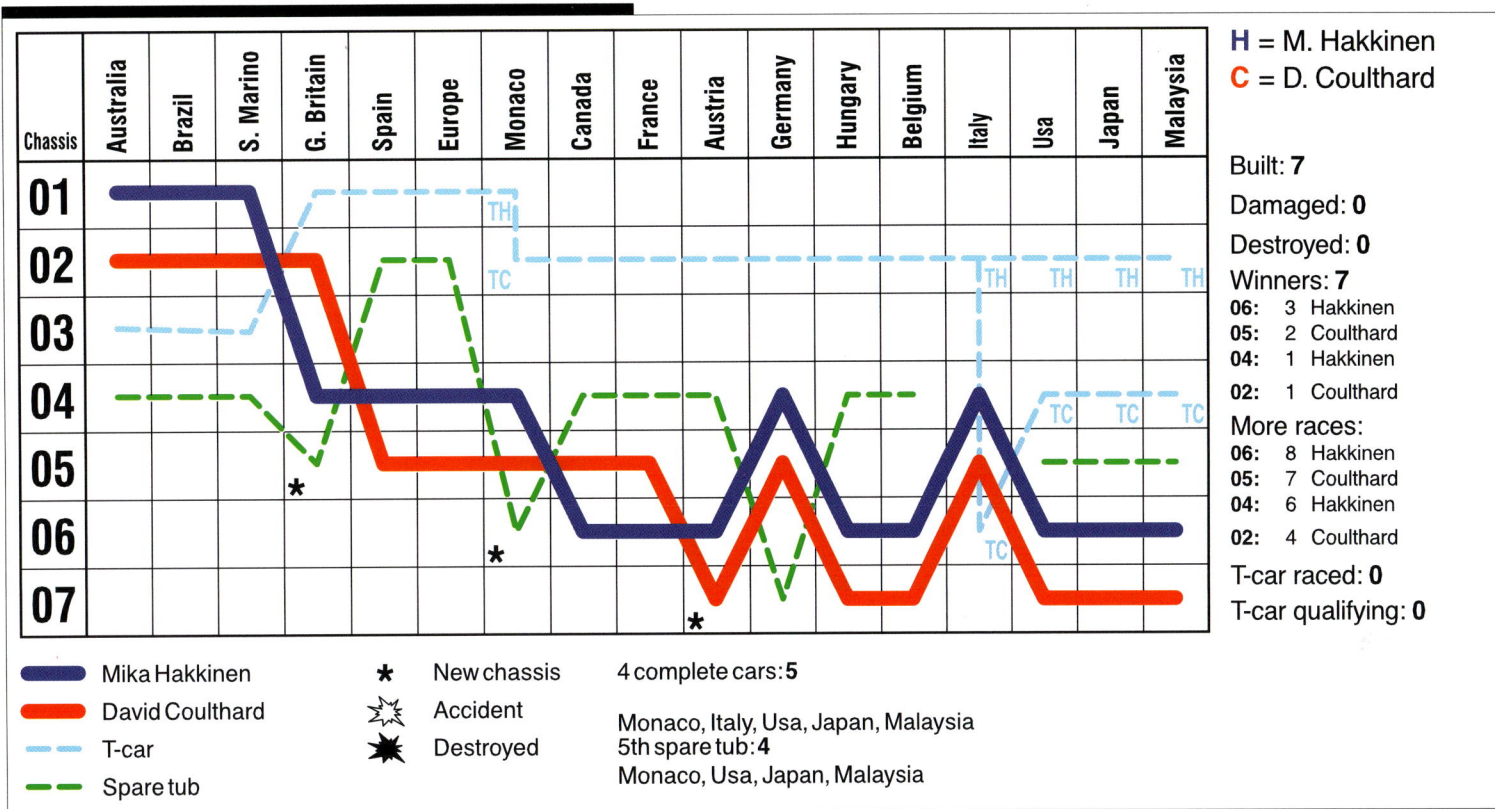

Chart — Chassis (01–07) vs races: Australia, Brazil, S. Marino, G. Britain, Spain, Europe, Monaco, Canada, France, Austria, Germany, Hungary, Belgium, Italy, Usa, Japan, Malaysia.

H = M. Hakkinen
C = D. Coulthard

Built: **7**
Damaged: **0**
Destroyed: **0**
Winners: **7**
- 06: 3 Hakkinen
- 05: 2 Coulthard
- 04: 1 Hakkinen
- 02: 1 Coulthard

More races:
- 06: 8 Hakkinen
- 05: 7 Coulthard
- 04: 6 Hakkinen
- 02: 4 Coulthard

T-car raced: **0**
T-car qualifying: **0**

Legend:
- ▬ Mika Hakkinen
- ▬ David Coulthard
- - - T-car
- - - Spare tub
- * New chassis
- ✸ Accident
- ✹ Destroyed

4 complete cars: **5**
Monaco, Italy, Usa, Japan, Malaysia
5th spare tub: **4**
Monaco, Usa, Japan, Malaysia

by the Williams 04 with Jensen Button in 15 GPs. Jos Verstappen's Arrows 04 took part in 14 events, then Minardi's 04 driven by Gastone Mazzacane in 13. Heinz-Harald Frentzen's Jordan 06 and the 01 BAR of Ricardo Zonta competed in 12. Then follow Jarno Trulli's 05 Jordan, Jacques Villeneuve's 04 BAR with 11, Johnny Herbert's 06 Jaguar, Ralf Schumacher's 02 Williams, the 02 Benetton with Giancarlo Fisichella and Alex Wurz and the 02 Prost of Nick Heidfeld, all of which competed in 10 Grands Prix each. Nine races for Rubens Barrichello's 202 Ferrari, Eddie Irvine's 04 Jaguar, the 05 Benetton with Giancarlo Fisichella, Jean Alesi's 03 Prost, the 07 Sauber of Diniz, the 03 Arrows with De La Rosa. The McLaren 06 driven by Mika Hakkinen was the only chassis to compete in eight GPs, while David Coulthard's 05 McLaren, Irvine's 05 Jaguar, the 03 Benetton of Wurz and Mika Salo's 05 Sauber all took part in seven races.

The most unfortunate chassis were the 04 and 05 Benettons and the 03 Prost, all three of which were damaged twice during the season. The teams that shouldered the most repair work were Benetton and Prost with five monocoques to put right, followed by Sauber and Arrows each with four damaged

chassis. In Austria, the French team had both its chassis damaged in a single accident, involving its two drivers.

Jaguar produced the most chassis; five from the season's first race, to which it took three complete cars (01 for Herbert, 04 for Irvine, 03 as the T-car and 05 as the spare chassis), leaving chassis 02 at the factory.

Williams took pre-series chassis number 00 to the first two races as the spare, after which it was used by the team for private testing. BAR never took chassis 06 to a race; that, too, was used only for private testing and entered at Monaco. The same was the case for the 01 Jordan, Frentzen's T-car, also at Monaco. Arrows, however, built chassis 06 to act as a laboratory at the end of the season.

This is the sequence of the construction dates of Benetton chassis: 01 (18 January), 02 and 03 (23 February), 04 (11 April), 05 (curiously, 28 February), 06 (25 April), 07 (21 June). Chassis 01 is the spare used in the first three races and then taken to races as the spare monocoque, enclosed in its own crate; 07 was never taken to a GP.

The team that raced its T-car most was Williams: chassis 02 competed in Australia, Brazil and San Marino, driven at all times by Ralf Schumacher, followed by Prost, Arrows and Minardi with three apiece: Alesi in Australia (03) and Italy (01), Heidfeld Monaco (01), Verstappen in Brazil (02) and Germany (04), and De La Rosa at Monaco (02). Benetton and BAR fielded their T-cars twice, with Wurz in Monaco and Belgium (03), Villeneuve in Monaco (02) and Zonta at Monaco.

The teams that used their T-cars cars most times in practice and warm-up were Arrows out of necessity 14 times, followed by Prost with eight.

Ferrari chassis covered the most miles, as can be seen in the graph over-page: 199 was used the most, having been driven 14,079.213 km, 201 for 13,151.433 km. The least used chassis was 204, having completed just 1,123.693 km. Of the eight chassis built, only one made its debut on a world championship circuit, 201 in Brazil; the others all appeared first either at Fiorano (198, 200, 203, 204, 205), Mugello (199) or Barcelona (202) during private testing.

FERRARI • *F1-2000* • N° 3-4

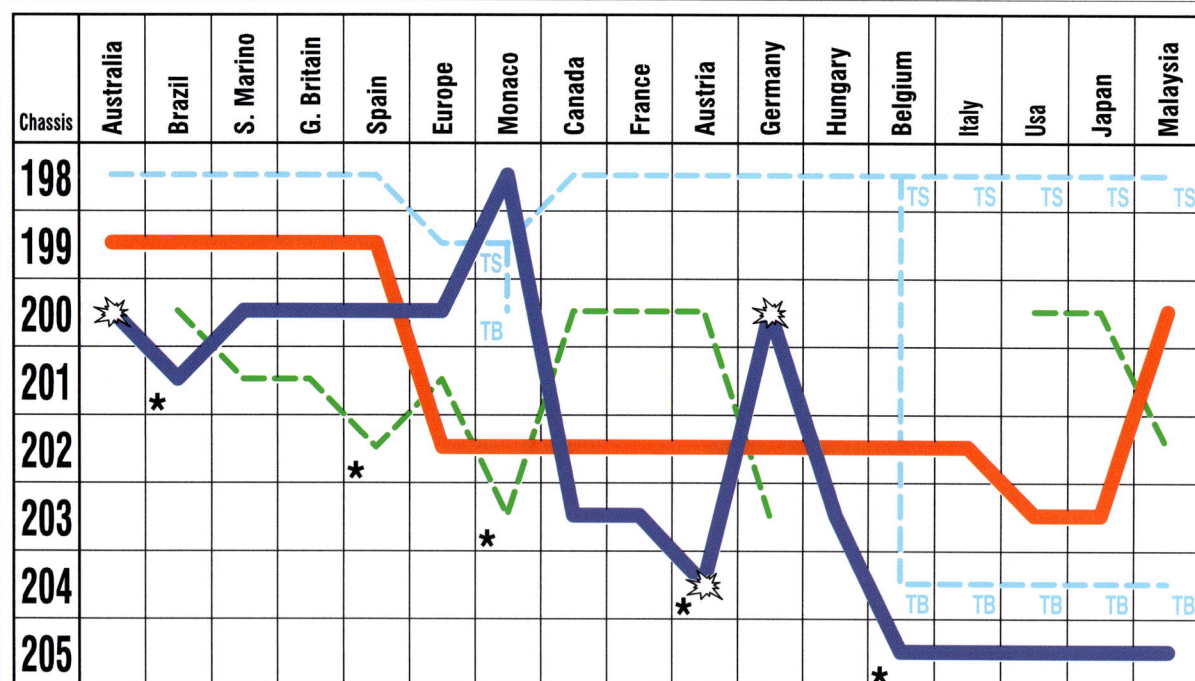

Chart columns (Grands Prix): Australia, Brazil, S. Marino, G. Britain, Spain, Europe, Monaco, Canada, France, Austria, Germany, Hungary, Belgium, Italy, Usa, Japan, Malaysia

Chassis rows: 198, 199, 200, 201, 202, 203, 204, 205

S = M. Schumacher
B = R. Barrichello

Built: **8**
Damaged: **3**
200: Brazil - Germany
204: Austria
Destroyed: **0**
Winners: **10**
205: 4 Schumacher
198: 3 Schumacher
203: 1 Schumacher
200: 1 Schumacher
202: 1 Barrichello
More races:
202: 9 Barrichello
200: 5 Schumacher
205: 5 Schumacher
T-car raced: **0**
T-car qualifying: **2**
198: Schumacher (Br.-Ger.)

Barrichello (Germany) qualified on Schumacher race car (200)

Legend:
— Michael Schumacher
— Rubens Barrichello
--- T-car
--- Spare tub
✳ New chassis
✸ Accident
✸ Destroyed

4 complete cars: **7**
Monaco, Hungary, Belgium, Italy, Usa, Japan, Malaysia
5th spare tub: **4**
Monaco, Usa, Japan, Malaysia

All teams, with the exception of Arrows and Minardi, brought four complete cars to Monaco. Ferrari did so on six additional occasions, in Hungary, Belgium, Italy, USA, Japan and Malaysia with a fifth spare monocoque in Monaco, the USA, Japan and Malaysia. McLaren brought four complete cars on two fewer occasions, not having done so for Hungary or Belgium, while it took the fifth spare chassis to the same races as Ferrari.

As a precaution, neither Sauber competed in the GP of Brazil, after a rear wing failed in practice. The break happened because of the different vibration frequency generated by the irregularity of the San Paolo track's asphalt.

The most reliable team "award" for 2000 goes to McLaren, which completed 1917 laps, equal to 89% of the total number of 17 Grands Prix, followed by Ferrari with 1860.4 or 87%, which can be easily seen from the graph on page 13. In it are recorded, in order, the laps concluded by every team, positions, the most frequent technical problems, accidents, miles and days of private testing during the season. On the basis of that data, it can be seen that Ferrari covered more private test miles than anyone else, dedicating no less than 125 days to on-development work, against McLaren's 77 and 31,560 km against the Anglo-German team's 23,107 km.

The least reliable team was Prost, having covered only 1,252 laps or 58% of the total, a team that also established a record of 17 retirements for mechanical failures, of which seven were engine problems, followed by Arrows with 1,294 laps or 60%, and whose Achilles heel was the gearbox, which forced six of the team's 12 retirements for technical reasons. Jordan managed 14 retirements, of which six were divided equally between the engine and gearbox for a total of just 1,390 laps or 65% of total distance potential.

Chassis	198	199	200	201	202	203	204	205
First run	09-02-2000	24-02-2000	01-03-2000	25-03-2000	24-04-2000	23-05-2000	08-07-2000	21-08-2000
Km completed	4,915.112	14,079.213	5,096.513	13,151.433	7,102.114	4,436.241	1,123.693	3,282.553

JORDAN • *EJ10* • N° 5-6

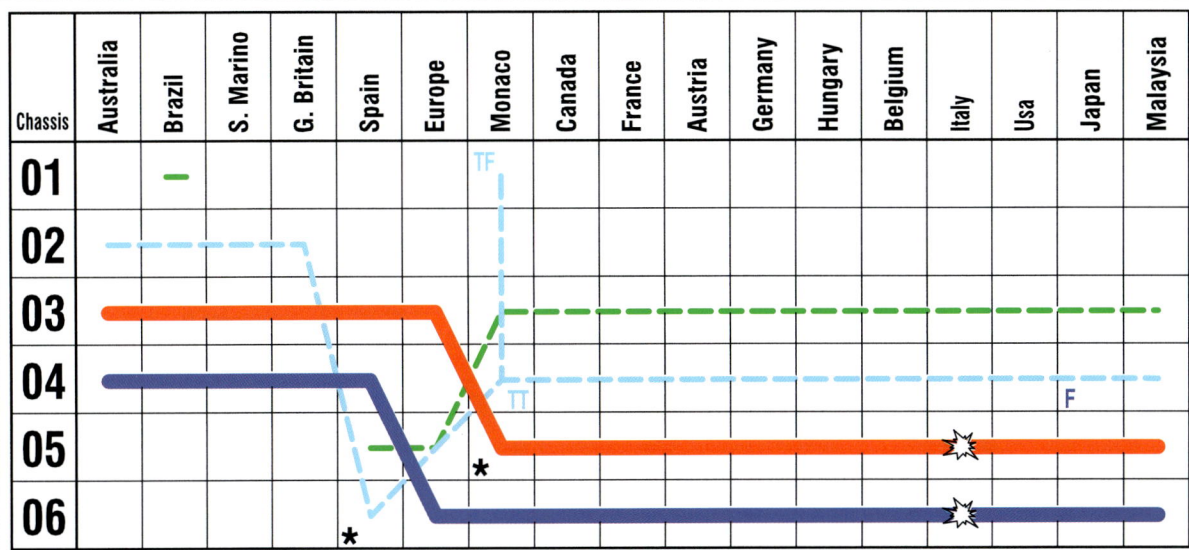

Chassis	Australia	Brazil	S. Marino	G. Britain	Spain	Europe	Monaco	Canada	France	Austria	Germany	Hungary	Belgium	Italy	Usa	Japan	Malaysia
01		—					TF										
02																	
03																	
04							TT									F	
05							*										
06					*												

F = H.H. Frentzen
T = J. Trulli

Built: **6**
Damaged: **0**
Destroyed: **0**
Winners: **0**
More races:
06: 12 Frentzen
05: 11 Trulli
T-car raced: **1**
04: Frentzen (Japan)
T-car qualifying: **1**
02: Trulli (Brazil)

	Heinz Harald Frentzen	*	New chassis	4 complete cars: **1**
	Jarno Trulli	✸	Accident	
	T-car	✸	Destroyed	
	Spare tub			

JAGUAR • *R1* • N° 7-8

Chassis	Australia	Brazil	S. Marino	G. Britain	Spain	Europe	Monaco	Canada	France	Austria	Germany	Hungary	Belgium	Italy	Usa	Japan	Malaysia
01																	
02							TH										
03																	
04																	
05							TI		B								
06								*									✸

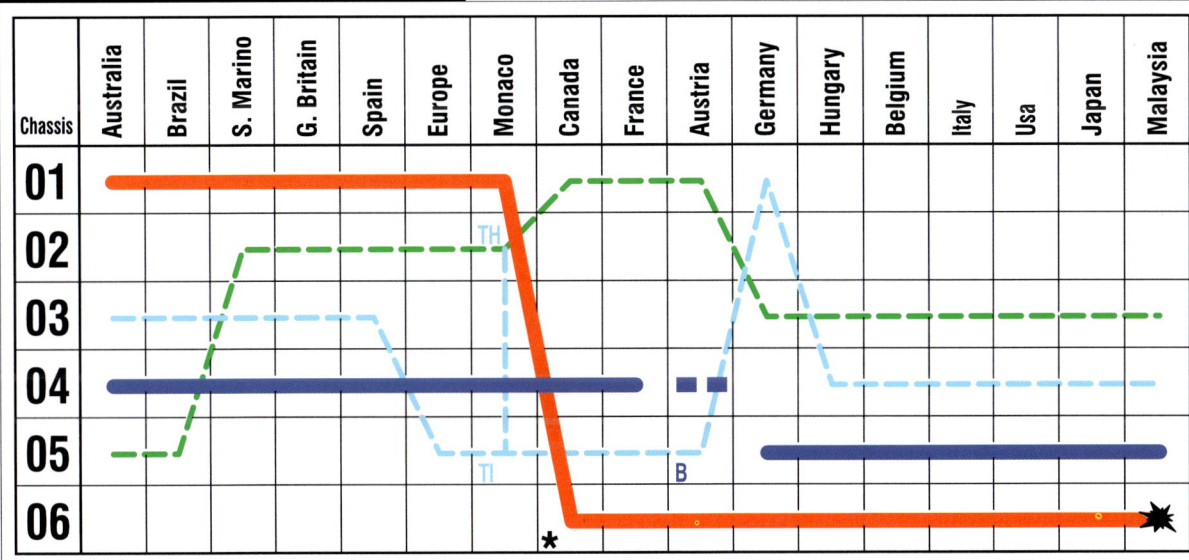

I = E. Irvine
H = J. Herbert
B = L. Burti

Built: **6**
Damaged: **0**
Destroyed: **1**
06: Malaysia
Winners: **0**
More races:
06: 10 Herbert
04: 9 Irvine
T-car raced: **1**
05: Burti (Austria)
T-car qualifying: **0**

	Eddie Irvine		T-car	*	New chassis	4 complete cars: **1**
	Johnny Herbert		Spare tub	✸	Accident	Monaco 5th spare tub: **1**
	Luciano Burti			✸	Destroyed	Monaco

WILLIAMS • *FW22* • N° 9-10

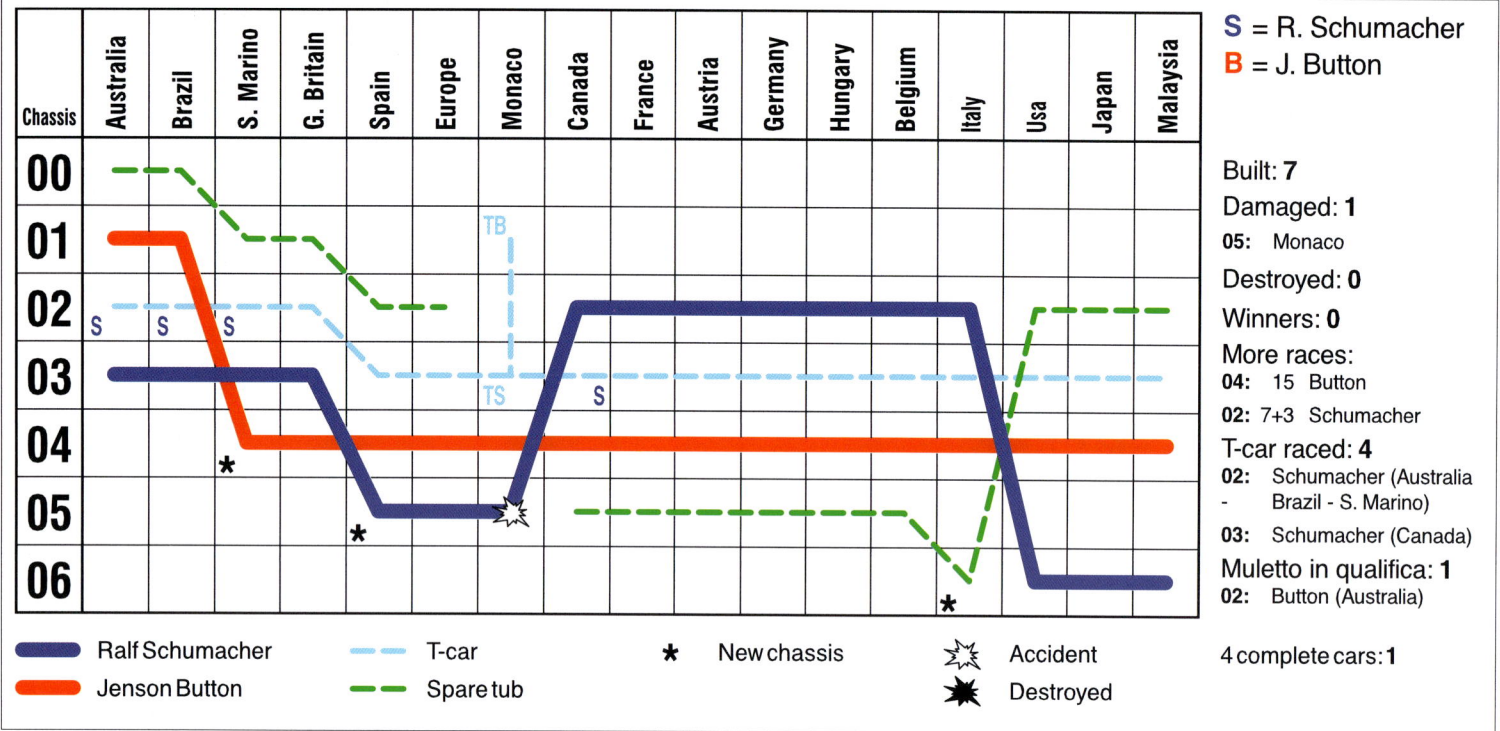

Chassis	Australia	Brazil	S. Marino	G. Britain	Spain	Europe	Monaco	Canada	France	Austria	Germany	Hungary	Belgium	Italy	Usa	Japan	Malaysia
00																	
01																	
02																	
03																	
04																	
05																	
06																	

S = R. Schumacher
B = J. Button

Built: **7**
Damaged: **1**
05: Monaco
Destroyed: **0**
Winners: **0**
More races:
04: 15 Button
02: 7+3 Schumacher
T-car raced: **4**
02: Schumacher (Australia - Brazil - S. Marino)
03: Schumacher (Canada)
Muletto in qualifica: **1**
02: Button (Australia)

Ralf Schumacher — T-car — * New chassis — Accident
Jenson Button — Spare tub — Destroyed
4 complete cars: **1**

BENETTON • *B200* • N° 11-12

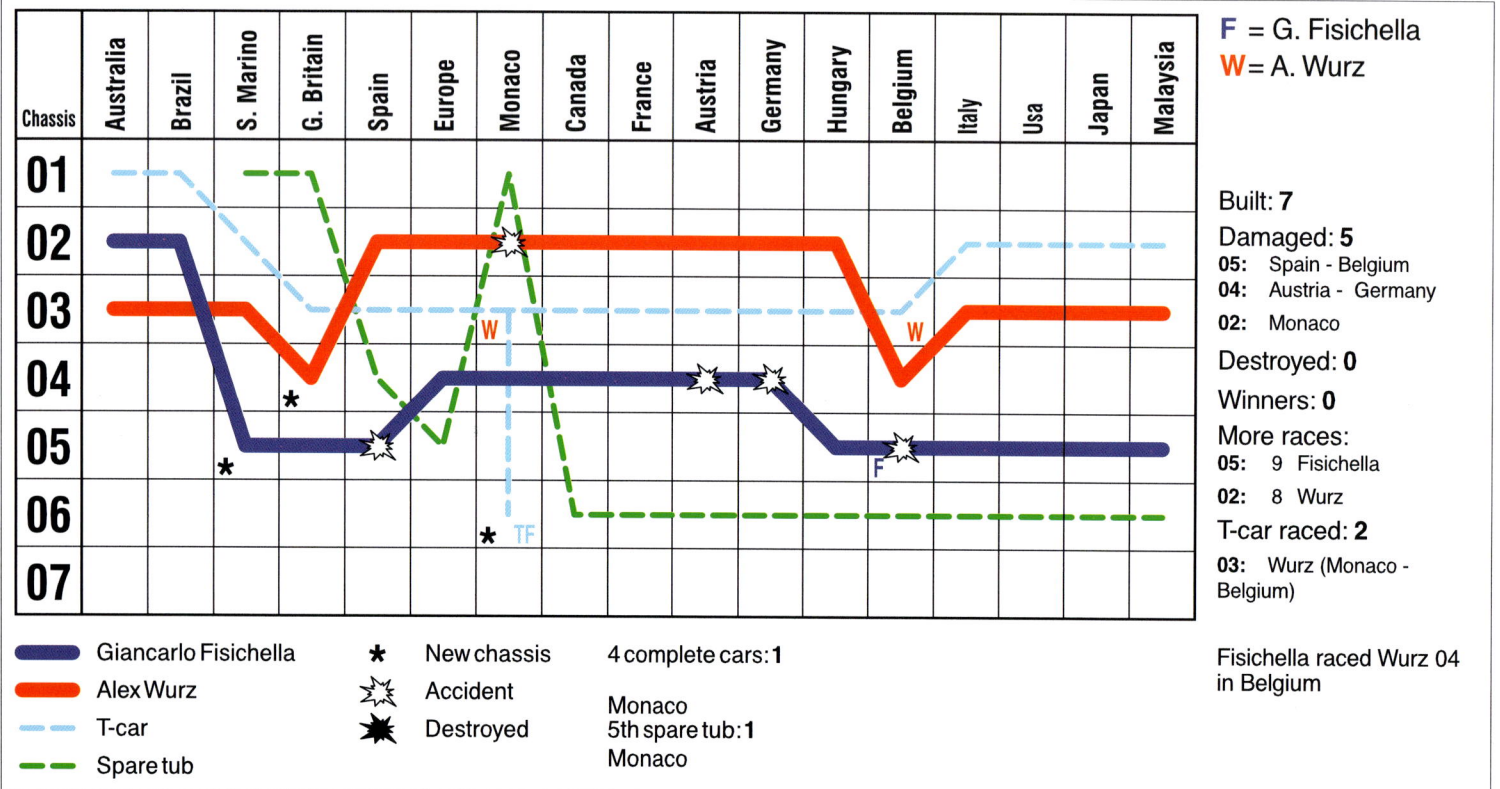

Chassis	Australia	Brazil	S. Marino	G. Britain	Spain	Europe	Monaco	Canada	France	Austria	Germany	Hungary	Belgium	Italy	Usa	Japan	Malaysia
01																	
02																	
03																	
04																	
05																	
06																	
07																	

F = G. Fisichella
W = A. Wurz

Built: **7**
Damaged: **5**
05: Spain - Belgium
04: Austria - Germany
02: Monaco
Destroyed: **0**
Winners: **0**
More races:
05: 9 Fisichella
02: 8 Wurz
T-car raced: **2**
03: Wurz (Monaco - Belgium)

Fisichella raced Wurz 04 in Belgium

Giancarlo Fisichella — * New chassis — 4 complete cars: **1**
Alex Wurz — Accident
T-car — Destroyed — Monaco 5th spare tub: **1** Monaco
Spare tub

PROST • *AP03* • N° 14-15

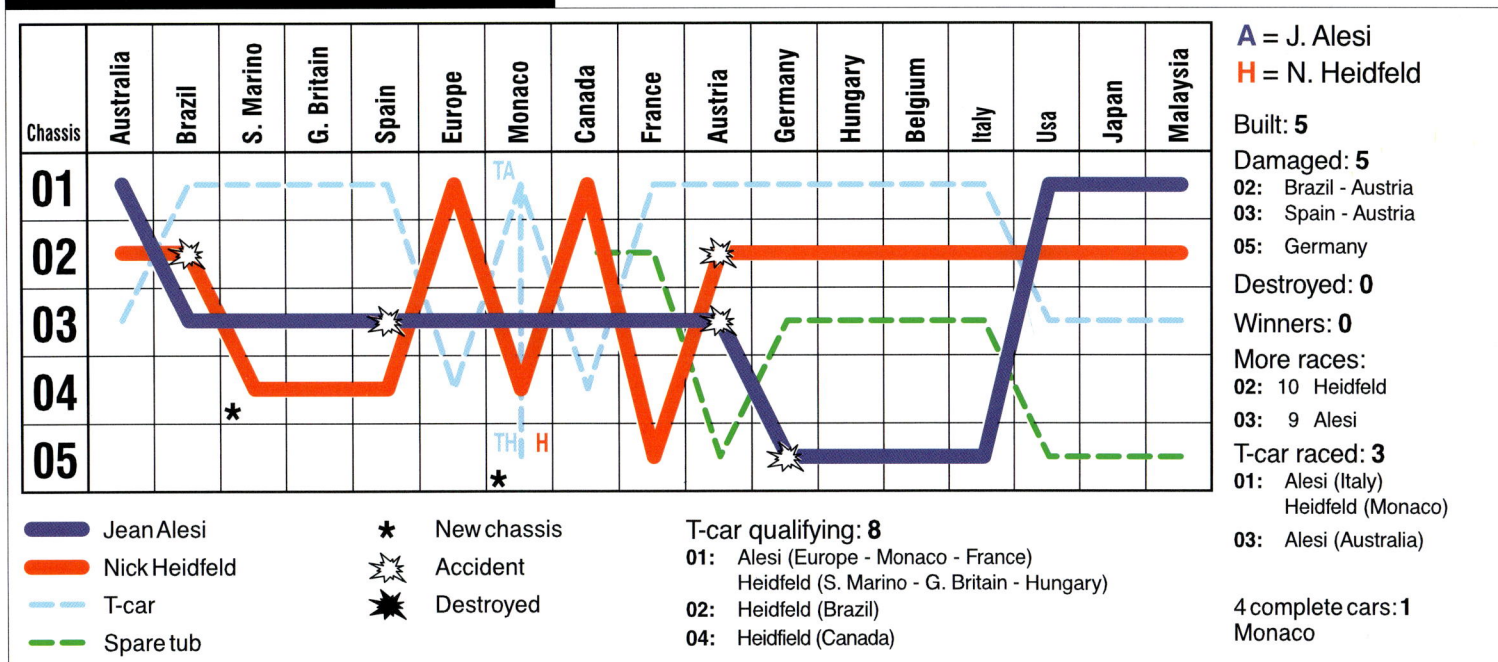

Chassis	Australia	Brazil	S. Marino	G. Britain	Spain	Europe	Monaco	Canada	France	Austria	Germany	Hungary	Belgium	Italy	Usa	Japan	Malaysia
01																	
02																	
03																	
04																	
05																	

A = J. Alesi
H = N. Heidfeld

Built: **5**

Damaged: **5**
02: Brazil - Austria
03: Spain - Austria
05: Germany

Destroyed: **0**

Winners: **0**

More races:
02: 10 Heidfeld
03: 9 Alesi

T-car raced: **3**
01: Alesi (Italy)
Heidfeld (Monaco)
03: Alesi (Australia)

4 complete cars: **1**
Monaco

— Jean Alesi
— Nick Heidfeld
--- T-car
--- Spare tub

* New chassis
✸ Accident
✸ Destroyed

T-car qualifying: **8**
01: Alesi (Europe - Monaco - France)
Heidfeld (S. Marino - G. Britain - Hungary)
02: Heidfeld (Brazil)
04: Heidfield (Canada)

SAUBER • *C19* • N° 16-17

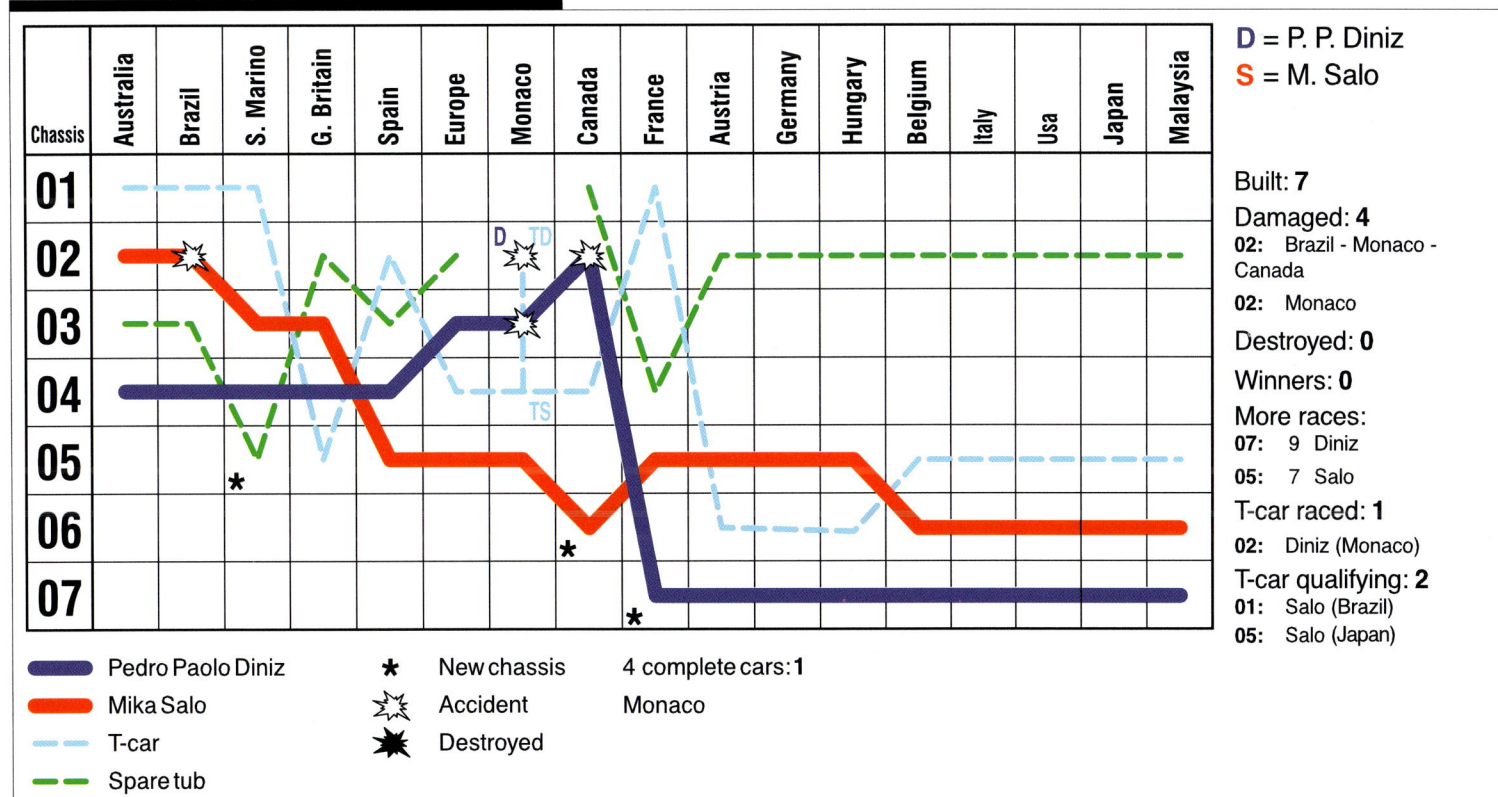

Chassis	Australia	Brazil	S. Marino	G. Britain	Spain	Europe	Monaco	Canada	France	Austria	Germany	Hungary	Belgium	Italy	Usa	Japan	Malaysia
01																	
02																	
03																	
04																	
05																	
06																	
07																	

D = P. P. Diniz
S = M. Salo

Built: **7**

Damaged: **4**
02: Brazil - Monaco - Canada
02: Monaco

Destroyed: **0**

Winners: **0**

More races:
07: 9 Diniz
05: 7 Salo

T-car raced: **1**
02: Diniz (Monaco)

T-car qualifying: **2**
01: Salo (Brazil)
05: Salo (Japan)

— Pedro Paolo Diniz
— Mika Salo
--- T-car
--- Spare tub

* New chassis
✸ Accident
✸ Destroyed

4 complete cars: **1**
Monaco

ARROWS • *A21* • N° 18-19

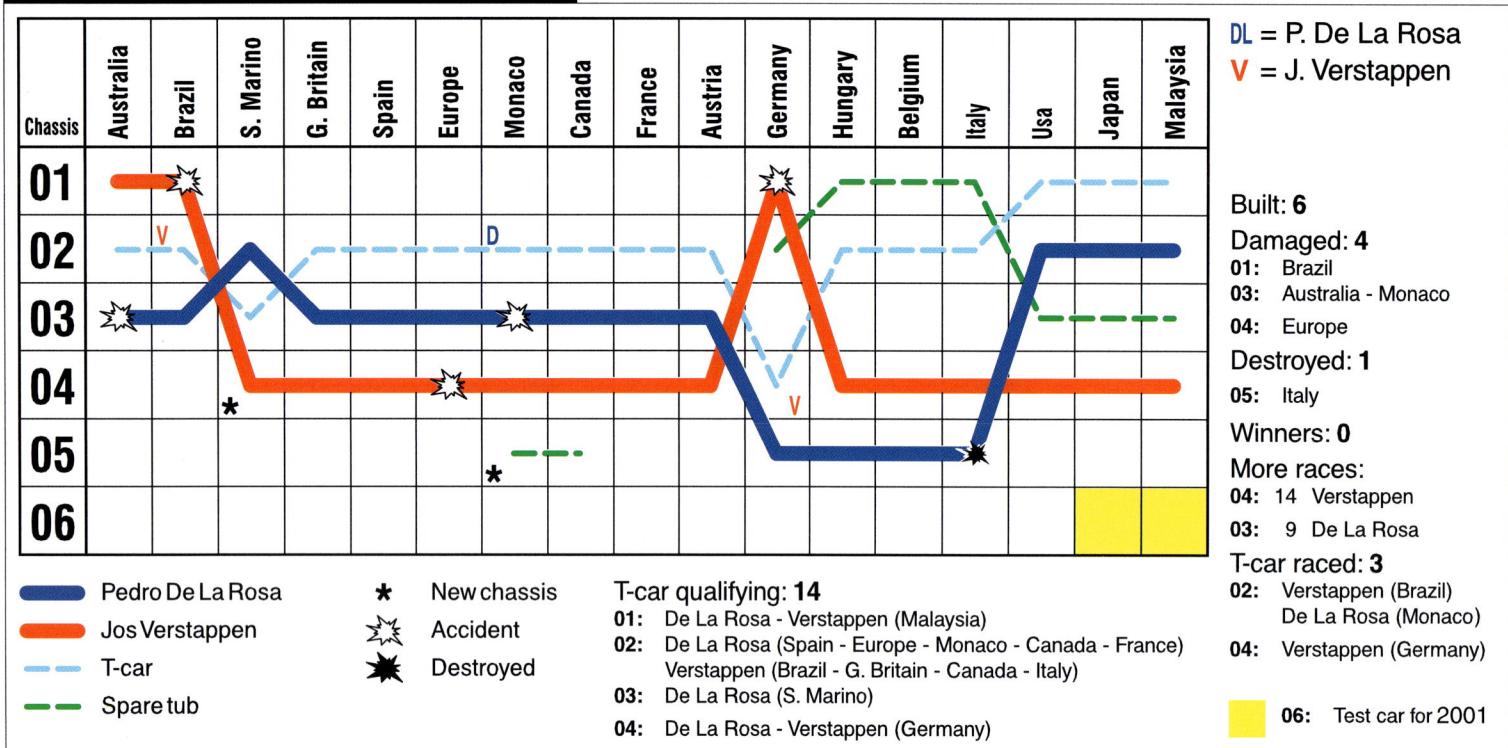

Chassis	Australia	Brazil	S. Marino	G. Britain	Spain	Europe	Monaco	Canada	France	Austria	Germany	Hungary	Belgium	Italy	Usa	Japan	Malaysia
01																	
02		V				D											
03																	
04			*								V						
05						*											
06																	

DL = P. De La Rosa
V = J. Verstappen

Built: **6**
Damaged: **4**
01: Brazil
03: Australia - Monaco
04: Europe
Destroyed: **1**
05: Italy
Winners: **0**
More races:
04: 14 Verstappen
03: 9 De La Rosa
T-car raced: **3**
02: Verstappen (Brazil)
De La Rosa (Monaco)
04: Verstappen (Germany)

06: Test car for 2001

Legend:
— Pedro De La Rosa
— Jos Verstappen
- - T-car
- - Spare tub
* New chassis
✶ Accident
✶ Destroyed

T-car qualifying: **14**
01: De La Rosa - Verstappen (Malaysia)
02: De La Rosa (Spain - Europe - Monaco - Canada - France)
Verstappen (Brazil - G. Britain - Canada - Italy)
03: De La Rosa (S. Marino)
04: De La Rosa - Verstappen (Germany)

MINARDI • *M02* • N° 20-21

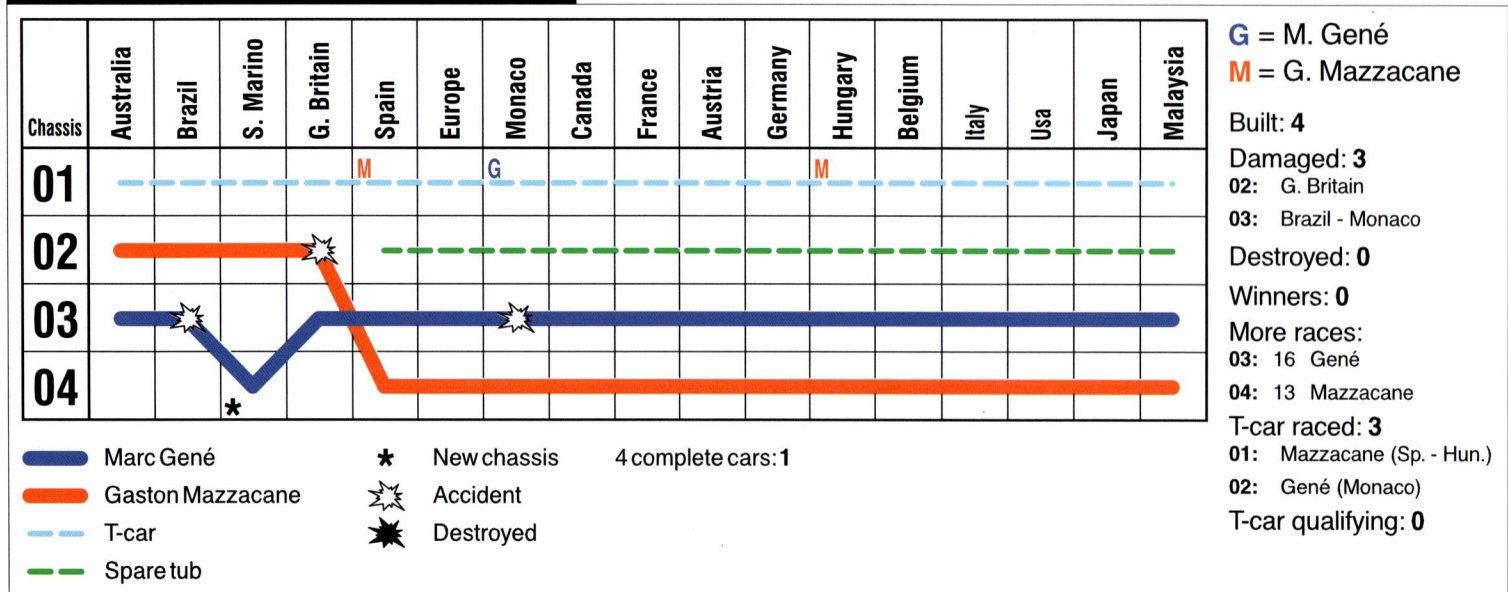

Chassis	Australia	Brazil	S. Marino	G. Britain	Spain	Europe	Monaco	Canada	France	Austria	Germany	Hungary	Belgium	Italy	Usa	Japan	Malaysia
01					M		G				M						
02																	
03																	
04			*														

G = M. Gené
M = G. Mazzacane

Built: **4**
Damaged: **3**
02: G. Britain
03: Brazil - Monaco
Destroyed: **0**
Winners: **0**
More races:
03: 16 Gené
04: 13 Mazzacane
T-car raced: **3**
01: Mazzacane (Sp. - Hun.)
02: Gené (Monaco)
T-car qualifying: **0**

Legend:
— Marc Gené
— Gaston Mazzacane
- - T-car
- - Spare tub
* New chassis
✶ Accident
✶ Destroyed

4 complete cars: **1**

BAR • *PR02* • N° 22-23

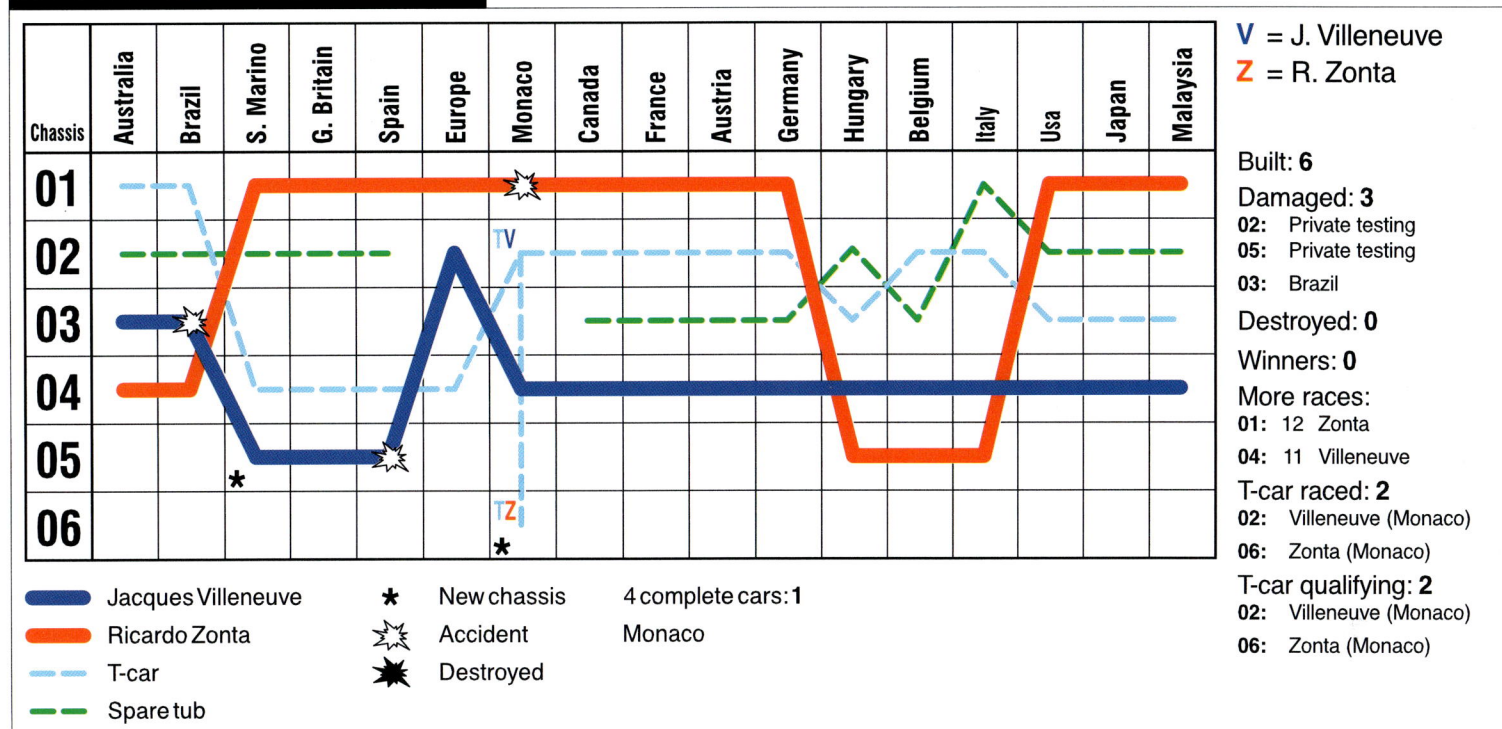

Chassis	Australia	Brazil	S. Marino	G. Britain	Spain	Europe	Monaco	Canada	France	Austria	Germany	Hungary	Belgium	Italy	Usa	Japan	Malaysia
01																	
02																	
03																	
04																	
05																	
06																	

V = J. Villeneuve
Z = R. Zonta

Built: **6**
Damaged: **3**
02: Private testing
05: Private testing
03: Brazil
Destroyed: **0**
Winners: **0**
More races:
01: 12 Zonta
04: 11 Villeneuve
T-car raced: **2**
02: Villeneuve (Monaco)
06: Zonta (Monaco)
T-car qualifying: **2**
02: Villeneuve (Monaco)
06: Zonta (Monaco)

Legend:
- ▬▬ Jacques Villeneuve
- ▬▬ Ricardo Zonta
- ┄┄ T-car
- ┄┄ Spare tub
- ✳ New chassis
- ✷ Accident
- ✴ Destroyed
- 4 complete cars: **1**
- Monaco

	laps completed (%)*	finishes	technical failures	accidents	test km	days
McLaren	**1917 (89 %)**	**29**	**4 - engine**	**1**	**23107**	**77**
Ferrari	1860 (87 %)	26	5 - hydraulic (2)	3	31560	125
BAR	1806 (84 %)	21	7 - engine (4)	6	22186	54
Minardi	1756 (82 %)	20	10 - engine (7)	4	7271	31
Benetton	1707 (79 %)	23	5 - engine (2)	6	17893	57
Williams	1702 (79 %)	18	11 - engine (6)	5	17828	64
Sauber	1649 (77 %)	23	3 - electronics (2)	6	21072	61
Jaguar	1641 (76 %)	21	6 - gearbox (4)	7	18989	69
Jordan	1390 (65 %)	15	14 - engine (3), gearbox (3)	5	18809	61
Arrows	1294 (60 %)	13	12 - gearbox (6)	11	12026	56
Prost	1252 (58 %)	10	17 - engine (7)	6	11296	57

* Each team had 32 starts. Except: BAR and Prost 33, Sauber 32.

TABLE OF CARS

		1 - 2 McLAREN	3 - 4 FERRARI	5 - 6 JORDAN	7 - 8 JAGUAR	9 - 10 WILLIAMS
CAR		**MP4/15**	**F1 2000**	**EJ10**	**R1**	**FW22**
	Designers	Adrian Newey Neil Oatley	Ross Brawn Rory Byrne	Mike Gascoyne Tim Holloway[c]	Gary Anderson John Russell	Patrick Head Gavin Fisher - Geoff Willis
	Race engineers	Steve Hallam[a] Mark Slade (1) - Pat Fry (2)	Ignazio Lunetta[a] - Luca Bal- disserri (3) - Carlo Cantoni	Sam Michael (5) Dino Toso (6)	Robin Gearing (7) Andy Le Fleming (8)	James Robinson[e] - Craig Wilson (9) - Tim Preston (10)
	Chief mechanic	Mike Negline	Nigel Stepney	Tim Edwards	Dave Boys	Carl Gaden
CHASSIS	Wheelbase	3080 mm*	3020 mm*	3050 mm	3050 mm	3140 mm*
	Front track	1490 mm*	1490 mm	1500 mm	1490 mm	1490 mm
	Rear track	1405 mm*	1405 mm	1420 mm	1405 mm	1405 mm
	Front suspension**	2+1 dampers and torsion bars	2+1 dampers and torsion bars	2+1 dampers and torsion bars	2+1 dampers and torsion bars	2+1 dampers and torsion bars
	Rear suspension**	2+1 dampers and torsion bars	2+1 dampers and torsion bars	2+1 dampers	2+1 dampers and torsion bars	2+1 dampers
	Dampers	McLaren-Penske	Sachs	Penske	Jaguar - Penske	Williams - Penske
	Brakes calipers	A+P	Brembo	Brembo[d]	A+P	A+P
	Brakes discs	Hitco	Brembo CCR	Hitco - Brembo	Carbon Industrie - Brembo	Carbon Industrie
	Wheels	Enkey	BBS	O.Z.	BBS	O.Z.
	Radiators	Calsonic-Marston	Secan	Secan	Secan	Secan
	Oil tank	middle position inside fuel tank	middle position inside fuel tank	middle position inside fuel tank	middle position inside fuel tank	middle position inside fuel tank
GEARBOX		Longitudinal magnesium	Longitudinal fabricated titanium	Longitudinal magnesium	Longitudinal magnesium	Longitudinal alluminium
	Gear selection	Semiautomatic 7 gears	Semiautomatic 7 gears	Semiautomatic 6 gears	Semiautomatic 6 gears	Semiautomatic 7 gears
	Clutch	A+P	Sachs - A+P	Sachs	A+P	A+P
	Pedals	2-3[b]	2	2	2	2
ENGINE		Mercedes - Benz FO110/J	Ferrari 049	Mugen Honda MF301	Ford Zetec CR-2	BMW E41/4
	Total capacity	2997.0 cmc	2997.0 cmc	2998.4 cmc	2998.0 cmc	2998.0 cmc
	N° cylinders and V	10 - V 72°	10 - V 90°	10 - V 72°	10 - V 72°	10 - V 72°
	Electronics	TAG Electronic	Magneti Marelli	TAG Electronic	Ford - Visteon	Bosch
	Fuel	Mobil	Shell	Elf	Petroscience	Petrobras
	Oil	Mobil	Shell	Elf	Texaco	Castrol
	Fuel tank capacity	140 l*	141 l*	152 l*	135 l*	135 l*
	Dashboard	TAG Electronic	Magneti Marelli	Jordan	Jaguar P.I.	Williams

11 - 12 BENETTON	14 - 15 PROST	16 - 17 SAUBER	18 - 19 ARROWS	20 - 21 MINARDI	22 - 23 BAR
B 200	AP03	C19	A21	M02	PR02
Pat Symons Tim Densham	Alan Jenkins[g] John Barnard[h]	Willy Rampf Leo Ress	Mike Coughlan Eghbal Hamidy	Gustav Brunner Gabriele Tredozi	Malcom Oastler Andrew Green
Alan Permain - Mark Heard (11)	Vincent Gaillardot[a] - Humphrey Corbett (14) - Gilles	Gabriele Delli Colli (16) Remy Decorzent (17)	Graham Taylor (18) Chris Dyer (19)	Gian Franco Fantuzzi (20) J. François Sinteff (21)	Jock Clear (22) David Lloyd (23)
Mick Ainsley - Cowlishawl	Pierre Gall	Urs Kuratle	Stuart Cowie	Gabriele Pagliarini	Alastair Gibson
3100 mm	3095 mm	3070 mm	3010 mm	3020 mm	3050 mm
1490 mm	1490 mm	1480 mm	1490 mm	1470 mm	1450 mm
1405 mm	1405 mm	1390 mm	1405 mm	1430 mm	1405 mm
2+1 dampers and torsion bars	2+1 dampers and torsion bars	2+1 dampers and torsion bars	2+1 dampers and torsion bars[i]	2+1 dampers and torsion bars	2+1 dampers and torsion bars
2+1 dampers	2 dampers and torsion bars	2+1 dampers and torsion bars	2+1 dampers and torsion bars	2+1 dampers and torsion bars	2+1 dampers and torsion bars
Dynamic Suspensions	Penske	Sachs	Dynamic Suspensions	Sachs	Koni
A+P	A+P	Brembo	A+P - Arrows	Brembo	A+P
Brembo	Carbon Industrie	Brembo	Hitco	Brembo CCR	Carbon Industrie - Brembo
BBS	BBS	O.Z.	BBS	Fondmetal	O.Z.
Secan - Marston	Secan	Calsonic	Secan - Marston	Secan	Marston
middle position inside fuel tank	middle position inside fuel tank	between engine - gearbox	middle position inside fuel tank	middle position inside fuel tank	middle position inside fuel tank
Longitudinal magnesium	Longitudinal	Longitudinal magnesium	Longitudinal carbon	Longitudinal titanium casting	Longitudinal alluminium
Semiautomatic 6 gears	Semiautomatic 7 gears	Semiautomatic 7 gears	Semiautomatic 6 gears	Semiautomatic 6 gears	Pneumatic 6 gears
A+P	A+P	Sachs	A+P	A+P	A+P
2	2-3[i]	2	2	2	2
Supertec FB 02	Peugeot A20	Petronas SPE 04A/B	Supertec FB 02	Ford Zetec - R	Honda RA 00E
2997.0 cmc	2998.3 cmc	2998.3 cmc	2997.0 cmc	2998.3 cmc	3000 cmc
10 - V 71°	10 - V 72°	10 - V 80°	10 - V 71°	10 - V 72°	10 - V
Magneti Marelli	TAG Electronic	Magneti Marelli	Magneti Marelli	Magneti Marelli	Honda
Agip	Total	Shell	Repsol	Elf	Nisseki
Agip	Total	Shell	Repsol	Elf	Nisseki
133 l	130 l	145 l	122 l	140 l	133 l
Benetton	Prost	Magneti Marelli	Arrows	Magneti Marelli	Bar P.I.

Notes and variations during the season:

a) Chief track engineer.
b) Only Coulthard.
c) Mike Gascoyne left the team after French GP.
d) 4 pistons caliper at the rear.
e) James Robinson left the team after the Hungarian GP.
f) Pat Simonds replaced Cristian Silk at the European GP.
g) Alan Jenkins left the team at Monaco GP.
h) John Barnard technical consultant.
i) Alesi used 2 pedals only at Australian GP.

* estimated value

** push-rod for all cars

	MERCEDES-BENZ	FERRARI	MUGEN-HONDA	FORD V10
Type	ILMOR FO110J	049/B-C	MF-301-HE	COSWORTH CR2
Total cube capacity	2997.1 cmc	2996.6 cmc	2998.3 cmc	2998.3 cmc
N° and cylinders V	10 a V 72°	10 a V 90°	10 a V 72°	10 a V 72°
Bore and stroke (mm)	93.50 x 43.65*	96.00 x 41.40*	95.00 x 42.30*	95.00 x 42.30*
Compression ratio	13.3 : 1*	13.2 : 1*	13.3 : 1*	13.2 : 1*
Number valves and return system	4 pneumatic	4 pneumatic	4 pneumatic	4 pneumatic
Maximum revs	17.400* (Q 17.600)*	17.600* (Q 17.900)*	17.400* (Q 17.600)*	17.500 (Q 18.000)
Maximum power	815 CV* (Q 830 CV)*	810 CV* (Q 820 CV)*	795 CV* (Q 810 CV)*	790 CV* (Q 795 CV)*
Bearings	6	6	6	6
Induction system	Moving trumpets	Moving trumpets	Moving trumpets	Fixed
Throttle	Electro-Hydraulic	Electro-Hydraulic	Fly by wire	Electro-Hydraulic
Electronics	TAG - Electr. Sys 2000	Magneti Marelli	TAG 300 Electr. Syst.	Ford Electr. Visteon VCS
Block	Light alloy	Light alloy	Light alloy	Light alloy
Lenght	570 mm	609 mm	625 mm	569 mm
Width	475 mm	530 mm	520 mm	506 mm
Height	458 mm	378 mm	450 mm	492 mm
Weight	92 kg*	102 kg*	110 kg*	97 kg
Project leader	Mario Illien	P. Martinelli / G. Simon	Tenji Sakaj	Nick Hayes
Race department staff	400 (F1 + CART)	150	160	~ 300
N° engine built in 1998	74	~ 110	+ 100	+ 100
Track responsable	Roger Higgins	Giuseppe D'Agostino	Tenji Sakaj	Jim Brett
N° of engines at races	10 - 12	12	9 - 10	10 - 12
Steps	4	3	5	3

Q = Qualifying
* Estimate value from Ing. E. Benzing
** Benetton and Arrows

BMW	SUPERTEC	PEUGEOT	PETRONAS	FONDMETAL - FORD	HONDA
E41 Phase 3/4	FB 02	A20 Evo4	Ferrari 048 04 A	ZETEC-R VJM2	RA000E
2998.0 cmc	2996.6 cmc	2998.3 cmc	2996.6 cmc	2998.3 cmc	2998.3 cmc
10 a V 72°	10 a V 71°	10 a V 72°	10 a V 80°	10 a V 72°	10 a V 80°
94.00 x 43.20	96.00 x 41.40	91.00 x 46.10	96.00 x 41.40*	91.00 x 46.10*	95.00 x 42.30*
13.2 : 1	13.2 : 1	13.5 : 1*	13.1 : 1*	12.8 : 1*	13.3 : 1*
4 pneumatic	4 pneumatic	4 pneumatic	4 pneumatic	4 pneumatic	4 pneumatic
17.300 (Q 17.500)	17.400 (Q 17.800)	16.400 (Q 16.600)*	17.000* (Q 17.300)*	16.300* (Q 16.500)*	17.400* (Q 17.600)*
785 CV (Q 800 CV)	780 CV (Q 800 CV)	780 CV* (Q 790 CV)*	785 CV* (Q 790 CV)*	715 CV* (Q 720 CV*)	805 CV* (Q 815 CV*)
6	6	6	6	6	6
Moving trumpets	Moving trumpets	Moving trumpets	Moving trumpets	Fixed	Moving trumpets
Electro-Hydraulic	Electro-Hydraulic	Electro-Hydraulic	Electro-Hydraulic	Electro-Hydraulic	Electro-Hydraulic
BMW Elektronik	Magneti Marelli	TAG - Electr. Sys 2000	Magneti Marelli	Magneti Marelli	Honda PGM-F1/IG
Light alloy	Light alloy	Light alloy	Light alloy	Light alloy	Light alloy
633 mm	623 mm	583 mm	618 mm	605 mm	625 mm
524 mm	542 mm	544 mm	538 mm	520 mm	525 mm
395 mm	388 mm	376 mm	378 mm	450 mm	445 mm
119 kg	115 kg	110 kg	110 kg	128 kg	98 kg*
M. Theissen/ W. Laurentz	Bruno Michel	Jean Pierre Boudy	Osamu Goto	Mark Parish	Takefumi Hosaka
+ 230	120	155	-	60	150
+ 90	80	100	+ 90	+ 60	+ 90
Werner Laurentz	Denis Chevrier	Guy Audoux	Osamu Gotu	Roger Griffiths	Katsutoshi Nishizawa
10	16 - 20**	11	8 - 10	8 - 10	10
3	4	3	2	2	5

ENGINES
2000

In 2000 mechanical engineering, already projected towards future innovations, the monothematic V10 formula had reached various stages of structural and metallurgical directional order for the usual purposes of evolution, moving along the road towards increments in rotation revolutions, within the limits permitted by the pistons maximum acceleration. If the primary result in the most evolved constructions was that of an increase over 1999 of *15-20* hp at the power peak, the second objective achieved with further lightened engines was a reduction in their barycentre, which is proportionally reflected in the centre of gravity of the entire vehicle. That is like saying the most recent progress these engines have made, took place by paying more attention to the dynamics of the car, since increased knowledge in the sector had permitted the appreciable exploitation of even small dimensional variations to increase the cornering speed of very sophisticated cars. It will, therefore, be preferable to ponder a number of considerations concerning the architecture of 2000 Formula One engines, before evaluating achievements in the pure functioning of those power units.

First of all, let us set out, in reasonably precise terms, the influence of each modification, such as the opening of the angle formed by the cylinders. In fact, to reduce the centre of gravity of the engine after having selected, for other reasons, low values of the bore/stroke ratio or of the connecting rod ratio, or after having compressed in an unlikely manner the spaces needed by the oil sump, or having decreased the diameter of the clutch (a real fly-wheel now, which has not been an issue for some time), nothing else remains but the sump arrangement of the cylinders. It is true; there would be much space to develop the valve timing organs which, with the modern pneumatic return of the valves, and the needs of the manifolds, oblige a notable height of the cylinder head. But, for now, it is felt this dimension remains an insurmountable constraint for all designers: while waiting for a significant increase in revolutions, which combine with the ascent to *20,000 rpm*, there are also other refinements of design and a further lightening of the engine to consider.

As a consequence, it is possible to hypothesise the standard dimensions of the current V10 and calculate the variations in height (the same goes for the width) with a simple little formula. It is sufficient to create an R radius and make it turn in the centre of the engine crankshaft, which coincides with the vertex of the angle formed by the axis of the cylinders. The product between this R radius and the cosine of angle ß, from time to time determinate, will provide both the *height H* and the *width W* of the engine, according to these conditions:

1) In the transverse section of the engine, edges are assumed in place of the normal connections, for the superior limit of the head, and on those edges, the *R* is measured.
2) The radius *R* is nothing other than the hypotenuse of a rectangular triangle, in which the smaller cathetus constitutes the semi-width of the head and the larger cathetus represents the sum of: one half of the stroke (in this example the lowest ratio of bore/stroke is selected $C/A=0.43$): the length of the piston con rod for a ratio of about *0.2*; distance of the piston pin from the crown of the piston, conventionally fixed at *20* mm; height of the head, estimated at *159* mm, an average value for 2000 F1 engines, obtained from various projections, for the acquisition of images in CAD (Computer Aided Design) programmes.
3) In determining the angle ß, at the value of a half of the "V" of the cylinders, subtract *16°*, equivalent to the breadth due to the stated semi-width of the head, in line with the CAD elaborations.

Having created this standard, it is possible to calculate the height and width characteristics of the V10 with different angles between the cylinders. Not already in absolute terms, but for relative values with the purpose of knowing how many millimetres an engine type can be lowered (and, consequently, widened) by enlarging the "V" of the cylinders. If, in a horizontal sense, the dimensions calculated in this way, between the outside edges of the head, can be approximated to the numbers usually provided by the constructors (a method of unified measurement does not exist) in a vertical sense, it is necessary to add the lower dimensions of the clutch (discs of *4.5* or *5* inches in diameter, with a radius of *57* to *63* mm) and, above, the height of the induction trumpets or other parts, where those elements are considered. But our interest is solely concerned with the concentration of the engine mass, without reverting to very complex methods, the following dimensional modifications of *R=320* mm, can foster a summary valuation of the position of the centre of gravity in an average ratio of *1:2.5* with the height calculated in this way: (see page 20).

Therefore, in the field of metallurgy, the last year of freedom from regulations for the aluminium-beryllium alloys (already abolished for brakes), gave another push to increasing revolutions, with a maximum of *18,000 rpm*, and

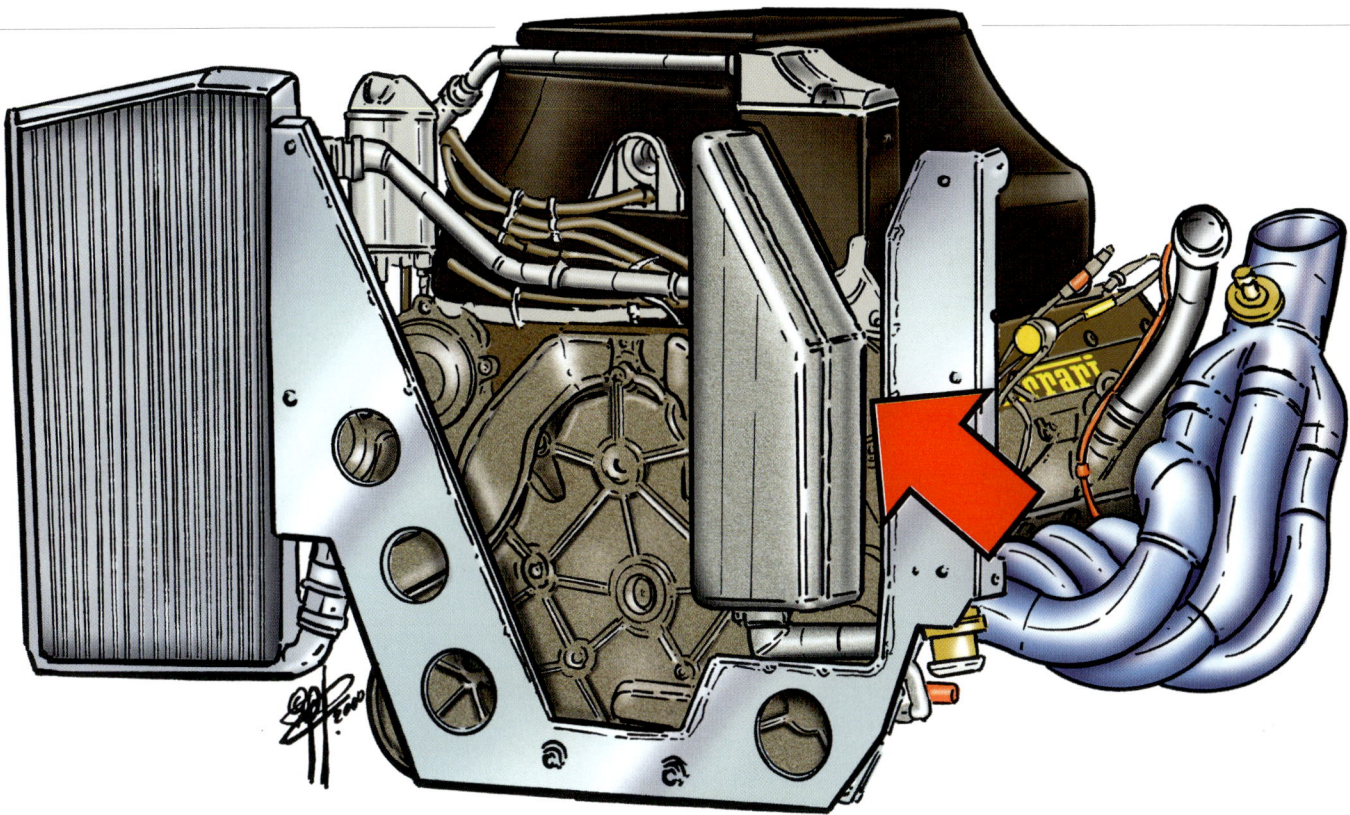

FERRARI

The 10 cylinder Ferrari 049 engine was one of the contributors to the Maranello manufacturer's triumph in both championships. With an 80° V, a weight of 102 kg and an accredited power of 820 hp in qualifying, 810 hp in race trim, it integrated perfectly with the revolutionary F1 2000 project. It was the first Ferrari engine to adopt the new disposition of the oil tank, placed in the frontal area and fitted inside the rear of the bodyshell. Note the asymmetric disposition and reduced dimensions of the tank itself, which required the installation of a supplementary element, fitted above the gearbox, to withstand the duration of the race.

BMW

The 10 cylinder BMW engine that powered the Williams caused some surprise on its F1 debut, by scoring a podium finish first time out, in Australia, and enabling Williams to return to the top of the constructor's championship table in a creditable third place by the end of the season. A result due more to the reliability of the 72° V10 engine, than the projective refinement of the platform, with decidedly generous physical dimensions, such as: 24 mm longer and as much as 17 kg heavier, in direct confrontation with the Ferrari 10 cylinder. Note the bigger oil tank (still within the limits of similar solutions adopted by other engine designers) compared to the size of the asymmetric tank fixed to the Ferrari engine.

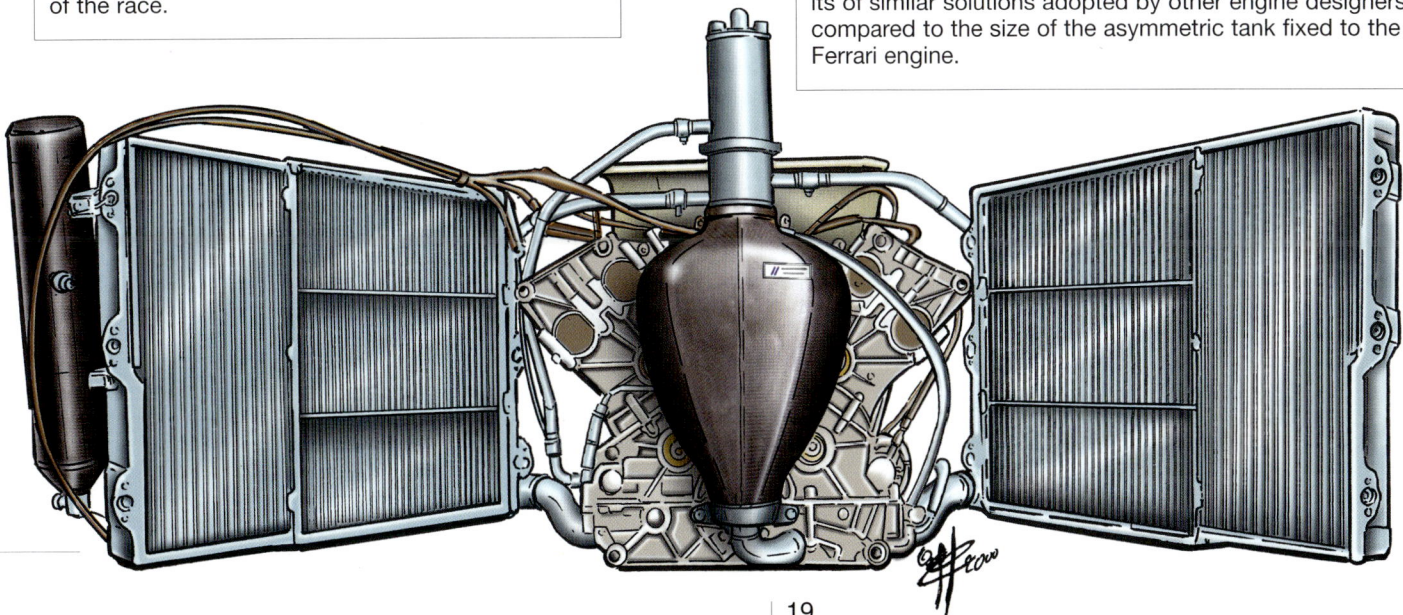

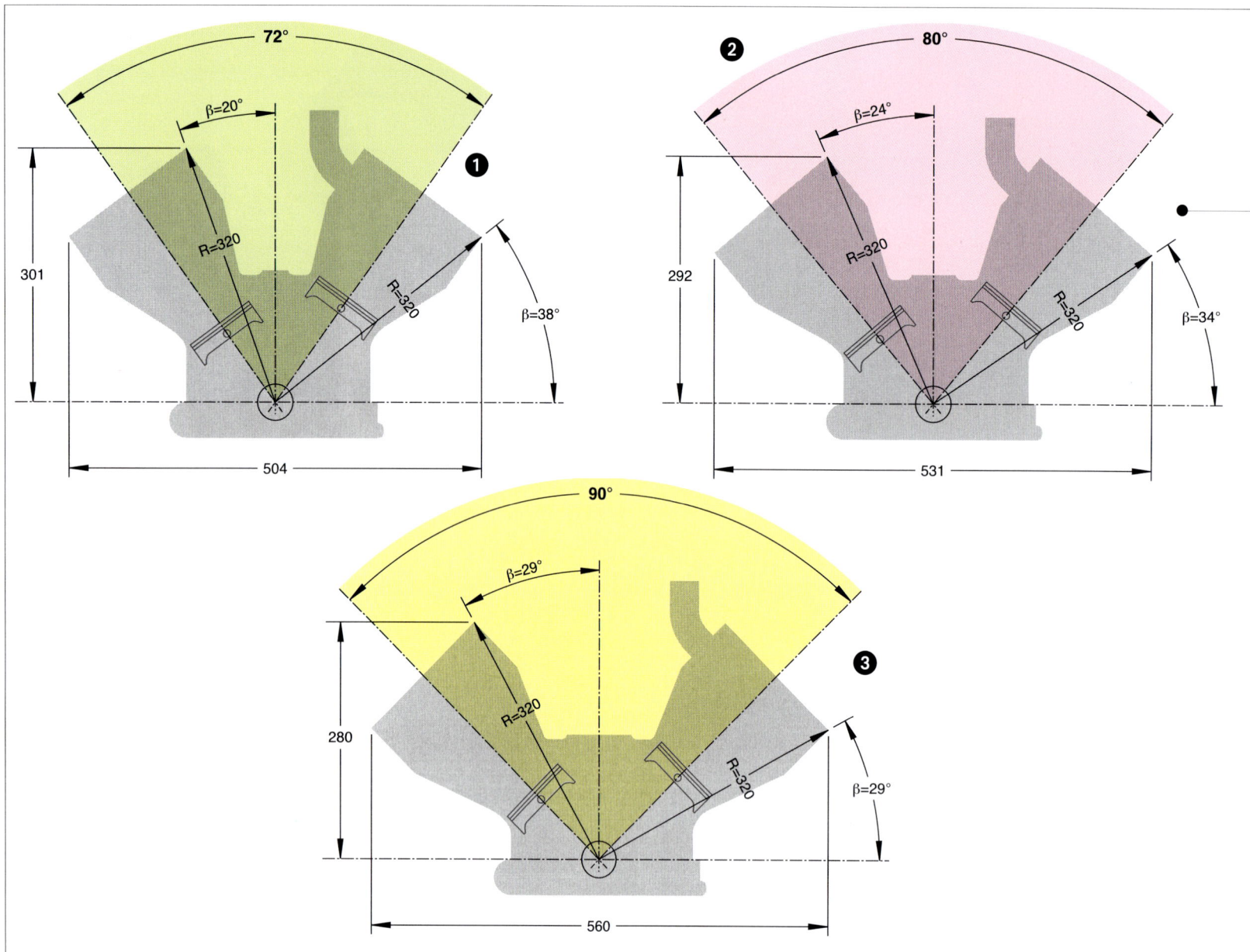

Angle	Variation of height measurements			Variation of width measurements		
V 72°	H = R cos (20) = 301 mm			W = R cos (38) x 2 = 504 mm		
V 80°	H = R cos (24) = 292	-9	-9 mm	W = R cos (34) x 2 = 531	27	27 mm
V 90°	H = R cos (29) = 280	-12	-21 mm	W = R cos (29) x 2 = 560	39	56 mm
V 100°	H = R cos (34) = 265	-15	-36 mm	W = R cos (24) x 2 = 585	25	81 mm

a reduction in weight to a limit of *92* kg, a value which merits comparison to the *165* kg minimum of three-litre engines of 30 years ago. This experimentation, prevalently concentrated on matching the pistons and cylinder liners in aluminium-beryllium (Ilmor-Mercedes, Honda and Cosworth), was important, both to permit a maximum acceleration of the pistons of close to *90,000* m/sec² and to reduce the total length of the engine by employing extremely thin walls, to the advantage of the car's distribution mass. And it has been a great stimulus for everyone: for the mechanical engineering school (the case of Ferrari) who did not take that route, but were still able to achieve almost equivalent results by the use of other, more or less traditional materials; for the same champions of aluminium

In these two drawings, showing the architecture of various engines, the different dimensions can be seen of the same power units in relation to the choice made of the angle of the cylinder banks. Of late in Formula One, the reduction of the centre of gravity factor has gradually become more determinate, and it is due to this factor that it has been necessary to widen the V of the engine to create a unit with a lower barycentre. The last drawing shows the comparison of the four solutions, more easily understood by the use of various colours in the upper graphics.

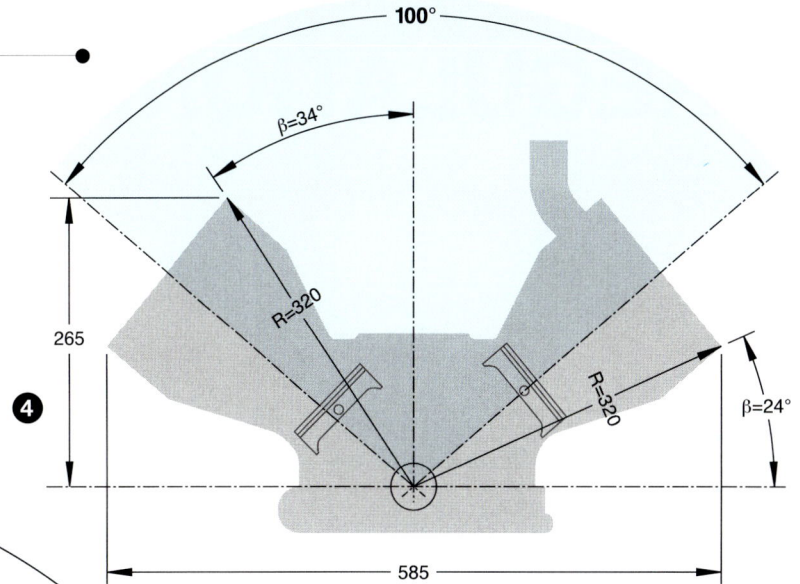

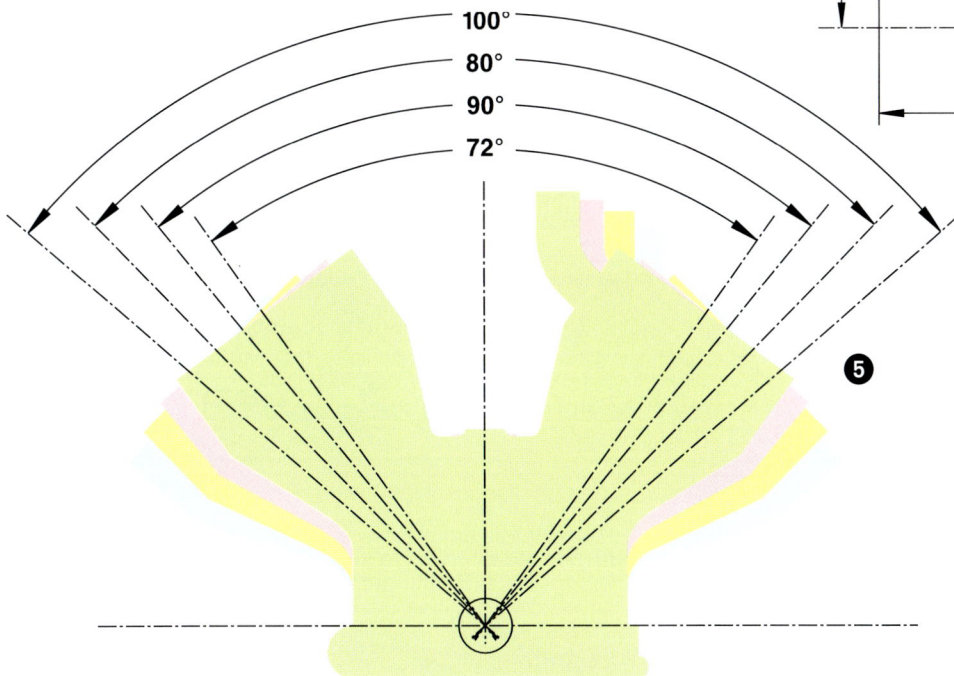

beryllium who, after historically notable progress, were able to maintain their positions even at the time of the elimination of the forbidden alloy before the season ended, to guarantee themselves a 2001 without a minimum of detraction.

Finally, an observation on the technical and functional characteristics of 2000 production (see table page 16-17): it can be seen that the estimated value of the bore has been subjected to some increase in the V10s of Ilmor-Mercedes, Honda, Mugen-Honda and Ford to permit increased revolutions while, against the trend, Peugeot returned to a smaller diameter (declared) to privilege torque and, above all, thermo-dynamic yield,

with a more collected combustion chamber. Of this, it should be remembered in the usual appraisal, that the *16,600* revs maximum of that engine is the equivalent of *17,000-17,500* of units with a diminishingly short stroke, in the light of principal indexes of mechanical exploitation. After which *25* m/sec of linear speed of the pistons has been overtaken in all cases of a medium-high C/A ratio and that the maximum speed of these components has reached *41* m/sec. It is also remarkable that, with these unitary cubic capacities and with these extremely high numbers of revolutions, the 10 cylinders of our era have been able to produce elevated levels of medium effective pressure (proportionate to the range of engine torque) with

values of *14.1-14.3* kg/cm² for the larger dimensioned stroke (Ilmor-Mercedes and Peugeot), and of *13.5-13.9* kg/cm² with a diminishing of the C/A ratio, the best results coming from Honda and Ferrari. That means an engine apparently on the limit of its performance can withstand further increases in revolutions – every *100* revolution step weighs like a millstone – without affecting the breadth of the field of utilisation. And that, in future evolution, with these parameters well consolidated and after the unjustified "euthanasia" of the *12*-cylinder, will continue to be rewarded for global performance, as well as for power increases bought with significant increases in revolutions per minute.
Enrico Benzing

THE NEW REGULATIONS

The 2000 season opened in search of regulation stability, after the revolution of '98, when the Federation introduced a limitation on the total width of the car and brought in grooved tyres. There were successive adjustments imposed in '99, including the addition of the fourth groove - for the front tyres, too - as well as numerous safety improvements. The only exception concerned a clarification on protection at the sides of the driver's head, substituted in previous years by more or less large fins for the purpose of getting around the '96 rules. Features that immediately created controversy and ill humour, as happened in '99 with Jordan (page 24, '99 Technical Analysis). Stability while waiting for the major 2001 revolution, of which only the need for greater severity of the roll bar protection crash test was notified in advance at the start of the year. At the invitation of the Federation, most teams brought forward to their 2000 cars the introduction of means by which to meet this rule. Only three teams did not accept Federation president Max Moseley's invitation: Prost, BAR and Sauber. It was odd that the Swiss team, at least, did not meet the new regulation after the accident involving Pedro Paulo Diniz, whose car's roll bar came away during the '99 Grand Prix of Europe and was the subject of an FIA intervention with decidedly more severe results.

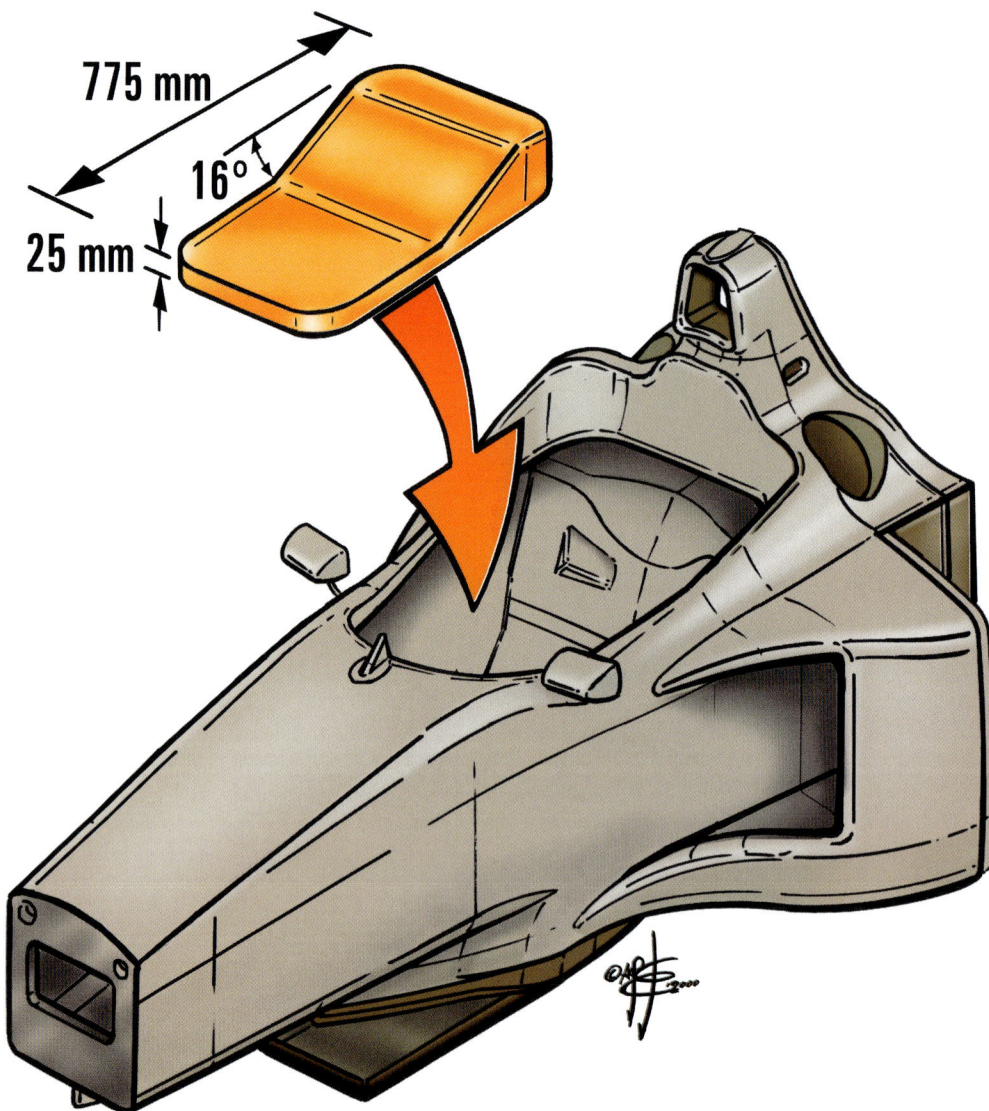

775 mm

16°

25 mm

COCKPIT OPENING

To stop the teams continuing to more or less blatantly get around the rule governing protection on the car at the sides of the driver's head, the Federation brought in a template or type of mask for the driver opening that, in substance, required a precise inclination of the protection structure, as shown in the drawing. In practice, the technical commissioners use a template that they place horizontally, at a height of 525 mm above the refuelling plane: that determines unequivocally the run of the chassis and the protection in the cockpit area. At 375 mm of the total 775 mm of the length of the cockpit opening, the inclination of the protection must be 16°. In that way, the Federation would have been able to banish all types of fins introduced in recent years to get around the protection regulations. But, as can be seen on page 26, this remained an unfulfilled objective, with the continued existence of suspect protection including Jordan's, the very team that, in a certain sense, inspired the new '99 restrictions.

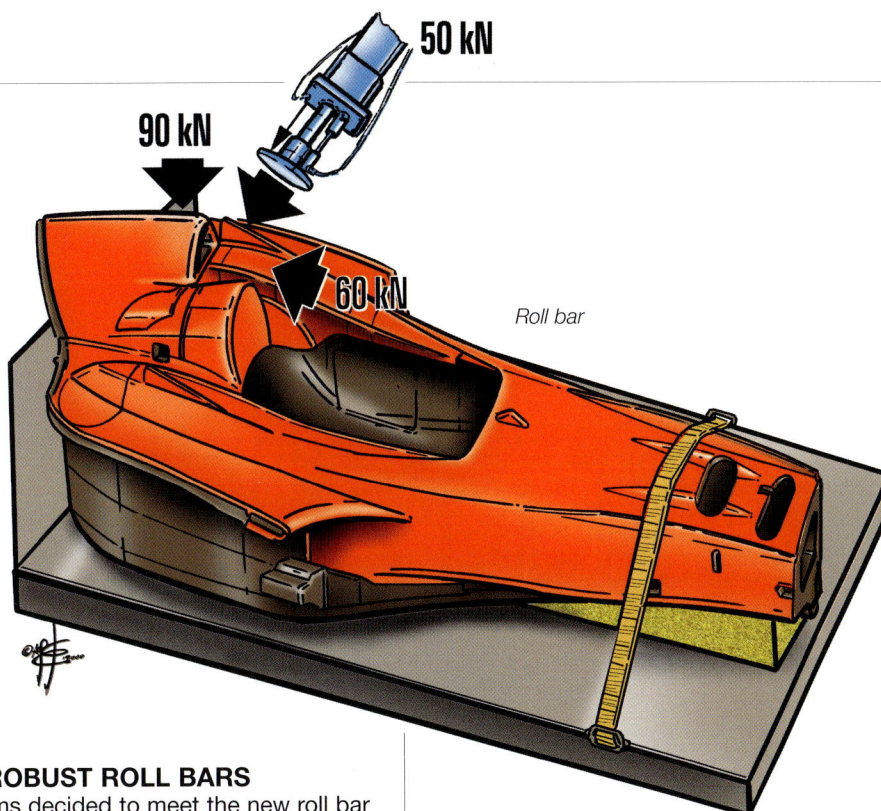

50 kN
90 kN
60 kN

Roll bar

MORE ROBUST ROLL BARS

Most teams decided to meet the new roll bar safety regulations earlier than required, on their 2000 models. The drawing shows the monocoque of the Ferrari, with its peculiarly shaped roll bar. In practice, to be able to meet the most severe crash test (50 kN lateral, 60 kN longitudinal and 90 kN vertical) the structure has a bigger surface and is inclined backwards. Below is the area of the protection structure for the cockpit, the subject of further major modifications that the Federation launched for 2001.

LIMITED ELECTRONICS

A drastic reduction of the various systems of electronic control should have come into force from the GP of Great Britain, with a view to bringing clarity to the possibility of using systems of programmed starting and traction control. At the centre of this limitation was the impossibility of managing, as intervening parameters, sensors fitted to all wheels, connected to others inside the engine. At first, it was even thought that the speed limiters in the pits and sensors that measure the speed of the wheels should be eliminated, while it was confirmed that they could not supply information with which to measure the rotation of the rears. The drawing shows a phonic wheel that with the sensors measures the rotation speed. In the end, severe limits were placed on the possibility of varying the parameters of the electronic accelerator of the air/petrol mixture and the differential. On the eve of the British Grand Prix, the pit speed limiter button was allowed back (on the left spoke of Hakkinen's steering wheel) connected to a small door of an aperture for the petrol filler, so as to easily measure any infractions.

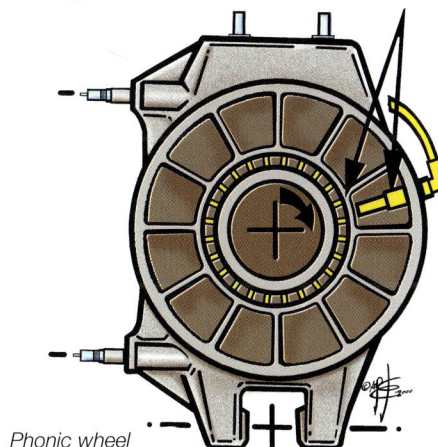

Phonic wheel

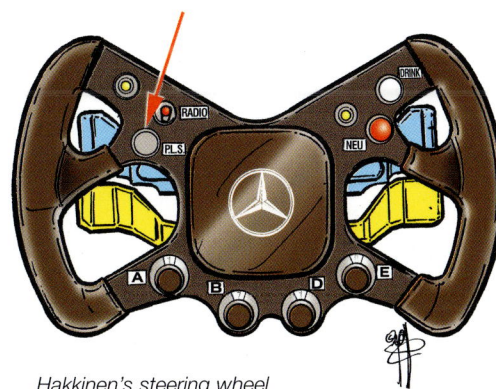

Hakkinen's steering wheel

TECHNICAL VERIFICATIONS

In Formula One, technical verifications are fundamental; the technical regulation in this respect is extremely precise and says: "The car must conform to the regulations for the entire duration of the event". A GP begins on Thursday afternoon with the scrutineering of the cars and ends only after the termination of verification at the end of the race. In fact, the most severe checks are carried out on the Thursday and after the race. The first important check tends to certify that all cars entered for the race respect all technical requirements. After qualifying and at the end of the race it must be established that no changes have been made to the cars and that the regulations have been respected. In the case of new monocoques, for example, the date the chassis passed the crash test must be established and be contained in microchips that tell the monocoque's life story, recessed into three different areas. At the track, this data is checked using a German Trovan reading device (see Technical Analysis '98, page 22). During official practice, quick random checks are conducted. This control work is carried out in synthesis throughout the weekend by technical commissioners, headed by Joe Bauer.

TECHNICAL CHECKS – THURSDAY

- Chassis read
- Protective roll bar
- Security of ballast
- Fuel tank safety valve
- Water or oil lines in cockpit
- Verification of the oil circuit and that the position of the oil reservoir does not extend beyond the rear axle
- Indication of neutral switch
- Two separate braking circuits and limitations in force
- Dimensions of the front and rear brake ducts
- Check various cockpit dimensions and fit the cockpit cross section template
- Extinguishing system and extinguisher switches for driver and marshals
- Switches in general (inside and out)
- Rear view mirror sizes
- Conformity of seat belts
- Rear light
- Headrest
- Position of the pedals to the axis of the car
- Presence of the rear impact absorbing structure
- Camera car
- Radio
- Conformity of the driver's helmet and overalls

Obviously, this is a brief summary of the checks carried out; each item could require a number of different measurements.

Reference Plane

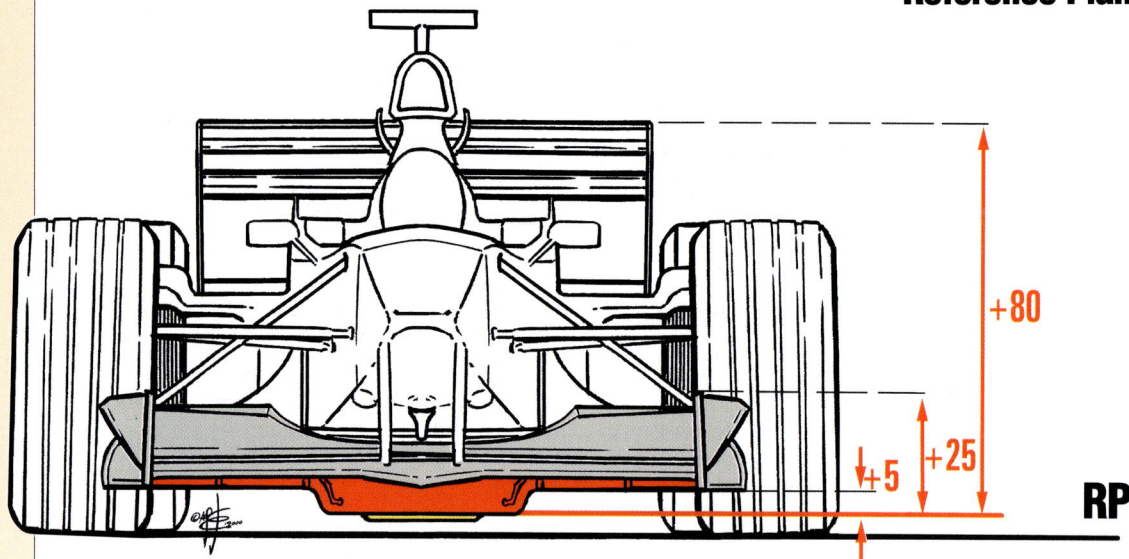

TECHNICAL CHECKS – FREE TESTING, FRIDAY (AT RANDOM)
- Software and electronic components
- Fuel sample
- Weighing
- Tyres

TECHNICAL CHECKS - SATURDAY
- Software and electronic units
- Fuel sample
- Weighing
- Tyres
- Bodywork around the front wheels
- Front wing height and overhang
- Rear wing height and overhang
- Stepped bottom

Random checks may be carried out of the:
Wooden plank
Body at various points
Front and rear wing deflection
Engine and its components
Gearbox and its components (reverse, number of gears, etc)
Brakes and caliper material
Rims
Driver cockpit exit time
Headrest
Removable driver's seat
All crash structures

TECHNICAL CHECKS BEFORE THE RACE
On all cars:
Thickness of brake discs
Tyres (five minutes before the start)

Random:
Software and electronics
Fuel sample

TECHNICAL CHECKS AFTER THE RACE
All cars:
Weight
Tyres

The first six cars to finish:
Front bodywork
Front wing (all dimensions)
Rear wing (all dimensions)
Stepped bottom
Wooden plank (thickness)
Wooden plank mounts
Rear bodywork
Fins in front of the rear wheels
Maximum height
Maximum width

All possible checks may be carried out, such as after Saturday practice.

REFERENCE PLANE
In '95 the Federation revolutionised the system for measuring the cars to more easily check dimensions: height measurements were no longer taken from the ground, a means that had sparked off considerable controversy in the past with teams circumventing the rules with systems that varied the cars' height from the ground. For the different levels, the reference point was to be the lowest part of the car, but take note: not the lower area of the wooden plank (a centimetre high and shown in yellow) but the area of the small step shown with a red line in the drawing.

The stepped area is 50 cm wide on the outside and the sides must be 5 cm higher than the central zone. It is from this that the term "stepped bottom" has been derived for current cars. In the same way, to reduce the negative lift, the whole front wing group must be at +5 cm in respect of the reference plane. To also limit the downforce, the front planes must be contained within +5 cm and +25 cm from the same plane and, therefore in practice, have a height of 20 cm. All the other height measurements must be compared to the Reference Plane, such as those of the rear wing, fixed at +80 cm.

TECHNICAL CHECKS – DURING PRACTICE
During each practice session, random checks may be carried out on between eight and 10 cars, using a special device made by the American company Buckeye Machine Fabrications which, since the tests' introduction in 1995, has been taken to each GP. The equipment weighs about 800 kg and cost $400,000.
The platform has two ramps (1) and scales made by Captels of France. At the centre there is a moving plane (3) to keep the car against the reference plane. The small pistons that raise themselves (4) mate with the six 50 mm diameter holes placed with extreme precision in the wooden plank, so as to check its

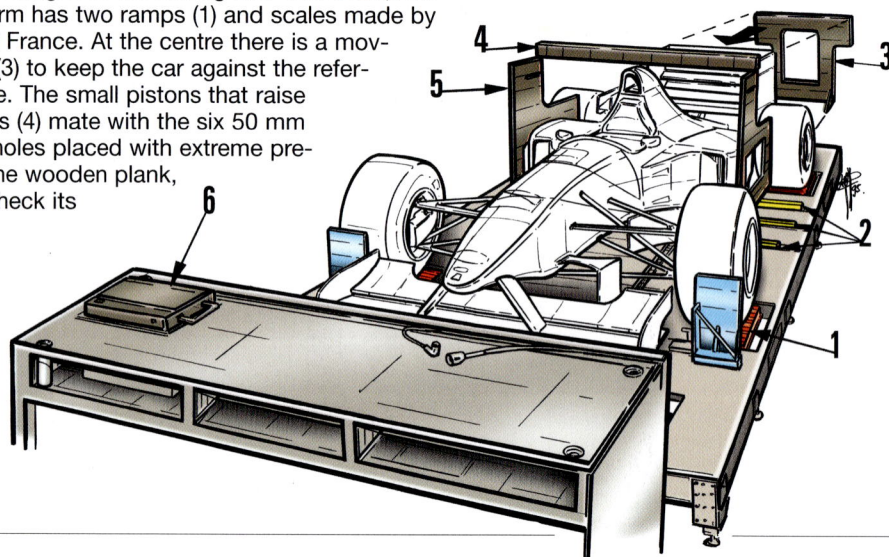

VERIFICATION OF THE FRONT WING

To limit the use of a 1997 system in which the front wing that bent in the peripheral area and sealed the front planes to the ground to increase downforce, a bending test was introduced for the '98 season. It entailed a 50 kg weight being fixed to each of the end plates.

VERIFICATION OF THE REAR WING

At the second GP of the '99 season, a second bending test was introduced for the rear wing, the construction of which had raised suspicions during winter testing. Cars had rear wing groups that bent backwards, guaranteeing a notable improvement in pure speed. The drawing illustrates the device introduced by FISA to apply pressure – 140 kg longitudinally – to the rear wing.

DISC BRAKES

Five minutes before the start of a GP, FIA's technical commissioners check the width of the brake discs which, from 1999, have been limited to just 28 mm on all cars before they join the grid. Of course, tyre seals are also checked.

effective width in a matter of seconds. In these points – and only these points – eventual plank wear must not exceed 10% of the plank's total thickness or a maximum of one millimetre. In (5) is indicated the hydraulic management part, with the various runners and jacks that adapt the platform to all the different cars. The checking operation takes a maximum of two or three minutes. Weight (1) measurements are taken and communicated by printer (6) to the driver, the regularity of the stepped bottom (2), the maximum width (4), height (5) and wing dimensions (3) with the help of special made-to-measure templates.

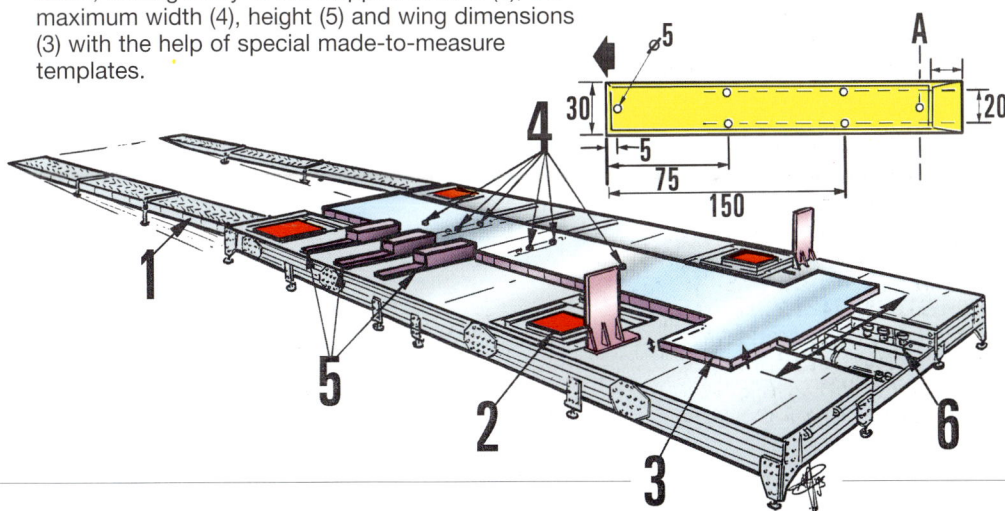

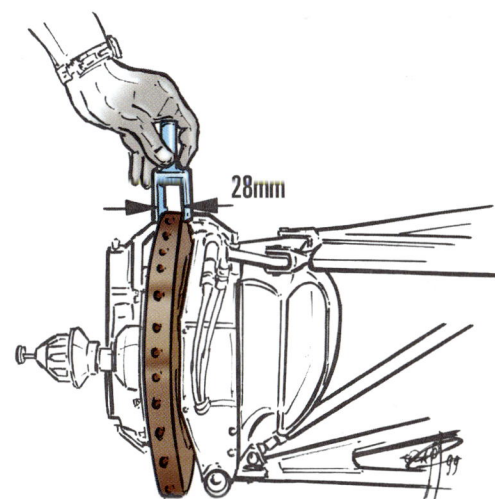

CONTROVERSY IN 2000

It was a relatively tranquil season from the point of view of disputes, which were concentrated on the first two races and the Grand Prix of Austria. On three occasions, in fact, there were three disqualifications involving two teams, Sauber and McLaren. The discontent at the beginning of the season concerned that which, by now, has become a recurring theme in the world of F1 and that is the drawing up, at times ponderously complicated, of the rules, and the bravura of the designers of the various teams in being able to get around them and extract advantages more or less manifestly legal. To tell the truth, the subject of protests at the beginning of the world championship was an area in which the Federation had corrected the casting of the draft rule on the protection of the sides of the driver's head of the cockpit, so as to avoid continuous interpretations which have been made from the moment it was introduced in '96. The noisiest controversy came about in the previous season, with an almost total lack of protection, represented by highly visible fins, the work of Jordan. To dispel all doubts, a modification was introduced for 2000 (art. 13.1.19), that permitted the teams to determine unequivocally, the shape and dimensions of this type of protection (page 22). Nevertheless in Australia, the first race of the season, controversy blew up again concerning the interpretation of this rule and, yet again, the most extreme example was by Jordan. Perplexity also surrounded the new concept of protection adopted by Ferrari, Minardi and, in part, by McLaren, who were legal as regards lateral height was concerned but, in practice, widened the inside area of the sides of the cockpit. Surprisingly, at the technical scrutineering on Thursday, the commissioners recognised irregularities on two other cars, Coulthard's McLaren and the Arrows, while the Jordans were judged legal, regardless of the fact that it was clear they did not respect the principal reason for the regulation: the introduction of a verification mask, which rigorously determined the point at which the protection had to incline upwards by 16°, 375 mm from the end of the tub, and the point at which the

same protection had to stop, at the end of the driver's helmet. The real disqualification at the opening race took place at the end of the Grand Prix with the Sauber of Salo, which was caught with the end-plates of the front wing of incorrect size. There was an even more incandescent end of race in Brazil, with five cars

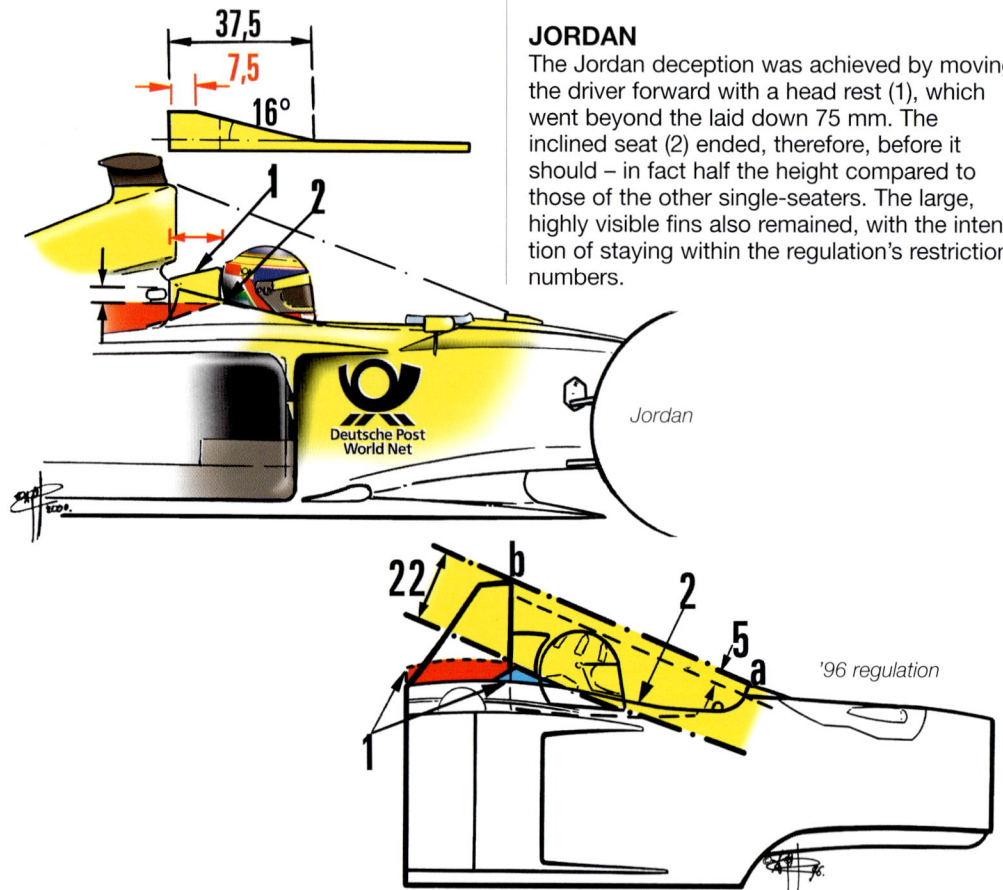

being investigated: the Ferrari of winner Michael Schumacher, the McLaren of second placed Coulthard, the Williams of Ralf Schumacher and the two Jordans, with only the McLaren disqualified due to the lack of height from the ground of the end-plates of the front wing. Instead, the excuse for the other single-seaters that were found to have their "wooden" planks damaged, was the exceptional irregularity of the track's asphalt, which provoked more abrasion than that expected by the teams. The final disqualification of the season took place at the Grand Prix of Austria, where McLaren was once more under the microscope through Hakkinen's winning car, found during the post-race verification to have the black box minus one of its seals, which Federation officials must apply to each car. A mystery that resolved itself with no effect on the drivers' championship, but with points being subtracted from the team's total in the constructors table, the perfect conformity of the black box having been established, in spite of the absence of one of the seals.

JORDAN

The Jordan deception was achieved by moving the driver forward with a head rest (1), which went beyond the laid down 75 mm. The inclined seat (2) ended, therefore, before it should – in fact half the height compared to those of the other single-seaters. The large, highly visible fins also remained, with the intention of staying within the regulation's restriction numbers.

Jordan

'96 regulation

THE '96 REGULATION

During the 1996 season, the Federation introduced protection for the side of the driver's head, which had to leave the driver's eyes free. The height and inclination were determined by a parallel of less than 22 cm of the union of the two protective roll bars, a regulation that immediately gave rise to many different interpretations. Some teams, like Williams, got around the obstacle by introducing vertical fins (1) with a view to respecting the regulation and lowering the height of the chassis in that area. Fins that were then used in subsequent seasons by all teams.

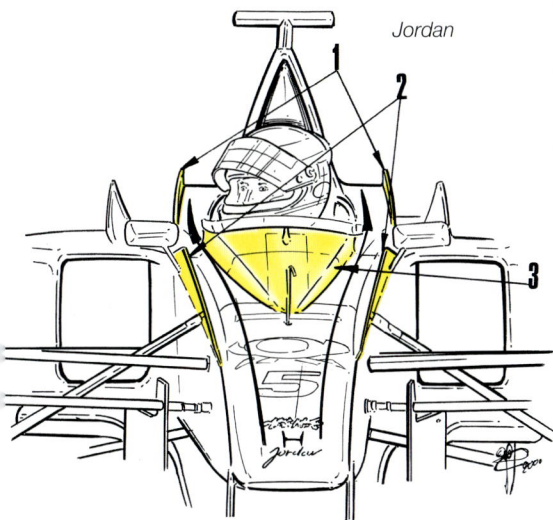

Jordan

JORDAN

From the front can be seen the various strata-gems used by Jordan, to get around the rule concerning protection at the sides of the cockpit, with prominent fins (1) at the sides of the driver's head and chassis (2) to be able to lower the section in the cockpit area. In the centre, there is a prominent piece of faring (3) with the job of deflecting the airflow towards the rear of the car.

ARROWS

The Arrows protection was manifestly irregular: too low at the sides of the driver's head and not responsive to the mask introduced by the Federation. To comply with the regulations, the British team had to add material inside the fins (as indicated by the arrows) in time for Friday's free practice sessions, undertaking to produce new protection in time for the second race of the season.

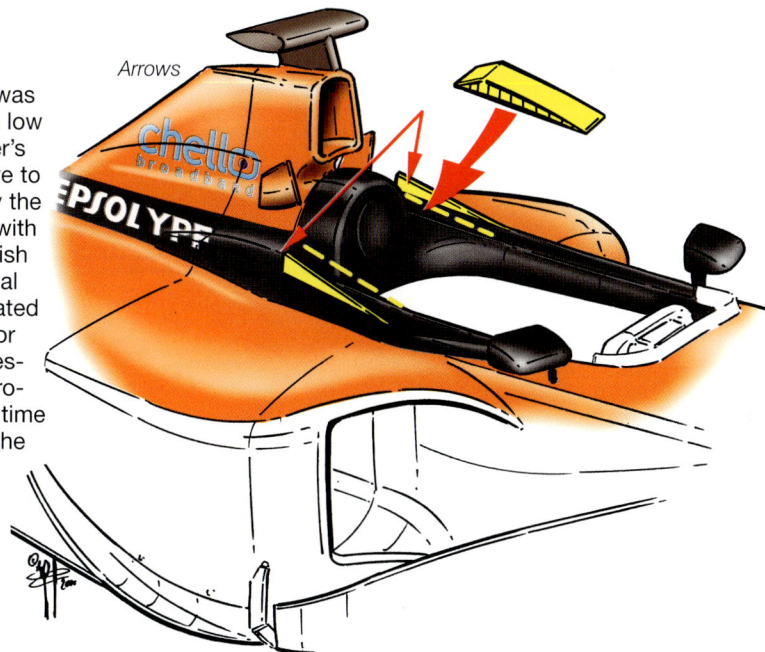

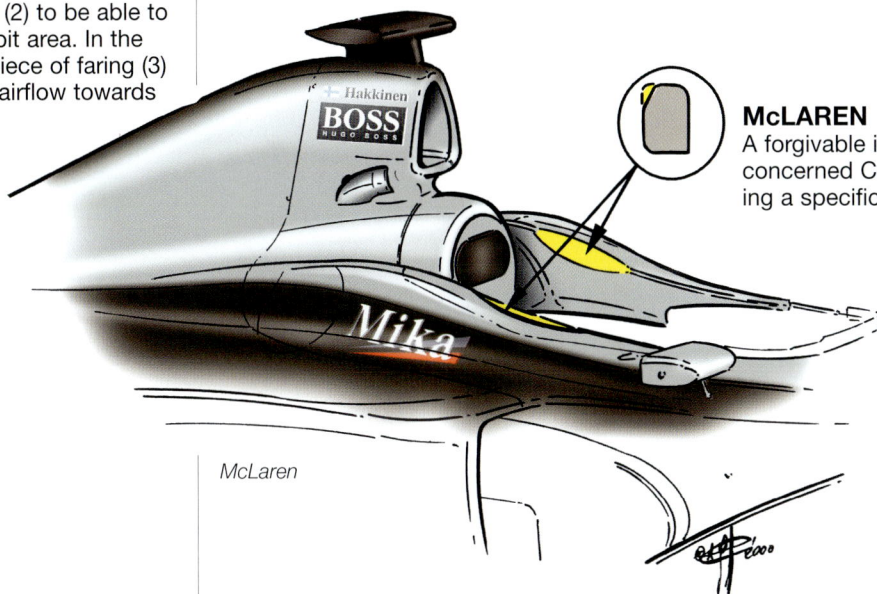

Arrows

McLAREN

A forgivable infraction by McLaren. It only concerned Coulthard's car on which, following a specific request by the driver, a small part was cut away to permit more lateral movement of the head. But the regulation demands a section of a constant 25 cm^2 above all in the areas at the sides of the driver's head. It was sufficient to add absorbent material in the lowered area to make the car identical to Hakkinen's and, more important, conform to the regulations.

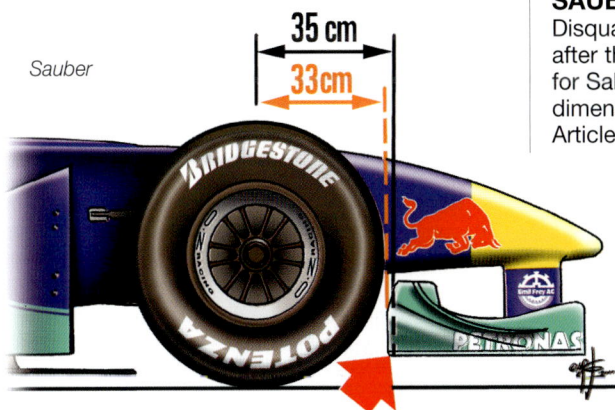

McLaren

Sauber

35 cm
33 cm

SAUBER, GP OF AUSTRALIA

Disqualification during post-race scrutineering after the first event of the season in Melbourne for Salo's Sauber, found to be irregular in the dimensions of the end-plates of its front wing. Article 3.11 of the technical regulations stipulates that the area in front of the axle of the front wheels must not be occupied by body parts for a limit of 35 cm from the axle itself. But the end-plates of the Sauber were 2 cm closer to the wheels: it was for that reason that the car was, rightly, disqualified, losing the Swiss team its sixth place.

27

50 mm

GP of Austria
Hakkinen

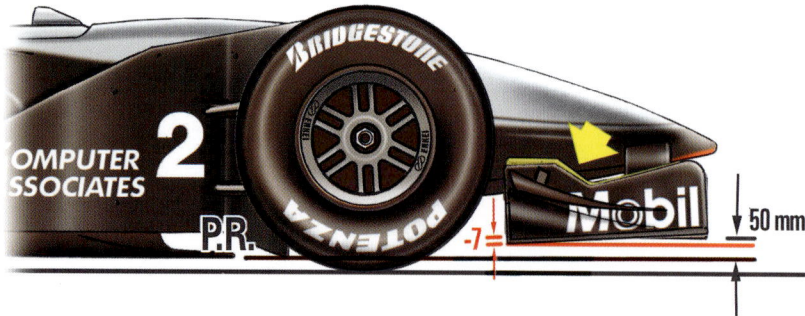

GP OF BRAZIL – COULTHARD

Scrutineering after the GP of Brazil was eventful, with five cars being investigated for not respecting art. 3.11 (Coulthard's McLaren) and art 3.13 (Michael Schumacher's Ferrari, brother Ralf's Williams and the two Jordans): the latter admitted a maximum tolerance in the use of the thickness of the so called plank of "wood" at the end of the race of 10%, in other words 1 mm. This rule has a famous precedent, the disqualification of Michael after winning the GP of Belgium in 1994. Because the car strayed onto the kerb, the plank of his Benetton was damaged by almost 2 mm in the area in which it came into contact with the red and white border of the track. From the GP of Japan of the same year, and to avoid such excessive severity, the Federation introduced 10 titanium pads, in specific areas of the plank, to side step useless disqualifications and also introduced the concept of discrétion in the application of the rules. The four cars involved were, eventually, absolved by the technical commissioners in Brazil, while McLaren was confirmed as irregular. In the case of Coulthard's car, the endplates of the front wing were guilty of being 7 mm lower (2 mm more than the eventual 5 mm tolerance) at the rear, compared to 50 mm high above the alignment, as prescribed by the rules.

GP OF AUSTRIA

Mika Hakkinen risked losing a fantastic victory in the GP of Austria, because one of the two seals that the commissioners had applied to the black boxes of all F1 cars was missing. On 25 July, about a week after the Austrian GP, the Federation decided to punish the team only, because it was guilty of not having verified the presence of the seal at post-race scrutineering. An omission on the part of the person whose job it was to apply the seal, even if it was never officially admitted, left the driver's championship untouched but lost McLaren the 16 points it had won during the race. The drawing shows the final check of the notorious black box, on the left-hand side of the MP4/15, which is carried out on the grid.

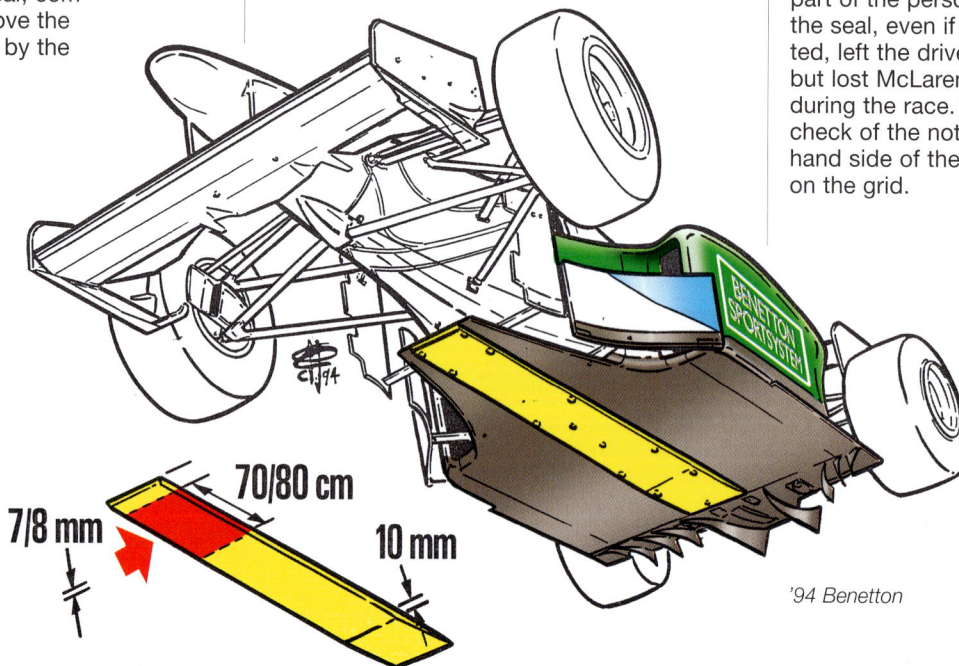

70/80 cm

7/8 mm

10 mm

'94 Benetton

NEW FEATURES
AND TRENDS

During the third season after the introduction of grooved tyres and the drastic reduction in the total width of F1 cars, (from 200 cm to 180 cm) the 2000 season concluded without major innovation, after seething with a vivacity of design in '98, the debut season of the new rules. Following gradual alignment with the new trends of '99, there was further consolidation of certain features in 2000. They included the value of the standardised wheelbase, oscillating between 305 cm and 310 cm; the need to design ultra-light cars in order to use heavy ballast rates in the search for optimum set-ups; the central position of the oil reservoir, used by three out of 11 teams in '98 and eight in '99 to, finally, 10 in 2000, with the single exception of Sauber, which adopted the 1999 Ferrari engine, therefore stuck with the old disposition of the oil pump. So there was a lack of obvious new features, although a number of new developments had initially caused some surprise, even if closer scrutiny revealed them to be revivals of at least two ideas that had already been used. It is not rare in Formula One to see a kind of reaching back into the past, sometimes using

notions tried years earlier, when they showed themselves to be of little advantage, but which suddenly return to favour, reinforced by changes in technical regulations or the different needs faced by the designers. That is the case with the chimneys, brought back to F1 by that genius of inventiveness, Adrian Newey, but already briefly seen on the Shadows of Elio De Angelis and Jan Lammers back in 1979, or the upper wishbone of the rear suspension, placed at mid-height to integrate the drive shafts inside it, as adopted by the McLaren MP4/15 but used earlier by Newey himself on the unfortunate Williams FW 16 of the late Ayrton Senna. The fashion of using steel wheel nuts of reduced section is also not really new: they first appeared at Indy and were brought to Europe by Alan Jenkins, who used them on the '97 Stewart. What were innovative were two developments presented by two second level teams: the fusion

of the gearbox in titanium, instead of magnesium or aluminium alloy, first introduced by Minardi and the double fixing (or pick-up points) of the lower wishbone, usually fixed in a single prominent central point, used for the first time by Sauber.

McLAREN MP4/15 – SHADOW '79 DN9

One surprise was the return of chimneys to discharge radiator heat, adopted for the McLaren MP4/15 of Adrian Newey, the most able designer of recent years in Formula One. He did nothing other than to take up an idea first introduced on another car, the 1979 Shadow DN9. To tell the truth, this development, by a now non-existent British team, of which the drivers were Elio De Angelis and Jan Lammers, had little success, while the McLaren chimneys not only remained on their cars for all races, they were also copied by Ferrari and Williams during the 2000 season.

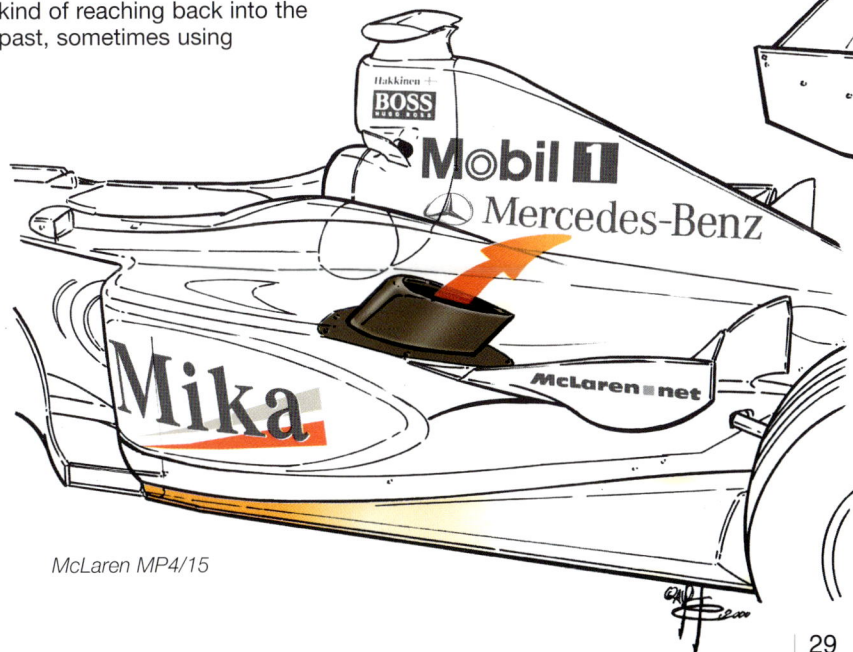

Shadow DN9

McLaren MP4/15

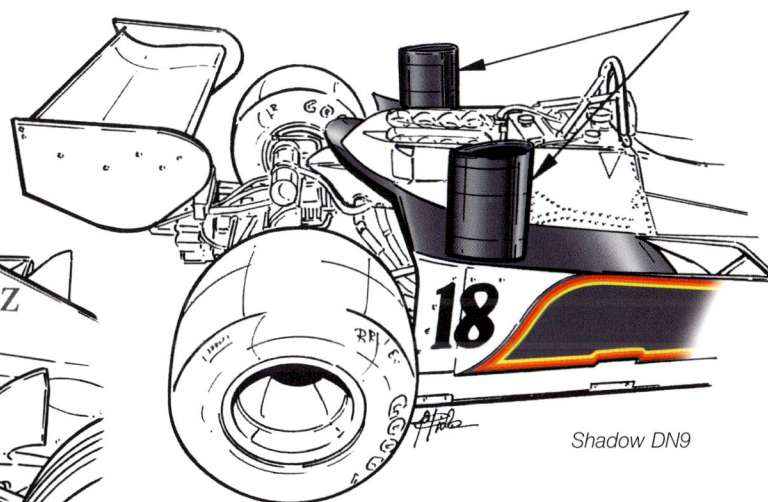

3   2   *Titanium*   1

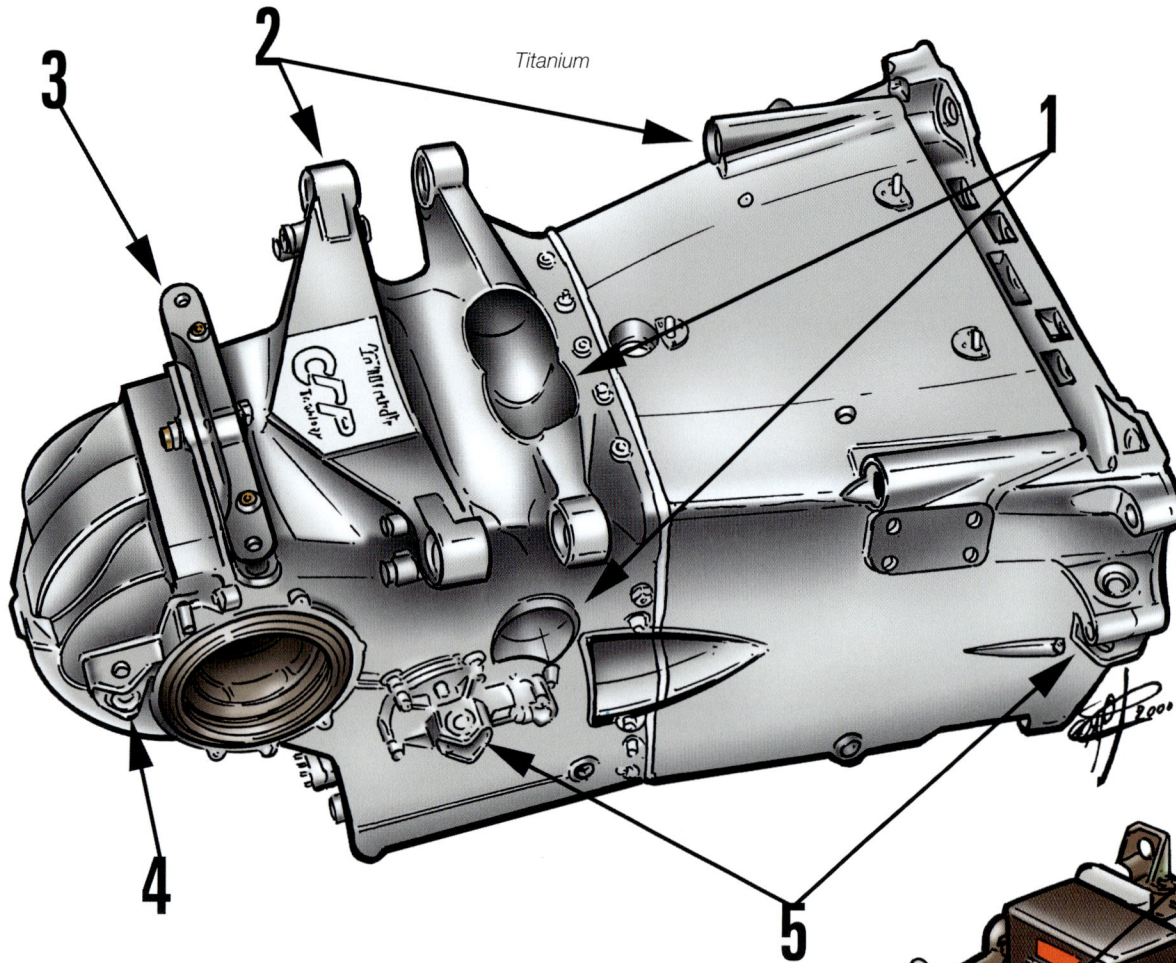

space-saving factor and a 30% increase in torsional rigidity. The weight-saving was also obtained due to a rationalisation of the steering link mounts of the suspension (2) the upper wishbone, (3-4) torsion bars, (5) lower wishbones included in the fusion, while they were external on the old box, applied (1-2) to the fusion in magnesium. The shock absorber housing (1) is visible in the drawing of the new gearbox, inclined in a V-shape and attached directly in a low position to the outside of the box.

4   5   1

MINARDI'S TITANIUM GEARBOX

The real new technical development of the season came from Minardi at the GP of Spain: the team introduced new technology for the construction of an F1 gearbox. It appeared after John Barnard's '97 Ferrari box with sheet titanium, and carbon fibre boxes by Barnard for Arrows and Alan Jenkins for Stewart in '98. In collaboration with CRP of Modena, the team, from Faenza, Italy, premiered a gearbox made entirely of titanium alloy, instead of the classic magnesium or aluminium alloy. The previous season, this technique was concentrated on the construction of uprights, which were later also used in 2000 by Williams - made by Don Casters Settas of Belgium - and BAR. The resultant weight reduction was notable at 25%, accompanied by a 20%

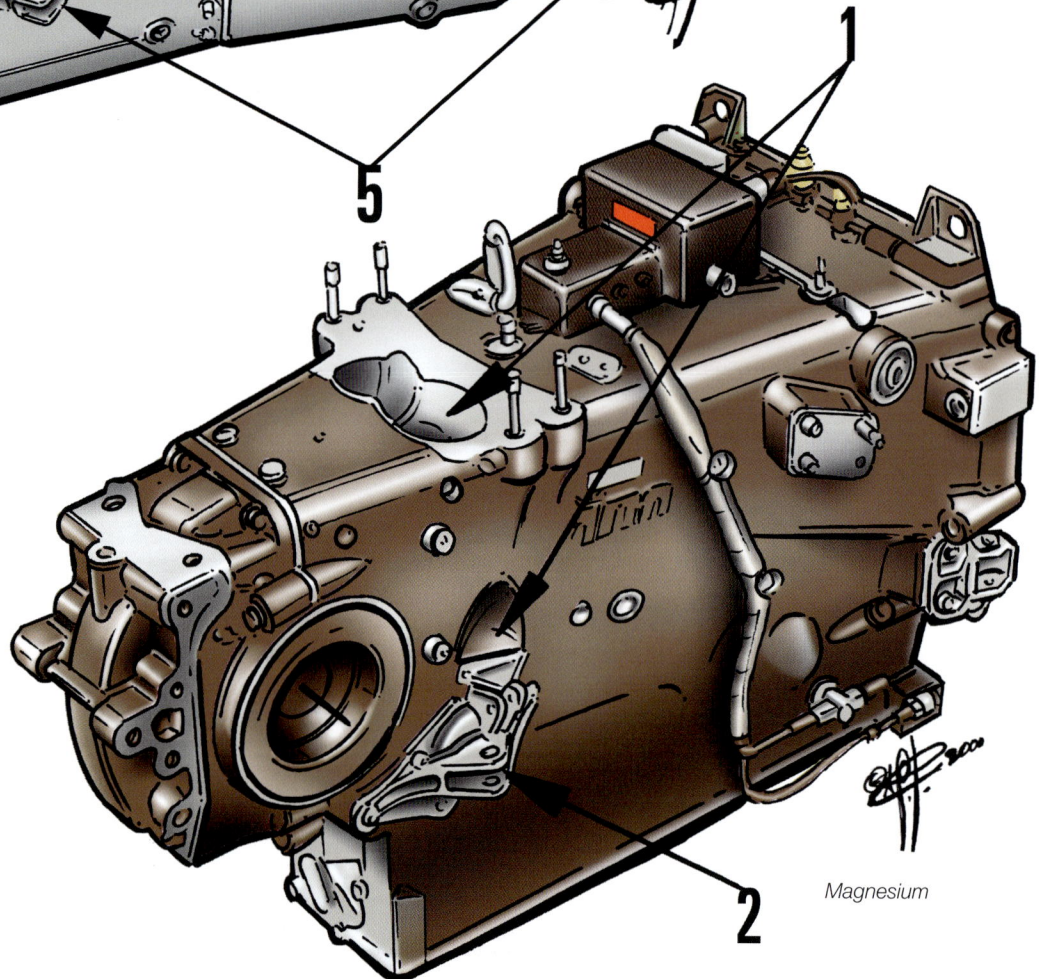

2   *Magnesium*

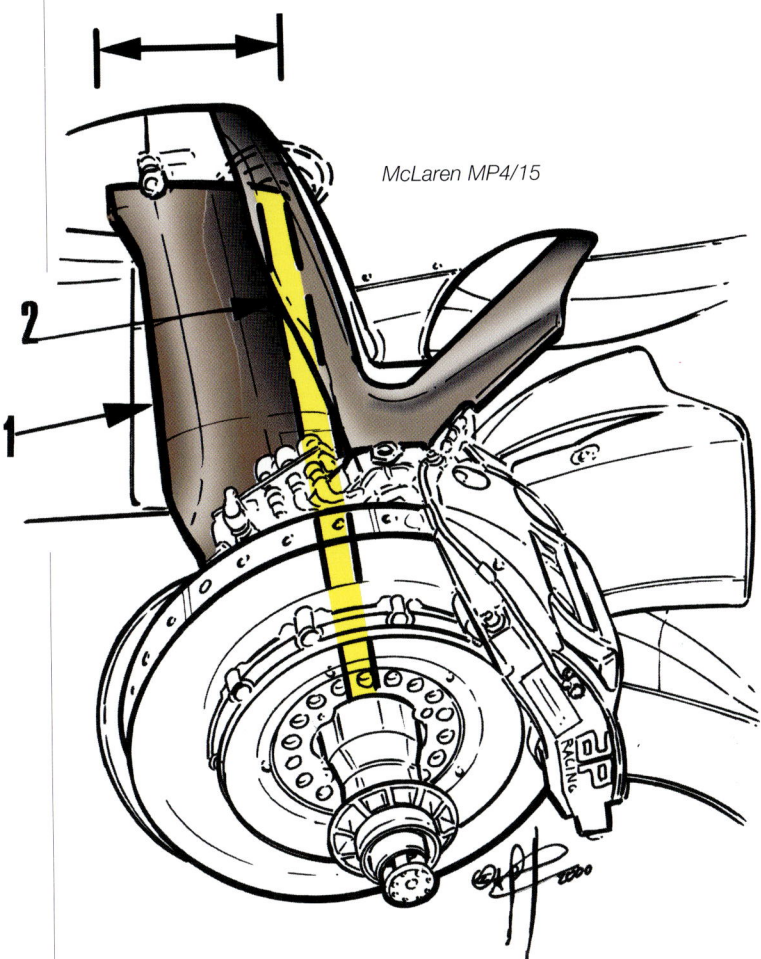

McLaren MP4/15

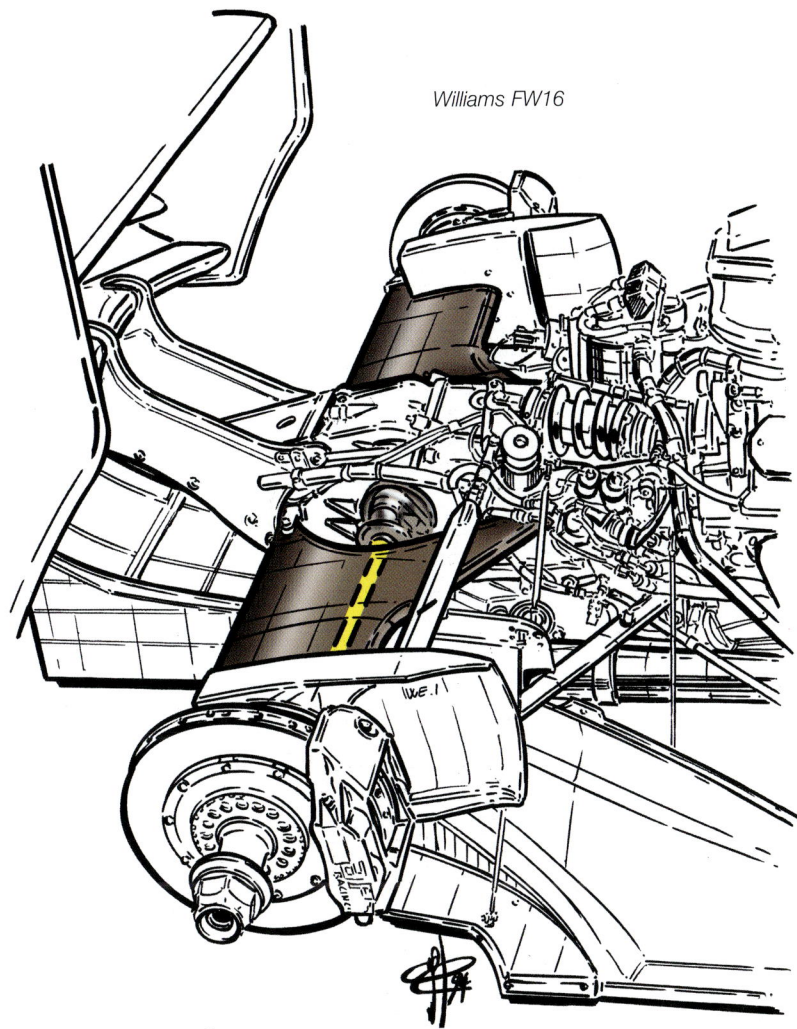

2

1

Williams FW16

McLAREN MP4/15 – WILLIAMS '94 FW16

For his MP4/15, Adrian Newey reintroduced an idea that he first used in 1994, when he was the technician in charge at Williams – the drive-shaft (2) hidden away inside a suspension arm. It was the upper wishbone (1) of the suspension on the FW 16 and was incredibly low: on the MP4/15 it was the convergence link. The arms were of carbon fibre in both cases, and were of notable size, with a winged section in profile. From this came substantial aerodynamic benefit, with a drastic reduction in the turbulence created by the rotating drive shafts in the open air.

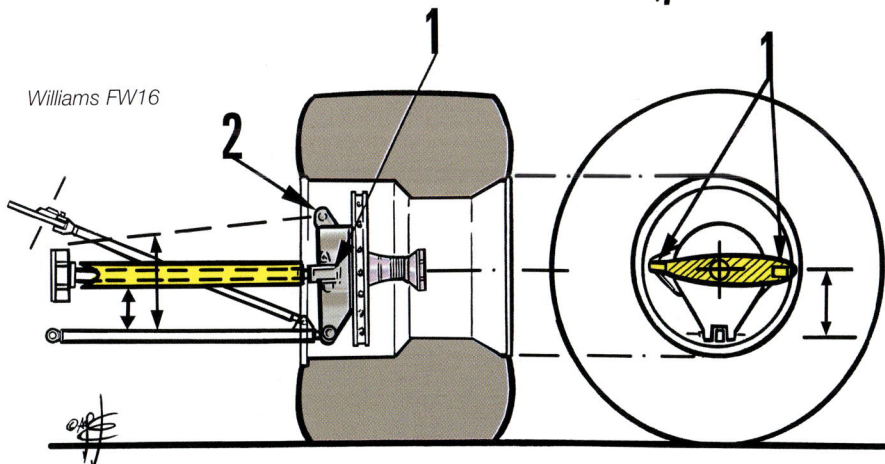

Williams FW16

1

2

1

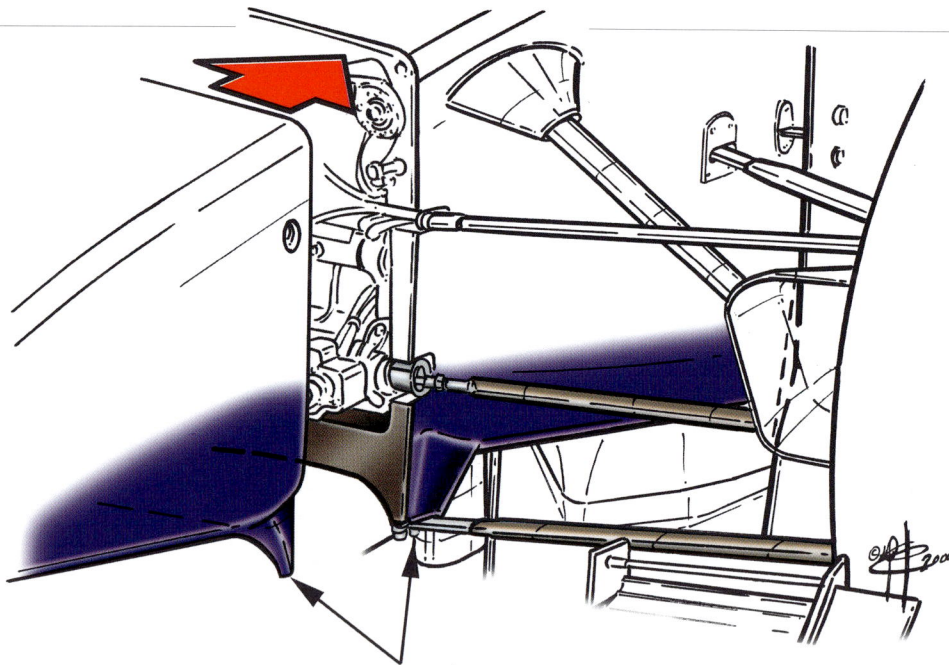

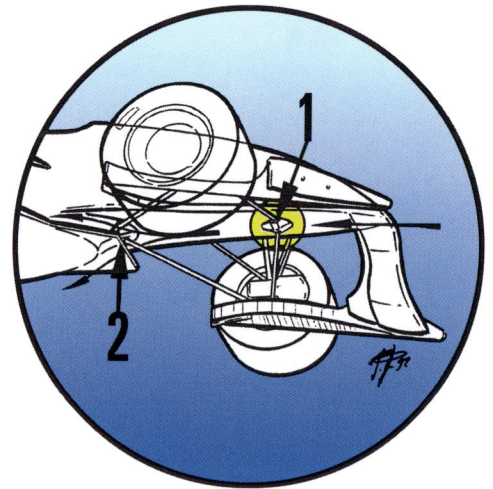

'92 Jordan

SAUBER

Sauber was the 2000 season's second team to have introduced something new, on its C19: it was a double mount, but outside the lower wishbone. With the introduction of the high nose on the Tyrrell 019 of J. Claude Migeot in 1990, it has been necessary to find an anchoring point outside the lower wishbone: it was Gary Anderson who came up with central anchoring, in a kind of little fin on the outside of the chassis of the '92 Jordan (drawing above). A system which is used right up to today by all current high nosed cars, but with various further sophistications, like the one introduced by John Barnard on the Ferrari 412 T2 in 1994 with knife edge mounts (drawing beside). So as not to disturb the airflow around the lower part of the car with central anchorage (in some cases very large, as with the Ferrari F1 2000), Sauber preferred to anchor the wishbones to two external but lateral mounts, leaving the central area completely free.

WHEEL NUTS

Introduced by Alan Jenkins on the Stewart in 1997, steel wheel nuts come from the United States, where they are used on Indy cars to provide a considerable weight-saving. Six teams adopted them for the 2000 F1 season: McLaren, Jaguar (ex-Stewart), Benetton, Arrows, BAR and Minardi, plus Williams who used a further noteworthy modified version. Another advantage offered by their employment is the possibility of using magnetised pistols with which to facilitate the change of wheels during a pit stop, producing a faster, more precise fitment.

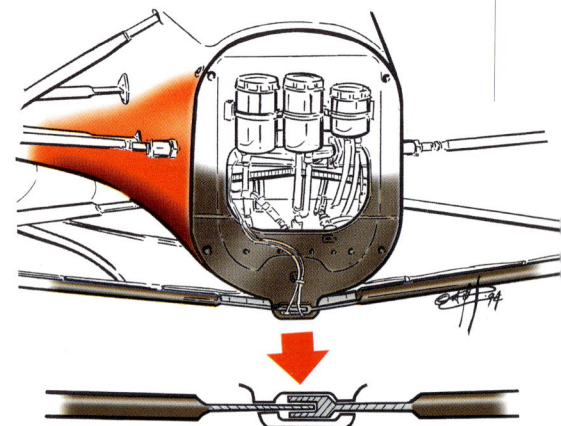

'94 Ferrari 412T2

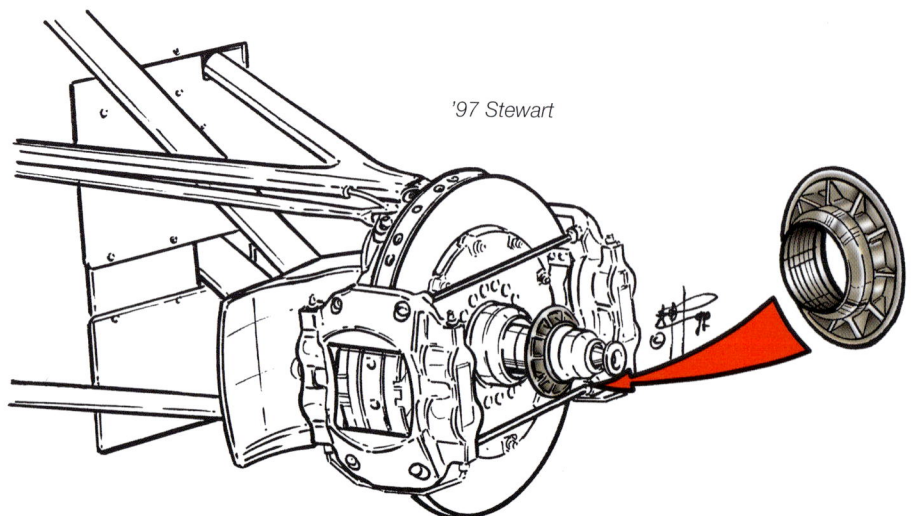

'97 Stewart

COCKPITS,PEDALS
AND STEERING WHEELS

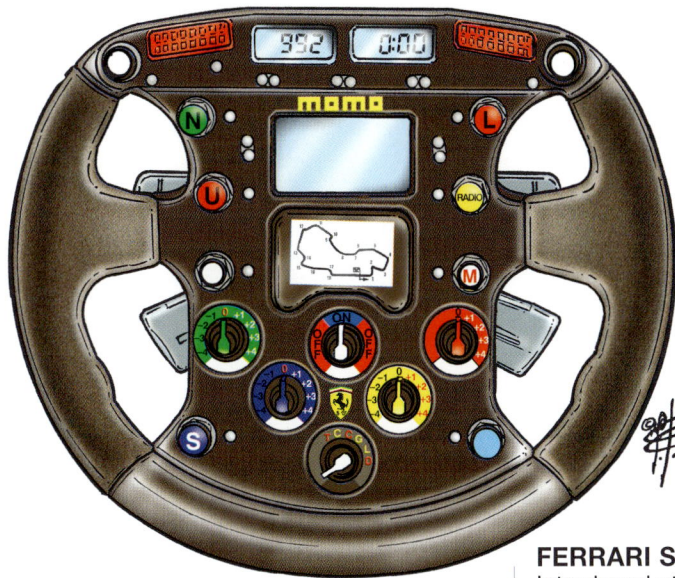

There were few new developments noted in this sector, among other reasons because it was penalised by the war that the teams have been waging for a number of seasons to stop people seeing inside their cars, cockpits in particular. Most kept the previous season's steering wheels, modifying only the functions of some switches. Starting with Ferrari, which introduced a new steering wheel at the '99 GP of Monaco and used it again in 2000. It was a wheel with all electronic components feeding into a central carbon fibre structure, completely demountable from the wheel itself. McLaren and Jordan did not change their steering wheels or the concept of their cockpits. The Federation introduced severe limitations on electronics from the GP of Great Britain, at first also banning the pit lane speed limiter, which would have caused the elimination of a push-button from the cars' steering wheels. This ban was not only rescinded on the eve of Silverstone, but the teams were also made to connect its insertion to the illumination of the car's rear light, to ensure the device was not used as an anti-spin system at the exit of slow corners. The only new developments came from Minardi and Prost. The former came up with a new idea with which to ease the drivers' entry into and exit from the car, with almost concave, scalloped

edges to the upper cockpit area at knee-height to allow their drivers to slip their legs into the car more easily. The second was linked to the move of Jean Alesi from Sauber to the French team, which resulted in Prost producing two different pedal set-ups and two different steering wheels. Alesi is the only driver not to use a clutch on the steering wheel and, after a brief experiment at the opening Grand Prix of the season, in Australia, he went back to just two rockers on the steering wheel and a third pedal for the clutch, as was on his '99 Sauber (see Technical Analysis '99, page 35).

FERRARI STEERING WHEEL
Introduced at the '99 GP of Monaco, the Ferrari wheel remained unchanged: it no longer had the square lower area in which to place a number of control paddles – six of them. The display was of the same dimensions, although the function of some buttons was different; they were moved to other locations, depending on the demands of the various circuits.

McLAREN STEERING WHEELS
McLaren also kept the same steering wheels as last season, tailored to its two drivers needs. Coulthard's (left) was still circular (1) in the lower area, and had much longer clutch levers (2). The position of some of the buttons on Hakkinen's wheel were different: for example, he preferred his drink button to be more accessible, up high on the right.

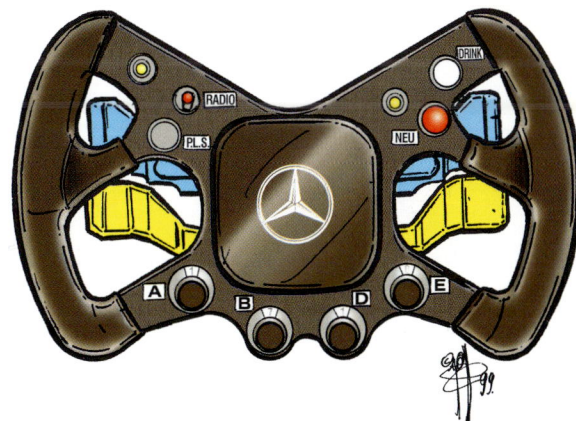

Coulthard

Hakkinen

1 2

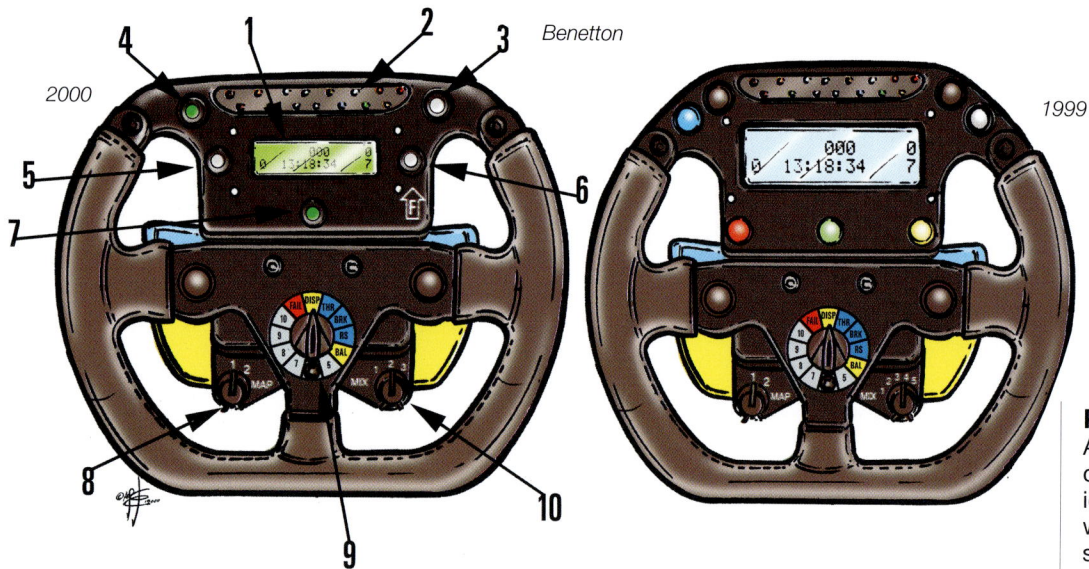

Benetton

2000

1999

BENETTON

The Benetton drivers' steering wheels were a clear derivation of the '99 unit, from which they differed only in the upper part, which housed a decidedly smaller display (1). The position of the lights (2) remained unchanged: they illuminated in sequence, to indicate the correct rpm during gear changes. The upper buttons in pairs in each part were: one, with the pit lane speed limiter to the right (3) and the radio (4) on the left. Neutral was button (5) while braking was administered by (6). Reverse (7) was in the centre. The lower area was modified to provide two forms of engine mapping (8) and a

different disposition of the control systems on the large central paddle (9) and, importantly, only three positions instead of five for blending the air and petrol fuel mixture (10).

JORDAN STEERING WHEELS

Jordan's steering wheels also remained unchanged with the exception of the rockers, shown in yellow, that operate the clutch. Those on Trulli's car were much longer than on Frentzen's.

Frentzen

Trulli

PIT LANE SPEED LIMITER

At first, buttons with which to action the cars' pit lane speed limiters were to be eradicated as of the GP of Great Britain, but they were later allowed to stay. The drawing shows the wheel of the Minardi, unchanged since '99.

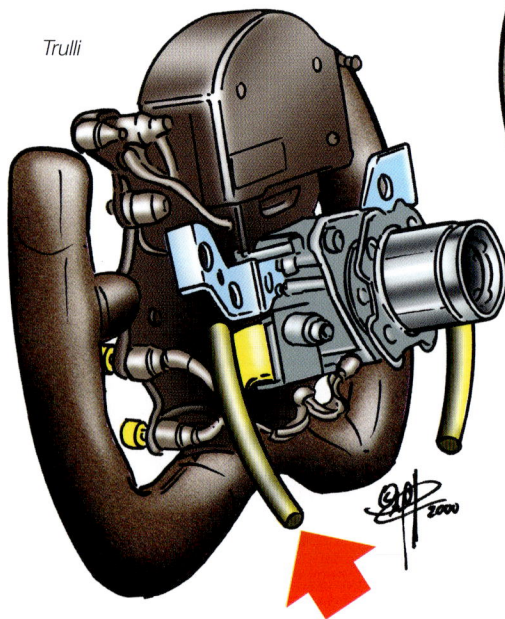

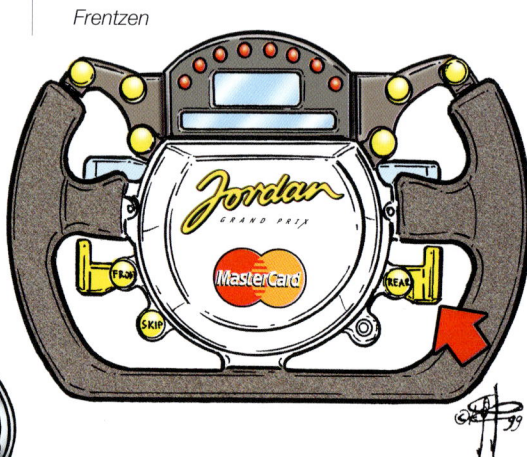

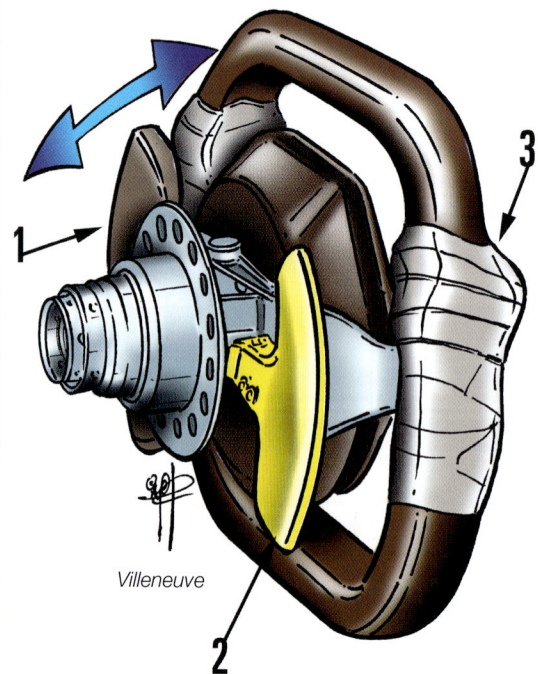

Minardi

VILLENEUVE

Jacques Villeneuve retained the ability to change gear with the lever on the right only (1): push it forward and it changed up, pull it back and it changed down. The large lever on the left (2) controlled the clutch. The Canadian habitually uses insulation tape to improve his grip on the rim.

Villeneuve

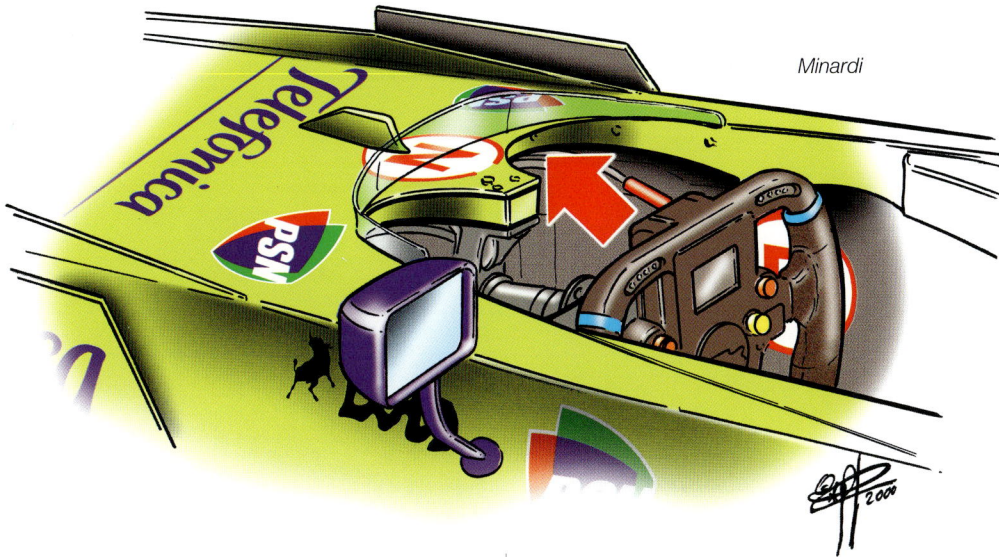

Minardi

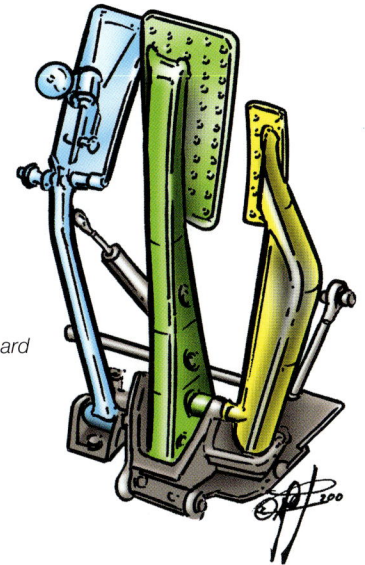

Coulthard

MINARDI

The Minardi modification to ease driver access to and from the cockpit was a new departure. The bulkhead that accommodated the steering wheel was made concave, like a double U, to make more room for knees. The idea also enabled the team to lower the height of the cockpit in that area.

PROST STEERING WHEELS
HEIDFELD-ALESI
ALESI PEDALS

Different Prost steering wheels. Heidfeld's was squarer and with four traditional rockers, the one for the clutch in yellow. Alesi had a wheel that was circular in the lower area, and with just two rockers. The Frenchman once again rejected a clutch on the steering wheel after testing that more modern arrangement again at the season's first race in Australia, and went back to being the only F1 driver to have a third full pedal for the clutch, as seen in the Prost cockpit drawing. On the left, Heidfeld's two-pedal set-up.

COULTHARD

As always, Coulthard also retained a third emergency pedal, although having an even larger dimension clutch rocker than Hakkinen's on his steering wheel. His clutch pedal was smaller than the others and was used only when necessary during a spin.

Alesi

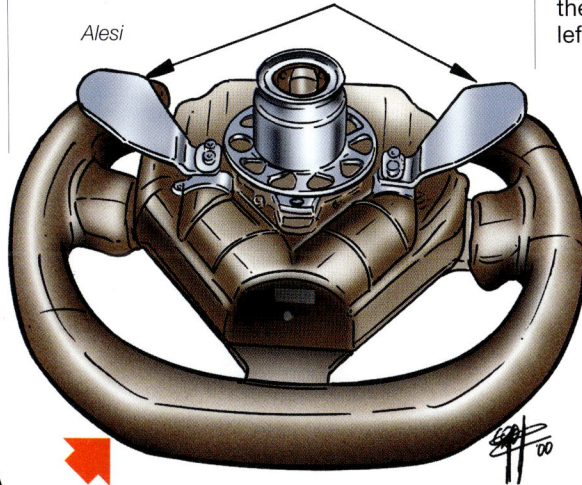

Alesi

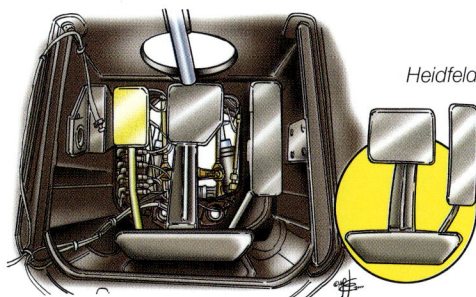

Heidfeld

FERRARI PEDALS

The two Ferrari drivers had considerably different pedal set-ups. Both had only two elements, but while Schumacher used a pedal for each foot some distance apart and, therefore, retained prominent lateral blocks, Barrichello used his right foot for both accelerating and braking. So the Brazilian's pedals were closer together and had no lateral blocks (1). To the left, on the chassis wall (2), there was also a small rest for Barrichello's left foot, which he hardly used when racing.

Schumacher

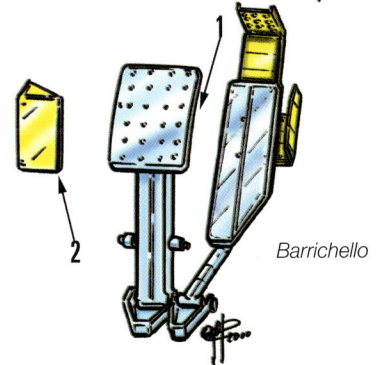

Barrichello

Heidfeld

TALKING ABOUT
BRAKES AND TYRES

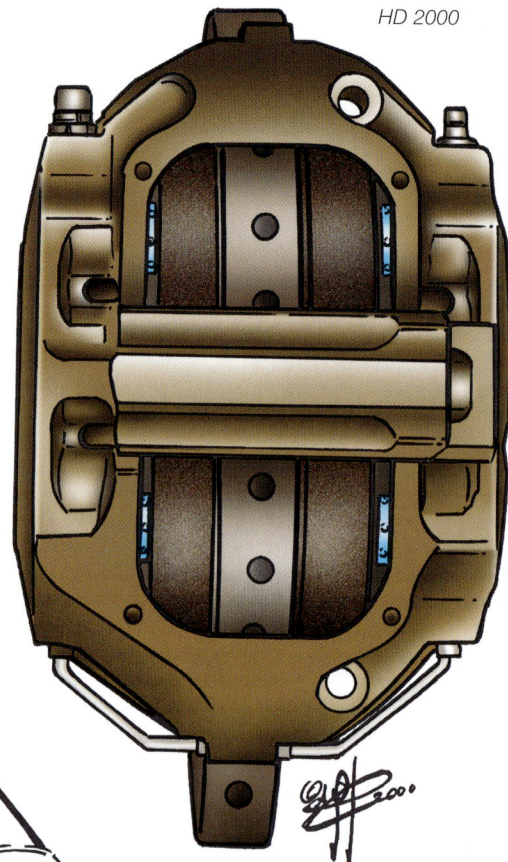

HD 2000

In the second season following the introduction of severe limitations on braking systems - maximum number of six pistons, discs only 28 mm thick and the prohibition of exotic materials like beryllium and Metalmatrix for the calipers - there were notable evolutions in the caliper field, particularly by Brembo, while A+P supplied a type derived from those of the previous season. A greater number of teams also used the new CCR discs, introduced at the GP of Belgium in '99, first exclusively for Ferrari, but which later became available to other teams. The division of the teams between the two calliper manufacturers was the following: Brembo - Ferrari, Jordan, Sauber and Minardi; A+P - McLaren, Williams, Benetton, Jaguar, Arrows, Prost and BAR. There were three suppliers of carbon discs: Brembo of Italy with its CCR, the French Carbon Industries and America's Hitco. Brembo's CCR discs were supplied to Ferrari, Benetton, Sauber, Minardi and Jordan - the latter from the GP of Canada - Herbert from the GP of Great Britain, alternating with CI, and Villeneuve from the GP of Canada. CI supplied Williams, Jaguar (but with Herbert using CCR) Arrows, Prost and BAR, Villeneuve having moved over to CCR in Canada. Hitco supplied their discs to McLaren and Jordan, the latter until the GP of Canada.

The two new developments of the season were represented by the two calipers introduced by Brembo: the first, called the HD 2000 (right drawing) was a traditional six piston unit in Avional aluminium alloy supplied to all teams, the only difference being that Ferrari was given a version with rapid engagement valves (bottom drawing), in place of bleeder caps, which had already been modified during the '99 season after Schumacher's dramatic accident at Silverstone. This modification was made available to all teams from the GP of San Marino. The second new caliper from Brembo, called the CCR2000, first appeared at the GP of Spain and is, in practice, a lighter version for qualifying, pro-

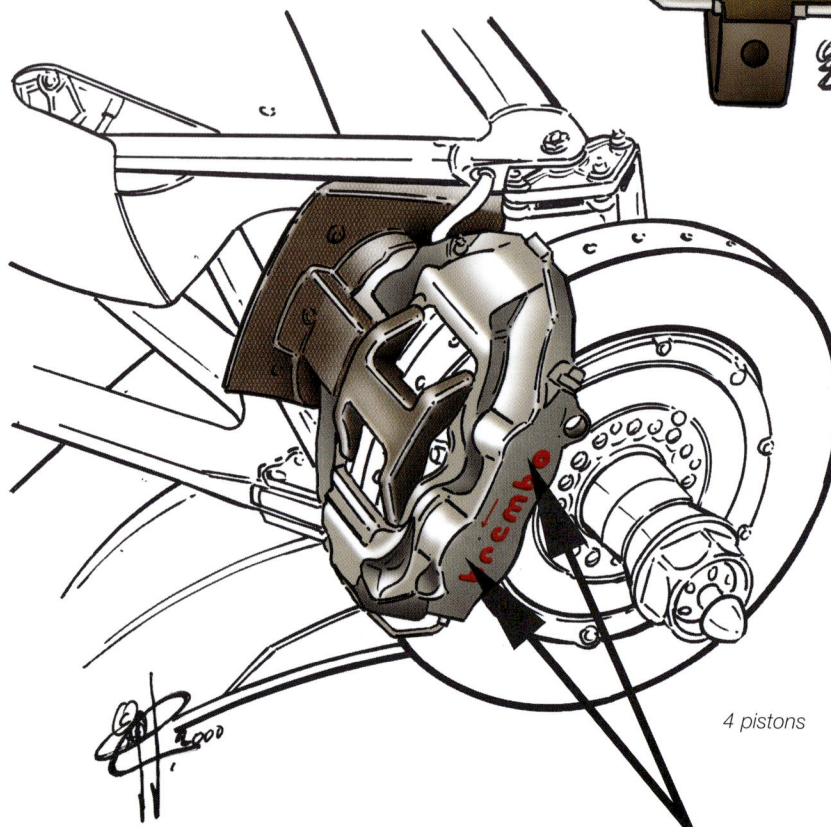

4 pistons

CCR 2000

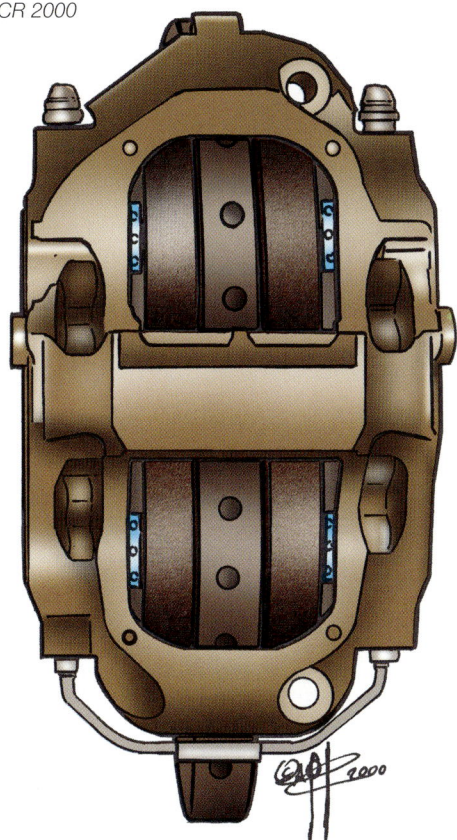

Canadian GP 2000 - Montreal

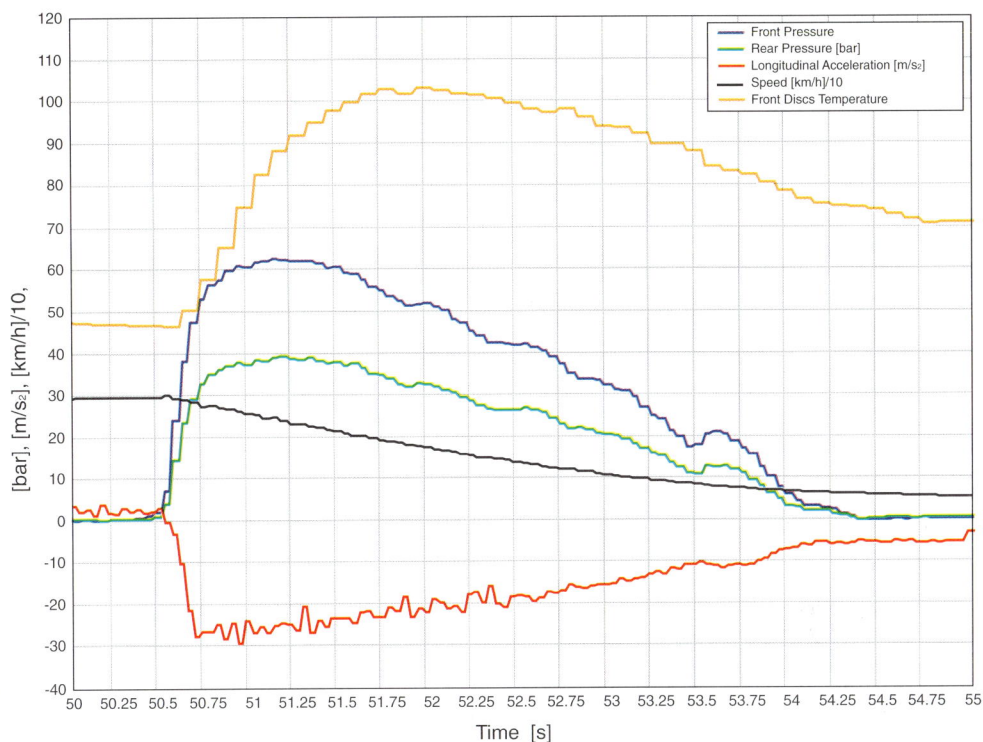

Legend:
- Front Pressure
- Rear Pressure [bar]
- Longitudinal Acceleration [m/s2]
- Speed [km/h]/10
- Front Discs Temperature

X-axis: Time [s]
Y-axis: [bar], [m/s2], [km/h]/10,

duced specifically for use with the thin 21 mm qualifying discs, instead of the usual 28 mm, introduced by Ferrari from the second race of the season. Jordan was the only team to ask for a caliper with four rear wheel pistons, for installation with the suspension upright group. All of these callipers had means by which to monitor the wear of discs and pads in real time.

The Montreal track is the hardest on braking systems and was the only circuit that caused the collapse of a disc, a Hitco on Frentzen's Jordan in '99. This circuit includes no less than six violent applications of the brakes at speeds that decrease from about 186-199 mph to 37-50 mph, in just 4.5 seconds.

The graph shows significant values taken of brake application number five on the Montreal circuit. Using the legend indicated on the graph, the base times are shown in abscissa in ordinate significant values.

It can be seen how a car reduces its speed from 186 mph to 37 mph in four seconds; to reduce kinetic energy, it is necessary that the front brake calipers exert a pressure of not much more than 60 bar and the rears close to 40 bar. A brake disc subjected to such pressure in just 1.5 seconds goes from an operational temperature of approximately 450°C to more than 1,000°C for about one second, subsequently stabilising itself at around 700°C in the following five seconds. The deceleration values to which the driver is subjected are also impressive. In the space of not much more than a second, they swing from 0.8 g positive to 3 g negative.

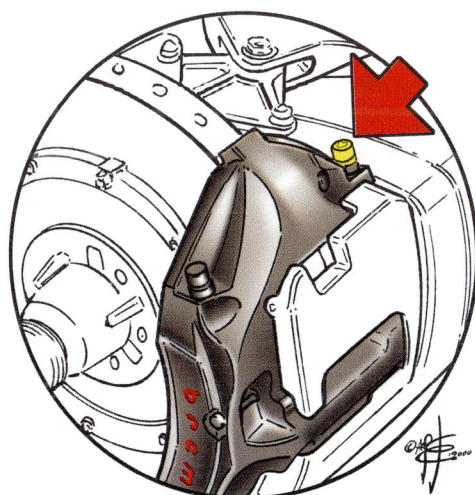

Rapid engagement valve

Australia

Canada

Brazil

S.Marino/qualify

Suzuka

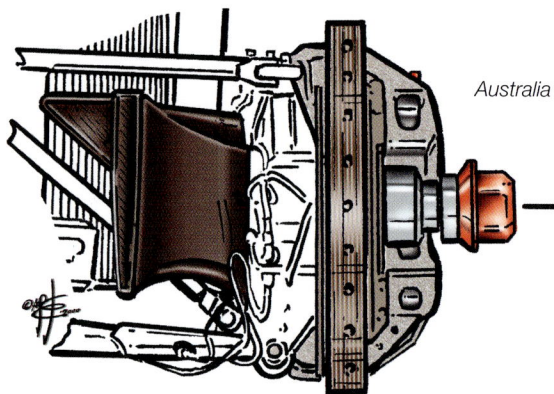

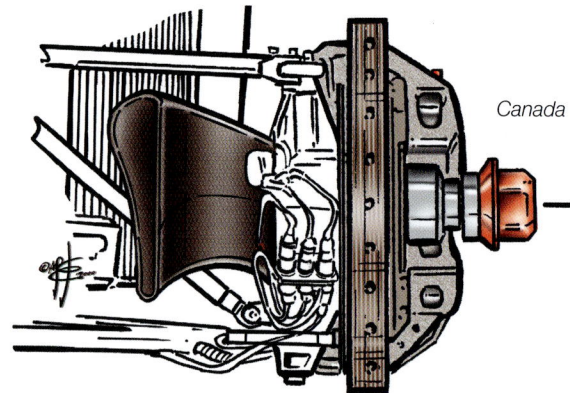

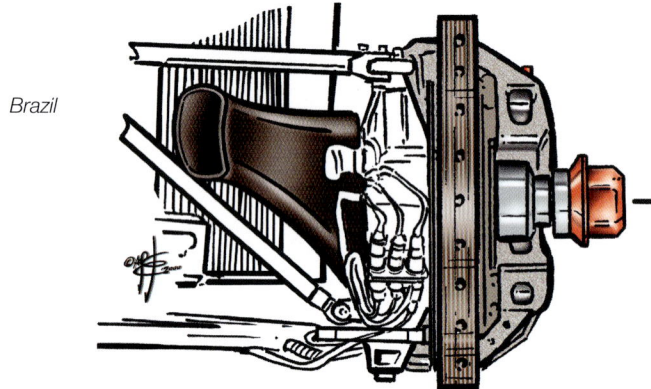

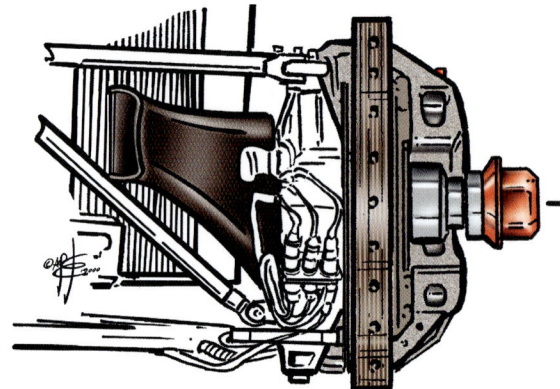

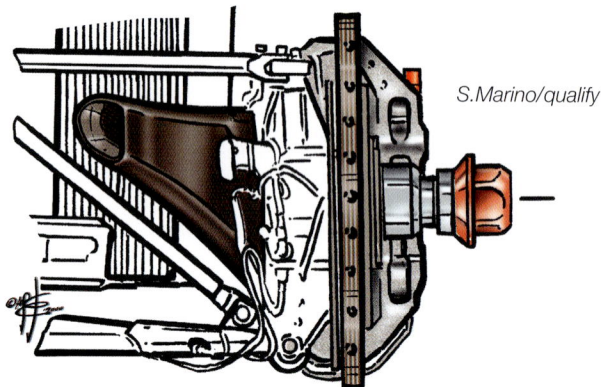

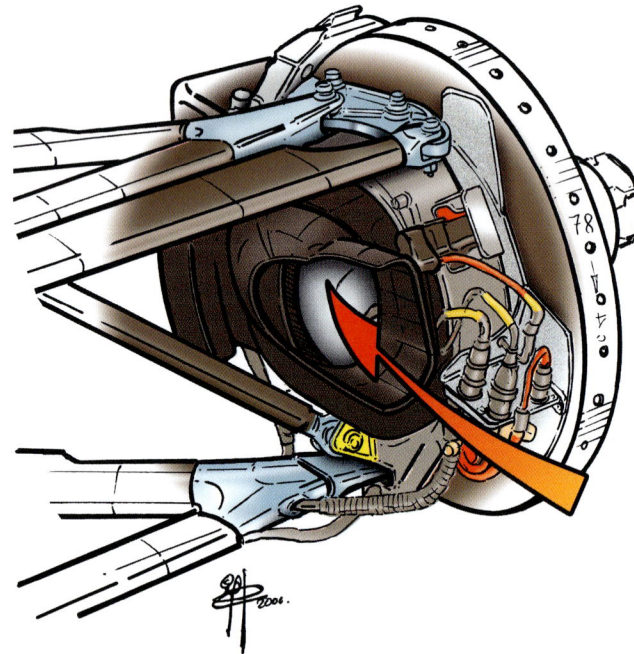

SEQUENCE FERRARI AIR INTAKES FOR BRAKE COOLING

This sequence of five drawings shows all the brake cooling ducts used by Ferrari during the season. The first at the top was derived from last season's and appeared at the opening race in Australia. The second, introduced at the GP of Brazil, was similar to the one used by McLaren in '99, with a rounded section that caught air above the push rod. The third was the small qualifying duct, which first came out at the GP of San Marino. An intake similar to the McLaren's was used for the first time in Canada, with a longer, narrower section. The last brake cooling duct was derived from the second, with the external part cut and used according to the different race cooling characteristics and shown in the final drawing, below right: it had a generous cut section to improve the cooling process. This version was used at Suzuka in the Grand Prix that decided the drivers' championship.

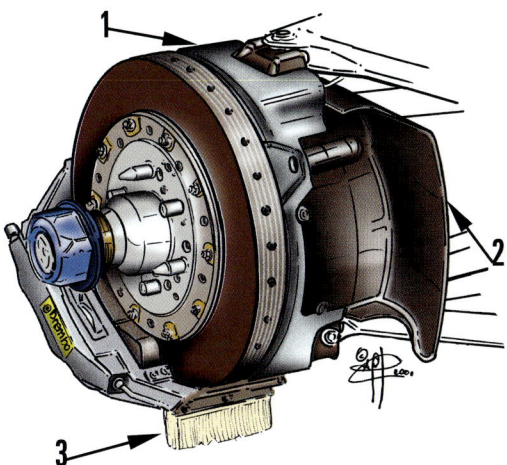

FERRARI AIR INTAKE FOR THE REAR BRAKES

Ferrari introduced an air intake to cool the rear brake discs: it had a circular faring (1) connected to the actual air intake (2). A further sophistication was tried out at the GP of Belgium: a small brush was installed to clean the inside of the rim, a feature that was not used in subsequent races.

QUALIFYING DISCS

Qualifying discs made their re-appearance for the first time since 1992, when they were used by Ferrari on the not very successful F 92, driven by Jean Alesi and Ivan Capelli.

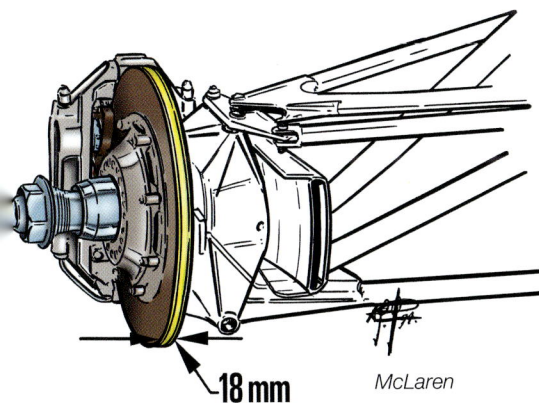

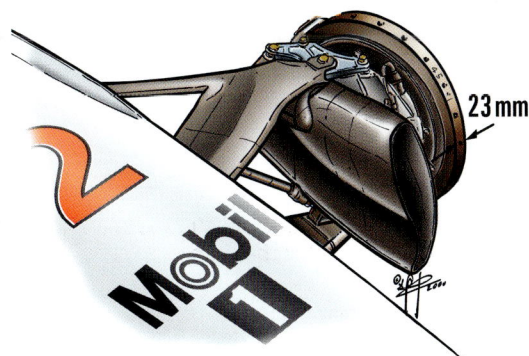

18 mm

McLaren

23 mm

They were full discs, without radial holes and were 18 mm thick. Those introduced by Brembo, first for Ferrari and then for all the other teams, were 21 mm thick (1) and, between disc and pad, meant a weight saving of 500 grams per wheel. The comparison between the standard discs and the qualifiers is also made on the basis of the new CCR calipers, 20% narrower (2) compared to the standard HD 2000 (above). The CCR caliper contributes a weight saving of 500 grams: 1450 against the 1950 of the HD 2000 and 1 kg when combined with qualifying discs, 3150 against 4150 grams. Brembo's qualifying discs were used by Ferrari, Sauber and Minardi: the Swiss team was the only one to

28 mm

21 mm

race with them, at Silverstone.

It was only in the last few races of the 2000 season that McLaren used 23 mm thick Hitco discs for qualifying, combined with lightweight calipers by A+P.

JORDAN

From the GP of Belgium, Jordan was the only team not to use the qualifying version of brake cooling air intakes (1) combined first with 23 mm Hitco discs and then Brembo's CCRs.

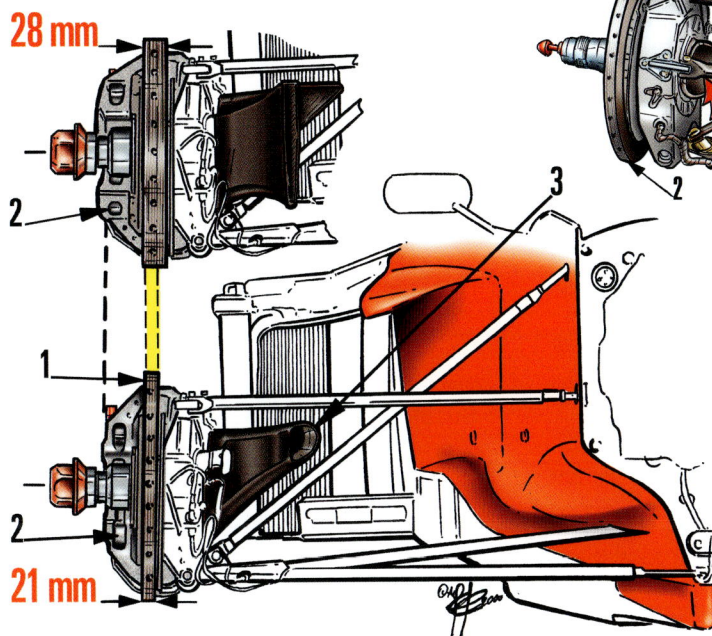

TYRES
2000

The 2000 season was a year of notable progress for Formula One tyres, even with the continuation of the Bridgestone monopoly and the equivalence of profiles and dimensions. Progress, clearly indicated by the improvement of lap times at almost all tracks, and in the regularity and stability of mileage, definable as the ability to prevent all forms of degradation of the tyre in use, but also to minimise the differences in performance (over/understeer) to the wear of the tread and under the influence of grooving, imposed by the regulations.

Obviously, every achievement in the area of performance has many implications for the chassis and engine. Then at times, as happened at Interlagos, Brazil, a reconstruction, even in part, of the track's surface produces surprising effects, both concerning increased grip, or how much the tyre adheres to the asphalt, and the exploitation of adherence, determined by the components linked to the roughness and the levelling of the surface. Talking of which, an evaluation of the principal responsibilities would be desirable; but regardless of how sophisticated the methods of calculation have become, from the revolution of 1961 (soft compound tyres and growing section) to today, absolute results are not obtainable, also because many functions of the tyres are incentives for the chassis. So one needs to rely on mathematical models realisable in the various sectors, to establish how much of an influence a determined increase in power has, all other conditions being equal, on lap times on all types of circuit, or how much work on the aerodynamics or kinematics characteristics affect the vehicle. In that way, with the usual approximations, it has been possible to establish that the contribution of the tyres at Δ% of lap times obtained during the 2000 season, compared to the limits of 1999, touched peaks of 80%, which must be considered really exceptional.

In the table that follows, the reference to the best improved results in qualifying has been chosen, this being the maximum expression also of driving, in conditions which are technically ideal and always equal to race material, as in the regulations. Of the 17 world championship Grands Prix, the 14 that are statistically valid have been used. Times related to the GP of Great Britain (constant rain) and the GP of Italy (re-design of the first two variants), have been omitted while Indianapolis, as a debut race, had no previous comparison data. Qualifying times on wet or just damp tracks (1999 or 2000), like those set at the GPs of Europe, France and Germany, were substituted with the technically comparable results of other sessions. While they are of debateable comparison, the times for the GP of Brazil were accepted, because normally the improvements to the track's surface are not separable from those resulting from the evolution of the tyres. In addition, as in the past, the percentage calculation was carried out for better immediacy of representation, with an inversion of signs, so that the positive Δ% represents progress and the negative Δ% a regress.

The first impression generated by the progress shown was that of change during the entire 2000 season, to a gradation of tyres that were increasingly softer than those used the year before. In a word, as if, in the usual classification made by the Bridgestone technicians, with four graduations *Extra-soft, Soft, Medium* and *Hard*, was constantly moved to a lower position. That appears technically founded, in as much that the scale provided does not refer exclusively to the hardness of the compound, but summarises the quality of the whole tyre. In fact, the characteristics of the elastomers used (there are special vectorial formulas for evaluations) did not seem much different than the previous ones, while the structural characteristics and carcass construction varied appreciably, developed to withstand a greater softness of compound. With a more compact grading, it was possible to reduce the gap that previous-

Circuits	Time, 1999 (seconds)	Time, 2000 (seconds)	Increase Δ%
Melbourne	90.462	90.556	-0.10
Interlagos	76.568	74.111	+3.21
Imola	86.362	84.714	+1.91
Barcellona	82.088	80.974	+1.36
Nürburgring	78.945	77.529	+1.79
Monaco	80.547	79.475	+1.33
Montreal	79.298	78.439	+1.08
Magny-Cours	77.912	75.632	+2.93
Zeltweg	70.954	70.410	+0.77
Hockenheim	102.950	101.658	+1.25
Budapest	78.156	77.514	+0.82
Spa	110.329	110.646	-0.29
Suzuka	97.470	95.825	+1.69
Sepang	99.688	97.397	+2.30
Average			+1.43

Circuits	Characteristics	km/h (Qual.)	Primary Choice	Index I
Indianapolis	Smooth; speed and pressure stress	203	New hard	0.7
Monza	Hardly abrasive; speed stress	249	Medium	0.6
Hockenheim	Smooth; speed stress	232	Medium	0.6
Silverstone	Medium rough, speed stress	216	Medium	0.6
Interlagos	Abrasive, some undulation	209	Medium	0.6
Imola	Slightly abrasive; little grip	210	Medium	0.5
Suzuka	Stressful and abrasive	220	New medium	0.5
Spa	Part road, abrasive	226	Soft	0.6
Zeltweg	Very limited degradation	221	Soft	0.6
Melbourne	Smooth and easy running	211	Soft	0.6
Montreal	Smooth and slightly abrasive	203	Soft	0.6
Monaco	Smooth with harshness	153	Soft	0.5
Barcellona	Very abrasive and stressful	210	Soft	0.4
Sepang	Moderately abrasive	205	New soft	0.5
Nürburgring	Smooth and slightly abrasive	212	Extra-soft	0.5
Magny-Cours	Flat and slightly abrasive	202	Extra-soft	0.5
Budapest	Medium abrasiveness	185	Extra-soft	0.5

ly divided the four levels, especially in the combinations, proposed for the majority of the grands prix and formed from *Medium* and *Soft* or from *Soft* and *Extra-Soft*, where the opportunity of choice was limited to just handling and not lap times. With micro-surgical precision, it has been possible to go into detail on the requirements of each circuit, to look for the most advanced rigidity characteristics, with the obligatory four grooves and dimensions of a *265* mm width of the front tread, *325* mm for the rear rolling area and *655* mm for the external diameter of both tyres.
Therefore, with the determination of a partially empirical index "I", it is possible to sketch out an evaluation of the global characteristics of the tyres on the basis of the nature of the cir-

cuits. The first term comes from the length of the tracts into which the race distance becomes divided, in the dominant practice of re-fuelling. Having chosen the most significant section of the circuit, (usually the first), the severity of use is determined according to the incidence of that tract or stint on the total distance, with added correction due to the granulometry of the asphalt and the generation of the stress of speed, which also influences rolling resistance. The 2000 seasonal picture can be summarised in this way.
As can be seen, the gradation *Hard*, proposed as an option only at Hockenheim and Monza, was never used and the new type *New Hard*, produced for Indianapolis with a higher index of year, was designed to withstand in complete safety - rather original for

Formula One - a banked bend of 9°, in which the inflation pressure had to go from an average of about *1.4* bar to *1.5/1.6* bar. It was very significant that the index was raised for all the softer material of 2000, to favour perceptible increases in mileage with great consistency of yield. As if that were not enough, for the end of the championship battle the intermediate category was reconditioned and can be called *New Medium* (Suzuka) and *New Soft* (Sepang), both containing important innovations in construction, and considerable ahead of the progress that it is logical to expect in 2001, with the return of the competitive stimulus of two different brands.

This diagram of lap times recorded by the two leading competitors in recent years, Hakkinen (McLaren-Mercedes) and Michael Schumacher (Ferrari), on the Suzuka circuit in the first part of the GPs of Japan of 1999 and 2000, perfectly summarises the progress made by Bridgestone tyres over the distance indicated, both in terms of absolute performance and in mileage. It is immediately evident that the Δ% increase in those times (*1.69%* for the limit in qualifying and *2.10%* for the fastest laps during the race) provide an average of 2% during the first stint of about 20 laps in both cases. But if the trend of 1999 is visibly descendant, that is with worse times as the race continues, as a typical index of tyre degradation, the progress indicated by the chronometer recordings of the 2000 Grand Prix seems totally the opposite, with constantly better results from the start to the first pit stop. That means that, in the latter case, there was no degradation of the tyres and the increases in performance followed, with great precision, the laws of progressive lightening of the car.

1999 vs 2000 Suzuka Race Lapchart

Generally, it is necessary to point out that the first appearance of the representation includes all the factors that concur with the improvement of performance, from the power of the engine to the efficiency of the chassis, as well as the tyres themselves. For the portion of the race examined in this graphic, nevertheless, it can be deduced that the contribution made by the progress of the latest generation of tyres has been preponderant, with an approximate 80% increase in Δ% of lap times. A historically important result, in spite of the *4* grooves imposed by the regulations to specifically limit too high an increase in performance, due to the greater cornering

speed. Therefore, for the second point under examination relative to handling, it is considered the ideal response of the tyres must always be the same, to vary the temperature and the consumption of the tread so that a great driver, at the wheel of an optimum car and in completely regular track conditions and race conduct, can constantly push himself to the limit. So with that kind of development of the race, there is nothing other than the weight of the car, prevalently in acceleration, to influence lap times. And it is well-known that some tortuous and demanding circuits can provide an improvement in lap times up to *0.04* seconds for every kilo of weight the car loses, in a range of weights such as those usually defined by the quantity of fuel being transported, while this value drops to about *0.02* sec/kg on the faster tracks. In the case of Suzuka in 2000, the almost linear progress of the improvement in lap times up to the 20th lap can make calculations an incidence in the order of *0.03* sec/kg, which appears considerable, especially as it was obtainable in the absence of tyre degradation.

Enrico Benzing

TYRES

The drawings show the two wet tyres supplied by Bridgestone during the season. On the left (18) the rain cover which, until the GP of Belgium, had the same pattern as that used during the '99 season but with shallower grooves, and was used as an intermediate. Note that the tread pattern is the same as the '99 design. On the right is the new intermediate pattern, which first appeared at Spa and was retained for the rest of the season.

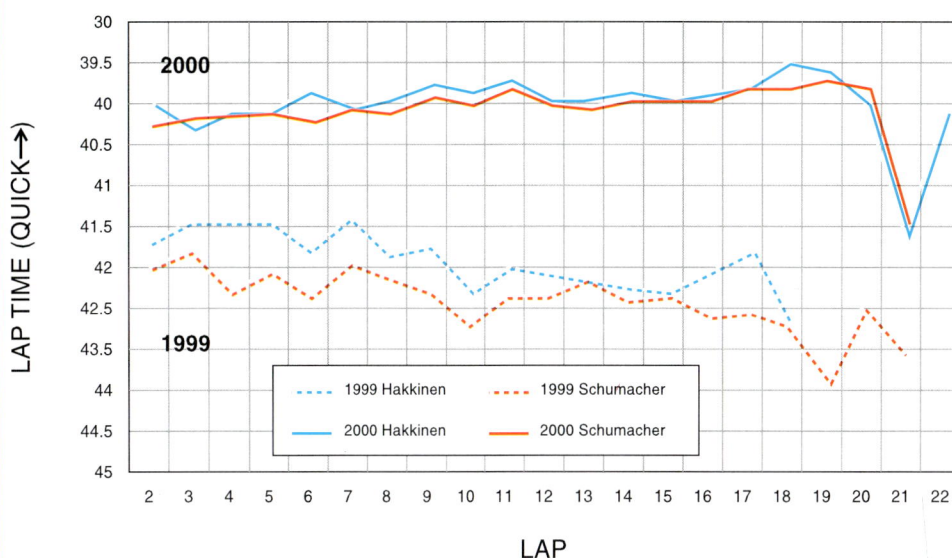

TALKING ABOUT SUSPENSION

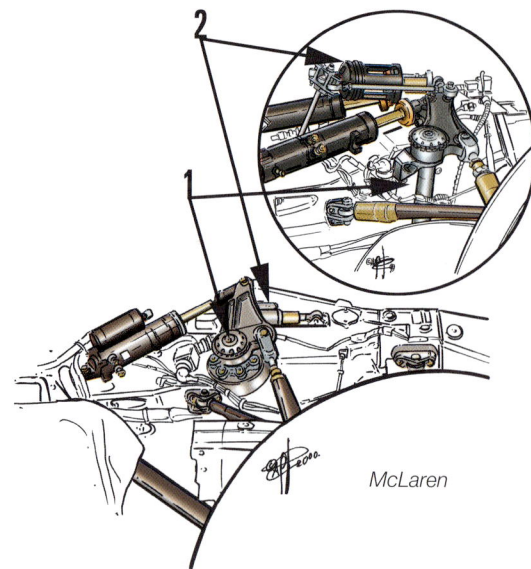

McLaren

All F1 teams uniformly adopted the lay-out of horizontal torsion bars and vertical shock absorbers on the front end, introduced by Ferrari and McLaren in '98, while four teams used coaxial springs with shock absorbers on the rear: they were Williams, Benetton, Jordan and Arrows. There were no major new developments in this sector which, among other things, has become increasingly difficult to analyse due to the growing trend among teams of concealing their cars' suspensions from prying eyes and lenses in every possible way, even during adjustments by the mechanics. Among the top teams, there was a different positioning of the McLarens' rear suspension's torsion bars, which retained their front lay-out almost unchanged, as did Ferrari. In spite of the mostly unaltered lay-outs, the various means of modifying suspension systems became slightly more complicated in 2000, due to a drastic reduction of 'clutter' during the design stage. There was a return to the past with the pull-rod lay-out, brought back to F1 front suspension after an eight year absence by Arrows. The last car to be fitted with a pull-rod front suspension was the Lotus 102 B of '92. There were new means of some suspension details' construction, including the cast titanium uprights of

Minardi, BAR and Williams, to mention them in chronological order of adoption. There was also a progressive advancement of the tendency to fit knife edge mounts for suspension arms, with Jordan also using this system for anchoring the push rod to the lower wishbone. On this point, the new development introduced by BAR during the previous season, with the push rod mount fixed directly to the upright and taken up in 2000 by Ferrari, was one of John Barnard's many innovations at the time of his Ferrari 412 T1 of '94. Another point to note as a new development, but certainly not for its validity, was the complicated lay-out of the Jaguar's rear suspension, which was responsible for a major scare during the last race of the season and of Johnny Herbert's F1 career.

McLAREN
The position of the MP4/15's rear suspension torsion bar was new compared to the previous season's car. 1) On the MP4/14 the bar was outside the gearbox casting, while on the MP4/15 it was lodged inside the suspension rocker. 2) The position of the third shock absorber was different – the bump stop placed in a small niche in the upper area of the gearbox.

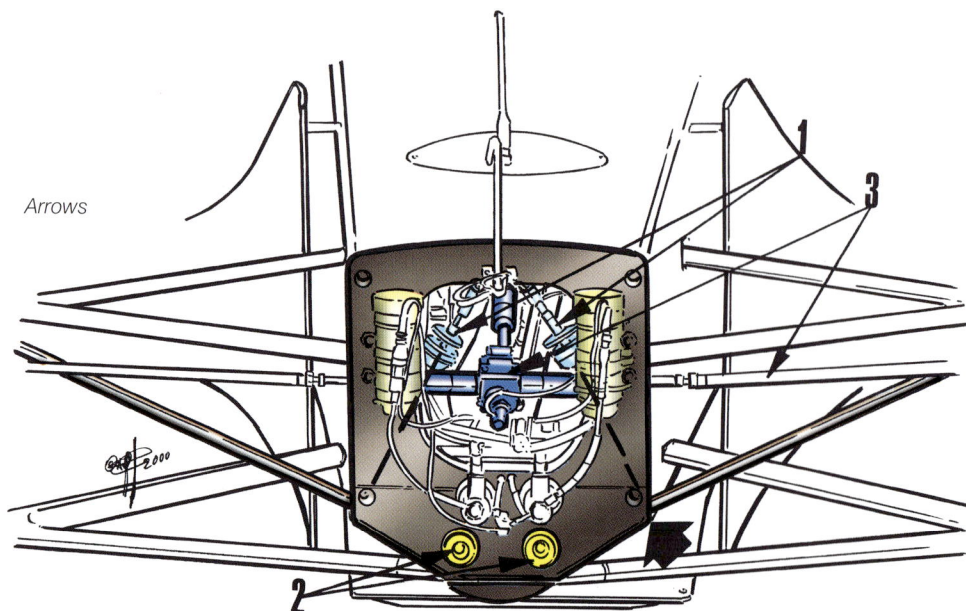

Arrows

ARROWS AND LOTUS
Arrows brought back to F1 the link lay-out, a connection between the upper wishbone and the lower push rod of the vertical shock absorber to take the place of the standard push rod and, therefore, with a lower wishbone linked to the upper point of the shock absorber. The last example of that front end lay-out goes back to the Lotus 102 B of '92. But then, the push rod was connected to a

LOTUS 102 B '92

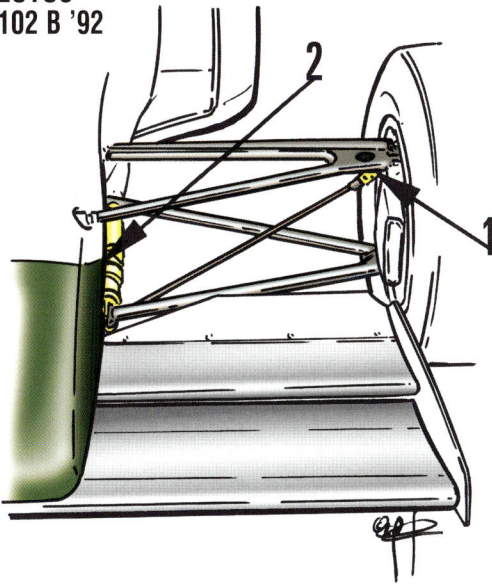

horizontally disposed shocker (2), while the Arrows shocks were vertical, even if severely inclined (1). That was how part of the advantage of moving the weight of the suspension lower. The horizontal torsions bars (2) were located very low down, while the steering linkage (3) was slightly lower, compared with the upper wishbone.

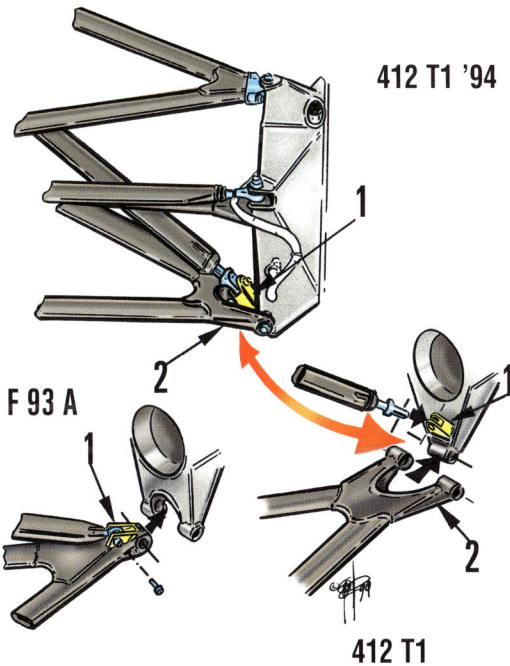

412 T1 '94

F 93 A

412 T1

FERRARI – BAR UPRIGHTS
At the GP of Monaco, Ferrari introduced an important new development on the car's front end, with the suspension push rod no longer connected to the lower wishbone but directly to the upright. It was a technique used by BAR in '99, rendering the suspension geometry more efficient, producing a steering angle of greater precision.

FERRARI 412 TI
It was John Barnard who gave the 1994 Ferrari 412 TI not only knife edge or small plate mounts that found great acceptance and are now used on all F1 cars. The anchorage of the push rod (1) was linked directly to the upright and no longer to the lower wishbone, which was the case with the 1993 F 93 A. The anchorage (2) of the upright to the lower wishbone was also different. All of these features were aimed at reducing the friction and to have a more precise control of the suspension geometry.

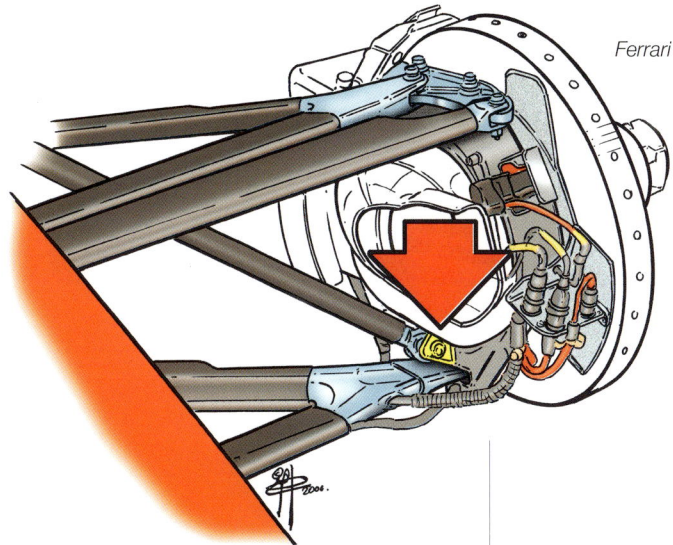

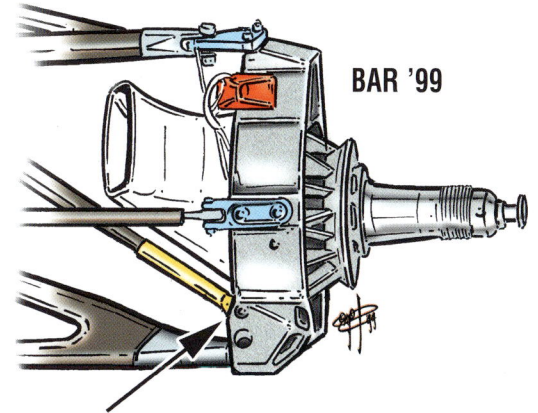

Ferrari

BAR '99

JORDAN
Jordan was the only team to substitute the uniball in the anchorage point between the push rod and lower wishbone with a knife edge mount of the push rod, made entirely of carbon fibre, as indicated with the arrow in the drawing. It should be pointed out that all the suspension arms were in carbon fibre.

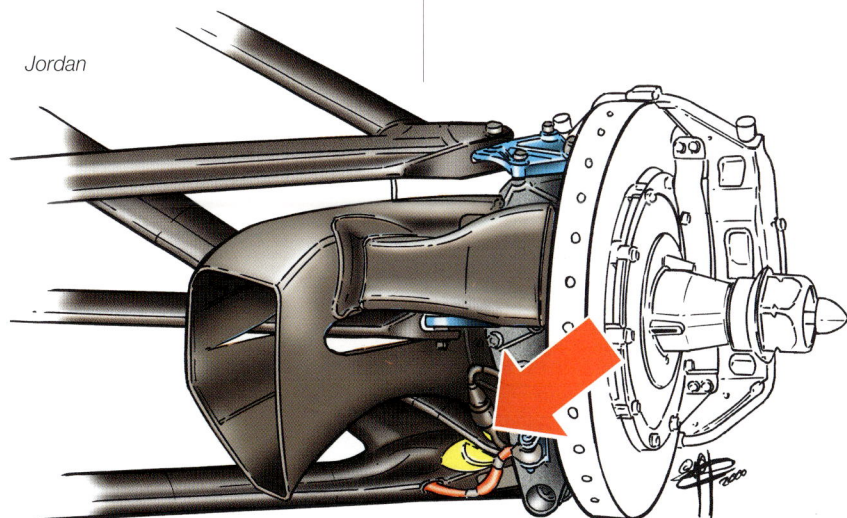

Jordan

MINARDI UPRIGHTS

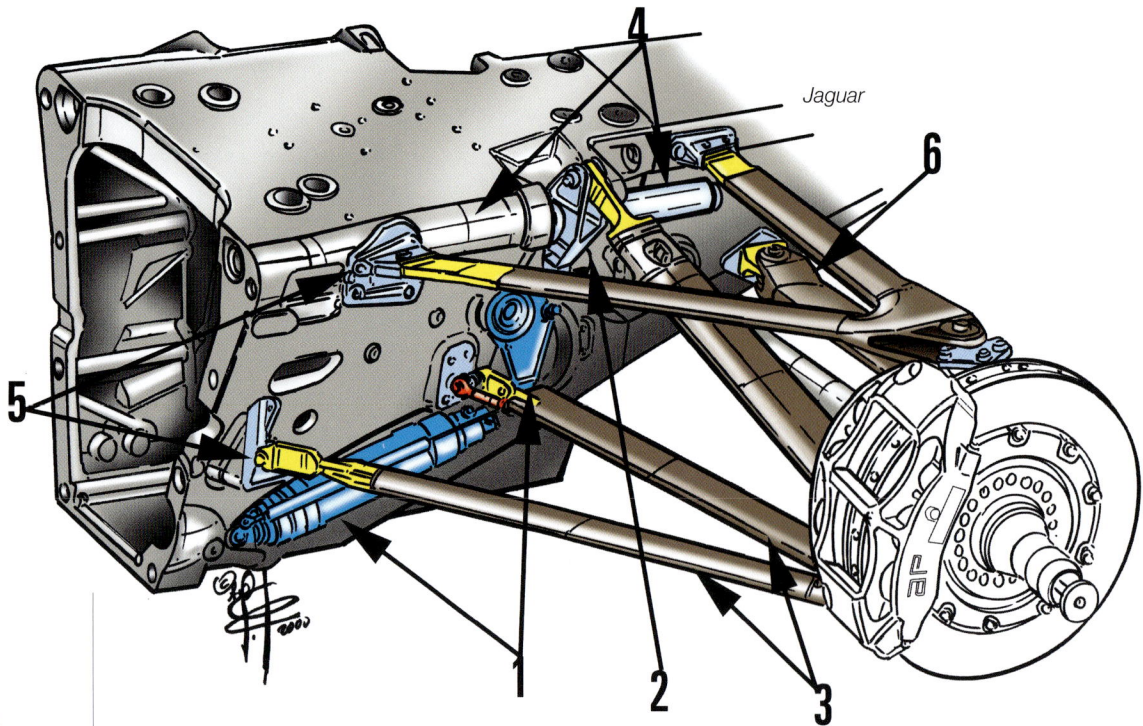

Minardi presented its second generation of uprights cast in titanium, which were around 20% lighter, made by CRP of Modena and used for both the front and rear suspension systems. The only elements that were not part of the single block were the small mount plates of the upper wishbone and the steering linkage. This feature was also adopted by BAR and Williams.

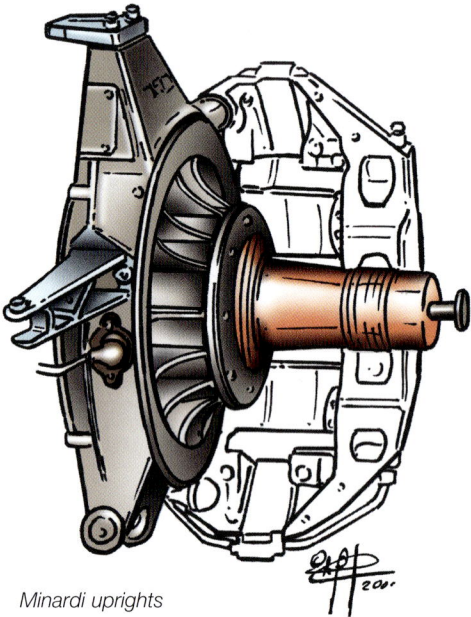

Minardi uprights

Jaguar

JAGUAR

Jaguar's suspension lay-out was extremely complicated and was designed to move its weight as low down as possible. The shock absorber, which is usually high above the gearbox, was moved to a niche down low and in an inclined position, to work with the push rod link through two rockers, one down low and the other high (2). Note the multi-link solution (3) with the lower wishbone substituted by two arms directly attached at two different points. The torsion bar (4) was positioned horizontally inside the vertical rocker. All the suspension mounts (5) were knife edge. 6) The toe-in link.

MINARDI'S REAR SUSPENSION

Even if it was a year old, Minardi's rear suspension was one of the most interesting in F1 and followed the lay-out of Ferrari's front suspension. 1) The long rockers exited the upper part of the casting. 2) The roll bar was identical to that used on the Ferrari's front end. 3) Horizontal torsion bars. 4) The shock absorbers were at an oblique angle and lodged inside the gearbox, as can be seen on page 30 of the "New Features and Trends" chapter.

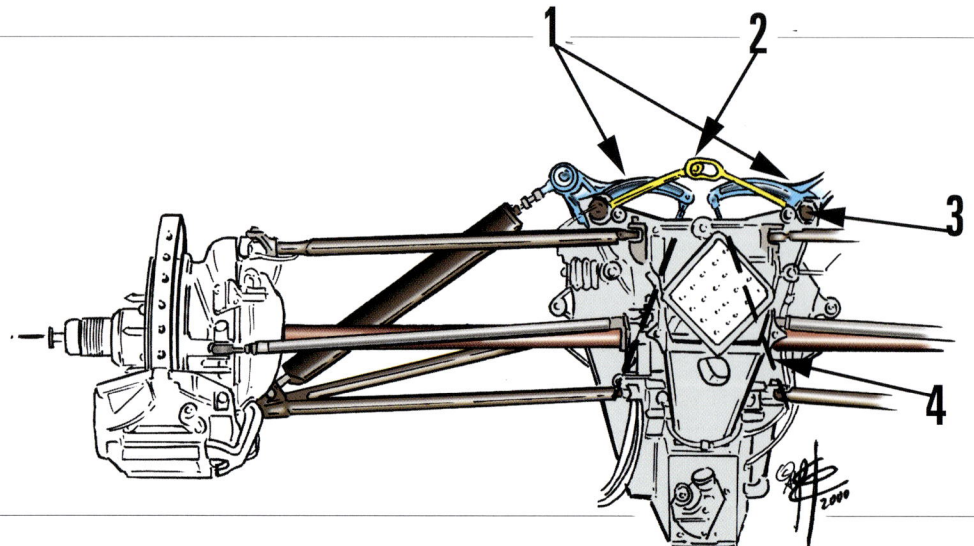

44

SAUBER

Torsion bars were also included in the Sauber C 19's rear suspension system. They were placed (1) on the outside of the casting and connected to the suspension rockers. 2) Third bump stop element connected to the roll bar. 3) The shock absorbers were placed above the gearbox casting. 4) Lower wishbone mounts. 5) Upper wishbone mounts and toe-in link (6).

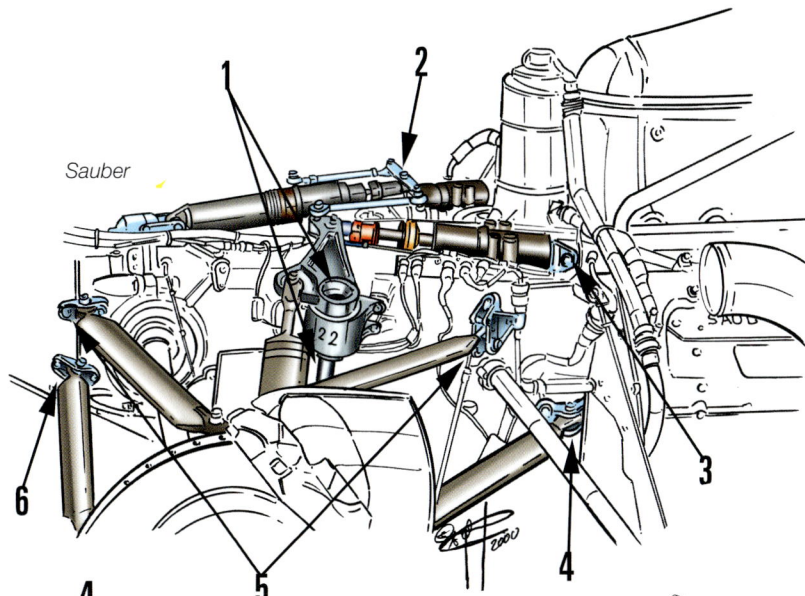

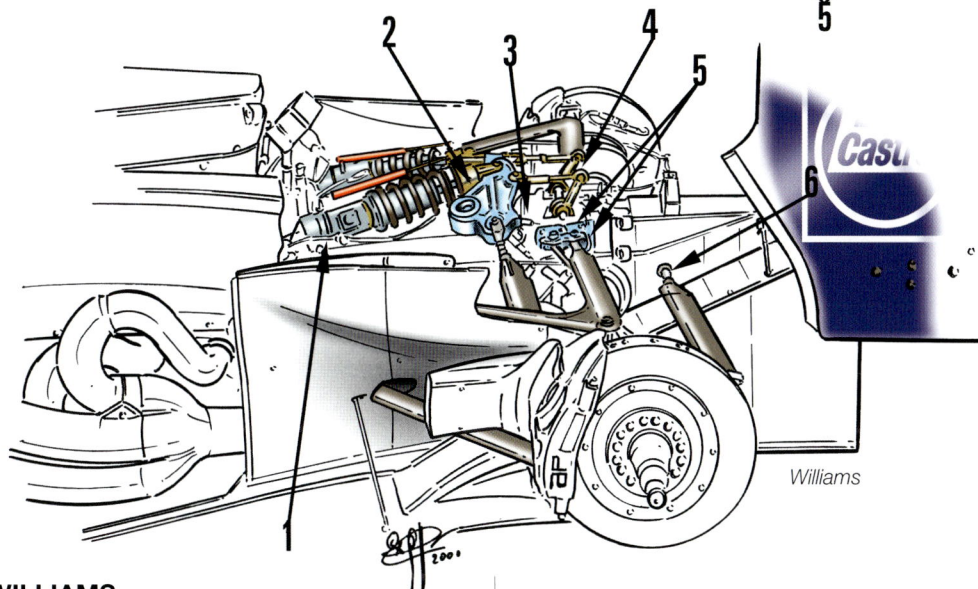

Sauber

Jordan

Williams

WILLIAMS

Williams continued to use coaxial springs (1) with shock absorbers, connected to a classic rocker (2) with two mounts for (3) a third bump stop element. The anti-roll bar (4) was very short and placed above the gearbox. The wishbone mounts (5) had two different anchorage points.

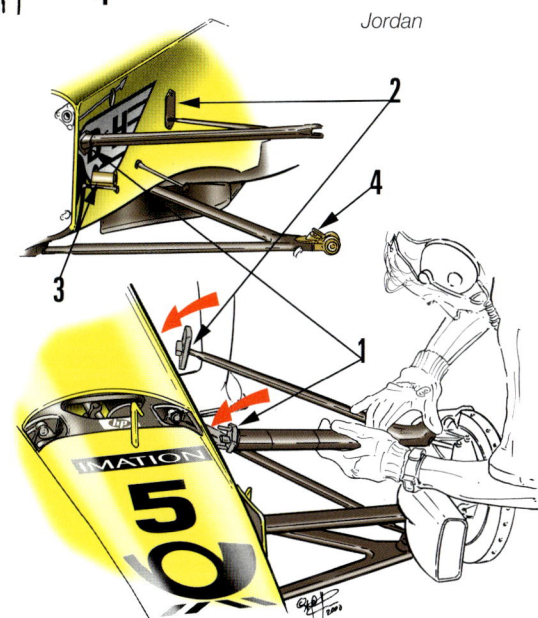

Benetton

BENETTON

The Benetton's suspension was similar to that of the previous year's car, differing in particular in the position of the third shock absorber-bump stop (1) that was previously placed up high and for 2000 was positioned mid-way. 2) Suspension rocker to which the shock absorber was connected (4), heavily inclined. 3) Horizontal torsion bar.

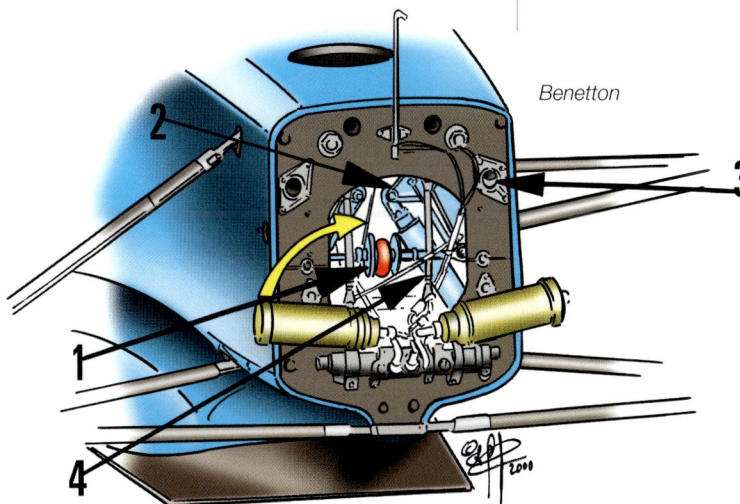

JORDAN

The drawing shows the operation for substituting the suspension's front wishbones, which have small plates and knife edge mounts. The upper wishbone is fixed to the chassis in front at the point (1) and behind in the point (2). The steering linkage can be unscrewed from the chassis at the point (3). Note the usual knife edge mount (4) of the push rod with the upright.

TALKING ABOUT
DOWNFORCE

end of the 2000 season, as was the reversed arrow-shaped wing adopted the previous season for hyper-fast circuits, like Hockenheim and Monza. The search for greater downforce stability is also noticeable from the only new feature of the season: the curious inclination of the lateral end-plates on the nose of the Jordan, the team that had the plane as close to the ground as possible. With the end-plates slightly inclined upwards at the rear, pitch sensitivity was reduced.

G.P.

It was a season that saw the different teams correct and improve measures already taken the year before, without any great inventiveness; so there was an intense search for aerodynamic refinement of individual details to improve efficiency. And it is precisely in this sector that major progress was seen, which can be measured in what has become two tables to permit a direct comparison of the various values obtained during the previous season. Most of the teams opted, in particular, for extremely well-balanced cars in the knowledge that, in the last season of Bridgestone's monopoly, they would not be able to count on very high adherence levels from the tyres. One of the principal objectives was to build cars that are easy to balance aerodynamically and are little affected by pitch sensitivity from the ground. Together with Williams,

Ferrari was, perhaps, the team that evolved most in this sector, obtaining high values of efficiency from its F1 2000: it should be remembered that aerodynamic efficiency is determined by the ratio between lift and the drag coefficient, Cz and Cx. Ferrari made progress with both the nose and body of the car, particularly as far as the fluid dynamics inside the side pods are concerned, and in the delicate zone in front of the rear tyres, where they attempted to reduce the aerodynamic blockage that affected previous models. Blockage that penalised the Rosse, in particular, at top speed due to the increased resistance generated by those areas and by the greater incidence of the wings. The F1-2000 had used a different ground height for its wing planes. The characteristic arrow-shaped wing, which was introduced for the third last race of 1998, was dropped at the

The most popular method for measuring aerodynamic forces in Formula One in the wind tunnel with model cars of reduced scale, is that of the use of a fixed frontal area to alter the test configurations. In that way, the determination of the coefficients of resistance, Cx, and of negative lift Cz (minus sign omitted) is the quickest, as well as being free from errors, which can be committed in the height of surfaces that vary only slightly. The results are not absolute, but relative to a common term of reference; and they are always acceptable because, once having chosen an intermediate value, the shift between the minimum and the maximum hindrance remains contained.

In the application of this principle, the wind tunnel can provide us with dimensionless coefficients, verified in a medium level car during the 2000 season, in line with the regulations

1999	Cz	Cx	S	Vel.km/h	D kg
Australia	2.496	0.981	2.54	297	1442
Brazil	2.511	0.942	2.67	305	1530
San Marino	2.421	0.912	2.65	306	1470
Monaco	2.661	1.000	2.66	290	1478
Spain	2.447	0.898	2.72	305	1516
Canada	2.257	0.832	2.71	319	1504
France	2.628	0.962	2.73	297	1520
G.Britain	2.436	0.872	2.79	310	1533
Austria	2.330	0.884	2.64	306	1429
Germany	1.908	0.697	2.74	345	1455
Hungary	2.647	0.990	2.67	300	1561
Belgium	2.418	0.850	2.84	315	1572
Italy	1.845	0.680	2.71	347	1435
Europe	2.586	0.938	2.76	305	1576
Malaysia	2.580	0.952	2.71	304	1562
Japan	2.633	0.991	2.66	300	1552

Values for average F1 750 HP car

Cz
Lift coefficient
Cx
Drag coefficient
Eff.
Efficiency
S
Speed
D
Downforce

2000	Cz	Cx	S	Vel.km/h	D kg
Australia	2.798	0.958	2.92	302	1578
Brazil	2.780	0.958	2.90	307	1585
San Marino	2.610	0.883	2.96	310	1563
G.Britain	2.775	0.965	2.88	310	1628
Spain	2.739	0.960	2.85	306	1616
Europe	2.733	0.920	2.97	307	1661
Monaco	3.137	1.084	2.89	292	1694
Canada	2.325	0.760	3.06	322	1540
France	2.475	0.847	2.92	300	1575
Austria	2.833	0.957	2.96	300	1548
Germany	2.166	0.693	3.13	350	1599
Hungary	2.939	1.020	2.88	300	1631
Belgium	2.587	0.836	3.09	320	1663
Italy	2.029	0.682	2.98	349	1513
Usa	2.571	0.846	3.04	321	1624
Japan	3.113	1.065	2.92	305	1630
Malaysia	2.946	1.044	2.82	306	1652

JORDAN
Throughout the season Jordan used front wing end-plates slightly inclined upwards towards the rear to reduce pitch sensitivity, sacrificing something in terms of obtainable maximum load downforce.

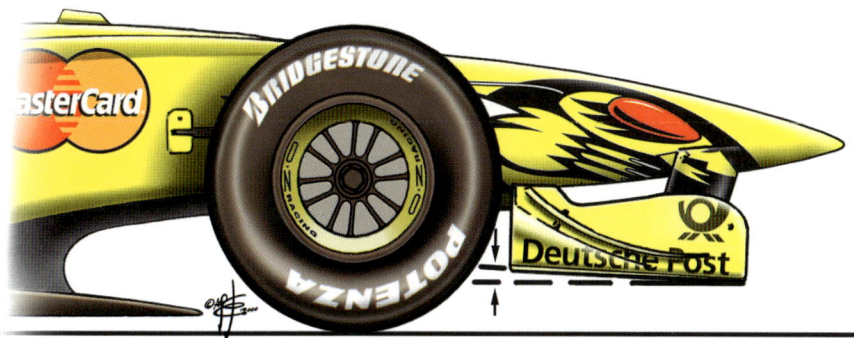

devised for every conformation of circuit. With absolute precision for the intermediate configuration, in which the value of the frontal area is exactly that which is assumed as a reference, and with a certain tolerance for the two extremes of set-up of minimum resistance and minimum down force, prepared for the fastest tracks, such as Monza and Hockenheim, and those of maximum aerodynamic load as are prepared for Monte Carlo. All the values are carried in the opposite page table, where the Cz/Cx ratios provide the grade of efficiency of the aerodynamic body, and where, with a rounding up of the values, the aerodynamic load per determined speed is added.

Those speeds, which determine, in squared proportion, the entity of the forces of negative lift for the Cz coefficients indicated, do not constitute the maximum values actually achieved by the average car selected for this example, but represent theoretical data, broadly indicative as the target of the season for the various types of tracks. Compared to the previous year, the Cz increases were on average *12%*, except for particular cases of considerable variation of availability of grip (gradation of the tyres and condition of the asphalt), while in more severe conditions increments of up to *18%* were achieved. That reflects the typical tendency to exploit the

annual increases in power not just to increase top speed, but to stress all the components linked to the capacity of the exploitation of adherence. And if the percentage of Cx usually increases (up to *10%* recorded in 2000), and those of Cz follow soon afterwards, the fact must be underlined that, in a number of circumstances, due to valuable improvements of shape in this phase of the evolution, there was no worsening in resistance, all to the advantage of aerodynamic efficiency.

Enrico Benzing

COMPARISON OF HIGH DOWNFORCE/LOW DOWNFORCE
In this drawing, it is easy to see the difference in resistance of the frontal sections of the Ferrari, set up with a small amount of downforce on the left (Hockenheim-Monza) and extensive downforce on the right (Monaco-Budapest). Note that the flap of the front plane is much bigger (1) and has greater incidence, the presence of an external triangular fin (2) of the second flap (3) in the lower part of the rear wing, and the "wall" of planes in the upper part (4). In comparison with the front wing, it can be seen how the Monaco flap is much bigger and squarer and has a large Gurney flap with an external triangular fin. Compared with the rear wing below, the high downforce feature is shown with dual planes to the front and much bigger principal chord planes (in red). Above is the Monza version, with a mini-plane combined with an equally small flap in the upper area.

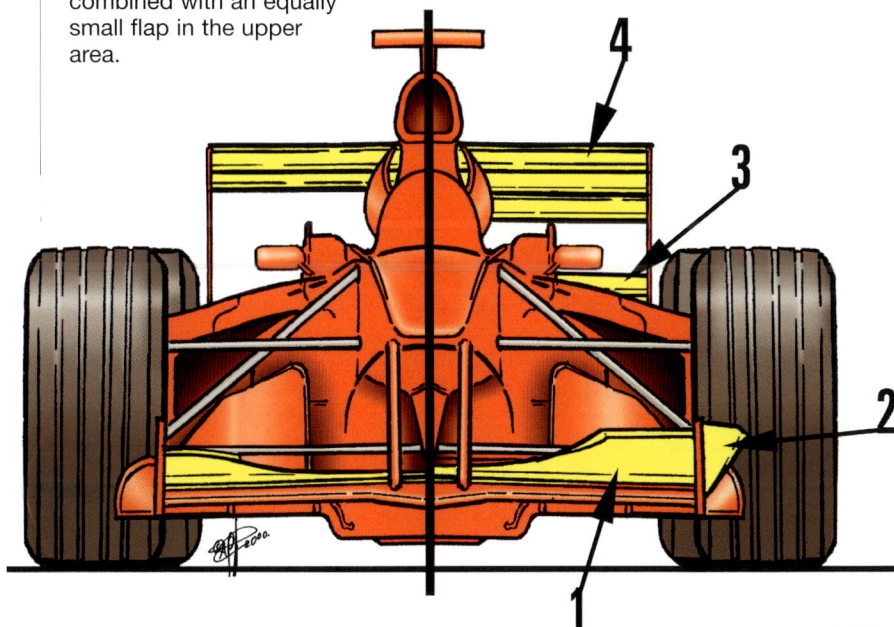

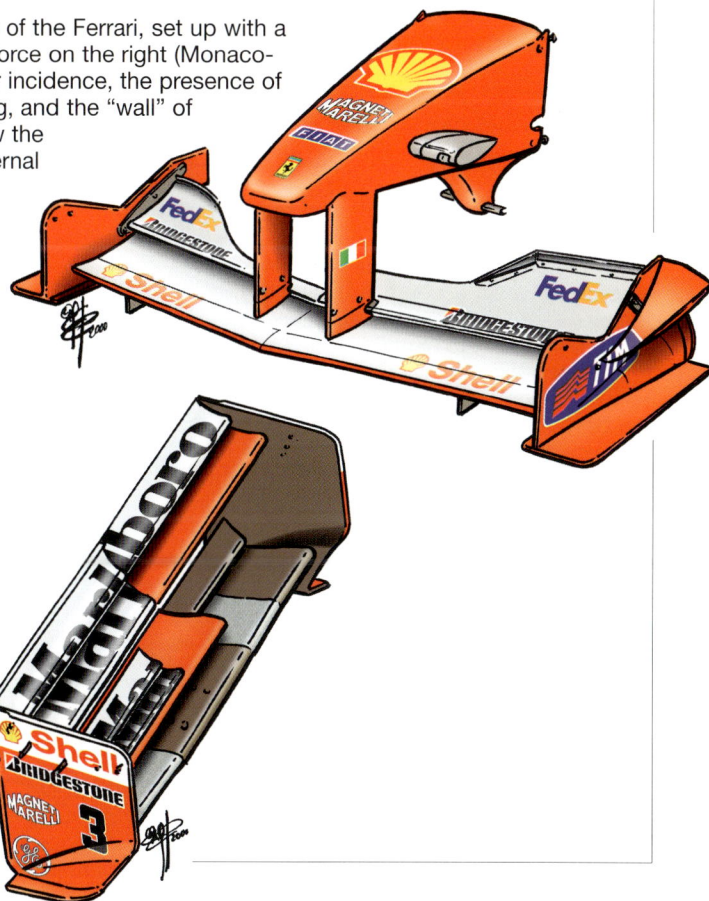

Australia

Brazil

Imola

Montecarlo

Canada

Austria

Germany

Monza

'99 Monza

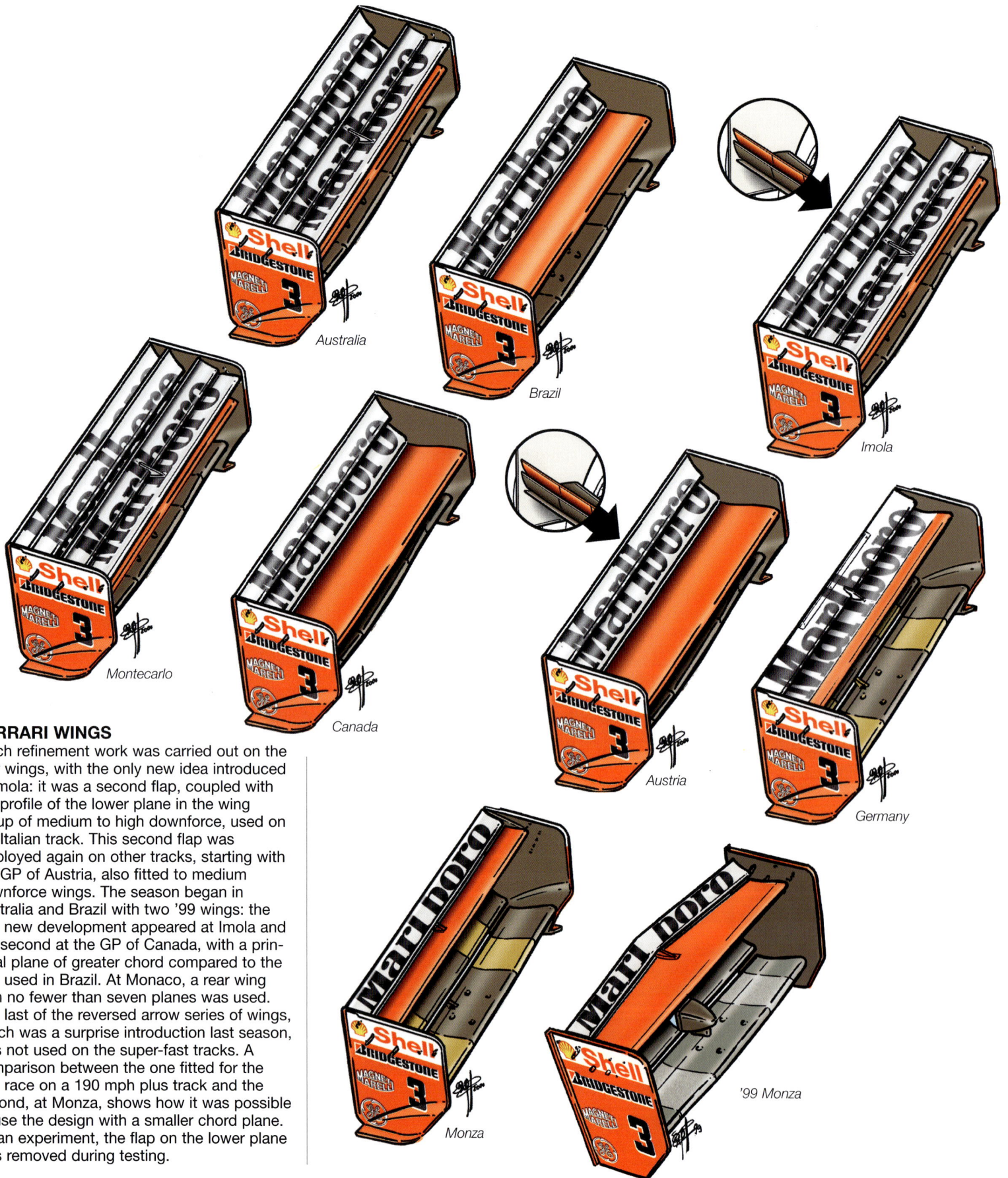

FERRARI WINGS

Much refinement work was carried out on the rear wings, with the only new idea introduced at Imola: it was a second flap, coupled with the profile of the lower plane in the wing group of medium to high downforce, used on the Italian track. This second flap was employed again on other tracks, starting with the GP of Austria, also fitted to medium downforce wings. The season began in Australia and Brazil with two '99 wings: the first new development appeared at Imola and the second at the GP of Canada, with a principal plane of greater chord compared to the one used in Brazil. At Monaco, a rear wing with no fewer than seven planes was used. The last of the reversed arrow series of wings, which was a surprise introduction last season, was not used on the super-fast tracks. A comparison between the one fitted for the first race on a 190 mph plus track and the second, at Monza, shows how it was possible to use the design with a smaller chord plane. As an experiment, the flap on the lower plane was removed during testing.

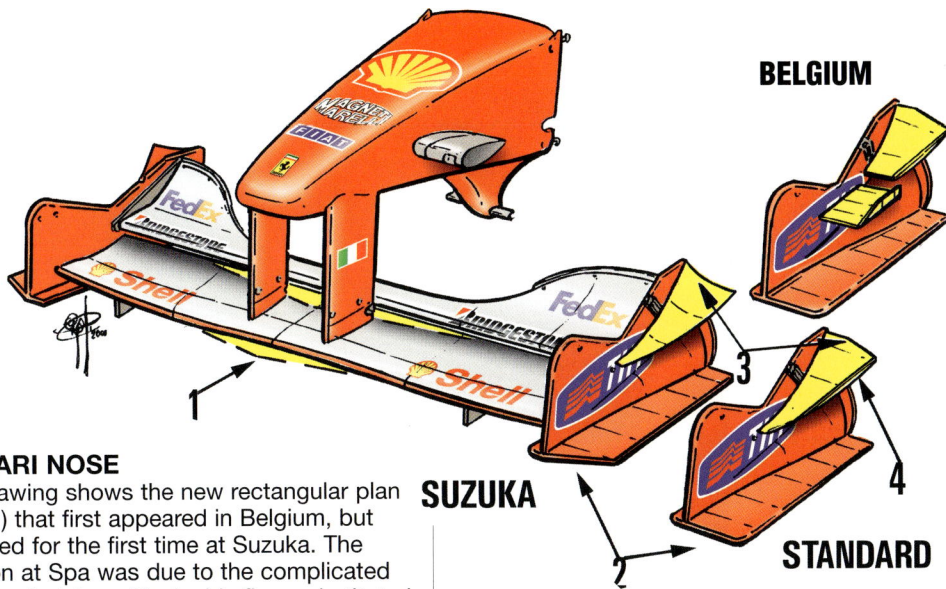

BELGIUM

SUZUKA

STANDARD

FERRARI NOSE

This drawing shows the new rectangular plan nose (1) that first appeared in Belgium, but was used for the first time at Suzuka. The rejection at Spa was due to the complicated lateral end-plates with double fins, substituted in Japan by elements cut in the external horizontal area (2) and with various lateral fins (3). They are more inclined and do not have the small lateral fins (4) of the traditional end-plates.

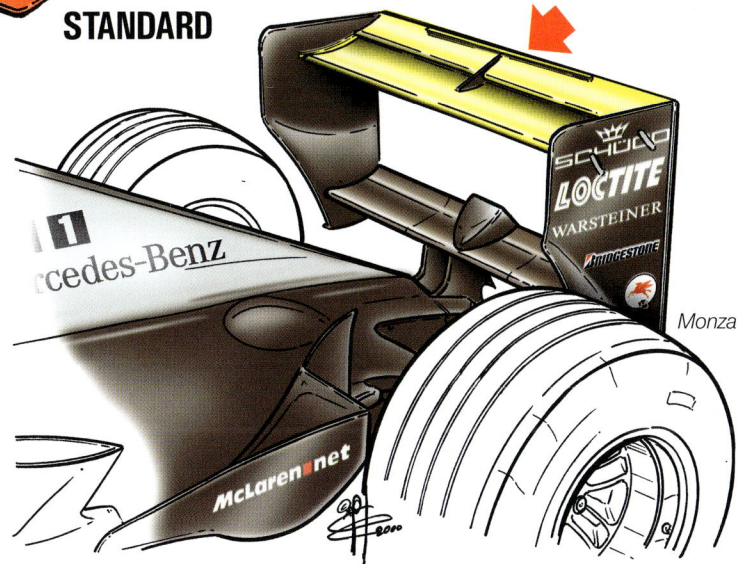

Monza

Canada

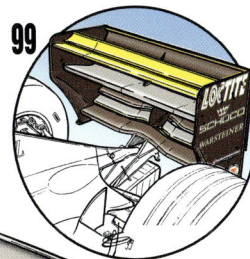

99

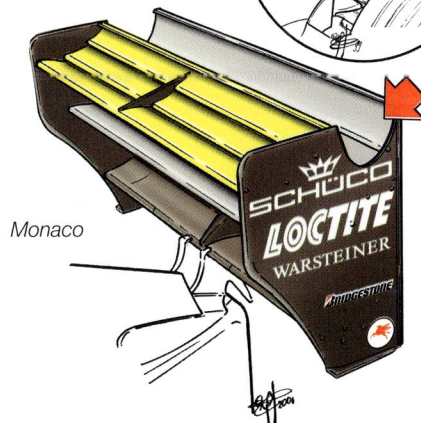

Monaco

Budapest

McLAREN WINGS

Two new developments at McLaren, both introduced at Monaco: they were the three planes up high to the front, in place of the traditional two, and the cut of the end-plate at the height of the flap to the rear, a technique already used by BAR at the GP of Spain. This end-plate was not used at Budapest, the other high downforce track. The Canadian version, without the flap on the lower plane, was often combined with a flap also in this area of the wing.

JORDAN 99

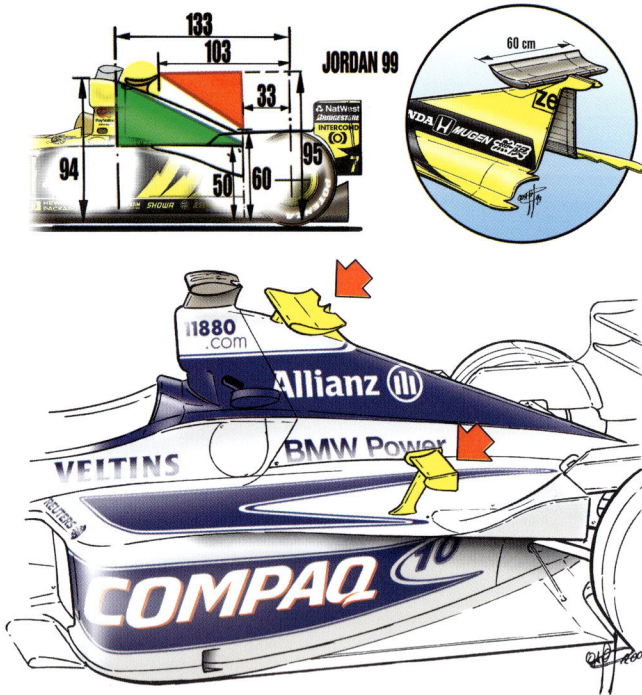

Williams Monaco

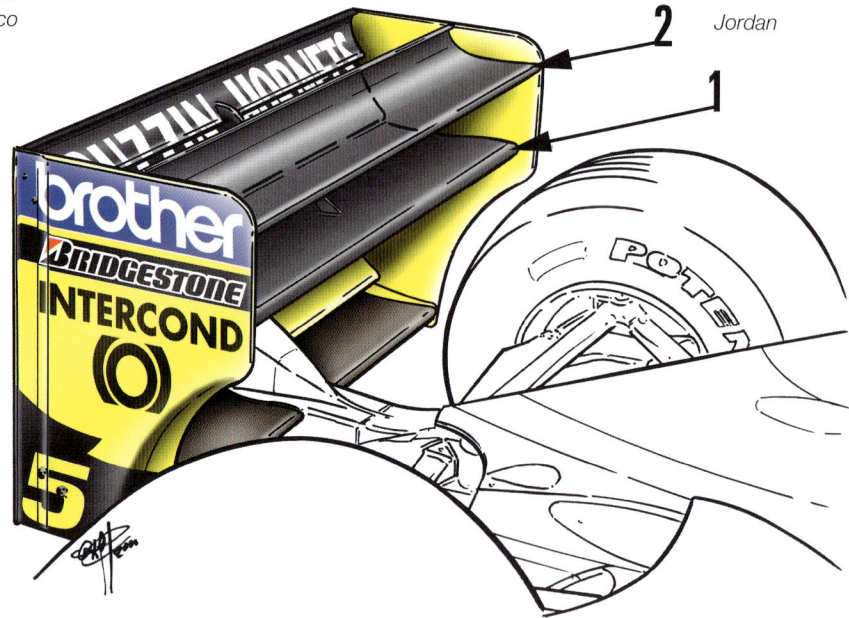

2

Jordan

1

HIGH DOWNFORCE

In most cases, the features introduced in '99 were seen again in 2000 with some small changes, illustrated in this mini-sequence.

WILLIAMS MONACO

Williams was the only team to use again the third small wing, brought back by Jordan the previous season, combined in this case with two new mini-planes placed above the sides, in the area in front of the rear wheels. The table above shows the '99 Jordan idea, and the drawing clarifies how there was a loophole in the regulations that permitted the use of the third small wing, introduced in '95 by McLaren and banned conceptually by FIA.

JORDAN

Jordan more or less brought back the rear wing used at Monaco in '99, with a single plane (2) in place of the usual two to the front, above the principal plane.

BAR

At the GP of Spain, BAR was the first to introduce this edge on its rear wing end-plate, which makes the wing flap more efficient in a corner.

WILLIAMS

Like McLaren, at Monaco and Budapest Williams used three planes in place of the usual two to the front. At other medium-high downforce circuits, a development was used that saw two planes placed low to the rear, with two more in the high front area.

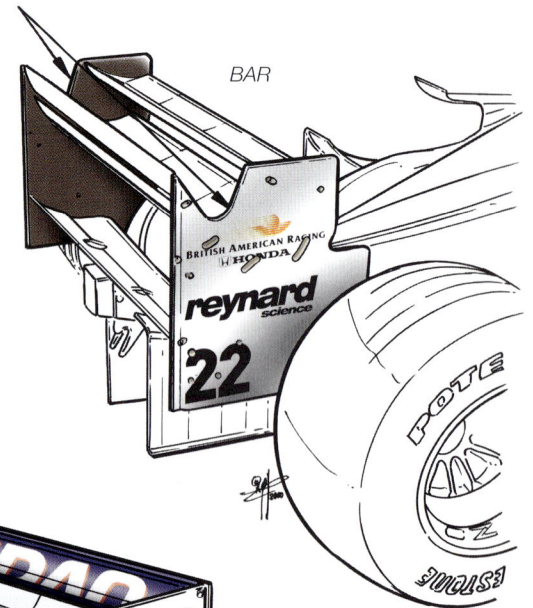

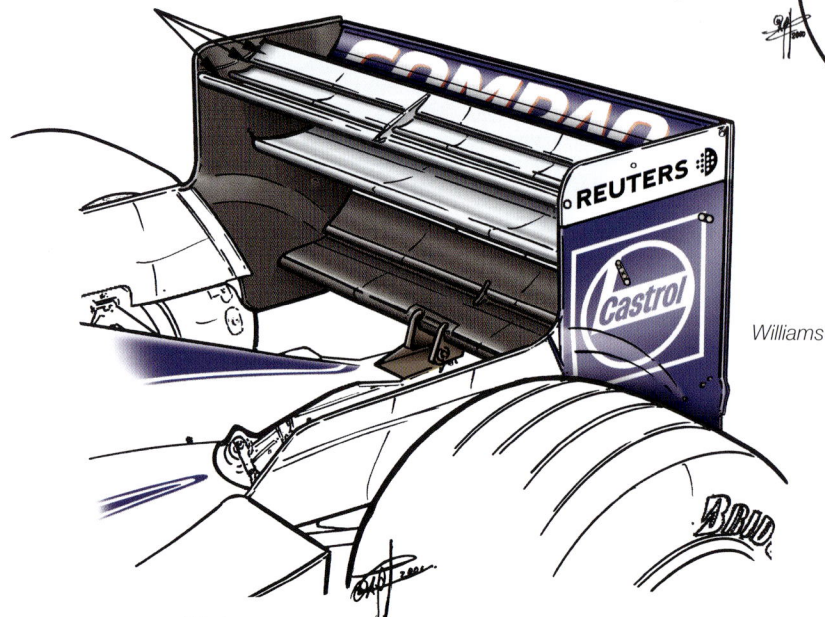

BAR

Williams

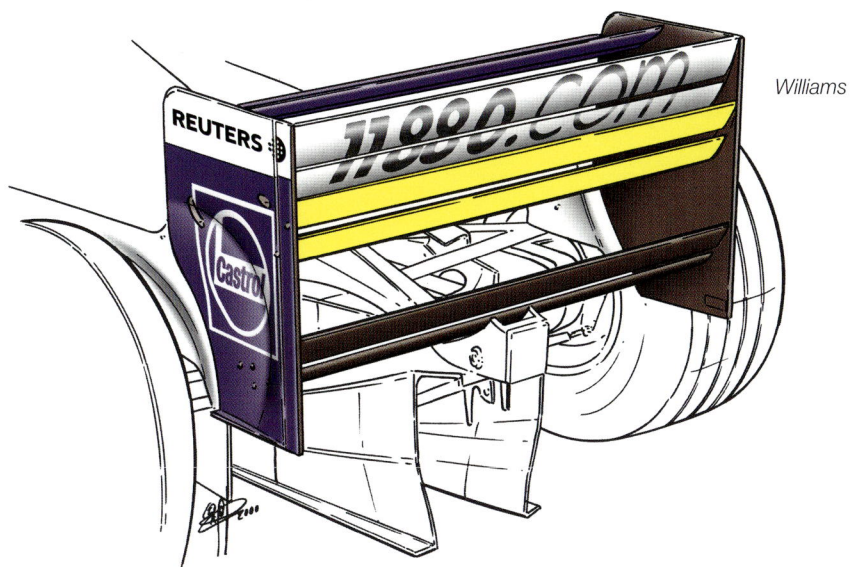

Williams

JORDAN, ARROWS AND MINARDI

A mini-flap with a small Gurney flap for the Jordan, with a principal plane that kept the traditional chord, the opposite to Arrows, which combined a mini-flap with a much reduced chord plane. The Arrows front wing probably had the least downforce used on the two fastest tracks. Those of Minardi and Sauber were the only examples with split flaps, a feature used in the past by Williams, Benetton and Prost.

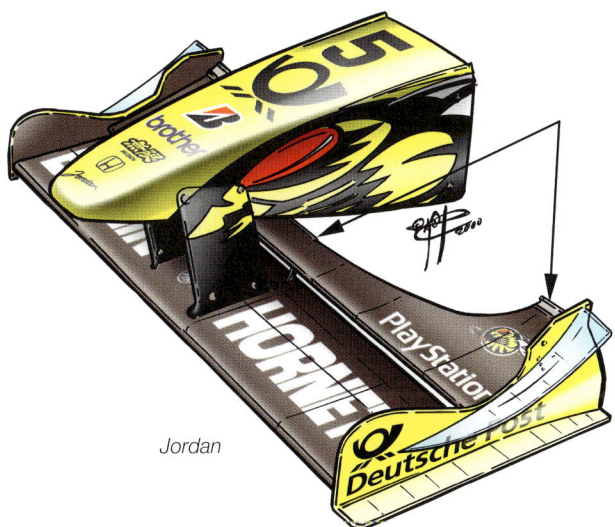

Jordan

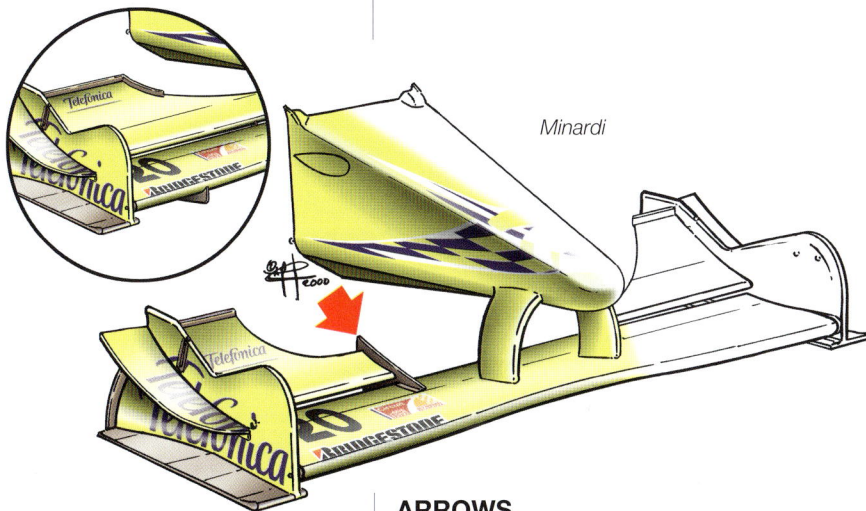

Minardi

ARROWS

On high downforce tracks, Arrows adopted these two small fins of the Minardi-Tyrrell type, a technique also used in earlier seasons by Jordan and Prost.

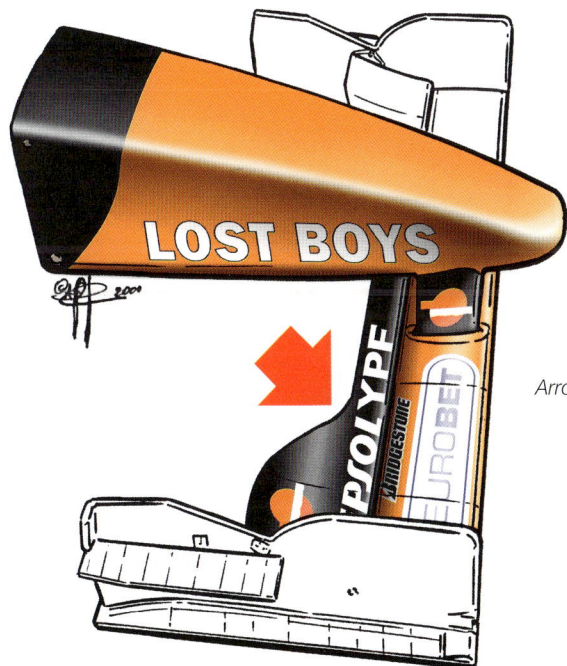

Arrows

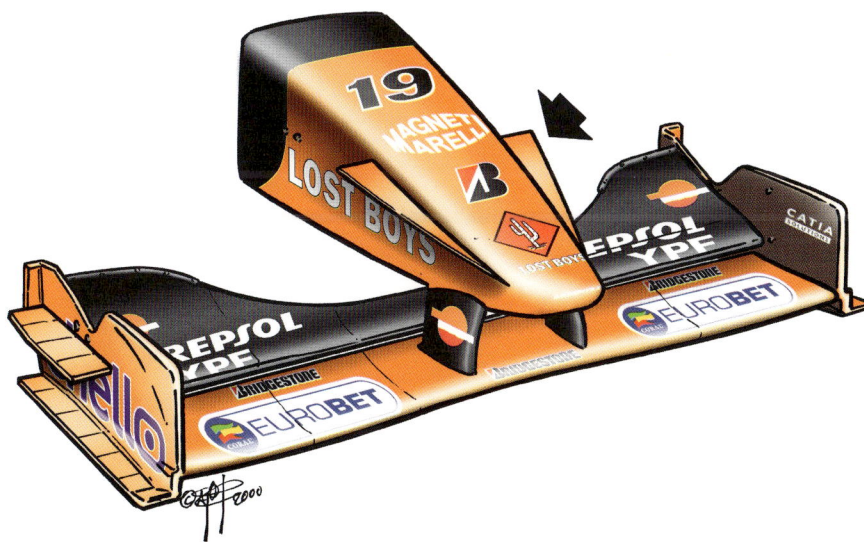

LOW DOWNFORCE REAR WINGS

No-one went over the top during the 2000 season; in fact, most teams used the principal plane configuration, with reduced chord and a mini-flap. Williams used only a single element down low, while Sauber retained the flap down low but, in particular, cut the extensions that linked the fins in front of the wheels to the end-plates of the rear wing. Note how the planes of the Benetton are straight. Jordan brought back the rear wing used the previous season, with a flap, which had a bigger chord, compared to the upper principal plane.

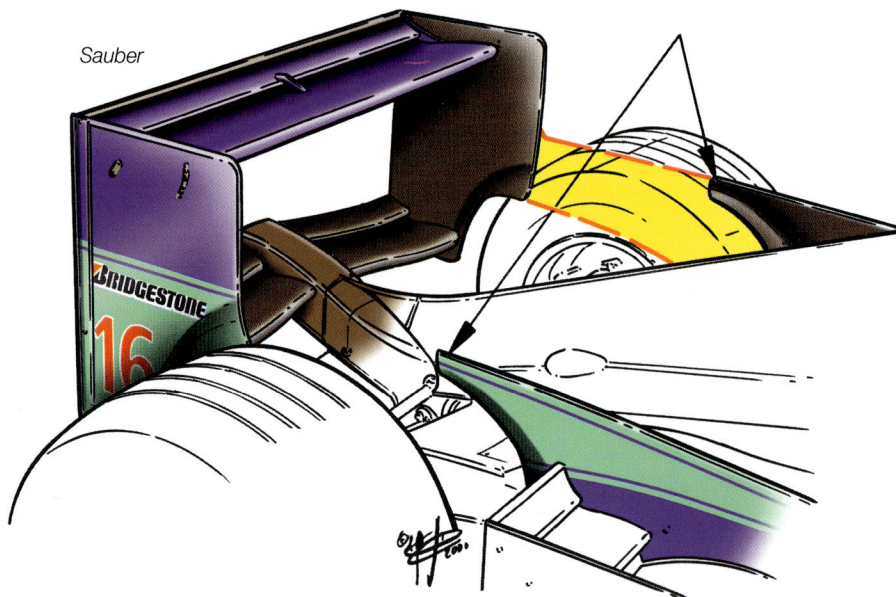

Sauber

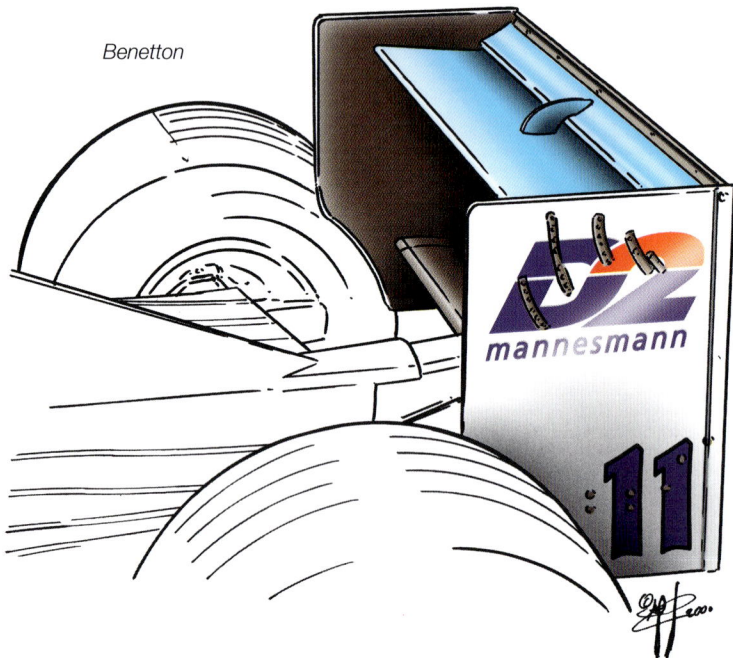

Benetton

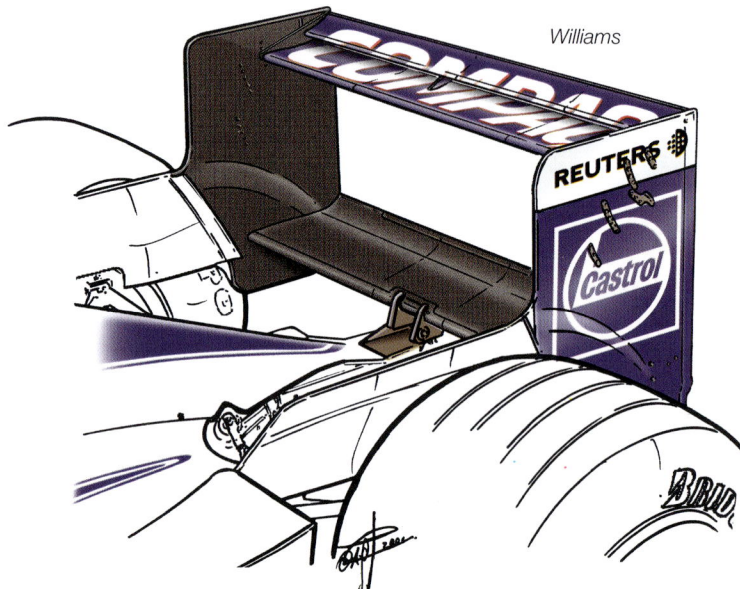

Williams

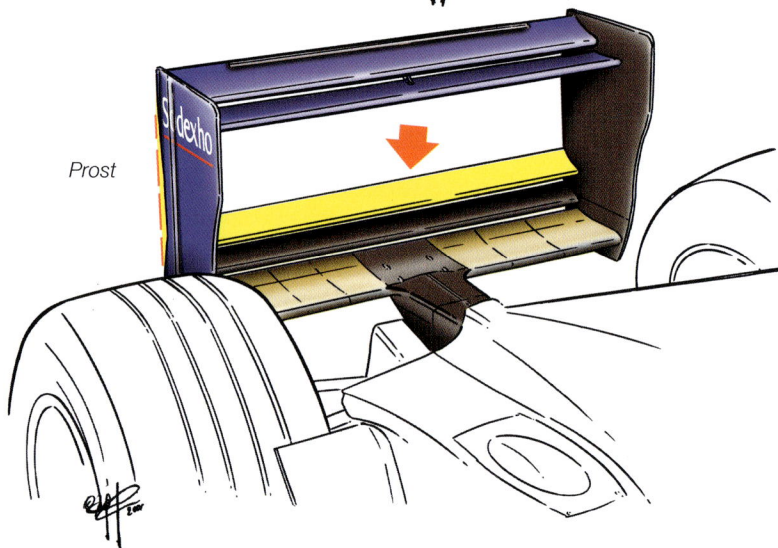

Prost

PROST AND MINARDI

The two teams that used the smallest rear wings were Prost and Minardi, who also fitted very narrow and profiled lateral end-plates, reminiscent of experiments conducted in seasons past. Prost was the only team to use two flaps in the lower area of the wing.

Minardi

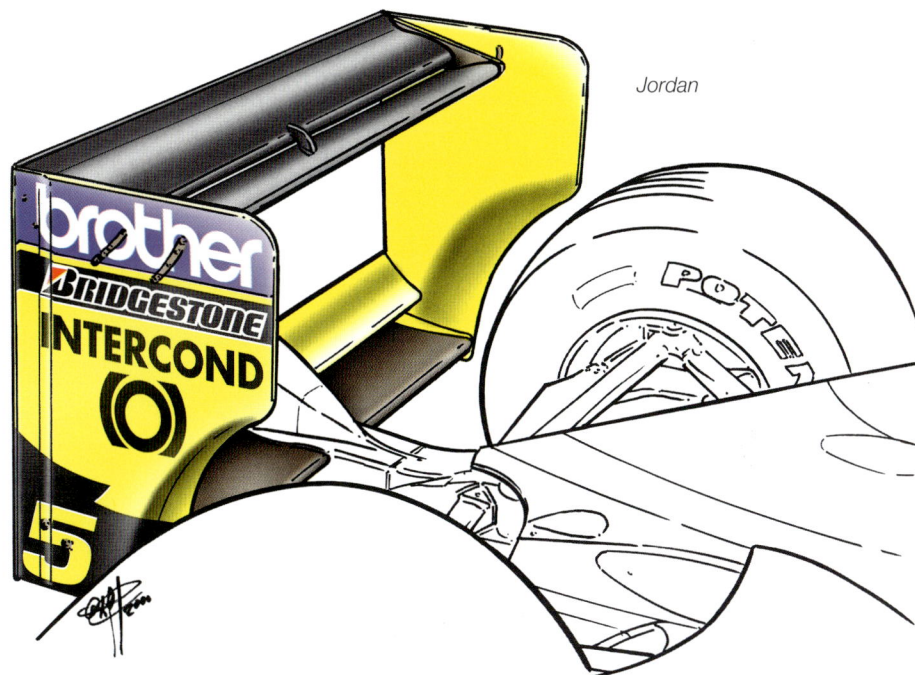

Jordan

'99 JORDAN AND '97 STEWART

The Minardi end-plates clearly recalled those seen the previous season on the Jordan, among others, which, in turn, had exploited the concept introduced by Stewart in '97. The Stewart wing certainly had the most down-force of those used at Monza in recent years. It had just one plane in the upper area, two mini-planes in the lower zone and these new end-plates.

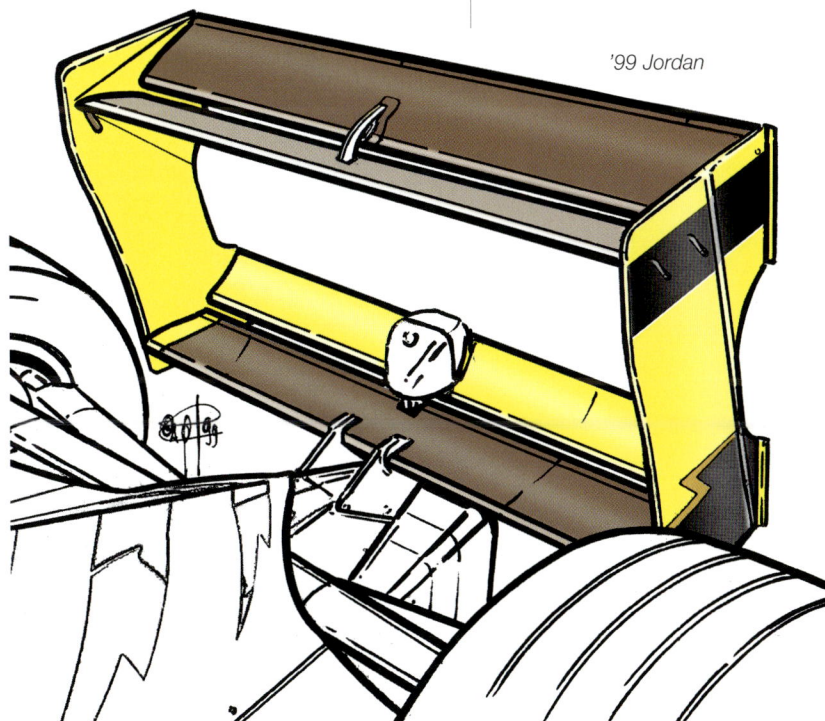

'99 Jordan

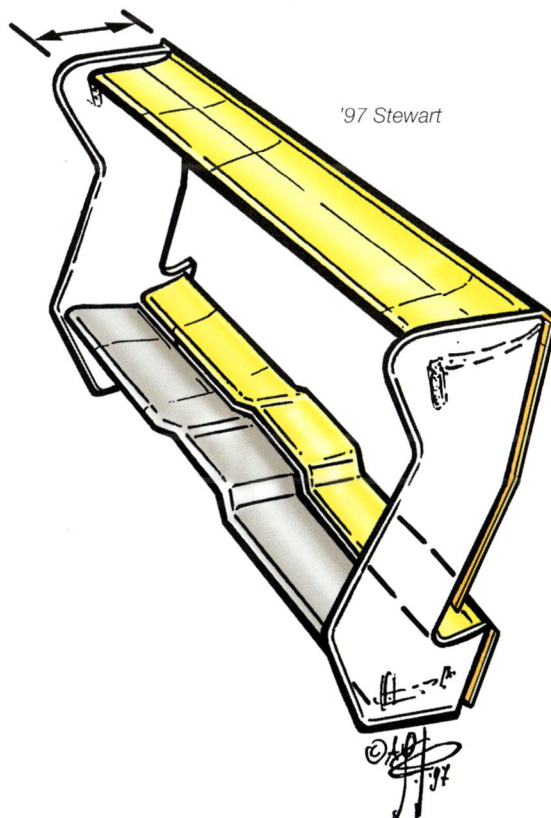

'97 Stewart

TALKING ABOUT
UNDERBODIES

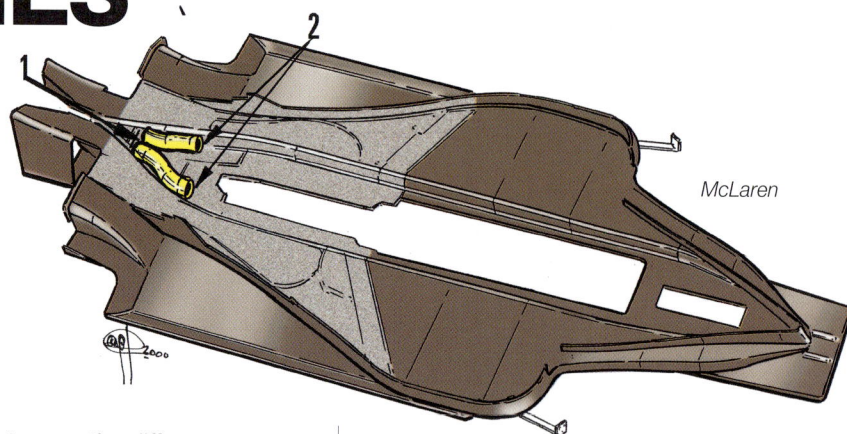

McLaren

The third season of stable regulations had its calming effect on the inventiveness of the designers, in the diffuser channel and underbody areas included. A new trend was born, of exhausts that blew from the upper part of the engine cover, a feature introduced by Ferrari at the '98 GP of Spain. Stewart and Prost went that way the following season, the latter from the GP of Belgium, making three teams that had adopted the system in '99. The number doubled to six in 2000: the teams were Ferrari, Jaguar (ex-Stewart), Prost, Jordan, Sauber and Minardi. The rest – Williams, Benetton, BAR and Arrows –retained the standard system of a row of lateral channels, with some slight variations. McLaren was the only team to have their cars' exhaust low in the centre of the principal section of the diffuser, using a '99 Williams idea that the Grove team dropped from that year's British GP. The McLaren-Mercedes system had a somewhat different lay-out to the Williams, with the ends of the exhausts extremely close to each other, almost paired, while on the FW 21 they were separated by a central fin of the gearbox faring (see drawing).

However, in most cases the different teams came up with systems similar to those they had used in '99, with one or two important exceptions, McLaren, Williams and Minardi. From the San Marino GP, Patrick Head's team introduced a lay-out that exploited a different interpretation of the rules, opening up a much bigger window in the vertical connection area, between the reference plane (central zone) and the stepped bottom, together with another new development that concerned the lateral channels and the usually flat area inside the rear wheels, as can be seen from the drawing. The Gustav Brunner-designed Minardi had a new horizontal fin in the same area inside the rear wheels and showed a certain inclination of the traditional plane. Most teams also produced single-piece underbodies, with the exception of Arrows and Benetton, which had

a small linked portion in the initial area of the side-pods. The Ferrari and BAR underbodies were of one single element, but with the divergent part and the front of the knife edge zone separate.
All teams freed the extractor's lateral channels of suspension components, with the exception of Prost, which kept the rear arm of the lower wishbone at mid-channel, in common with the '99 Williams.

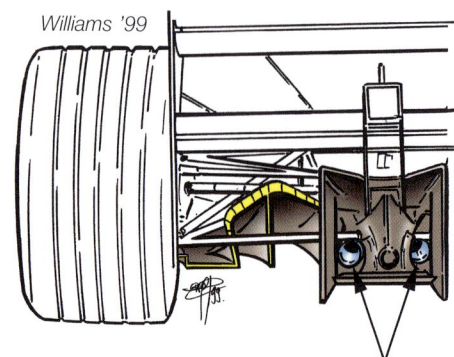

Williams '99

McLAREN

Adrian Newey gave the MP4/15 exhausts that exited from the lower area of the central tunnel (1), using a reviewed and corrected version of the system introduced in '99 by Williams. On the McLaren, the terminals exited almost paired, while on the Williams they were set slightly apart. Note in the detailed drawing how the section of these terminals was neither round nor oval and were of a different length at the openings, (2) with the group of five tubes per cylinder bank.

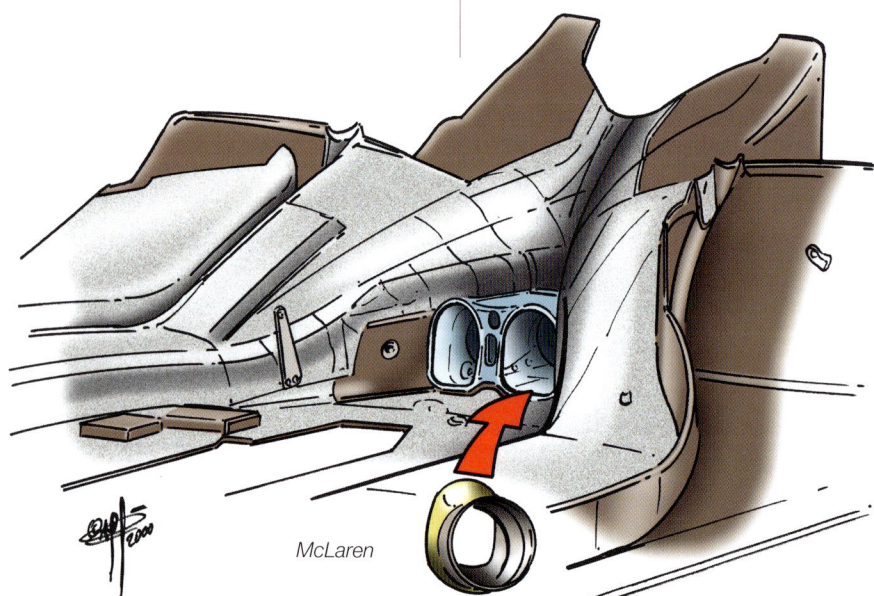

McLaren

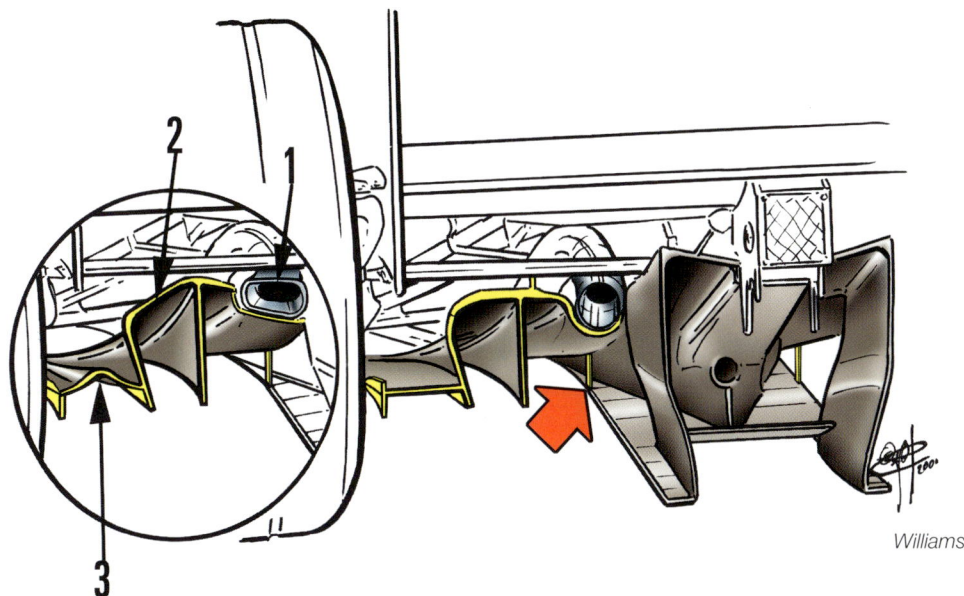

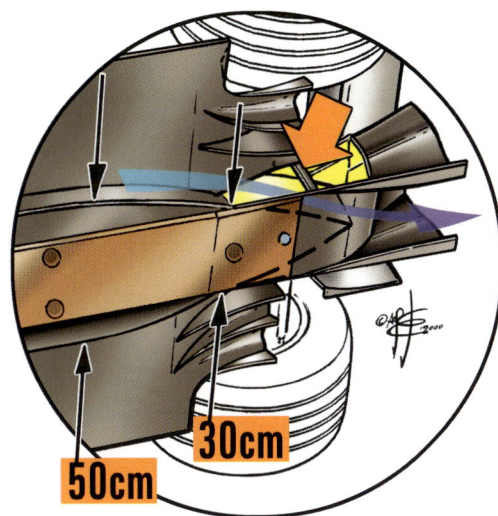

Williams

WILLIAMS

The most interesting new development came from Williams, with the exploitation of a bigger window in the vertical linkage wall, between the reference plane and the stepped bottom, which ended at the point (1) indicated by the white line. A greater flow of air was guaranteed through the central channel, as can be seen when compared to the traditional design. This new feature was introduced at the GP of San Marino and was retained, even with the introduction of the new diffuser that appeared at the GP of Hungary. However, the exhausts (1) were notably modified and given a flat section, the lateral channels (2) inclined upwards and the plane near the wheels, which is usually horizontal, noticeably curved up (3), a technique used only by Williams for the remainder of the season.

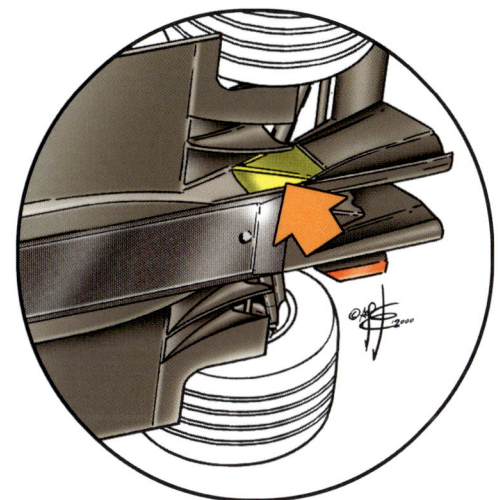

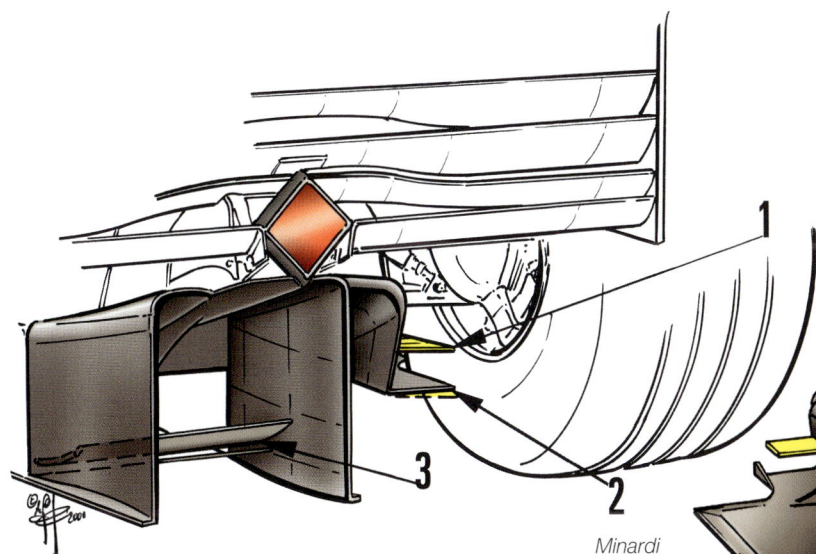

Minardi

MINARDI

The team came up with a new idea for the area inside the rear wheels. A small horizontal plane (1) was added, while the lower part was slightly inclined upwards (2). The central channel had a small flap (3). The arrow in the overall drawing indicates the small knife edge zone to the front of the sides, a little narrower than the 140 cm allowed by the regulations.

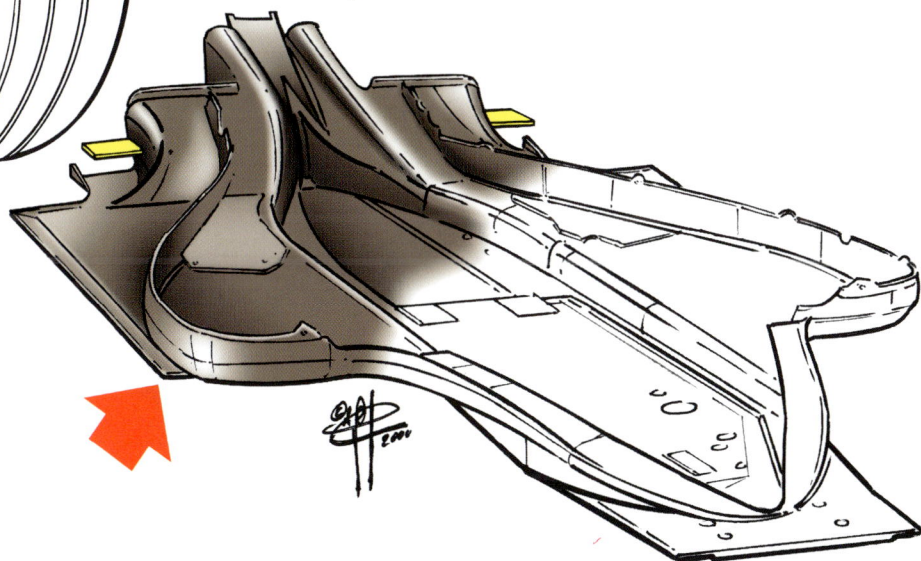

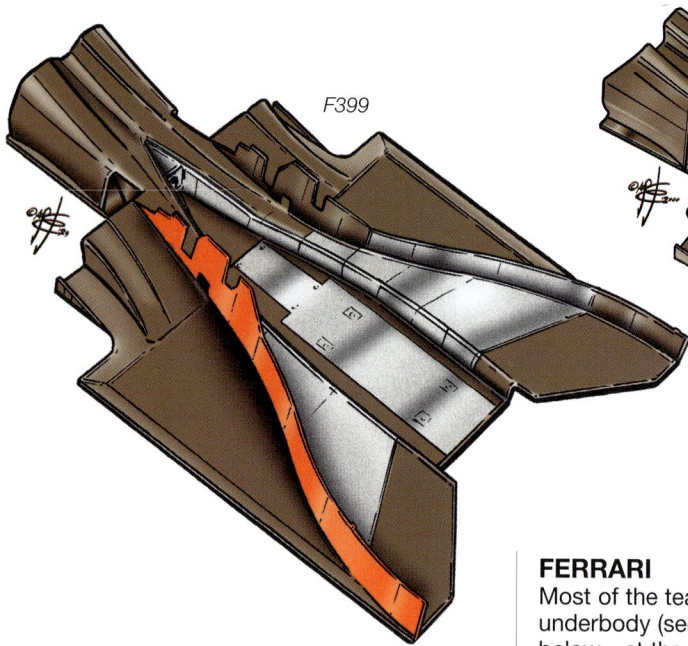

F399

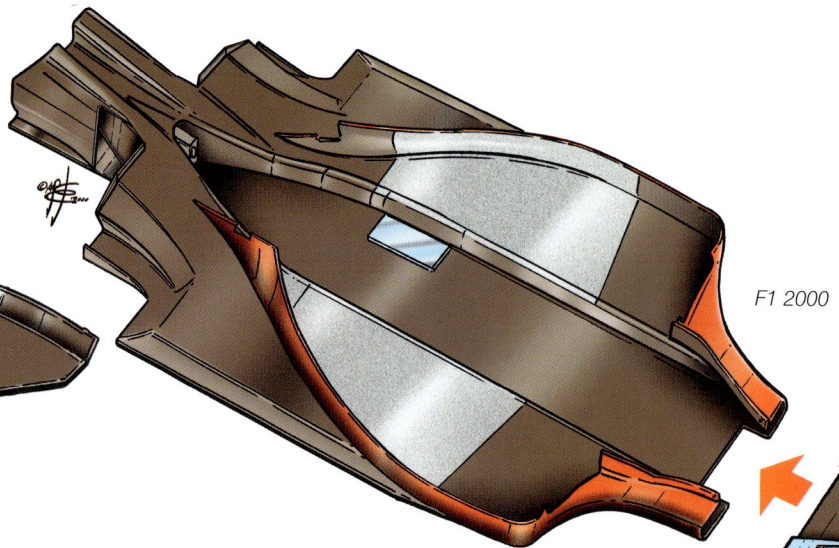

F1 2000

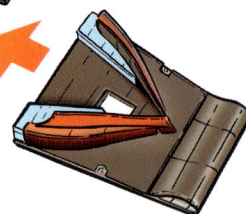

FERRARI

Most of the teams produced a single piece underbody (see also the Jordan drawing below…at the side…). The difference can be seen between the stepped bottom of the F 399 and the F1 2000's single-piece underbody, with the exception of its knife edge part of the divergence, also used to position ballast in the furthest forward, lowest possible part of the car.

BAR

BAR also had the knife edge area separated from the rest of the underbody. Note the two small vertical fins, similar to those used from the start of the season by Williams.

JORDAN

The underbody of the Jordan holds no secrets when seen from above and below. It is easy to see how it was made in a single piece, with the two lateral fins (1) actually connected in the area at the entry to the flanks themselves. Air entered (2), in part, via the block of the underbody. Derived from those used the previous season, small vertical fins (3) were also retained at the sides of the internal area of the rear wheels.

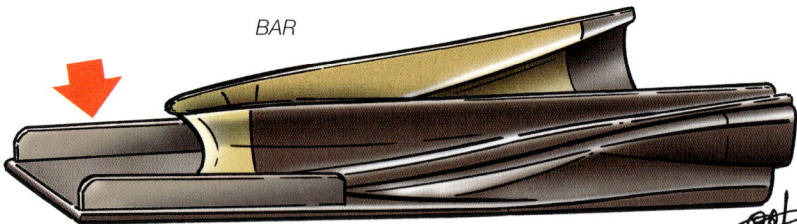

BAR

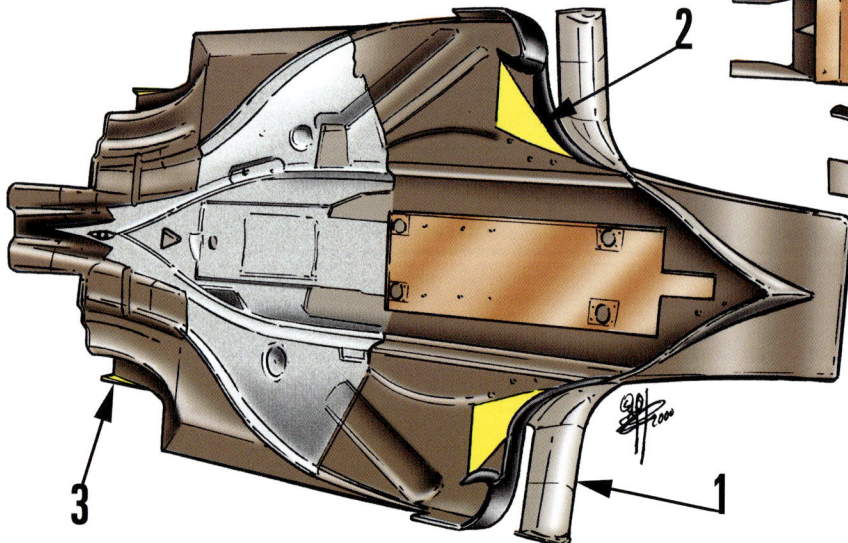

2

3

1

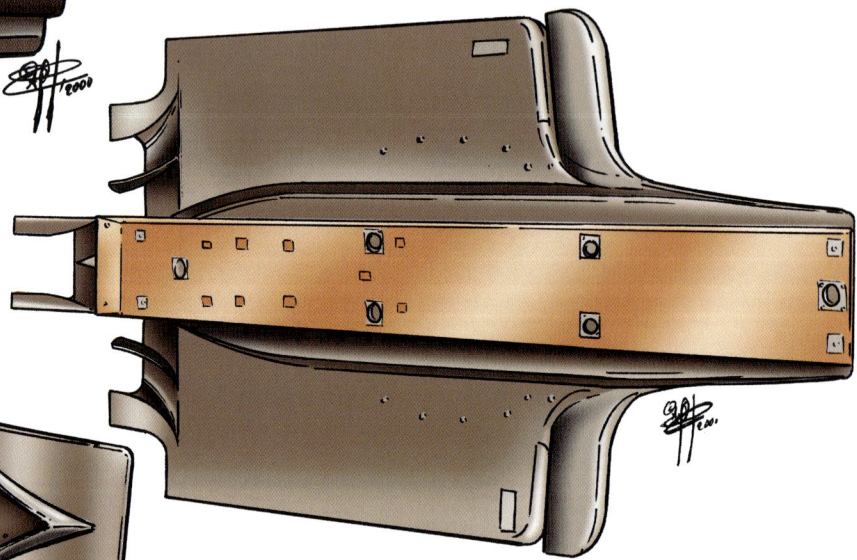

Jordan

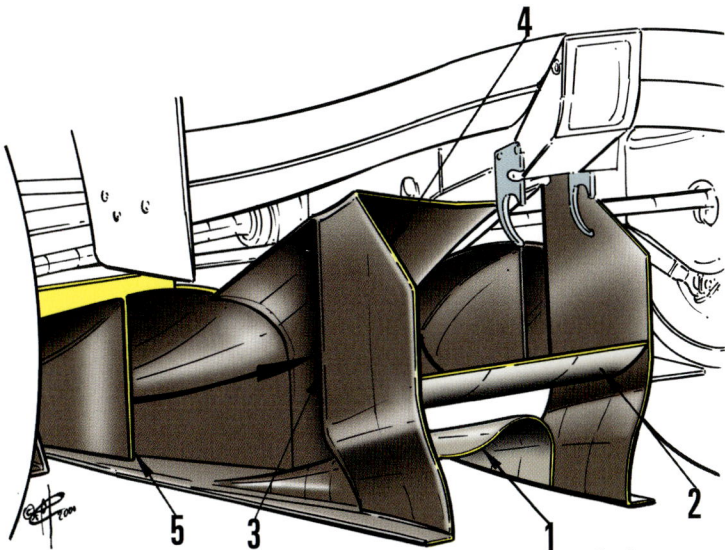

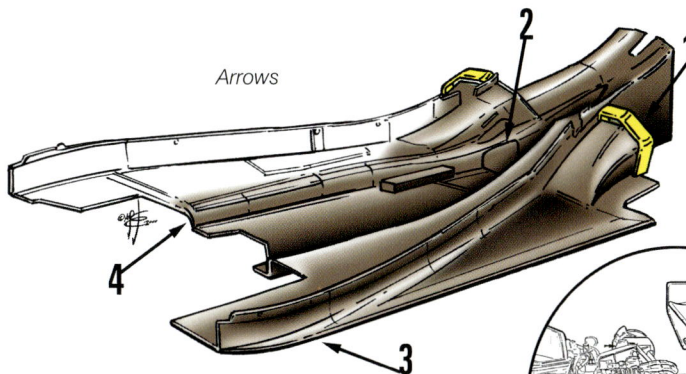

Arrows

Sauber

Stewart '97

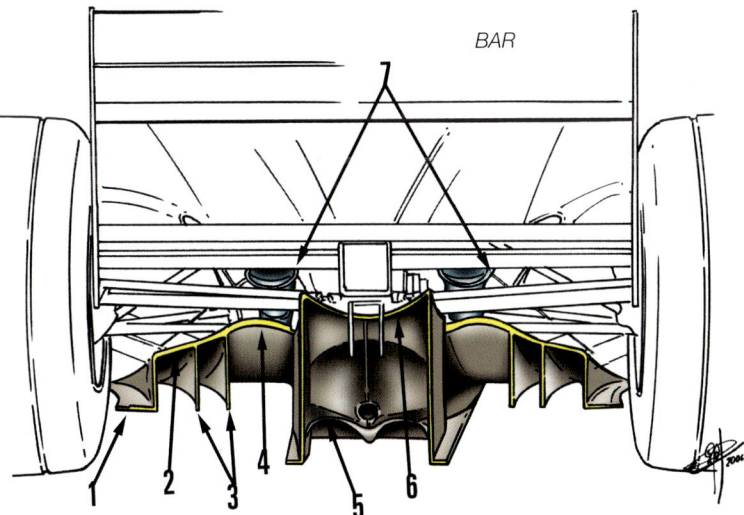

SAUBER

The diffuser of the Sauber C19, evolved from the '99 car of which it retained the curiously curved shape (1) of the central channel, topped by a small flap (2). The lateral window (3) was very wide, with just one middle plate (5) in the lateral channels. The central diffuser was cut in the upper area (4). A new idea for the lateral channels was introduced at the GP of Belgium. A small flap was added, similar to the one used throughout the season by Arrows.

BAR

The diffuser of the BAR was similar to that of their '99 car, of which it retained most features. 1) The smooth area inside the wheels was slightly inclined. The lateral channels remained divided into three sections (2-3), the central section extremely narrow. Note how the inner channel climbs (4). The lower arched area of the central diffuser (5) was retained, the upper section concave (6). The periscope exhausts were of oval section (7) and passed through the suspension.

PROST

Prost was the only team with the rear arm of the suspension wishbone that encroached on the lateral channels, which were square and heavily curved upwards. Note the odd Gurney flaps in the plane area inside the two wheels, indicated in yellow.

ARROWS AND '97 STEWART

Arrows placed a small flap to the rear of the lateral channels (1) introduced by Hegbhal Hamidy, when he worked with Alan Jenkins at Stewart in '97. Tom Walkinshaw's team used a stepped bottom, cut in the central area inside the wheels (2). The closely linked shape (3) of the lateral zone of the initial low part of the flanks was odd. Arrows and Benetton were the only teams to have the underbody divided into two sections, without the initial part of the flanks.

BAR

Prost

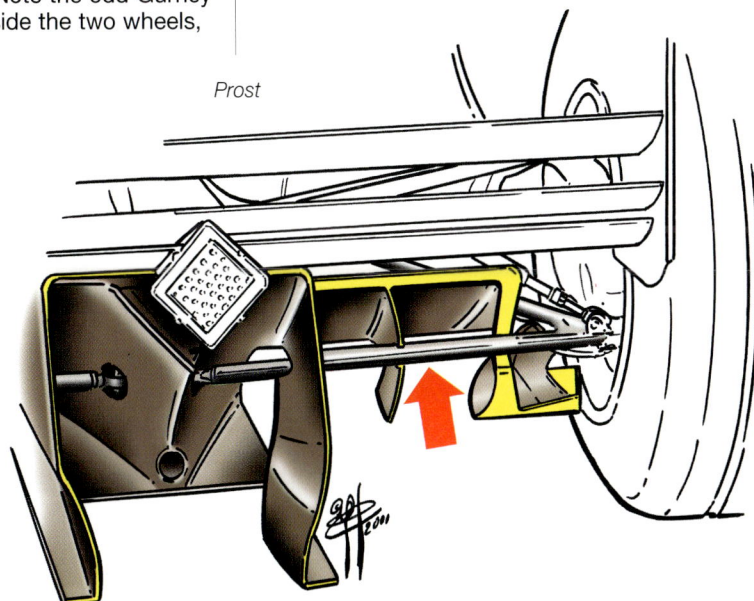

TALKING ABOUT
NOSES

In an increasingly difficult working environment, the chapter analysing the season's F1 car noses is one of the more interesting and remains one of the few elements changes to which can be easily seen outside the pits. In the overall complexity of the constituent parts that make up the nose, its shape influences the aerodynamics of the entire car, among other things. Aerodynamic efficiency, the ratio between downforce and penetration, is mainly determined by the effectiveness of the elements that comprise the nose, as is the car's sensitivity to the variation in height from the ground. Even determinate choices of the plane of the rear axle extractor are based on the imposition data of the nose of the car in the wind tunnel, a discovery made in the years of the ground effect cars and, obviously, consolidated in recent seasons in which the Federation has intervened decisively as regards the front part of the car, with the raising of the front planes by +5 cm from the reference plane, and with a narrowing of the track. Nevertheless, in the third year after this revolution, there was a further alignment of the measures that consolidated themselves in '99, and a reduction of inventiveness, which has inevitably had its effect on the analysis of this sector. If an ulterior tendency has come to strengthen the situation, it is the search for better aerodynamic stability, to the detriment of the maximum downforce obtainable, a road that Ferrari took, in particular, followed later by others. More teams decided not to pursue the exploitation of the maximum 140 cm width of the front planes permitted by the regulations, and erred towards a reduction so as to create a new alignment with the internal area of the tyres, which were moved 10 cm per unit closer to the car's body after the introduction in '98 of the narrow, 180 cm track place of the previous 200 cm. In practice, only Williams and Benetton maintained large front planes of about 140 cm, while McLaren dispensed with that choice from the GP of Great Britain, as can be seen from the series of MP4/15 wings. In the last two races of 2000, Ferrari dropped

Australia

Monaco

the arrow-shaped front planes introduced at the '99 GP of Europe and returned to the rectangular plane used previously, even if only in testing for the GP of Belgium.

FERRARI
Certainly, the area in which the F1 2000 improved, compared to the old F399, was its aerodynamic configuration. That produced a 10% increase in efficiency, an extremely important value, which confirms just how much work was done in the Maranello wind tunnel. The analysis of the season's Ferrari noses confirms that statement. Starting from the base of the arrow-shaped planes, all other

parameters were optimised, including the slightly increased height of the principal plane from the ground in both the central and peripheral areas, to reduce pitch sensitivity. That produced a plane which, when seen from the front, seemed sinuous in appearance. The lateral end-plates were rather generous in the horizontal area, so as to reduce the total width of the planes and create an optimum alignment with the wheels, an area in which the brakes' air intake also played an important role in increasing global efficiency. The position of the plane, compared to the end-plates, is such as to create, in both the front and lower areas, a sort of wall that

Canada

Belgium

Monza

Suzuka

improves aerodynamic stability. An indication of the improvement in efficiency was shown by the absence of intermediate vanes in the lower part of the planes in fast track noses, the purpose of which was to claw back something in terms of downforce. The convex outer area, surmounted by a large triangular fin with a small outer longitudinal Gurney flap, remained. Six different types of nose were used, of which three were derived from the same model, and were different from each other only in that the flap with which they were combined is concerned. These elements underwent a remarkable revolution, with four different types of flap introduced during the season.

NOSE SEQUENCE AUSTRALIA-MONACO-CANADA-BELGIUM-MONZA-SUZUKA

For most of the season the arrow-shaped nose, with its intermediate vane in the lower area, was used. During the early races, the flap was fairly square and had a large Gurney flap. At Monaco, those two factors underwent a variation, with a notable increase in their surfaces, and without the need for the Gurney flap in the central area of the plane, as used in '99. The first variation appeared at the GP of Canada, with a more rounded flap, again surmounted by a small Gurney flap, which followed the shape of the plane in the peripheral area. On the fast circuits of Hockenheim and Monza, lateral end-plates without the triangular fin (which was retained on the nose of the

McLarens) were used, combined with a much smaller chord flap. The first major new development appeared at the GP of Belgium with an experiment, first abandoned and later revived for the season's last two races. The rectangular plane nose appeared again at Spa, combined with different lateral endplates with double fins, in place of the arrow-shaped plane. But at Suzuka, the straight-shaped plane made its return, although it was combined with an external fin in the lateral end-plates similar to the standard version and to that of McLaren.

59

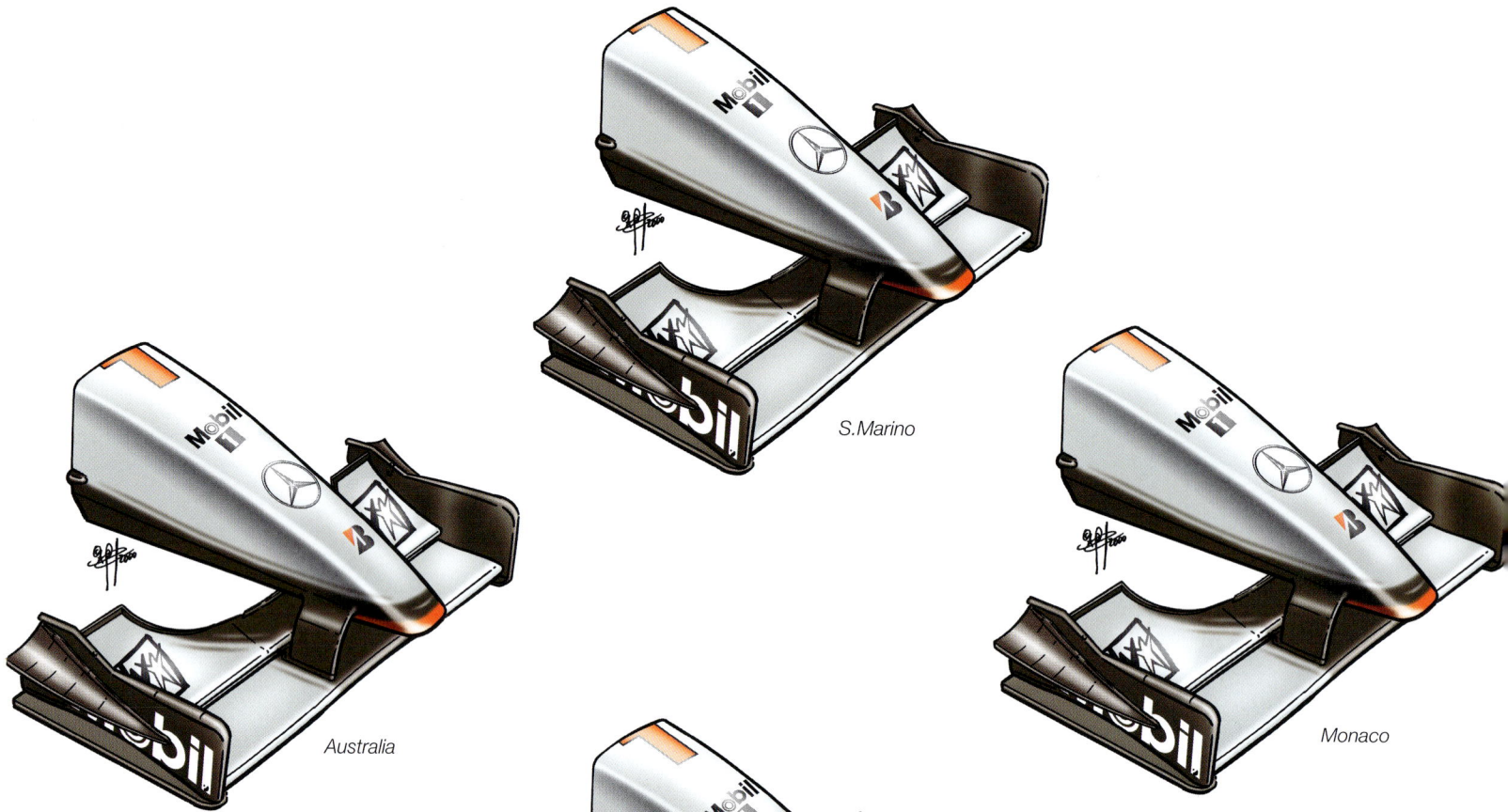

S.Marino

Australia

Monaco

Great Britain

Monza

McLAREN

The start of the season saw the use of a wing similar to the previous year's, with a full-width plane and the lateral end-plates inclined inwards towards the rear. The flaps remained rather square for the entire season, without the peripheral area cut, as with the flaps used for many races during the '99 season (Technical Analysis '99, page 60). An important new McLaren development was introduced at the GP of Great Britain, with the appearance of end-plates closer to the centre of the car, to reduce the total width of the planes and give the lower outer parts an ample knife-edge zone. The external triangular fins were of a different shape, too - longer and slightly less curved. The end-plates were also used for fast circuits, for which Ferrari decided not to employ their large triangular fins. The last two drawings show the two different versions: for Monaco, the flap with maximum chord and fitted with lateral and central Gurney flaps; and for Monza, a flap with much reduced chord but slightly higher than the one adopted during the previous season in which, among other things, straight end-plates were used, without either the external convex shape or the triangular fin.

McLaren

Williams

McLaren

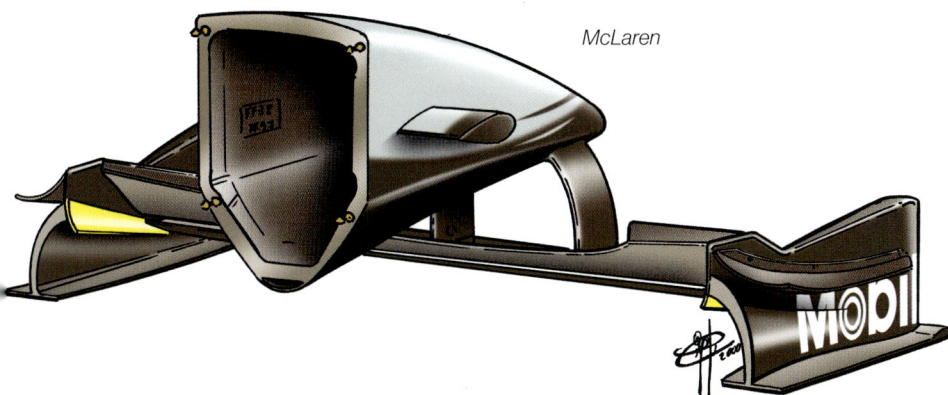

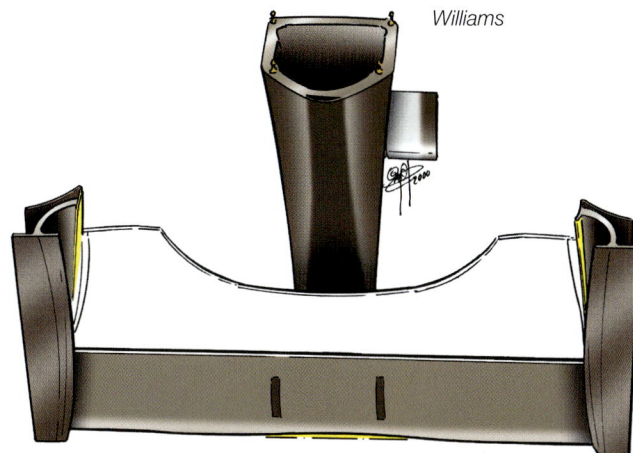

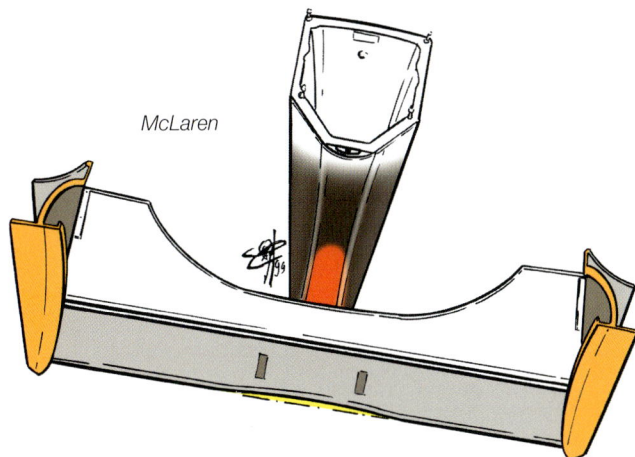

McLAREN AND WILLIAMS

McLaren and Williams remained faithful to the complete absence of the small intermediate vanes in the lower part of the planes, as can be seen in the rear view of the MP4/15's nose, as well as in the drawing below, which makes the comparison with FW22. In the underneath view of the McLaren wing, there is a new feature compared to the almost identical unit used in '99, the presence of a small deflector (indicated in yellow) inside the convex area. The Williams nose, seen from underneath, appears almost identical to that of the '99 car, with the same triangular cut in the horizontal part of the external end-plate.

FERRARI IN BELGIUM

In Belgium, there was the surprise momentary abandonment of the arrow-shaped nose, replaced by a new unit with straight planes (1), both for the principal element and the flap. The lateral end-plates were also new, with the substitution of the single triangular fin (see drawing) by dual fins, of which the number two was almost of traditional cut type, and the number three a small horizontal plane vaguely like the '98 Stewart. The latter two new developments were subsequently dropped and removed from the version used at Suzuka.

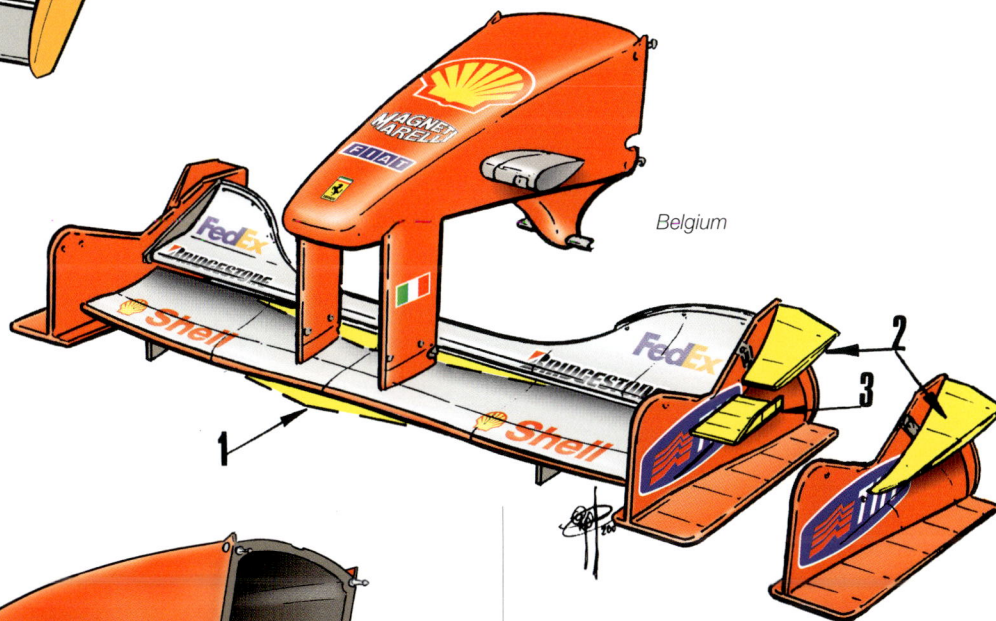

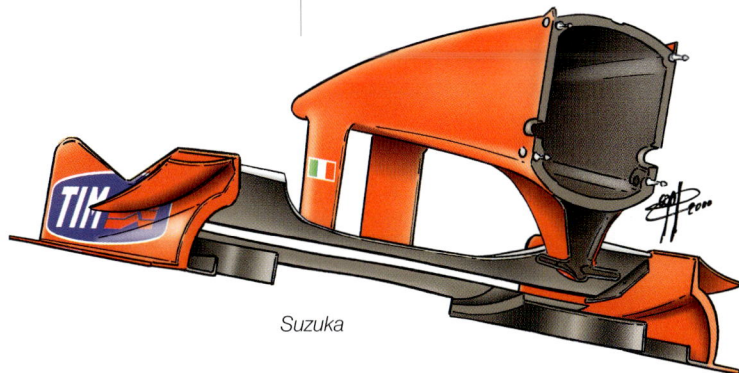

Belgium

FERRARI AT SUZUKA

A view from underneath the nose, with straight planes used during the last two decisive races of 2000. The two intermediate vanes can be seen, positioned about 20 cm from the larger external units. The central bulb that fares the fin under the chassis was much pronounced, its purpose being to become a mount for the lower wishbone of the suspension.

Suzuka

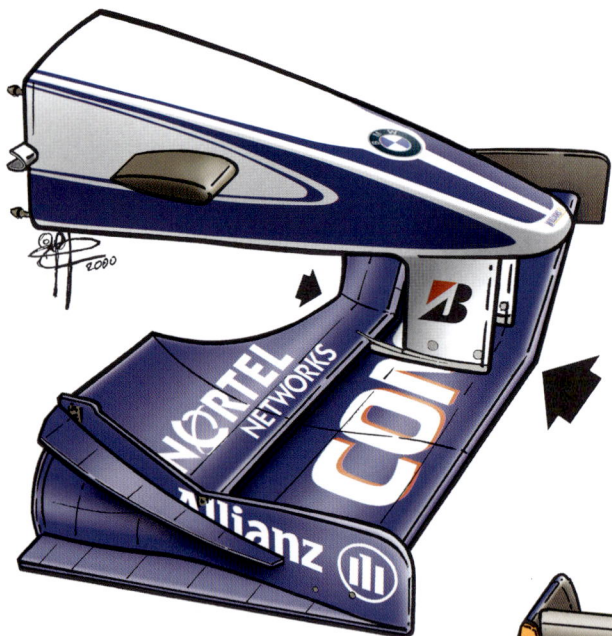

Williams

WILLIAMS

The nose planes of the Williams, devoid of external end-plates. This version is the standard unit with the rectangular plane, while at the side can be seen the slightly arrow-shaped nose, introduced at Indianapolis: the flap, too, has the same shape, although with a much less accentuated V, compared to the arrow-shaped nose of the Ferrari. In the view from underneath the end-plates, the small triangular step of the horizontal part can be seen, almost identical to that of the '99 end-plates.

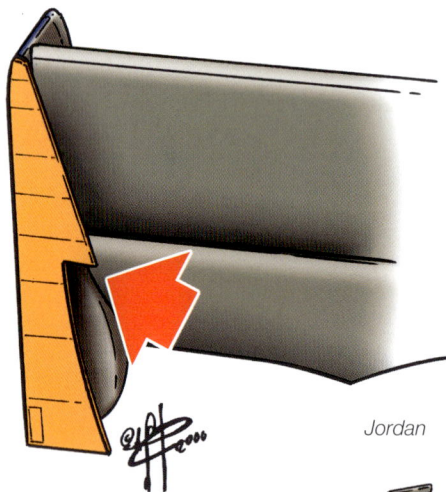

Jordan

JAGUAR

Large intermediate vanes for the Jaguar, with the lateral end-plates narrowing at the rear: note how these units have a horizontal small step area inside, and a large vertical Gurney plate in the external terminal area.

JORDAN

Jordan's bare plane, which also had a completely straight wing fitted close to the ground. The lateral end-plates were significantly concave in the central area and given a triangular fin, which was transparent to meet sponsorship needs.

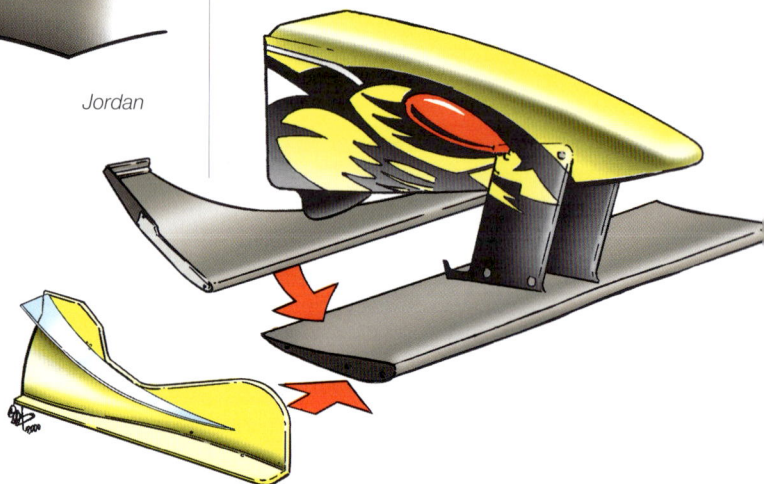

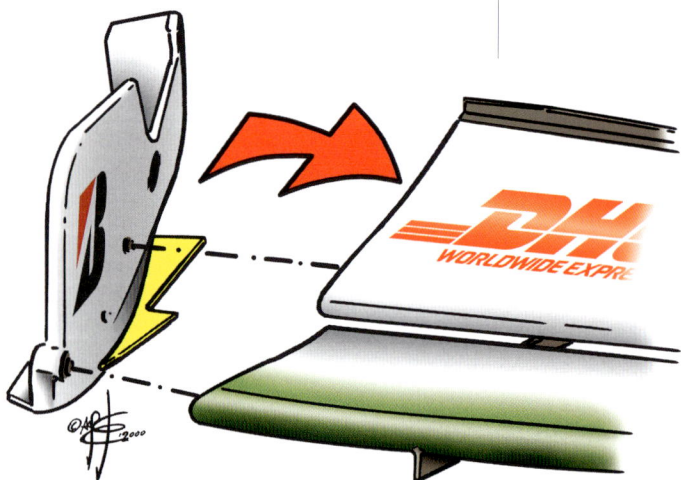

Jaguar

BENETTON

Benetton was one of the few teams to keep a full-width plane in the front, with lateral end-plates that close themselves towards the inside of the rear area. The flap is reminiscent of the McLaren '99, with its concave external area. Note, too, the curious rounded cut of the long and small intermediate vanes, which are sharply curved towards the outside.

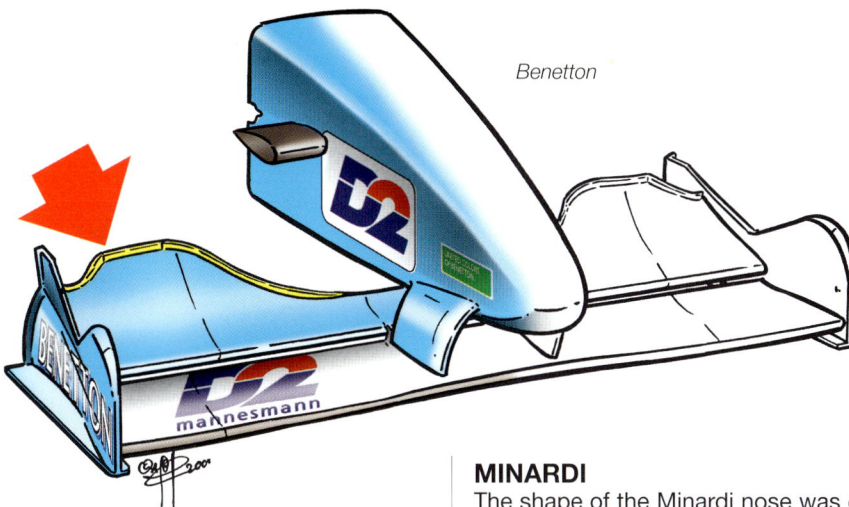

Benetton

MINARDI

The shape of the Minardi nose was curious, not so much for its various components (plane, flaps and end-plates) as much as for the contour of the central area, extremely square in the upper zone and with the slightly convex end-plates.

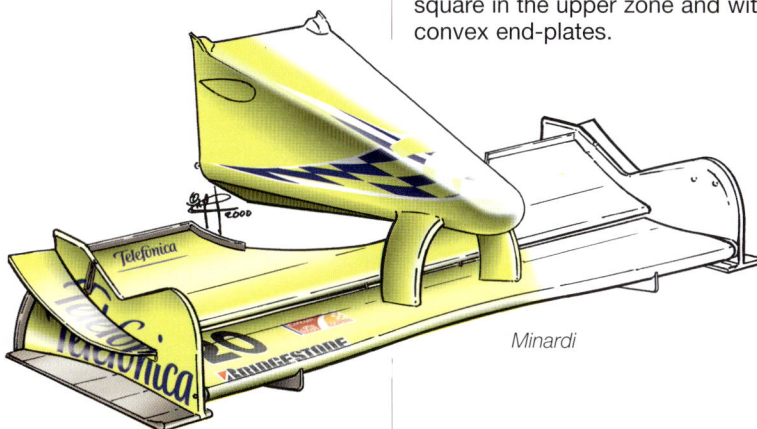

Minardi

SAUBER

Sauber maintained the skewed shape of the intermediate vanes for the third season, shown without flaps in this drawing. The lower parts of the end-plates can be easily seen, moved more towards the centre of the upper area. To the left, the absence of the flap shows the concave area of the external end-plates.

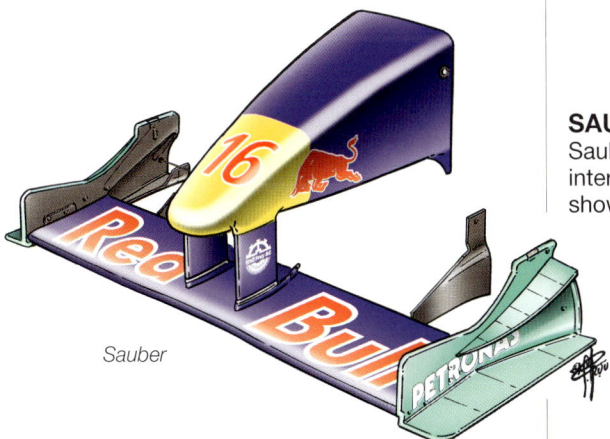

Sauber

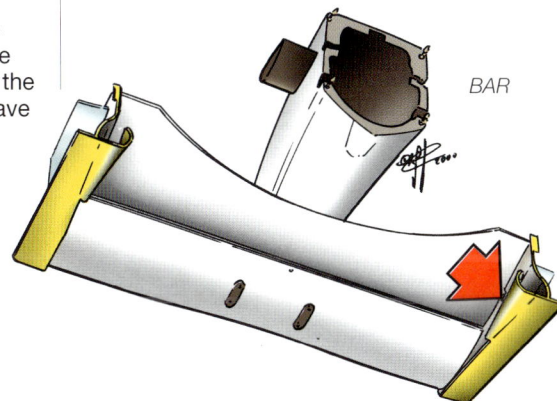

BAR

PROST AND BAR

Large intermediate vanes on the Prost, contrary to the BAR which were, like McLaren and Williams, without intermediate vanes, as can be seen in the underneath view. Note the rounded section of the horizontal zone, which curves slightly in the upper area. Prost used several lateral end-plates: the one shown in the drawing has a triangular external fin with an extremely small lateral Gurney flap in the terminal area.

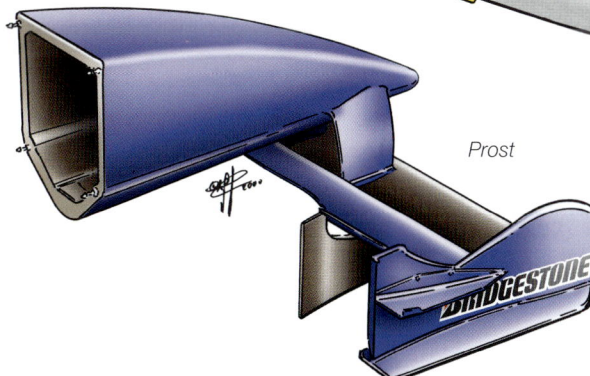

Prost

THE TWO RIVALS

Once again, the fight for the world championships took place between Ferrari and McLaren. No other team was able to win a single Grand Prix. But the epilogue was different from those of previous seasons. Ferrari succeeded in its historic campaign to once again win the world drivers' title after 21 years, and following a '99 season in which it won the constructors' championship. It was a full house for Maranello, with the drivers' title

secured at Suzuka a race before the conclusion of the season and the constructors' 14 days later at Sepang. All credit to a car that, while following the lay-out of the previous model, was designed for the first time to the limit of the regulations in all sectors. A car à la Adrian Newey, the designer of the defeated rival. In the drawings that compare the two cars, it can be seen how both represent developments of their '99 predecessors. The

Ferrari retained its high nose, aerodynamic typology in the central area, with low barge boards that were markedly concave in the lower area, high exhausts and the general lay-out of the suspension. The physical dimensions of the chassis were at the limit permitted by the regulations, with notable reductions in all sections, to the advantage of aerodynamic penetration. Both cars were built with the objective of reducing weight to the

minimum, so that the teams could have the fullest flexibility in the deployment of ballast when determining the cars' set-up for the characteristics of the different circuits. While maintaining the car's low nose and general lay-out the McLaren, with barge boards behind the front wheels and rather high side-pods, incorporated the greatest number of new features. Among them were the chimneys, copied from its rival Ferrari, which

appeared at the GP of France and were used for only two races, Hungary and Malaysia: new elements also included low exhausts that blew through the central section of the diffuser. The evolution of both cars during the season was minor, particularly for the Ferrari, due to a design by Rory Byrne that did not have to be substantially corrected. One should also not forget the successful race strategies developed by Ross Brawn, which

often made the difference between the Rosse and the McLarens, as was the case with Michael Schumacher's victory in the GP of Japan. In the see-saw battle for the drivers' title between Schumacher and Hakkinen, Mercedes-Benz engine mal-functions took their toll on the Finn's performance, even if globally McLaren was the team that covered most laps during the course of the 2000 season: 1,917 against Ferrari's 1,860.

THE SECRETS
OF 2000 F1

The car that brought the world drivers' title back to Maranello has no particular secrets, as it retraces the basic design of the F399 both as far as its architecture in general and suspension are concerned. But one of the secrets that led to Ferrari winning both the drivers' and constructors' world championships was by getting its race tactics right, and that was the work of a group headed by Ross Brawn. Tactics in which the car and its development project were always the protag-

onists, given that the car's fuel tank capacity, one of the most important parameters on which calculations are based for the various strategies, is decided on while the car is being designed. On several occasions, the winning move was to delay a refuelling pit stop and obtain an advantage over an opponent, as was the case at the GP of Japan, at which Michael Schumacher won the drivers' title with one race in hand. To establish race strategy, the team starts work on the Friday of

race weekend, when 60 litres of petrol are poured into the cars' tanks against just 10 for qualifying, in which teams attempt to privilege maximum performance and, therefore, make the car as light as possible. On Friday, consumption is established, as are the negative effect of 10 kg of fuel on a car's lap time, the abrasiveness of the asphalt and, therefore, the deterioration of the tyres so as to decide the number and most advantageous moment in which to programme race pit stops. Other

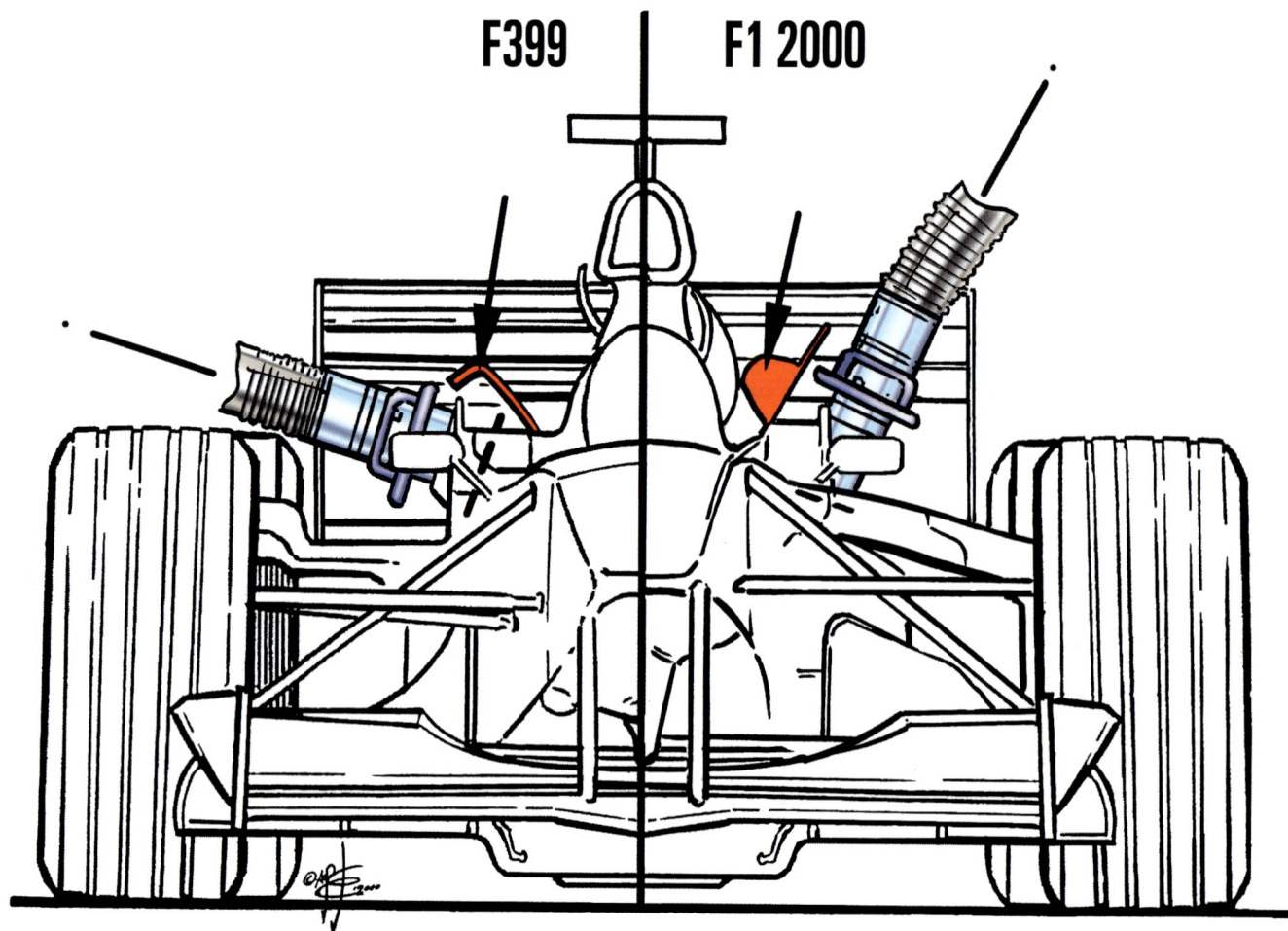

F399   F1 2000

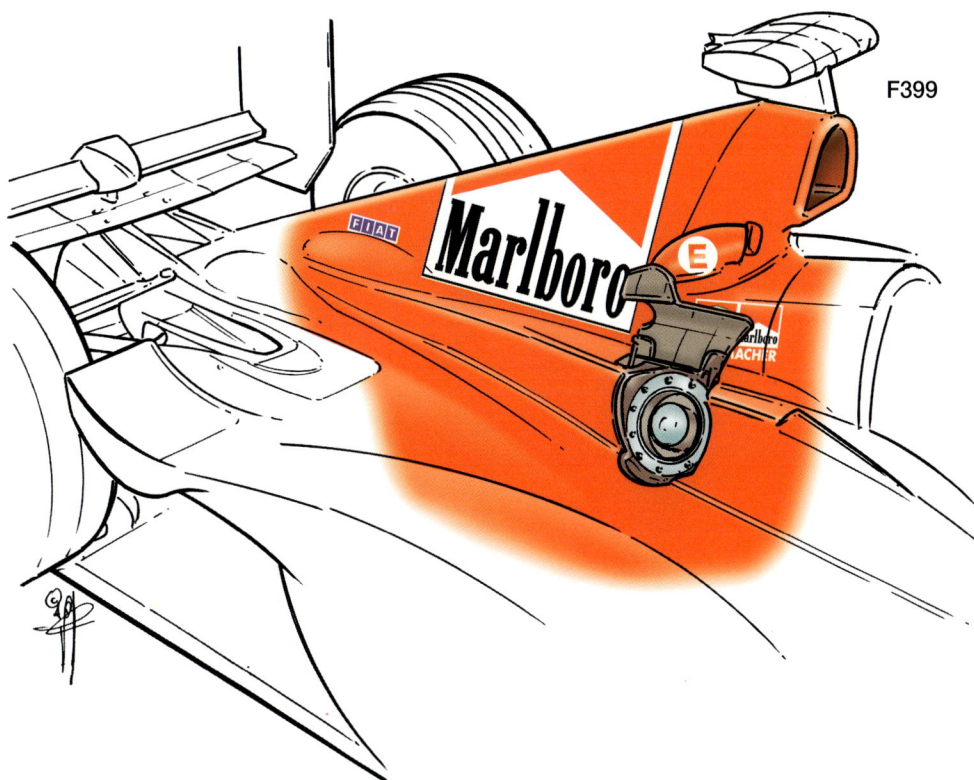

F399

factors taken into account in this area of variables are the type of circuit, the deployment of the pits, length of the pit lane and the permitted speed in it, the answers to all of which help to determine the time it takes for a car to make a pit stop. At Suzuka, the winning strategy was of two pit stops instead of one, in part because the extra weight of 10 kg of petrol would mean a loss of 0.42 seconds per lap, a severe penalty at most circuits and one that dictated the 'less fuel at the start and two pit stops' strategy in Japan. In races with two pit stops, it is extremely important to be able to vary the timing of the second stop. The table on the following page includes all the parameters that determined the Schumacher Ferrari's winning strategy. In discussions before the race, Schumacher and Brawn opted for the first stop on the 22nd lap, but delayed it until the 23rd, and that was determinate. When race leader Hakkinen came into the pits on lap 22, Brawn timed the Finn's pit stop: from that, he was able to deduce the quantity of petrol Hakkinen had taken on board for the second phase of the race. It was decided to let Schumacher stay out for three laps more than Hakkinen, to take advantage of the lightness of his car compared to the heaviness of the Finn's fully fuelled McLaren. When Schumacher stopped on the 23rd lap, only 10 kg of petrol were pumped into his car. So when Hakkinen stopped for a second time on the 37th lap, Schumacher was able to capitalise sufficiently in three laps and build the lead, which still

enabled him to get back into the race five seconds ahead of Hakkinen after the German's second pit stop. The table was produced with the help of Japanese engineer, Kazuhito Kawai, and English journalist James Allen, both television commentators, a Microsoft Excel simulation programme similar to the one used by Ferrari, plus a cross sec-

tion of information received from the various teams, tyre manufacturers and telemetric data. Race strategy also comes into the equation from the car's design stage for another reason: the need to facilitate work during a pit stop, even if the F1-2000 showed itself to be less versatile in this area than the F 399, as illustrated in the following pages. In a direct comparison of pit stop operations, it can be seen how the more horizontal position of the petrol filler cap, "hidden" inside the fairing at the side of the F1-2000's cockpit for aerodynamic reasons, can create some insertion problems: one difficulty emerged quite clearly at the GP of Spain, when chief mechanic, Nigel Stepney, the refueller, was injured. A tall man, his height helped him to take up the obligatory position with the refuelling tube, which must fall vertically from above the shoulder: but with the F 399, the tube could be held more easily under the arm with a slight angulation instead of in the horizontal position (drawing on page 68).

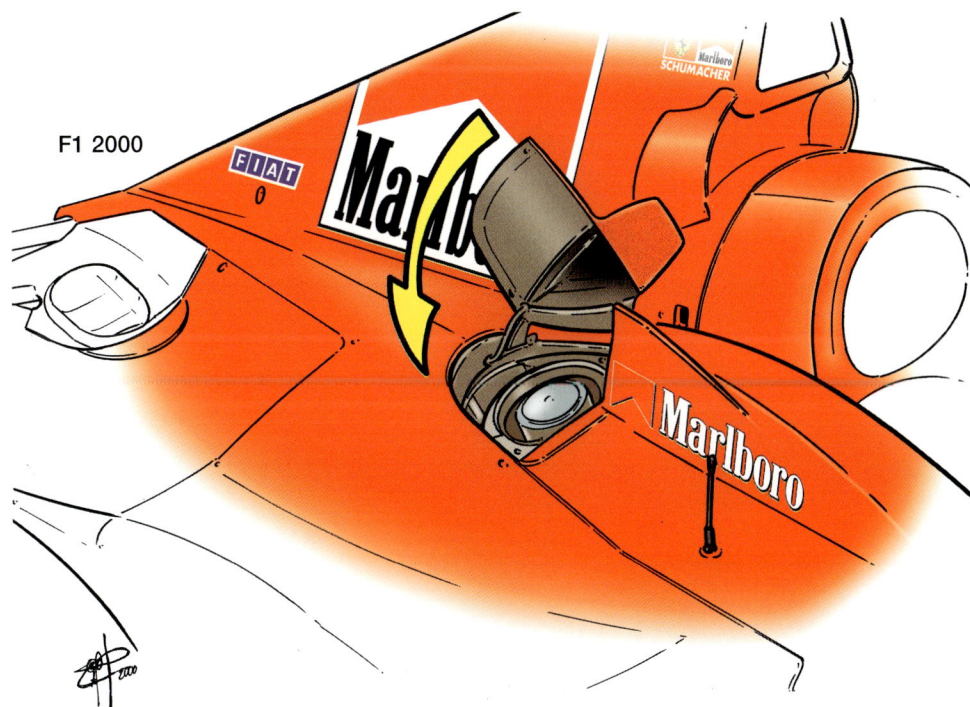

F1 2000

Timer for re-fuelling

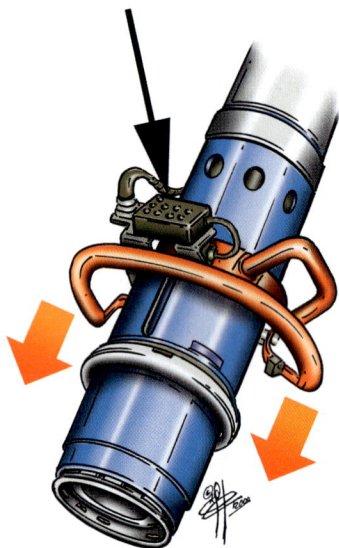

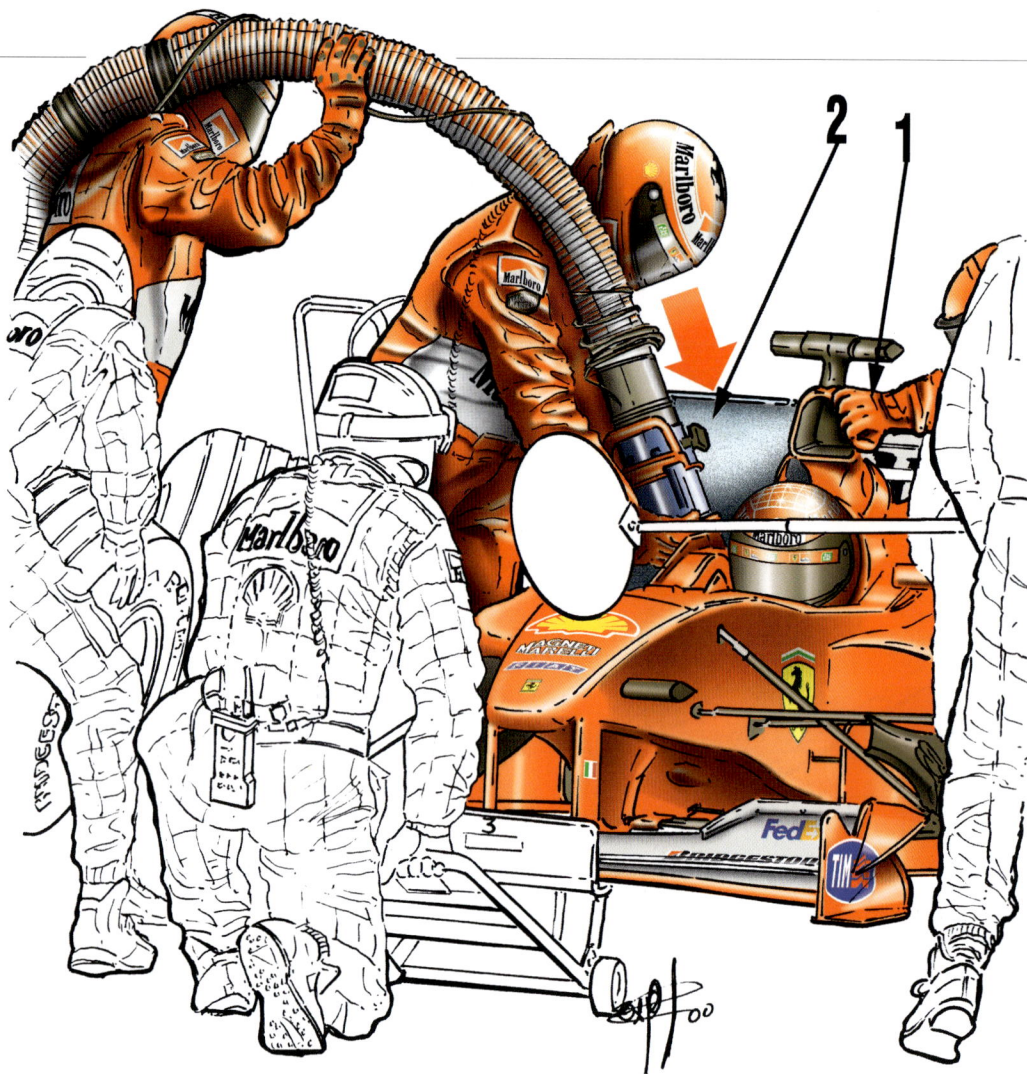

2000 SUZUKA SIMULATION

Number of Laps	53	Fuel comsuption (kg/lap)	3.02
Total fuel needed (kg)	162.48	Tyre Deterioration (sec/lap)	0.04
Reference lap time (sec.)	99.5	Fuel Load at Ref. Lap Time (kg)	10.0
weight effect of 10 kg fuel (sec.)	0.42	Extra Time needed for Stop (sec.)	18.0

1 Stop-Total Time (min.)	Start				1st Stop	Out		Goal
90.189	0	1	2	15	27	28	29	53
Refueling amount (kg)	88.0				78			
Fuel remaining in car (kg)		82.56		40.28		74.98		-0.52
Est. Lap Time (sec.)			102.46	101.33			102.14	100.06
Stationary Time (sec.)					11.40			

2 Stop-Total Time (min.)	Start				1st Stop	Out			2nd Stop	Out		Goal
89.957	0	1	2	15	23	24	34	39	40	41	42	53
Refueling amount (kg)	74.0				55.0				40			
Fuel remaining in car (kg)		68.56		26.28	2.12	54.10		8.80	5.72	42.76		6.524
Est. Lap Time (sec.)			101.87	100.74			101.27	100.05			100.79	99.83
Stationary Time (sec.)					8.78				7.07			

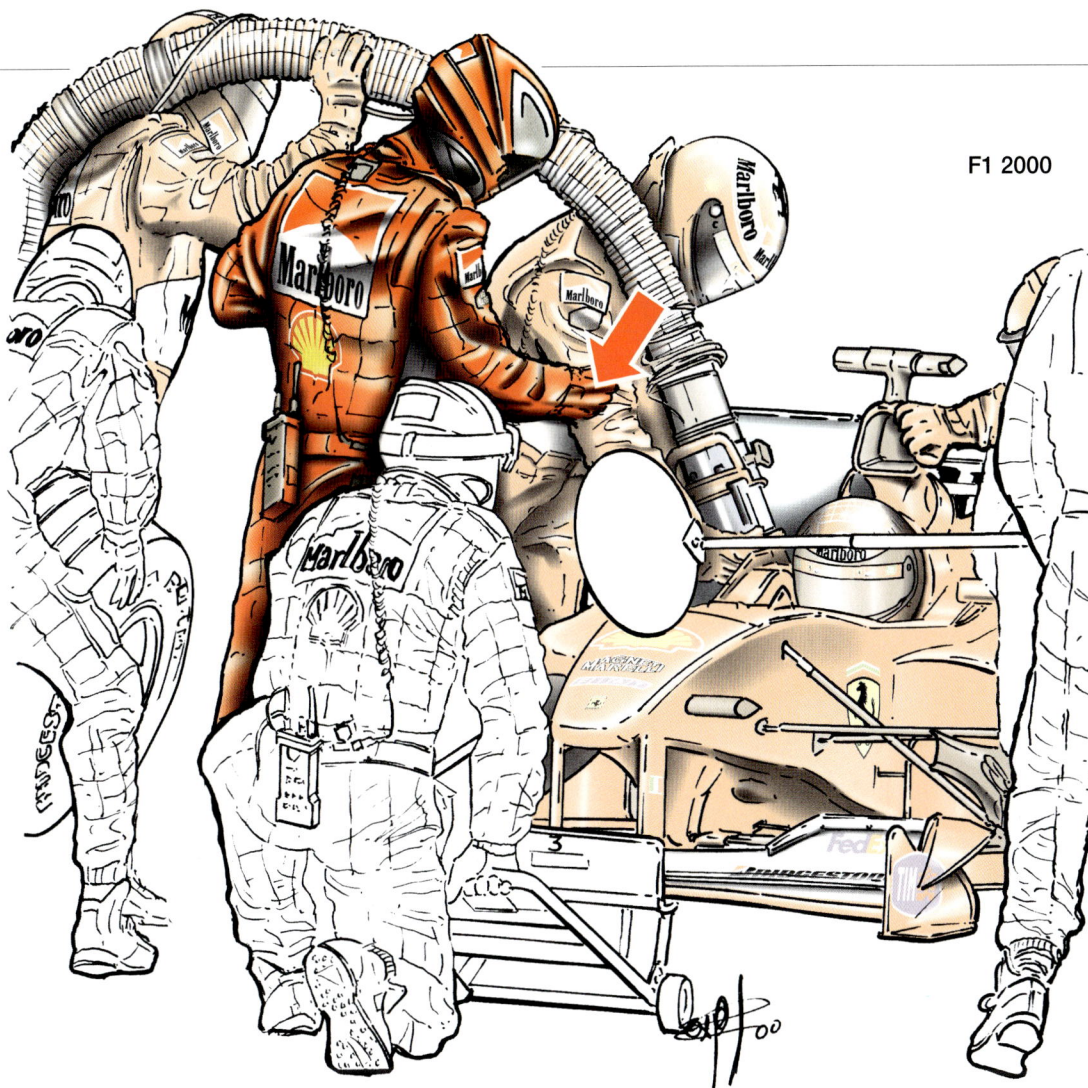

F1 2000

F1 2000 RE-FUELLING

In these two sequences, we see how refuelling was modified after Stepney's accident, and his substitution by Pietro Timpini. In the first illustration (opposite page), the hand of the mechanic is also shown (1) strongly counter-balancing the opposite side of the car, as the refuelling tube falls vertically. Behind, there is an anti-heat flange held by another mechanic to stop petrol from spilling over onto the exhaust. The second illustration (left drowing) shows a mechanic supporting and helping the re-fueller throughout the manoeuvre, in particular during the detachment of the tube, which requires considerable strength.

RE-FUELLING TUBE

The re-fuelling technique has changed. Until '99, the amount of petrol to be poured into a car during a pit stop could be calculated in advance, so that only the required quantity went into the tank. That method, with which it was not possible to make a mistake, was later stopped. From the 2000 season, it was decided to make team tactics more elastic, filling the tank to the top. The amount of fuel to be pumped into a car was calculated using a timer (regulations dictate that the flow must be 12 litres per second) with the possibility of varying the time of insertion at any moment. The mechanic keeps a check on his fuel delivery by watching a series of LEDs (as indicated by the arrow) that light up every two tenths of a second. The risk in this second tactic is one of human error: unless the refueller keeps a keen eye on the LEDs during the delicate refuelling operation, he could inject the wrong quantity of petrol into the car.

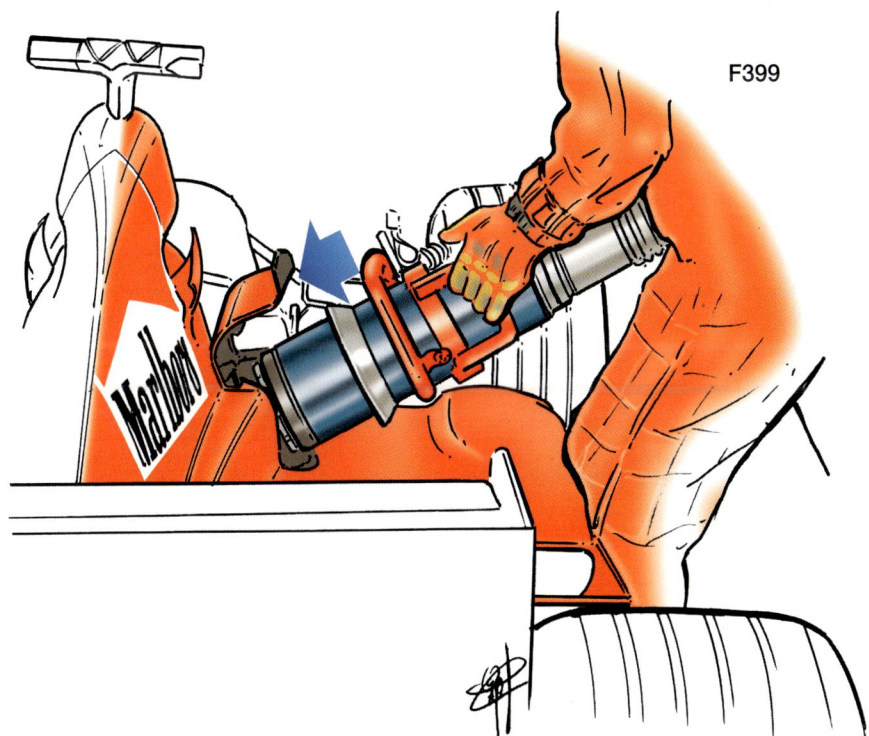

F399

FERRARI

The F1 2000 will pass into history as the car that was able to bring the drivers' world championship back to Maranello, for the first time since 1979. Designed by Rory Byrne under the direction of Ross Brawn – the two architects of Michael Schumacher's first two world titles at Benetton – the F1 2000 was, perhaps, the most innovative car of this last season. Only the high nose of the old F399 remained, increased by a lower part that is even higher off the ground, compared to that of the F399, and the general disposition of the suspension and the construction techniques of the gearbox. For the rest, it was a project on the limit in every area, starting with the interpretation of the chassis dimensional regulations to lower the centre of gravity and, even more striking, the minimum weight. The latter (as for their leading opponents) was substantially below 50 kg less, enabling them to use ballast as an additional element to optimise the adaptation of the car to the different characteristics of the various circuits. More than anything else, Ferrari worked hard on aerodynamics, which were once again slightly inferior to those of their rival, McLaren, though not so much as in previous seasons. For this reason, there was no need for radical changes, as were made regularly in previous years. And it was this limited development, which was apparent from the outside of the car from one race to another, which testified to the high level of efficiency of Ferrari's basic project. The F1 2000 was born McLaren-style, by exploiting the interpretation of the regulations to the letter. The car immediately showed it was a winner from its debut in Australia, and needed only minor revisions and adjustments during the remainder of the year. This drawing shows the F1 2000 at the time of its presentation: it was a car little modified during the season, as shown in the following pages. In the aerodynamic area, five large front wings: Australia, Imola, Canada, Hockenheim and Suzuka, three rear wings that can be classified as medium, high and low load, with slight variations regarding the position of the flap. Three different diffuser planes: the first used for almost all of the season, one specifically for ultra-fast circuits and the third, which made its debut at the GP of Belgium. As far as the shape of the body is concerned, in France a chimney was introduced, and flip ups in front of the rear wheels were tried, as illustrated in the series of engine covers on pages 74 and 75. Weight distribution was modified from the GP of Great Britain. A number of new front suspension developments made their debut at the GP of Canada, with an arm mount attached directly to the upright, and diverse rear wishbone mounts to the gearbox, brought in mid-season, together with a modification to the central shock absorber.

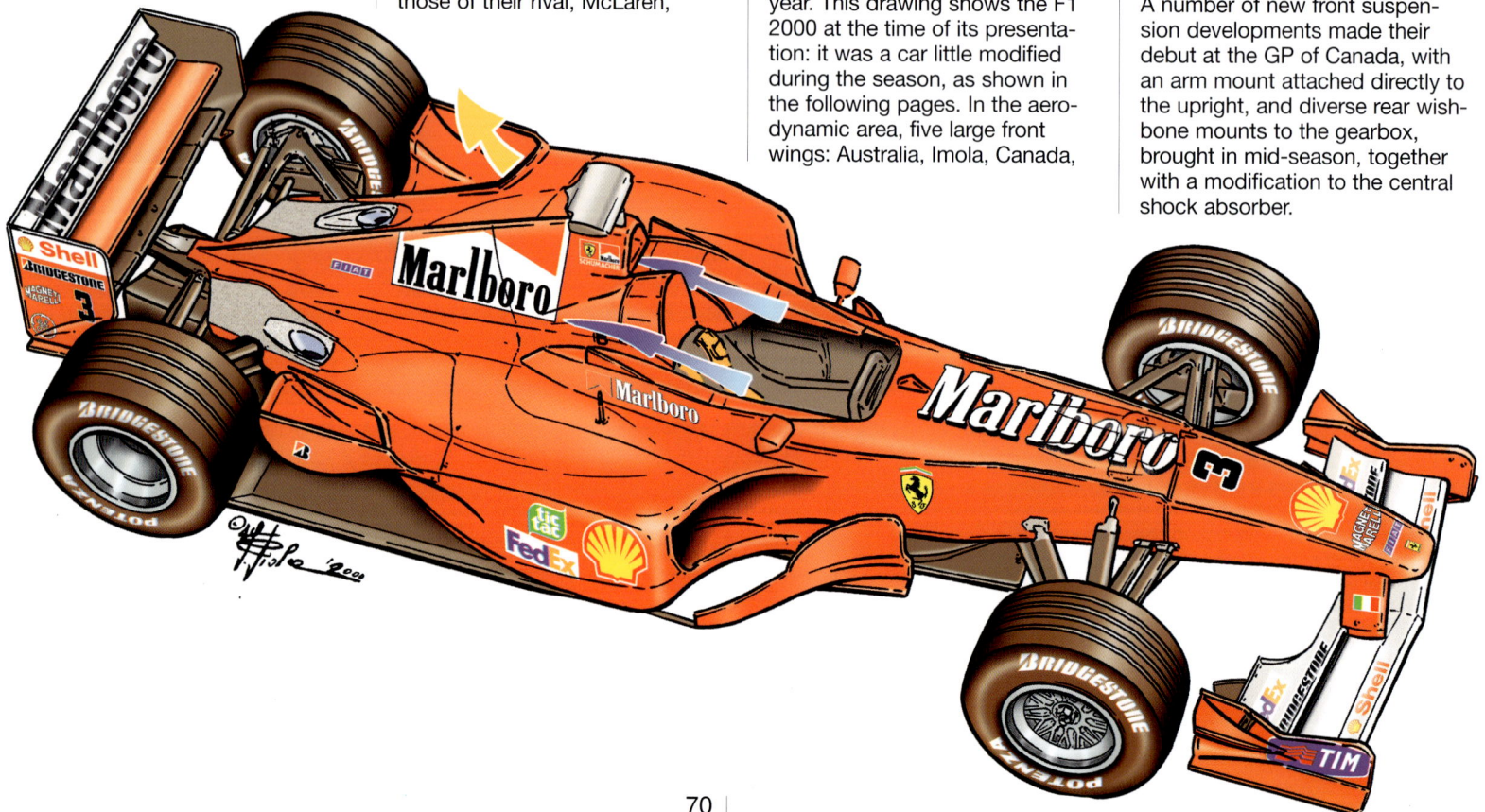

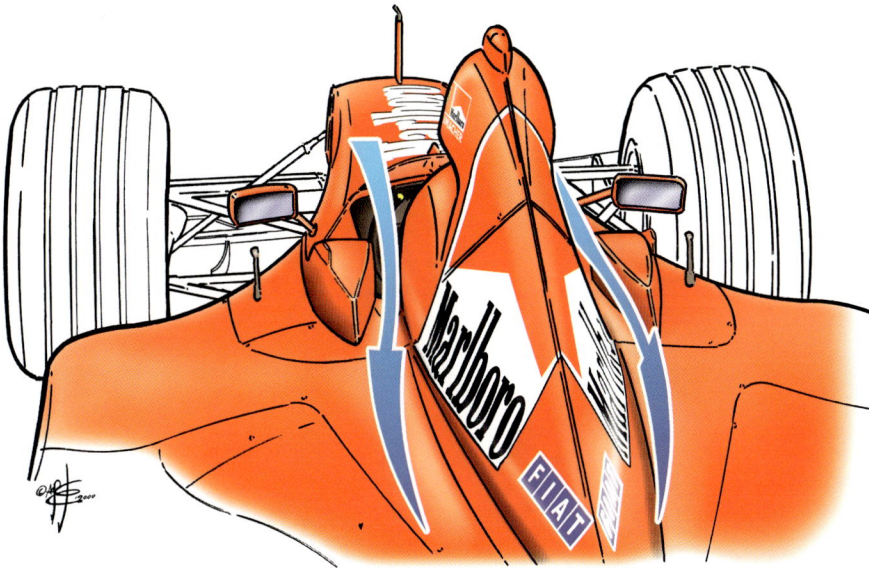

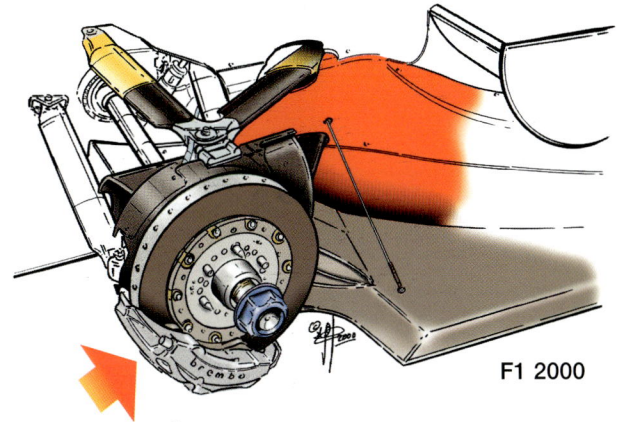

F1 2000

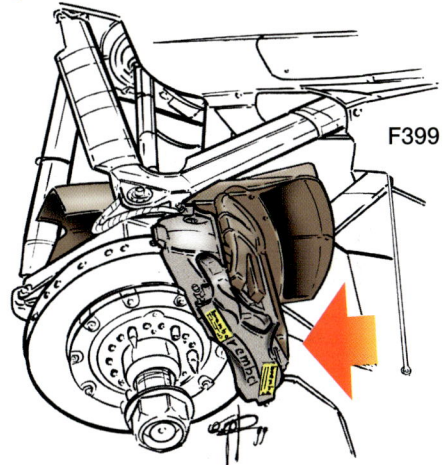

F399

PROTECTIONS

The search for the maximum efficiency of the aerodynamics, exploiting the rules to the limit, is evident in the devices adopted for protection at the sides of the cockpit, which are, in practice, separated from the body of the car to improve the air flow towards the rear wing.

BRAKE CALIPERS

One of the principal objectives of the design of the F1 2000 was a drastic reduction of the centre of gravity in every area of the car. The example of the rear brake calipers enables easy evaluation of this concept: on the F399 (below) the calipers were in the high front part of the disc: on the F1 2000, they were placed low, almost horizontally.

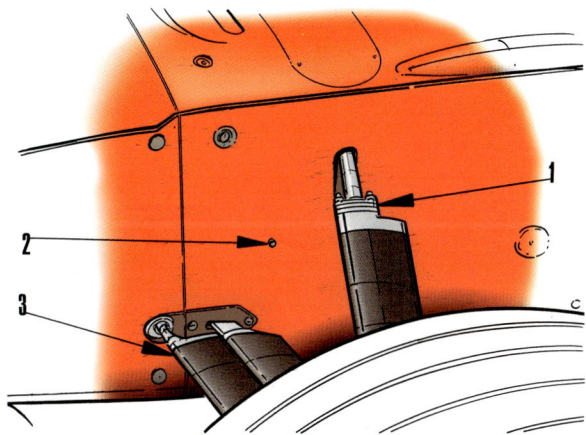

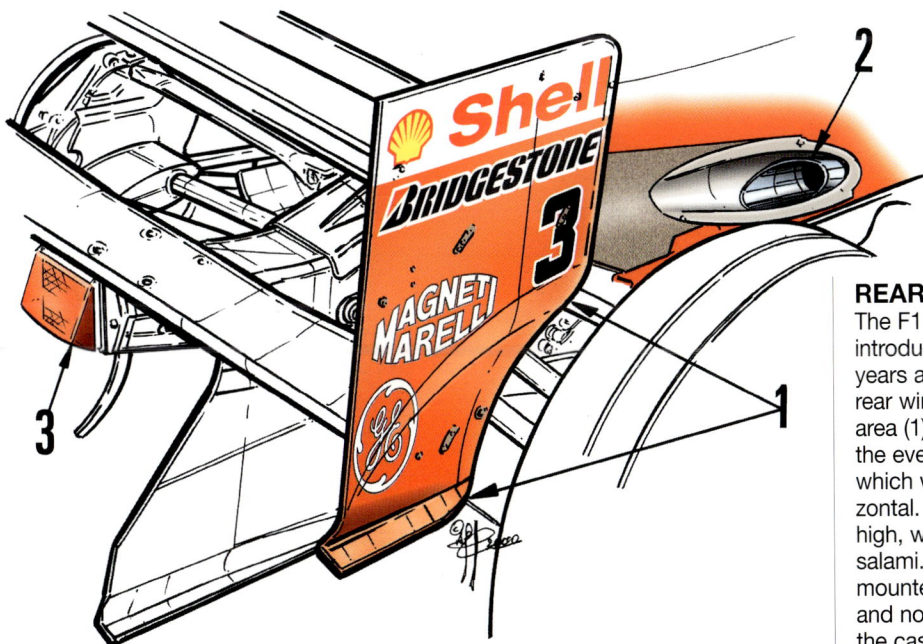

REAR END-PLATES

The F1 2000 adopted features introduced by Adrian Newey two years ago for the end-plates of the rear wing, scooped out in the lower area (1). The new development is in the even bigger knife-edge area, which was no longer perfectly horizontal. (2) The exhausts pointing high, with terminals like slices of salami. (3) The rear light was mounted behind the lower planes and no longer above them, as was the case with the F399.

FRONT SUSPENSION

A new system for regulating the height of the car from the track surface, achieved by varying the number of spacers mounted at the anchorage point (1) of the push rod. In (2) is indicated the reference applied to the chassis to measure the height from the ground. Below are indicated both the steering linkage (3) and the upper wishbone in carbon fibre.

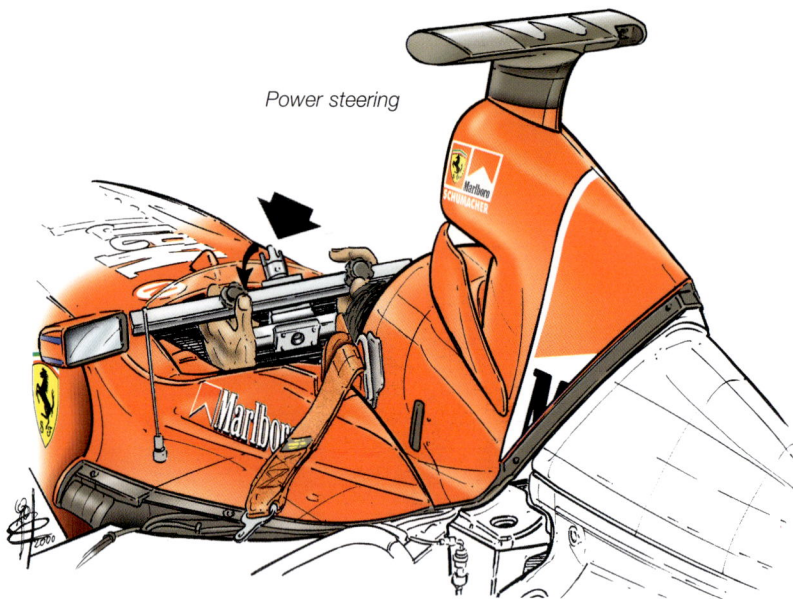

Power steering

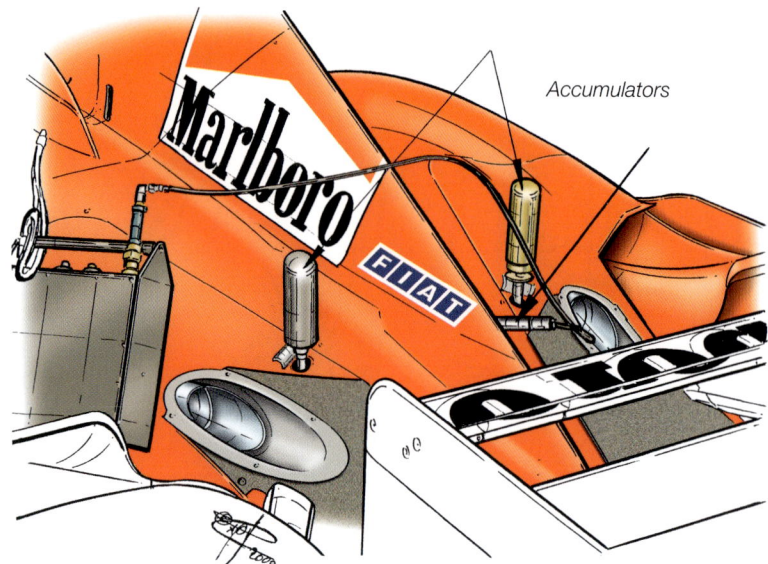

Accumulators

POWER STEERING

To ensure the perfect alignment of the steering, a mechanic sitting in the F1 2000 using a spirit level. The job was done just a few minutes before the beginning of morning free practice.

GP OF AUSTRALIA

In Friday's free practice, Schumacher slightly damaged his race chassis, which was repaired during the night in the area of the side body mounts, as indicated in the circle. A cosmetic repair, as the German was able to start the race with that chassis.

ACCUMULATORS

To avoid being unable to start the car on the grid, compressed air accumulators were fitted, to make up for an eventual lack of pressure in the hydraulic circuit, so that the butterflies open regardless.

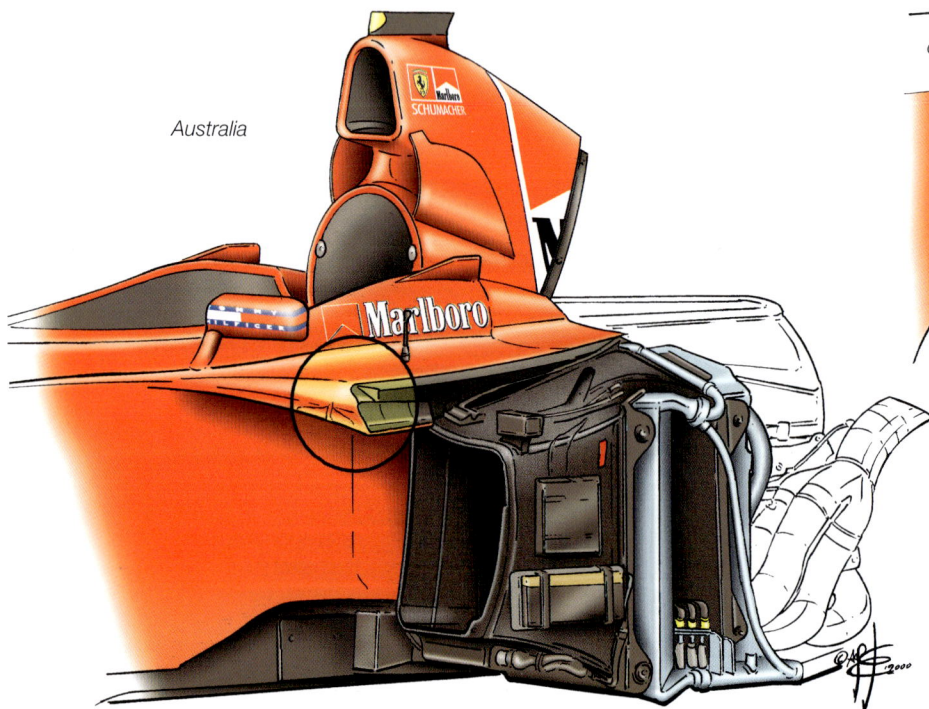

Australia

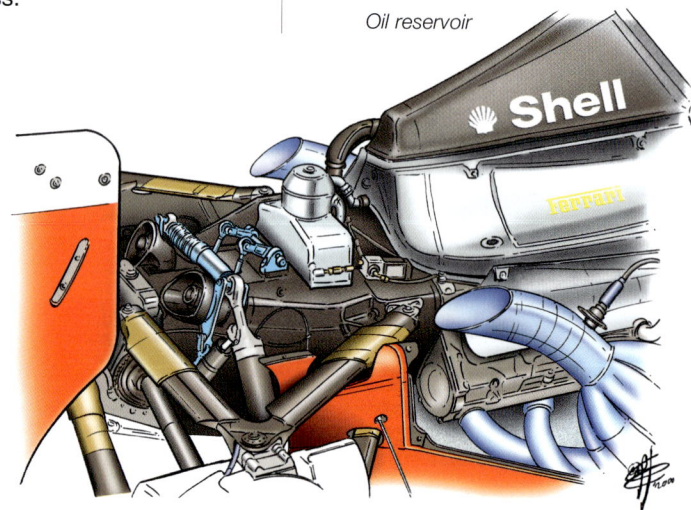

Oil reservoir

OIL RESERVOIR

From the first race in Australia, an oil circuit degassifier was placed above the gearbox, while the reservoir remained dimensionally unchanged in its new position, between the chassis and the engine.

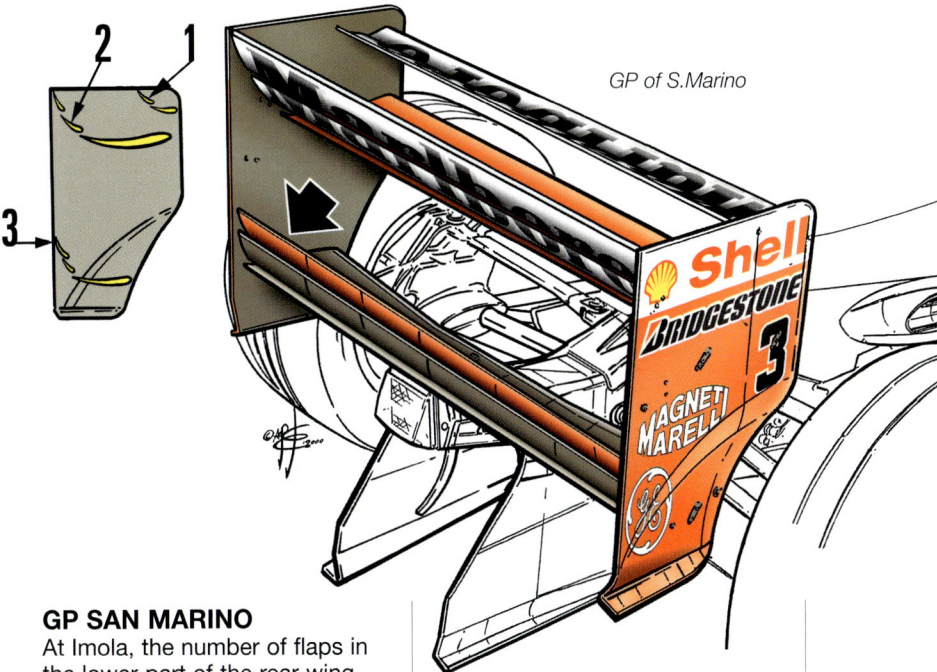

GP of S.Marino

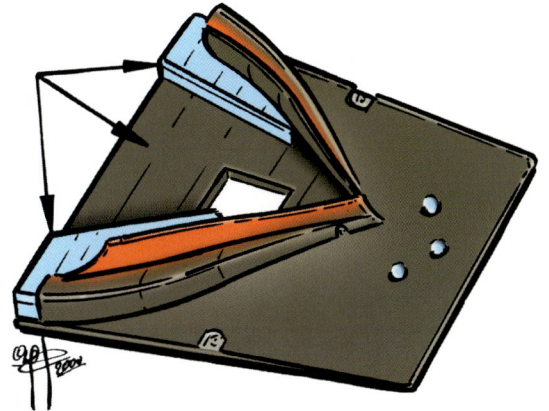

Ballast

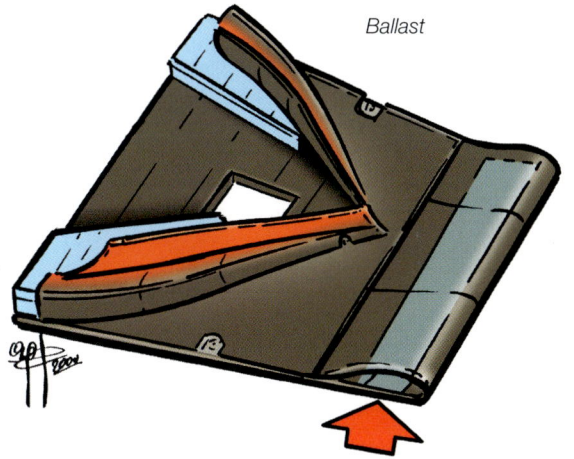

GP SAN MARINO

At Imola, the number of flaps in the lower part of the rear wing were increased, with a new second element shown here in red (3). A feature that eliminated the one used in 1999 with a profile at mid-height between the two principal planes. High up, there remained the double profiles on the edge of the in-going side of the principal group.

BALLAST

To reduce rear tyre wear at the GP of Great Britain, ballast, usually fixed inside the divergence of the knife-edge zone, was moved further ahead. It was slotted into the inside of the point separated, however, from the bottom platform, as can be seen in the drawing below. A point that has a decidedly round edge.

TOPPING UP

The oil was topped up by a little "nourrice" on the left, near the reservoir, which had also been moved to the left, hidden away inside the chassis.

Topping up

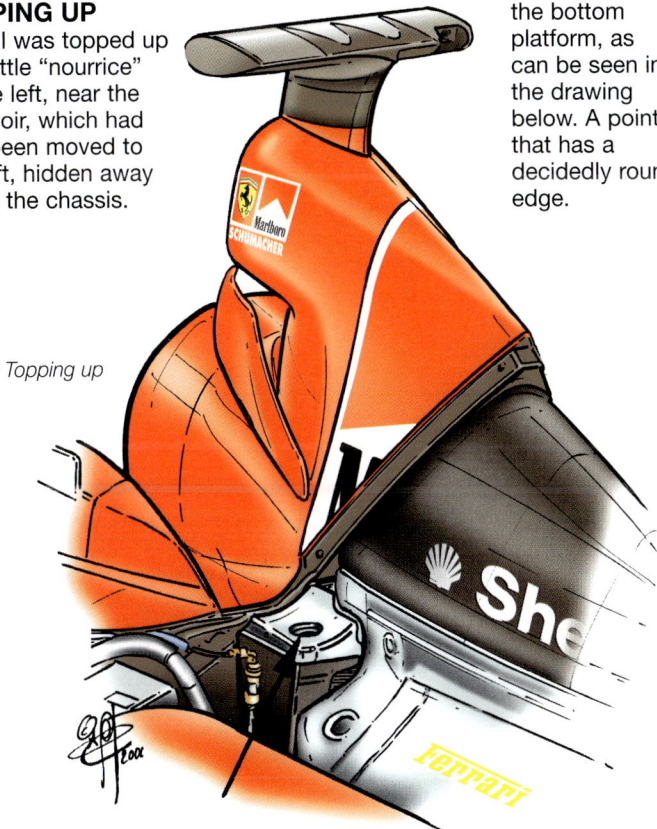

BOX

A curious shape for the engine's induction system box with manifold, determined by the larger dimensions of the protective roll bar, which is inclined backwards and also acted as the initial part. At the sides, the box covers the cylinder heads.

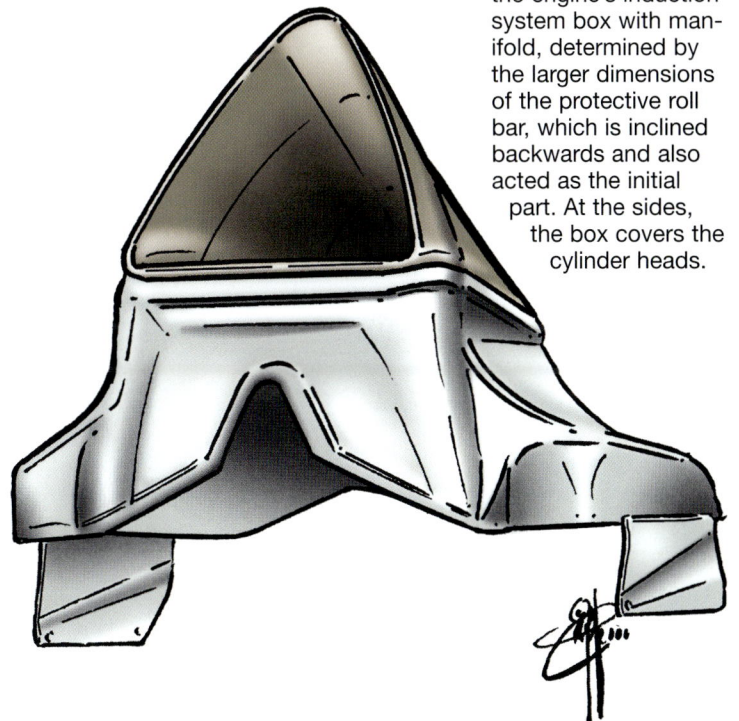

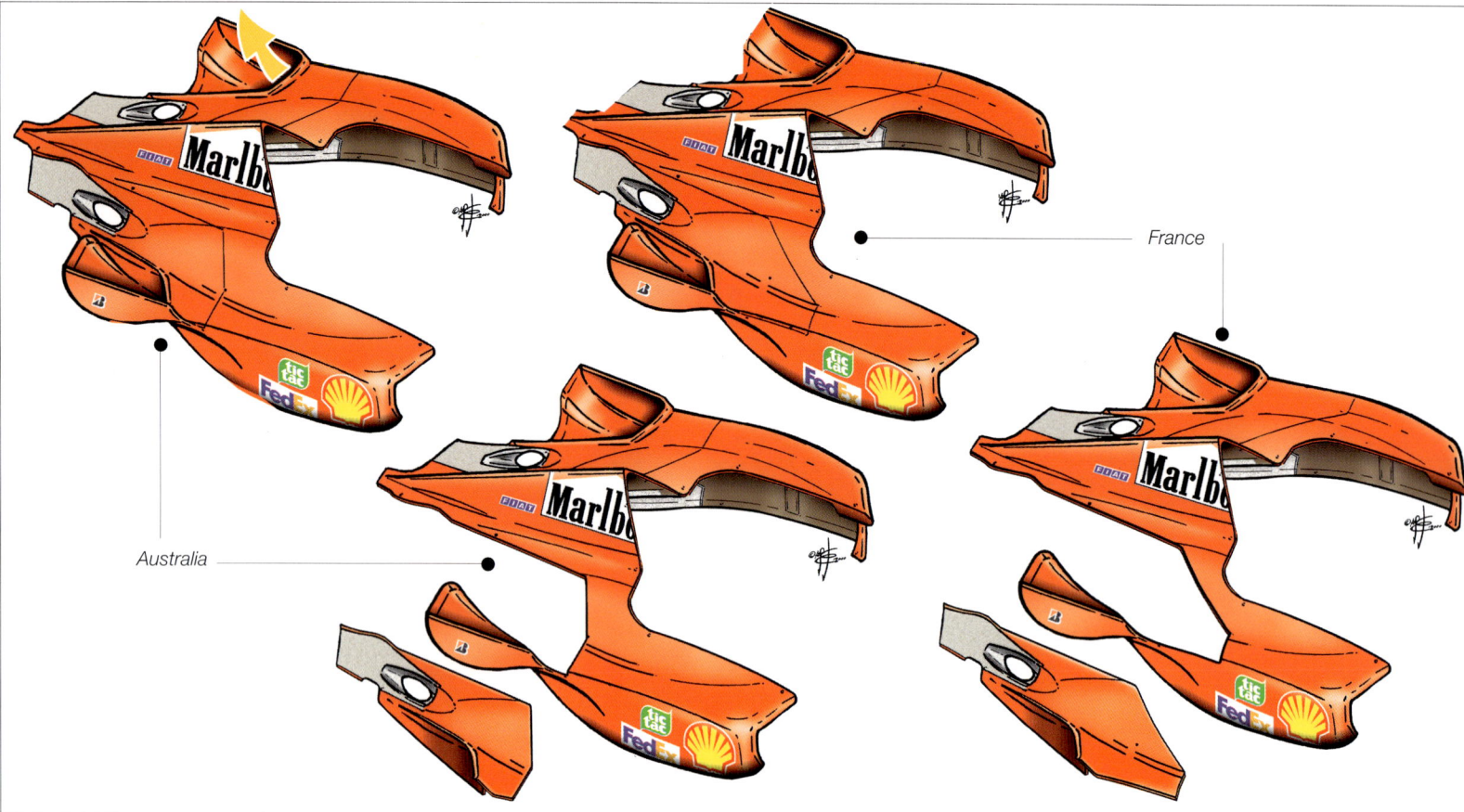

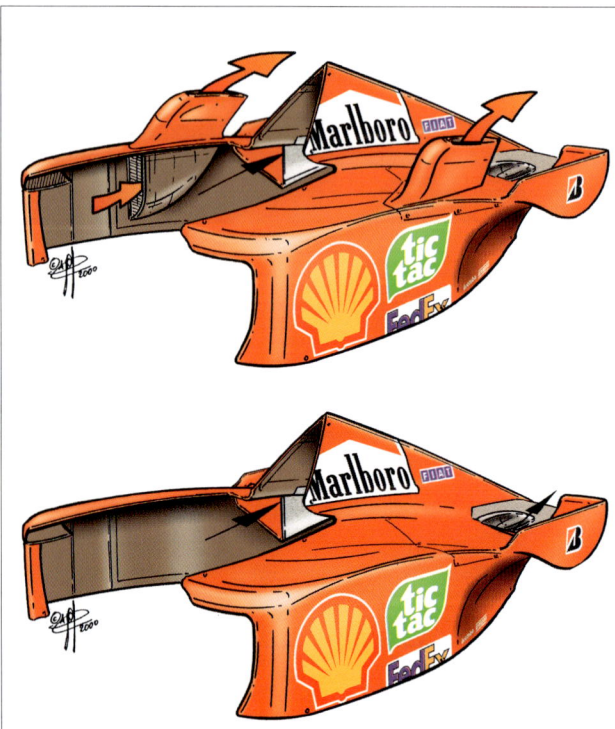

France

Australia

CHIMNEYS

Chimneys appeared for the first time at the GP of France, but they were not used in a race until much later, at the GP of Hungary, as well as the last GP of the season, in Malaysia.

ENGINE COVER

In this view from underneath, the internal heat protection can be seen, plus the terminal part of the exhausts, which remained pointing upwards, as on the F399, for the whole season.

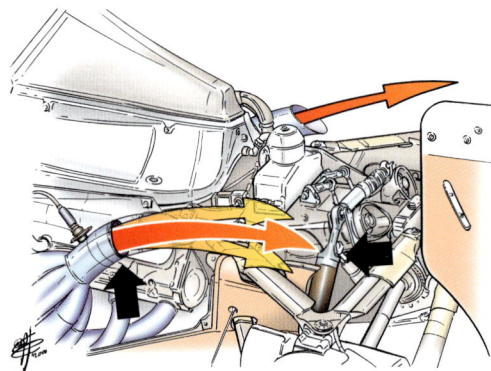

GP OF MONACO

A break in the left hand exhaust terminal caused Michael Schumacher's retirement at the GP of Monaco. The break had, in fact, changed the direction of the intense heat from the exhausts, "cooking" the push rod link of the suspension, indicated here between two arrows.

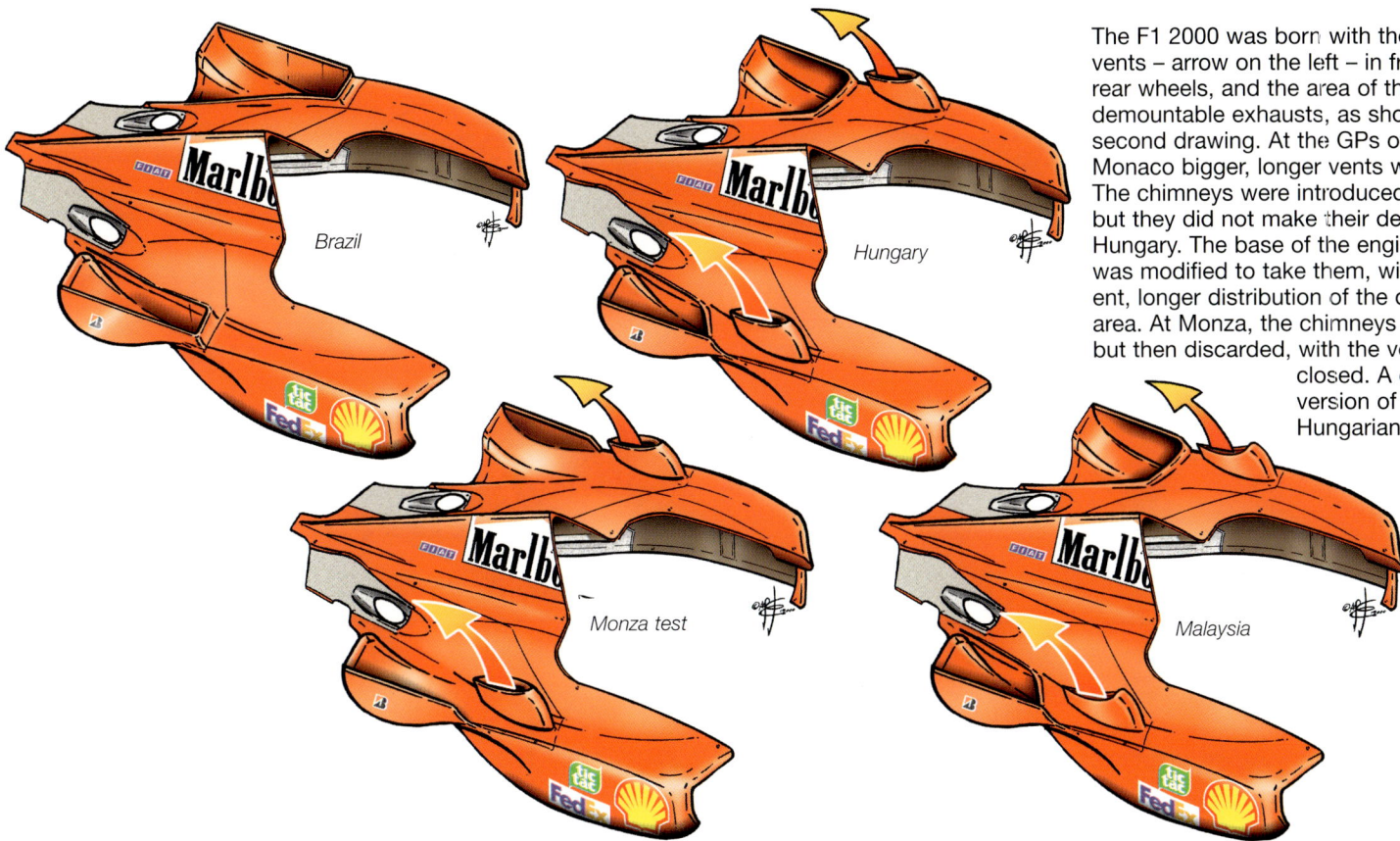

The F1 2000 was born with the hot air vents – arrow on the left – in front of the rear wheels, and the area of the demountable exhausts, as shown in the second drawing. At the GPs of Brazil and Monaco bigger, longer vents were used. The chimneys were introduced in France, but they did not make their debut until Hungary. The base of the engine cover was modified to take them, with a different, longer distribution of the outside area. At Monza, the chimneys were tried but then discarded, with the vents closed. A cut down version of the Hungarian chimneys was used in the Malaysian race.

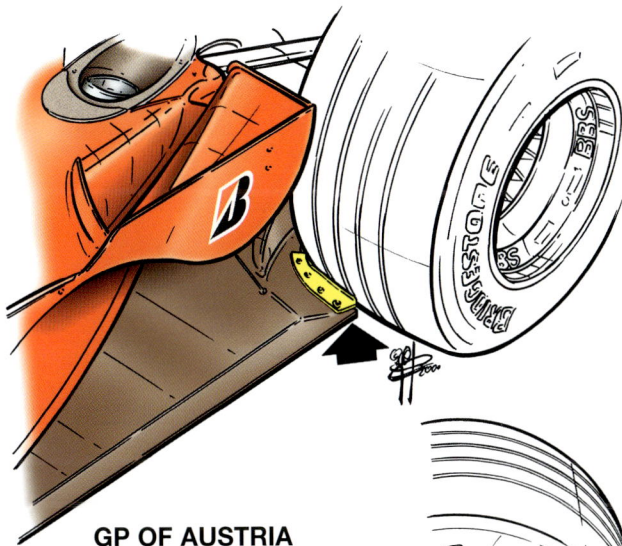

Brazil

Hungary

Monza test

Malaysia

GP OF AUSTRIA

At the Austrian GP, a seal was introduced for the flat part of the bottom platform in the area that almost touches the rear wheel. It is similar to the one adopted by Benetton in the 1999 season from the Monaco GP, and is described in the 1999 Technical Analysis on page 29.

TEMPERATURE SENSORS

In an attempt to keep rear tyre temperatures under control – a critical factor with the F1 2000 – from the Austrian GP, sensors were fitted to the upper part of the fin in front of the wheels. At Monza, these (6) sensors were fitted in the low area, in front of the wheels.

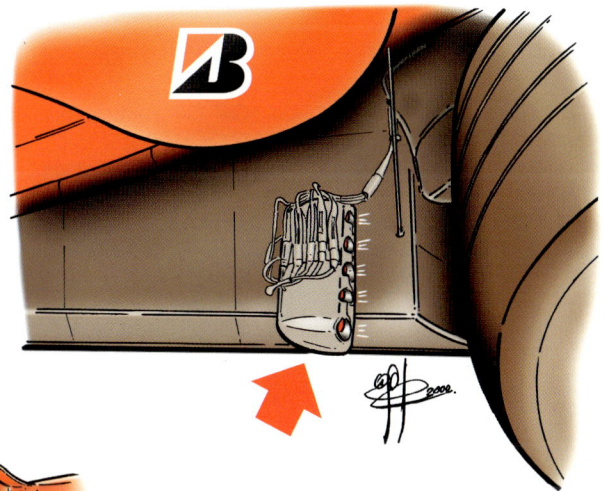

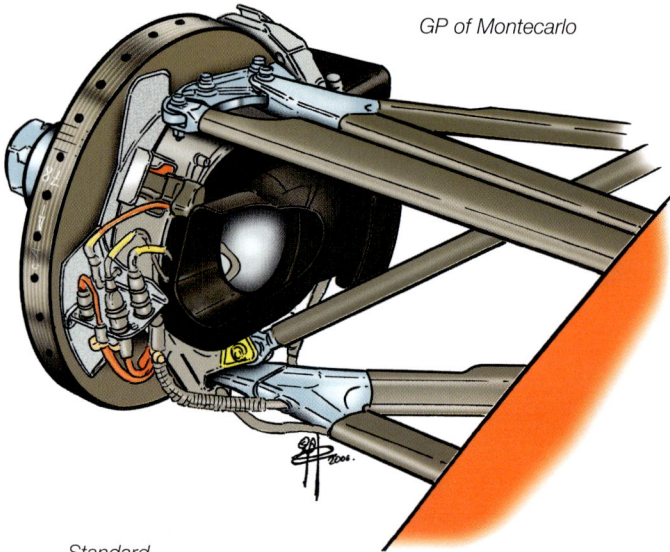

GP of Montecarlo

Standard

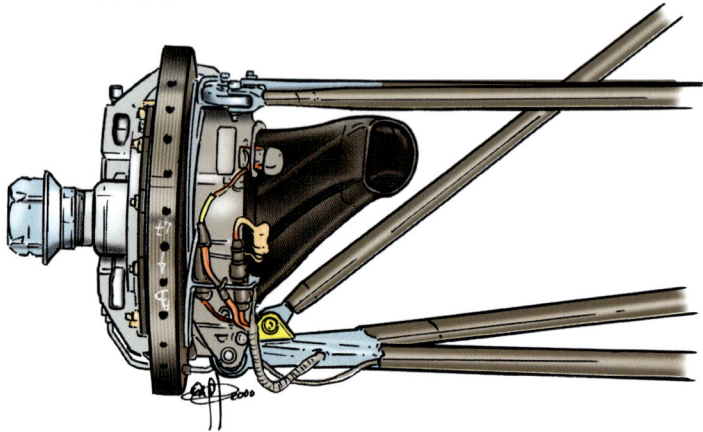

GP of Austria

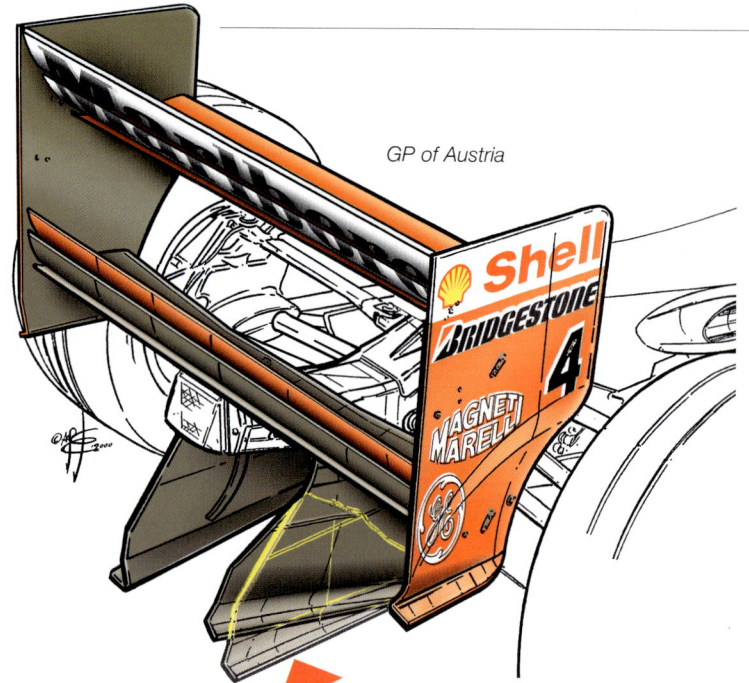

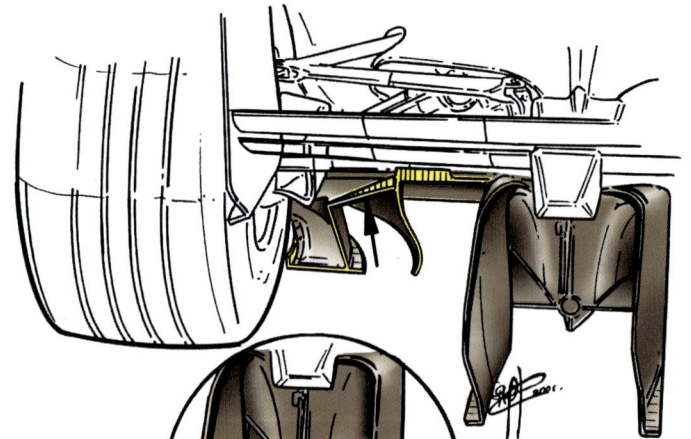

GP of Belgium

UPRIGHTS

An important new development, which was barely noticeable, on the front suspension, was introduced at the GP of Monaco. The lower anchorage point of the strut, usually fixed to the lower wishbone was, instead, moved directly onto the upright, as indicated by yellow. A similar feature to that introduced by BAR and which permits greater efficiency of the suspension geometry, with a more precise control of the steering angle.

GP OF AUSTRIA

In the accident at the first corner of the Austrian GP that involved the two Ferraris, Barrichello's car damaged the right hand side of the central diffuser. But that did not stop the Brazilian taking a fine third place.

GP OF BELGIUM

A new diffuser and a rather unfortunate front wing made their first appearance at the Belgian GP. The first had a rounded central area in the lower part and was kept for the race. But the nose with a new wing, which abandoned the delta lay-out (1), for the first time this season, and a new end-plate, were dropped. Compared to the earlier example, it had triangular-cut fins (2) cut and, further down, a small horizontal fin (3) of the Stewart type '99, but with a small lateral Gurney flap.

ENGINE

The drawing shows a spare engine, assembled with clamps in aluminium so as to simulate its exact position in the car. Note the small asymmetric oil reservoir: the drawing on the right shows the compactness of the installation of the engine, with its exhausts angled upwards, directing their heat away from the gearbox area.

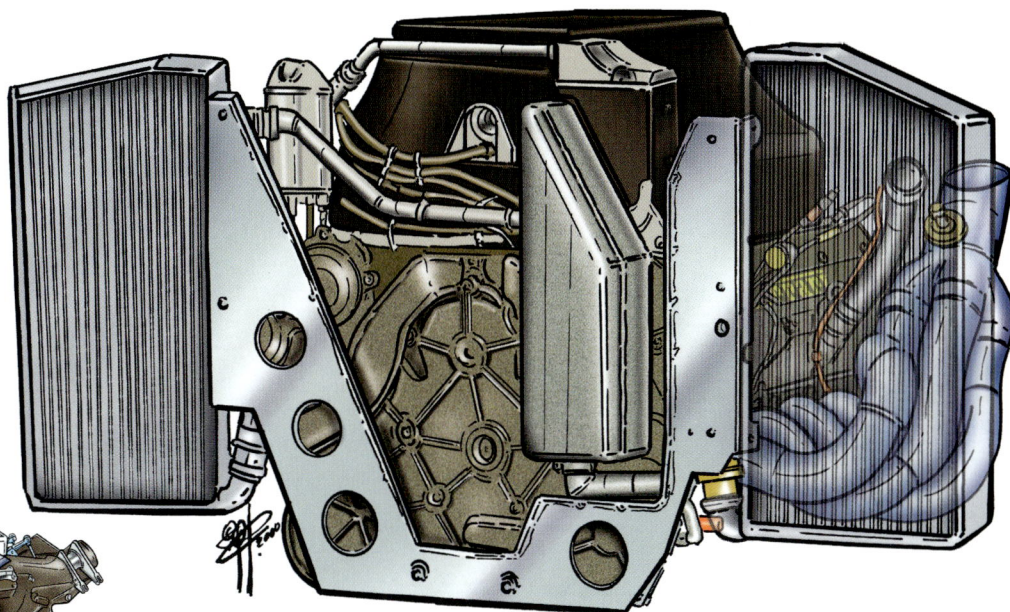

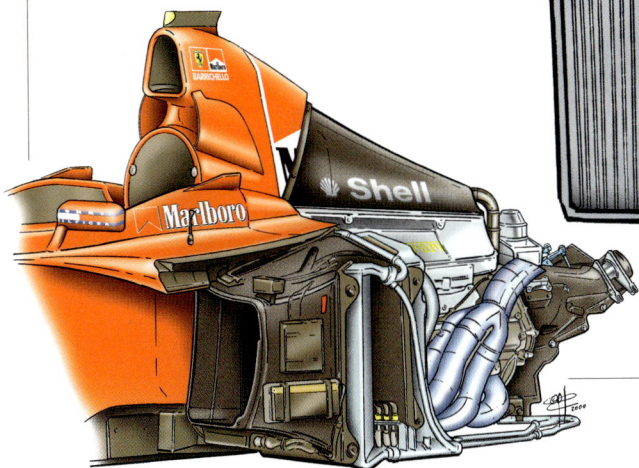

GP of Belgium

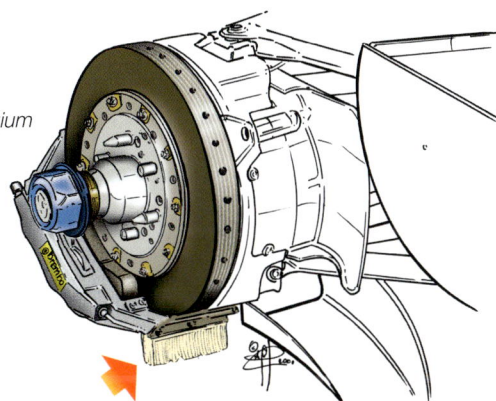

MONZA TESTS

During testing for the GP of Monza, many different ideas were tried out to prepare the cars as well as possible for the GP of Italy. (1) A new front wing without fins (2) on the outside of the lateral end-plates. (3) Sensors to measure the speed and pressure of air towards the engine air intake. (4) Funnels connected to the closed vents in front of the rear wheels. This idea was not used again. (5) Added sensors, which also remained during qualifying. (6) New rear wing.

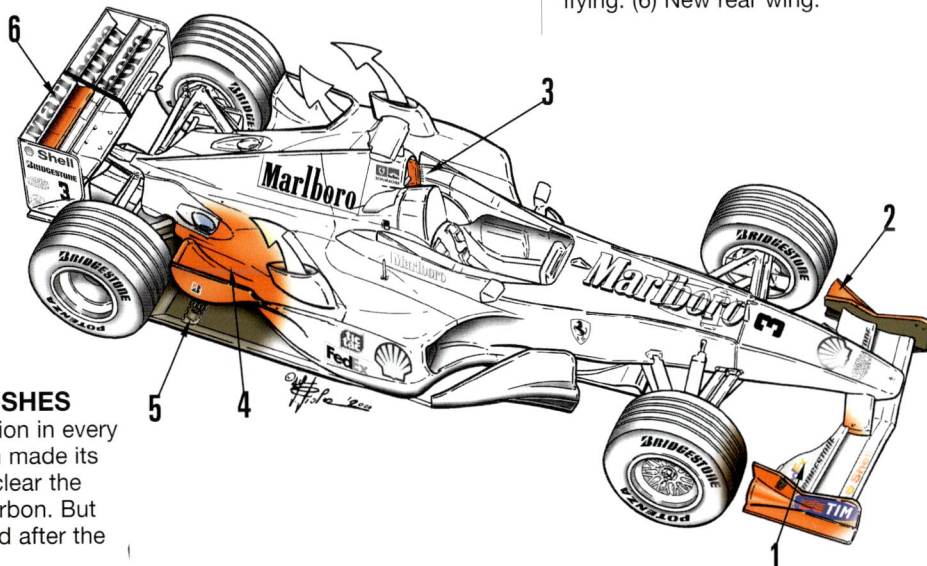

HUNGARIAN CHIMNEYS

Introduced in France, the chimneys were first used in a race in Hungary. Unlike McLaren, these devices were coupled to traditional hot air outlets, in front of the rear wheels. During the previous season, large openings were made in the engine covers, which severely damaged the car's aerodynamics.

BELGIAN GP BRUSHES

Searching for perfection in every area, this small brush made its debut in Belgium to clear the rims of brake disc carbon. But this idea was dropped after the race.

F399
'99 Suzuka

COMPARISON BETWEEN THE F1 2000 AND THE F399

In these drawings comparing the F1 2000 and the F399 cars as they competed in the last races of their respective seasons, it can be seen how the basic high nose philosophy has remained the same. The front wings are different: the F1 2000's is no longer of the arrow-type and has no intermediate vanes. The stepped bottom of the F1 2000 is practically constituted of a single piece, for reasons of rigidity and weight.

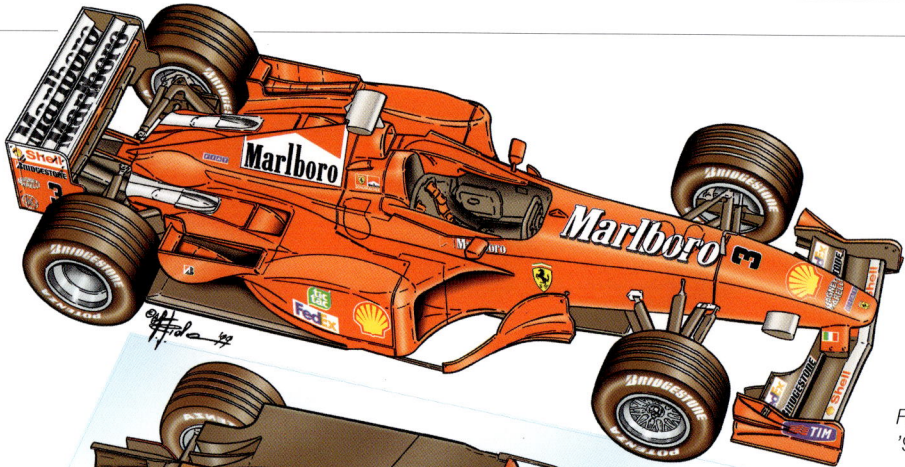

F1 2000
Sepang 2000

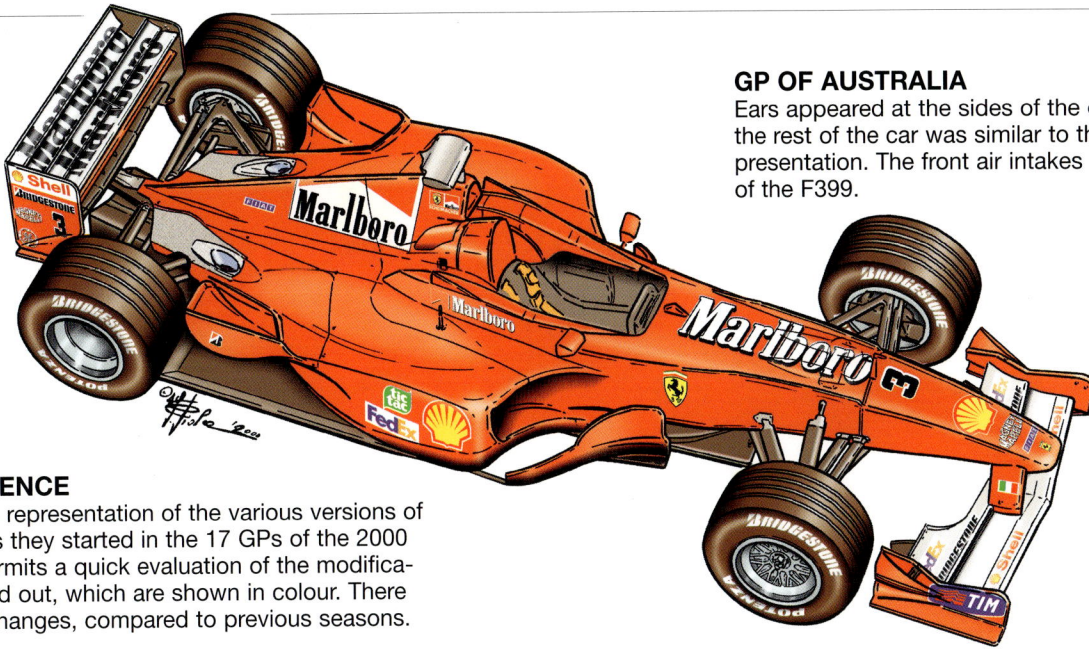

GP OF AUSTRALIA

Ears appeared at the sides of the engine's air intake, while the rest of the car was similar to the one at the pre-season presentation. The front air intakes of the brakes were those of the F399.

GP SEQUENCE

This simple representation of the various versions of the cars, as they started in the 17 GPs of the 2000 season, permits a quick evaluation of the modifications carried out, which are shown in colour. There were few changes, compared to previous seasons.

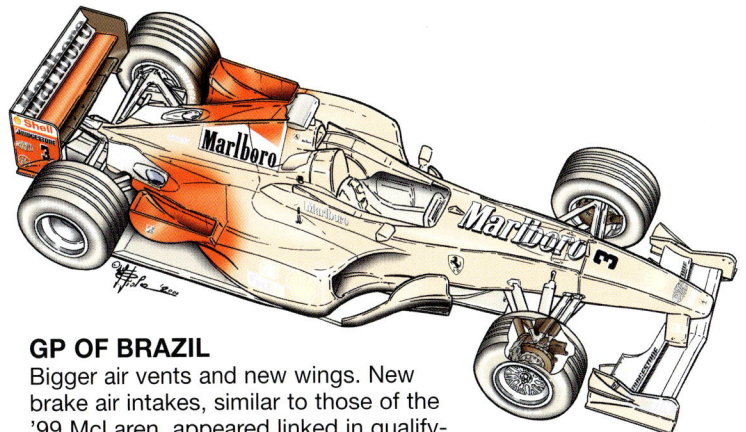

GP OF SAN MARINO

New rear wing with the addition of a second flap in the lower area, bigger brake air intakes.

GP OF BRAZIL

Bigger air vents and new wings. New brake air intakes, similar to those of the '99 McLaren, appeared linked in qualifying to thin, 22 mm discs.

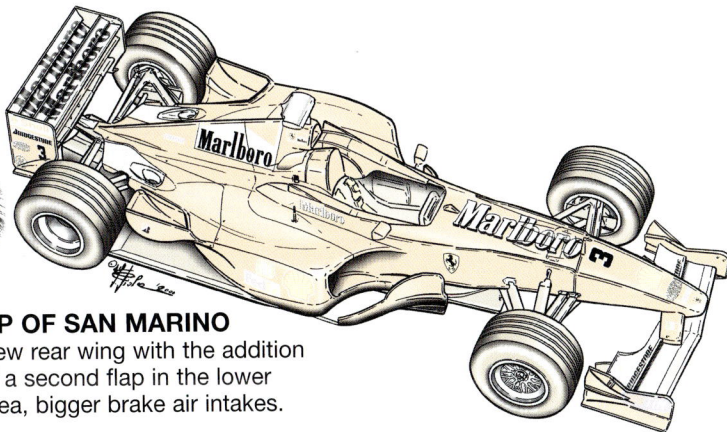

GP OF GREAT BRITAIN

Different weight distribution, with the addition of about 30 kg of ballast in the knife-edge zone under the chassis, to lighten the rear axle.

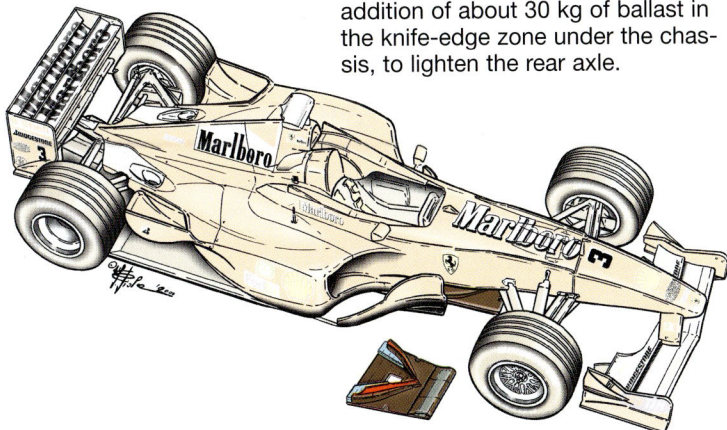

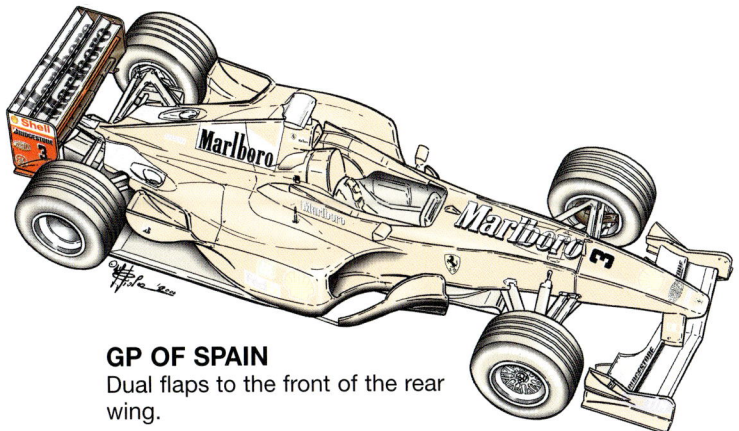

GP OF SPAIN

Dual flaps to the front of the rear wing.

GP OF EUROPE

New engine and lighter calipers for qualifying, combined with discs that had been in use since the GP of Brazil.

GP OF MONACO

Maximum downforce wing, new flap for the front wing and reinforced suspension arms.

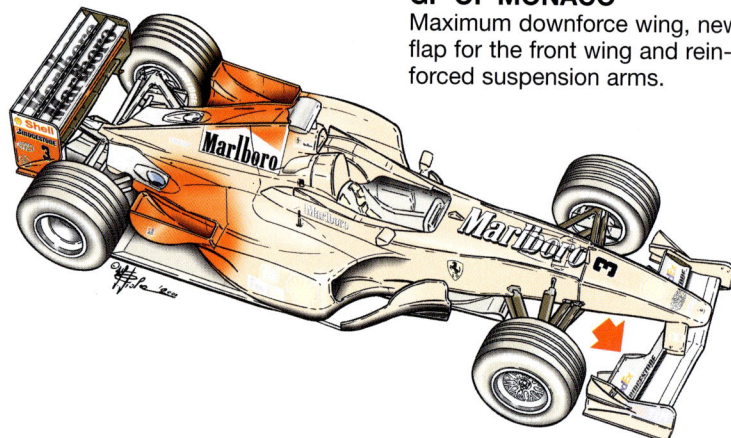

GP OF CANADA

New mount directly onto the upright for the front push rod link, rounded front wing flap and new rear wing.

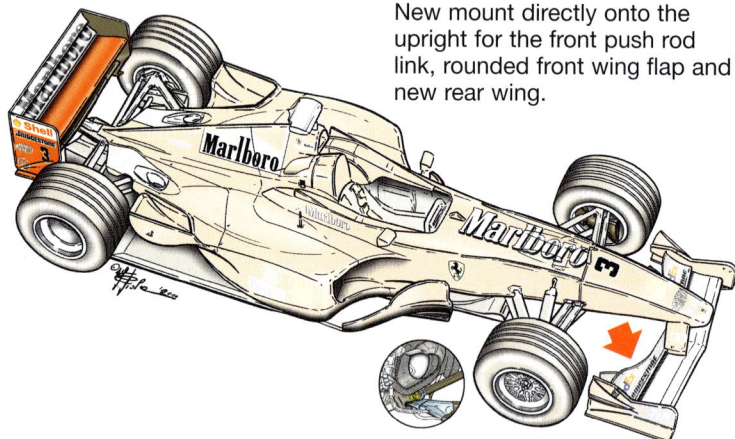

GP OF FRANCE

Introduction of chimneys in testing and the debut of a "wooden plank" in Stellite, to reduce friction and wear. New barge boards behind the front wheels.

GP OF AUSTRIA

Sensors to check rear tyre operational temperatures, fitted inside the flip-ups in front of the wheels. Seal in the lower area, used only in testing.

GP OF GERMANY

Reduced chord for the rear wing, front end-plates without fins and diffuser plane for ultra-fast tracks, with more inclined lateral channels.

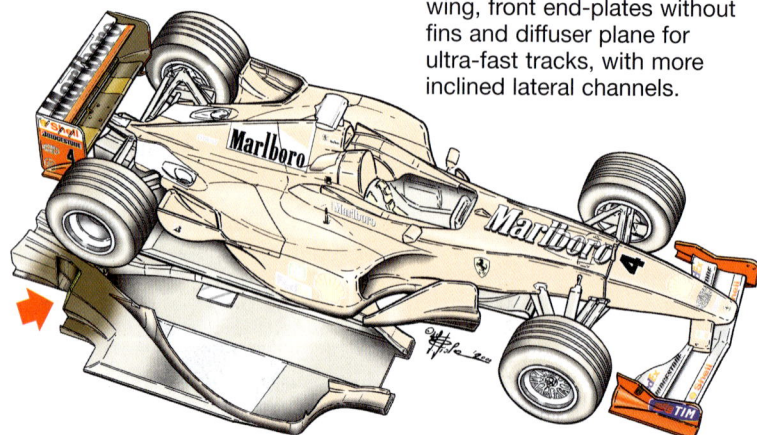

GP OF HUNGARY

Race debut of the chimneys, to expel the excessive heat of the Hungaroring track.

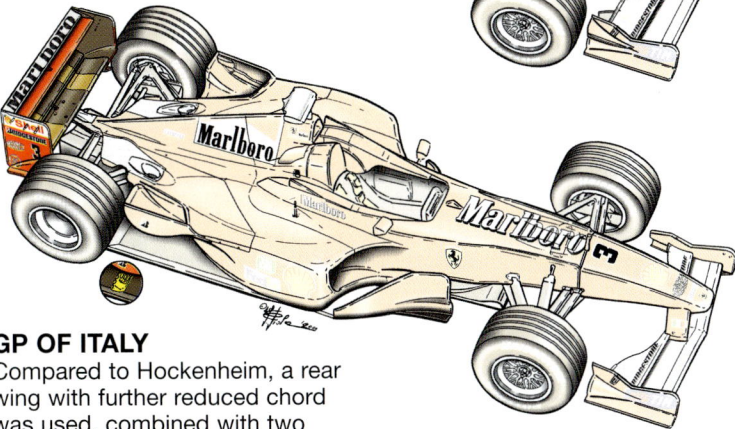

GP OF BELGIUM

Many modifications, even if the new nose (straight plane, new end-plates) was not used in the race. Overall, the new diffuser was modified in the central tunnel area, the "B" engine was also used in the race and a small brush was attached to the rear brake calipers.

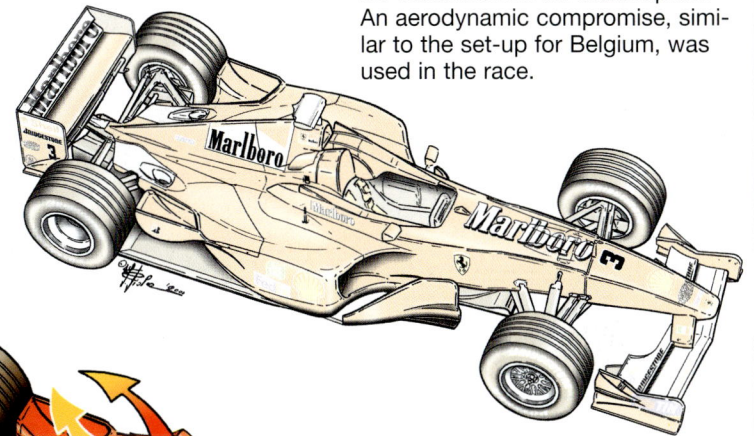

GP OF THE USA

No modifications for Indianapolis. An aerodynamic compromise, similar to the set-up for Belgium, was used in the race.

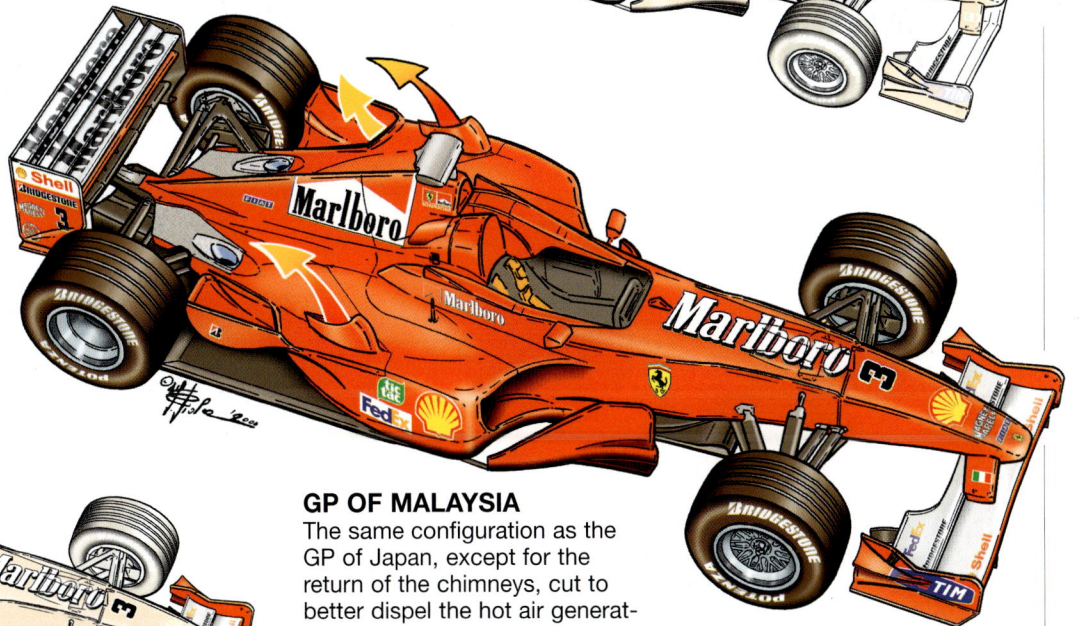

GP OF ITALY

Compared to Hockenheim, a rear wing with further reduced chord was used, combined with two planes in the lower area.

GP OF JAPAN

New front wing derived from the one rejected for the GP of Belgium. It had a straight plane, but with external fins bent into a new shape.

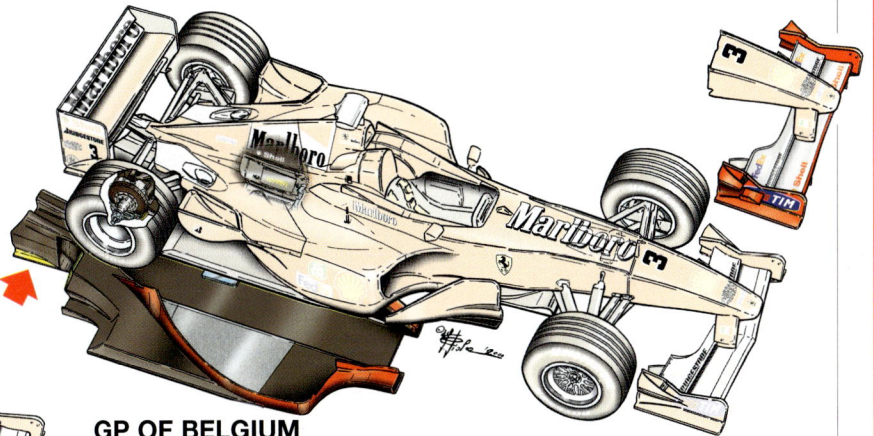

GP OF MALAYSIA

The same configuration as the GP of Japan, except for the return of the chimneys, cut to better dispel the hot air generated by the excessive heat of the Sepang track.

McLAREN

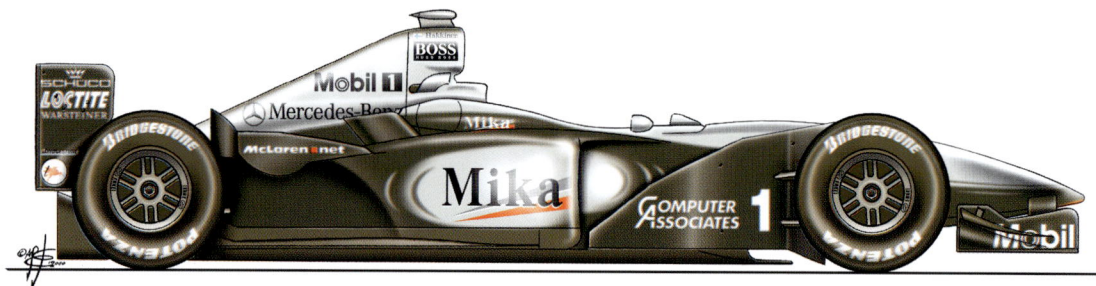

The inferior mechanical reliability of the 10-cylinder Mercedes-Benz engine cost Mika Hakkinen dearly: he saw his dream of winning three consecutive world titles evaporate into thin air one race before the end of the 2000 season. At Suzuka, Michael Schumacher beat his Finnish rival with superior race tactics after a season of highs and lows for both drivers. At zero points after the first two GPs and, therefore, with a deficit that became a turning point before the return to Europe, at the GP of Canada Hakkinen was no less than 22 points behind Schumacher. But then Schumacher went through a black period during the hot summer, scoring no points in three successive races, culminating in being overtaken by the Finn at the GP of Hungary: 68 points against 64, further consolidated at the GP of Belgium (78 to 70) with a masterpiece of a three-car overtaking manoeuvre, the lapped Zonta sandwiched between the two title contenders. But a breakdown at the United States GP followed by Ferrari's overwhelming finale of the season's last three races got the best of a car that, on occasions, showed itself to be more competitive than the Rossa. Adrian Newey optimised concepts that appeared on the MP4/14 the previous season, maintaining the dimensions of the car's wheelbase and weight distribution practically unaltered. More ballast could be loaded after reducing the car's weight in all sectors, starting with the 10-cylinder Mercedes, designed by Mario

Illien. But the big news was the introduction of "chimneys" in place of the usual hot air vents, open in the upper areas in front of the rear wheels. A development that was immediately heralded as innovative, but in the end turned out to be a re-worked old idea, obviously reviewed and corrected, of a feature introduced back in 1979 by Shadow, even if as a brief and unsuccessful experiment. Newey also revived

the low exhaust lay-out that discharges in the confined area of the central tunnel, first introduced and later abandoned by Williams in '99. The front suspension remained unchanged, except for the return of the steering arm placed inside the upper wishbone. For the rear axle, the torsion bars were positioned inside the fusion of the gearbox, produced in cooperation with Mercedes. There was another

rear suspension development seen earlier on another of Newey's cars, the Williams FW 16, which had the drive shafts fared inside the upper wishbone and moved lower. But in the case of the MP4/15 they were hidden inside the toe-in link that also functioned as a flap in respect of the lateral channels of the diffuser. McLaren was to have introduced radical changes to the gearbox and differential, but changes in the regulations, confirmed by the Federation before the GP of Belgium, stopped that programme.

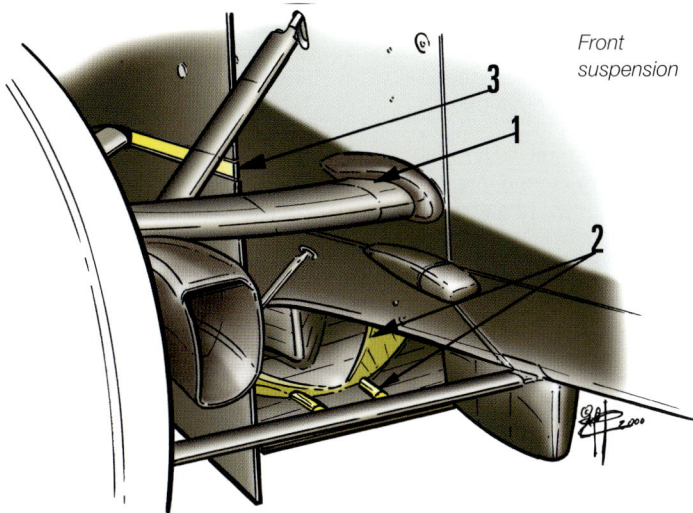

Front suspension

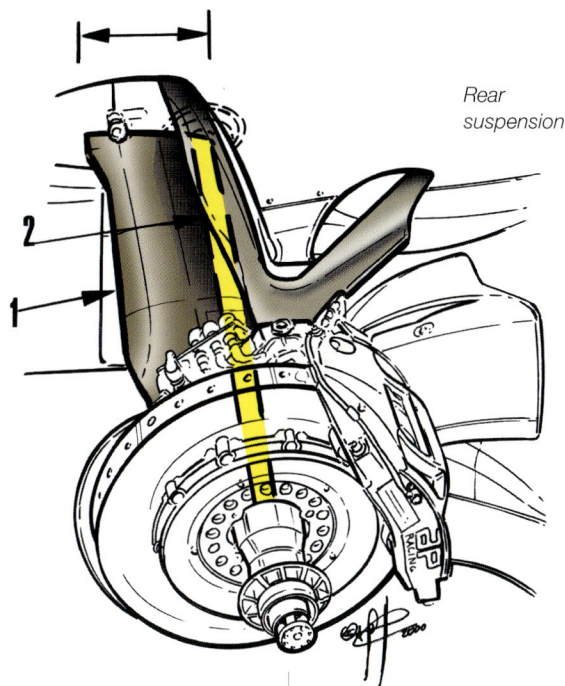

Rear suspension

CAPTIONS

The nose of the new MP4/15 was shorter and slightly higher than that of last year's car, but maintained the same inclination of its upper area. The shape of the two wing pillars was different, rather like an upside down V, but wider, more angular and a little longer. The front suspension went back to having the steering linkage counter sunk inside the winged profile of the upper wishbone. The large barge boards behind the front wheels were removable, like those used in private testing, to facilitate the work of the mechanics. The fins in the upper part of the chassis were bigger, an indication that the monocoque had been further lowered in that area, but not excessively so like Jordan. The central area near the cockpit was completely renewed and, of course, the small fins at the sides of the driver's head disappeared, banned by the Federation's new regulations. In their place was very rounded form of protection: it was concave inside, a feature that very much resembled another adopted by McLaren in 1996. The hollowing-out coincided with an accentuated tapering of the area under the engine's air box, where fins were in a position similar to that of last year's Ferrari. The most important new development started with the two "chimneys" in the area above the radiators before the fins in front of the wheels, which resembled those of the '98 McLaren. The purpose of the two big air vents, which were about 20 cm high and nick-named chimneys, was to "shoot" hot air in the low pressure zone under the rear wing in such a way as to not interfere with the wing's efficiency. Note the considerable advancement of the so-called Coca Cola area, which began with a small knife-edge zone at the start of the side-pods, becoming slightly narrower. The engine cover was extremely low at the rear, due to the faring that covered the rear suspension rockers (given a new position for the torsion bars) were more noticeable. The seven-speed gearbox was made in cooperation with Mercedes-Benz. The rear end no longer terminated in a point, but with a small square horizontal plane that also acted as a cover for the central section. Two exhaust pipes based emerge from this area, an idea abandoned by Williams in '99. Great care was taken to ensure an almost constant emission, to avoid variations in downforce.

FRONT SUSPENSION

The steering linkage (1) went back to its position inside the faring with a winged profile of the upper wishbone, while in '99 it had been moved to a lower position as from the GP of Austria. The large barge boards behind the wheels (2) were demountable, to facilitate eventual substitution, a matter that cost Coulthard more than an hour's work during testing for the '99 GP of Europe. The knife-edge zone under the chassis was also new, with two large protrusions (3).

REAR SUSPENSION

To improve aerodynamics the plane, with notable chord dimensions, (1) that act as toe-in link, also has the drive shafts enclosed within it (2) as was the case with the FW16, designed by Adrian Newey in '94.

OIL TANK

The central disposition of the hexagonal-shaped oil reservoir on the MP4/15 remained unchanged and the radiators continued to be laid out fan-style and oriented towards the front. The drawing shows the double vents of the exhaust from the engine block, the point at which there could be a device for controlling the exhausts' hot air flow.

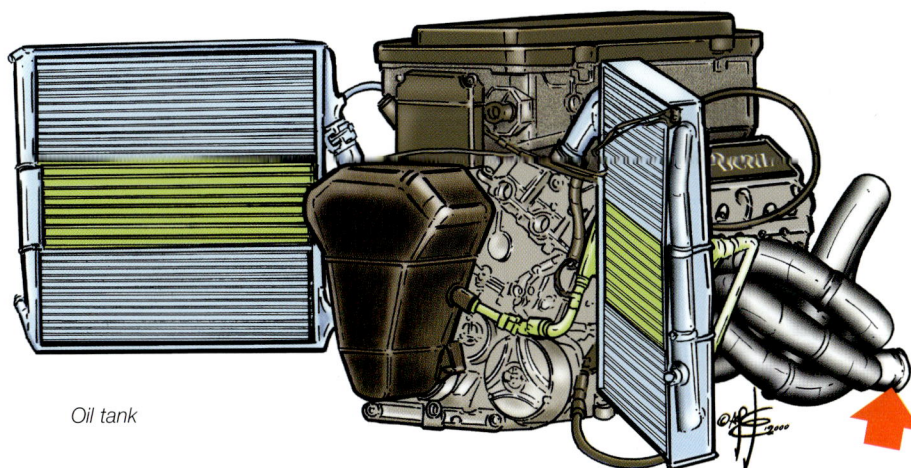

Oil tank

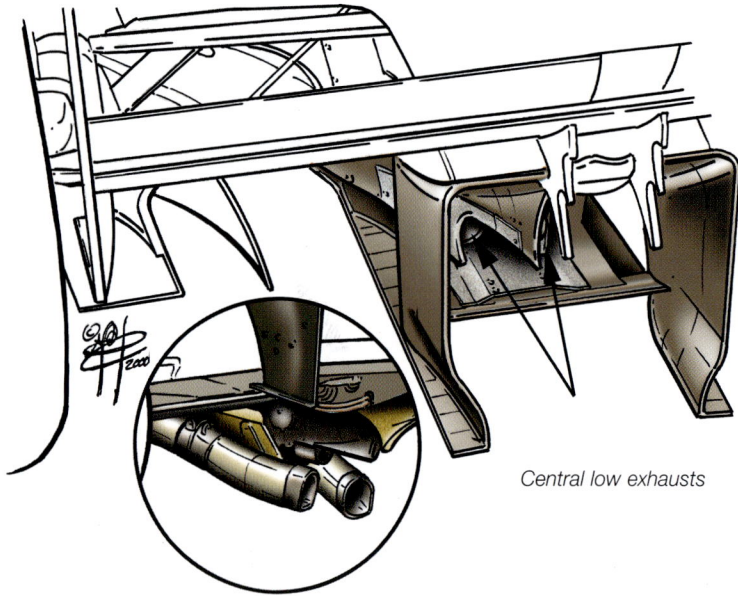

Central low exhausts

CHIMNEYS

One of the MP4/15's new features were the chimneys used to dispel hot air from the radiators with the lower, lateral area of the body completely closed. Four versions were used: one standard, one with a slit (1) in its base, one large chimney (2), one medium (3) one cut to improve cooling, which was used in Hungary and Malaysia, and one for qualifying, shown in the bottom drawing. The comparison with the standard chimney at the side shows how much more tenuous is the qualifying version. Chimneys were not used at one qualifying session in 2000: the GP of Europe.

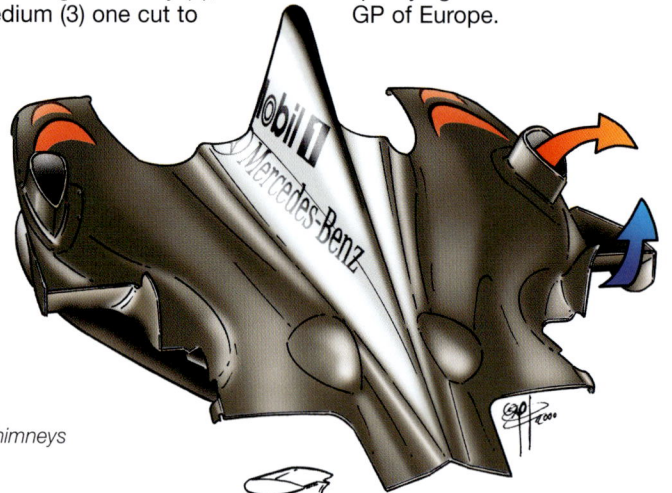

Chimneys

EXHAUSTS

For his MP4/15, Adrian Newey adopted the central low exhaust system introduced by Geoff Willis on the '99 Williams, a development that sees the two terminals even closer together. The terminals are illustrated, without lower faring, in the circle. They do not have a perfectly oval section.

FRONT SUSPENSION

The MP4/15's front suspension was practically the same as the '99 season's car, with the long push rod (1) connected to the inside vertical shock absorber; the only difference was the steering linkage (2) inside the upper wishbone in carbon fibre.

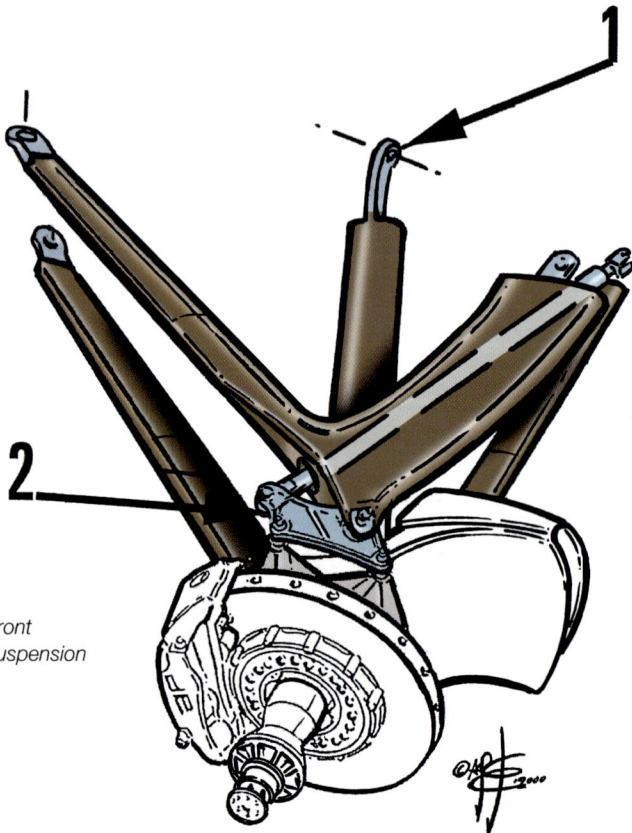

Front suspension

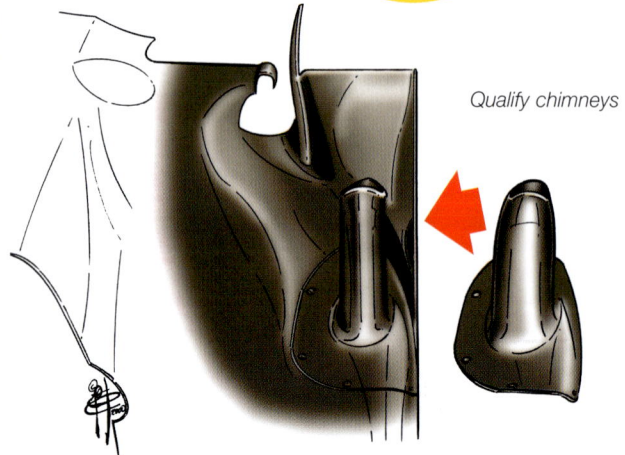

Qualify chimneys

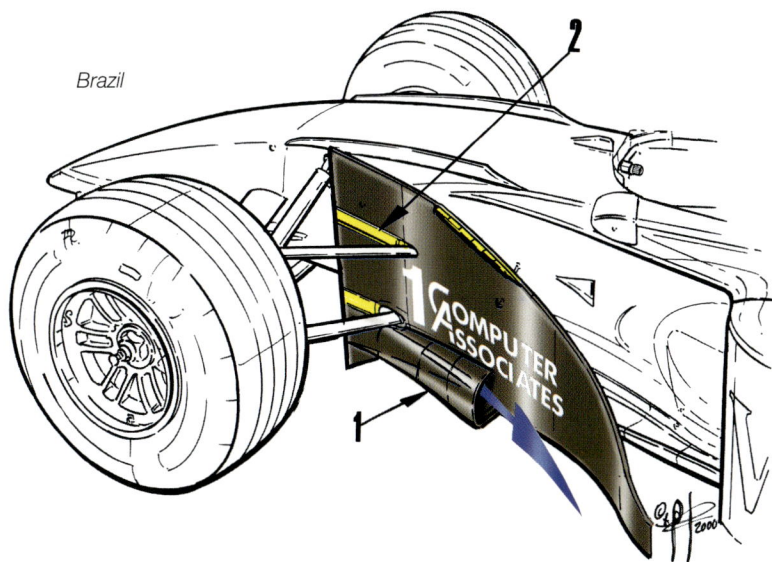

Brazil

Coulthard

BRAZIL
At the GP of Brazil, the barge boards behind the front wheels were modified: the lower area had an additional lateral blower (1). For easy substitution, these units were removable (2), like those used in private testing.

FRONT UPRIGHT
The front upright in titanium was very attractive, with its small wings for ventilation: the coupling flange with brake disc was in carbon fibre.

BRAKE COOLING AIR INTAKES SEQUENCE
The first illustration on the left was the biggest intake, used on circuits that were hard on the brakes and by Coulthard on medium tracks. The second is the new brake air duct, very long and thin, introduced in Canada and used on high severity circuits, but where it was also important to have good aerodynamic penetration. The third was for medium tracks that are not harsh on brakes, while the fourth is the smaller air intake for qualifying.

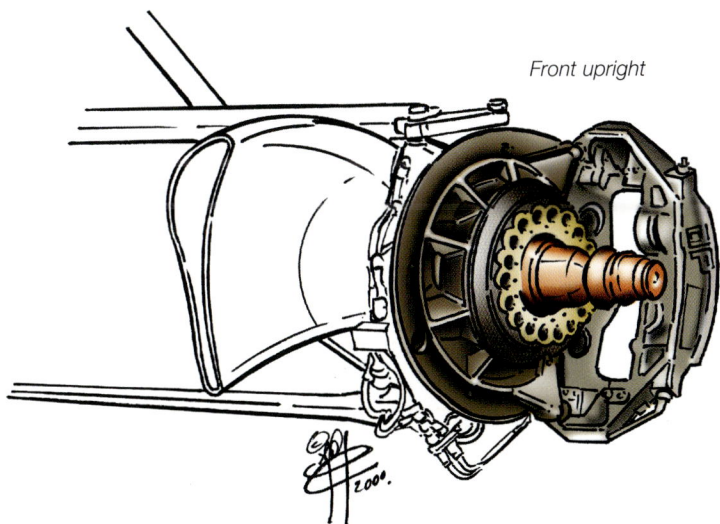

Canada

Medium tracks

Front upright

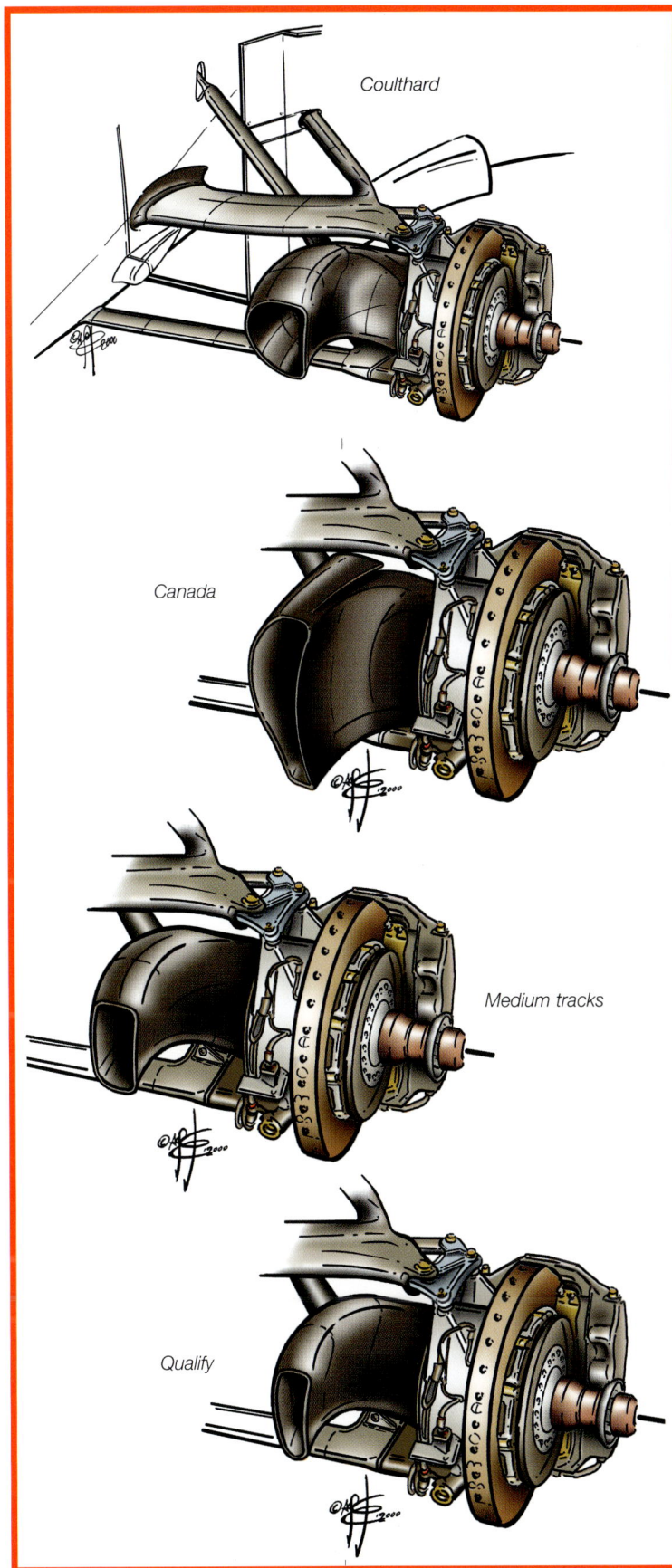

Qualify

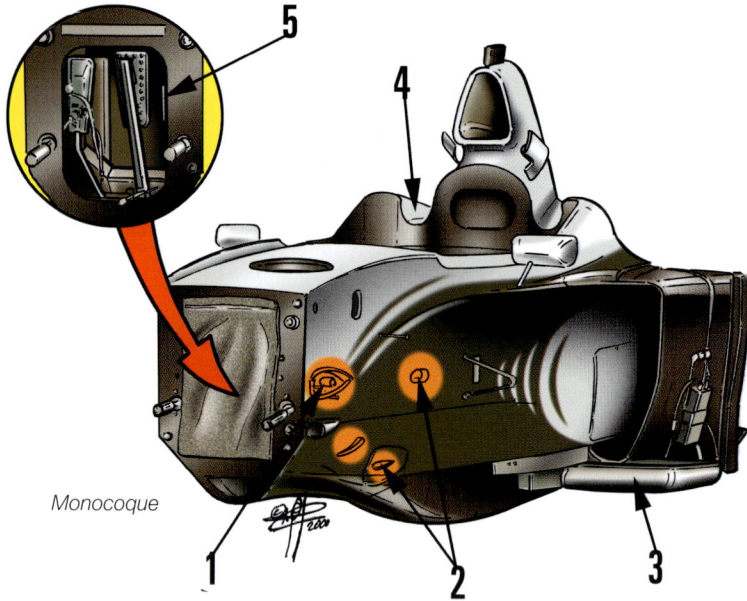

Monocoque

MONOCOQUE

The MP4/15 monocoque's lower part is very tapered. The mountings are coloured in orange. McLaren also adopted the low protection fins (3), debuted by Benetton in '98. Above is shown the concave area (4) at the sides of the cockpit, where the driver's head protection was also located. The pedals are shown in the circle. The Coulthard car had a slender brake pedal; the third small clutch pedal (5), illustrated in the cockpit chapter, can just be seen.

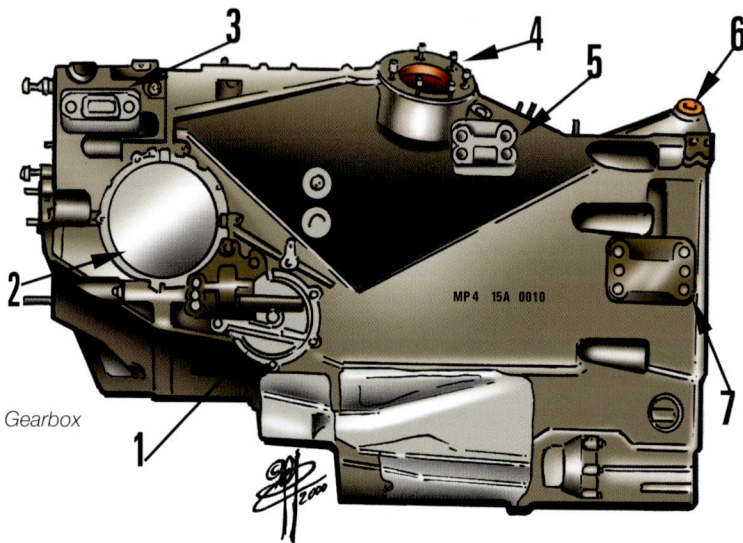

Gearbox

GEARBOX

The cast gearbox of the MP4/15 was of the traditional type. 1) Sequential selector. 2) The differential group fitted with overhang. 3-5) The upper wishbone mounts. 4) Mount for the suspension rocker with coaxial torsion bar. 6) Shock absorber mount. 7) Front mount for the lower wishbone.

Rear brake air intakes

REAR BRAKE AIR INTAKES

McLaren used two types of air ducts with which to cool the rear discs, one that was simple and was used on circuits that are less severe on the braking units, and another that incorporated extensive faring of the upright.

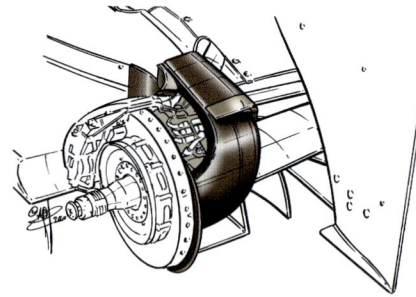

Canada

CANADA

A new rear wing, with three planes in the upper area and only one in the lower, was introduced in Canada.

REAR SUSPENSION

The layout of the rear suspension was very simple, with the torsion bars attached directly to the interior of the rockers. The drawing shows two of the three different rockers, each of which was used dependant on circuit characteristics to provide different levels of suspension progression.

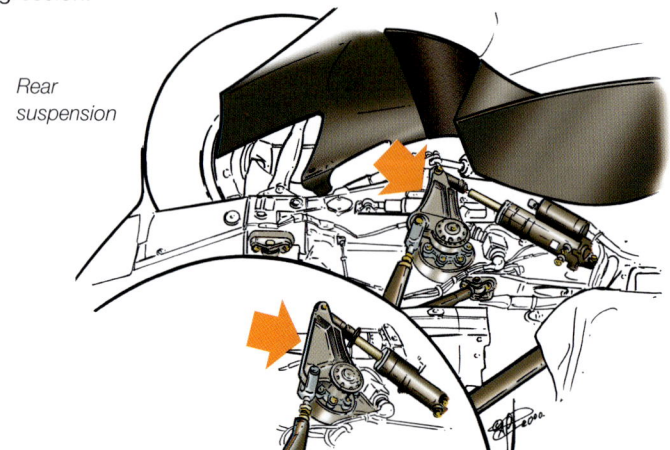

Rear suspension

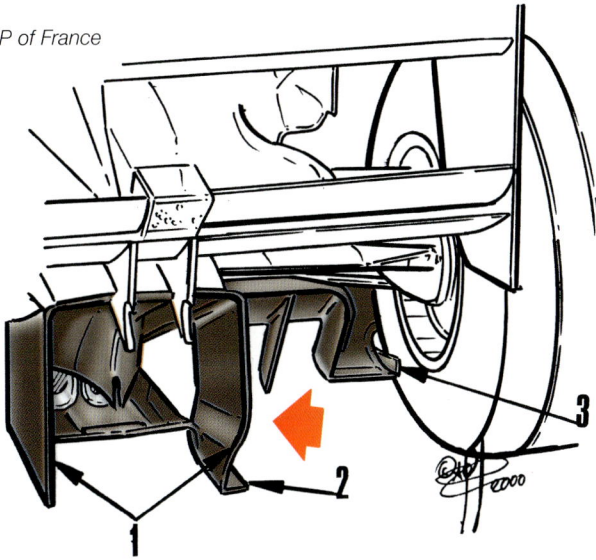

GP of France

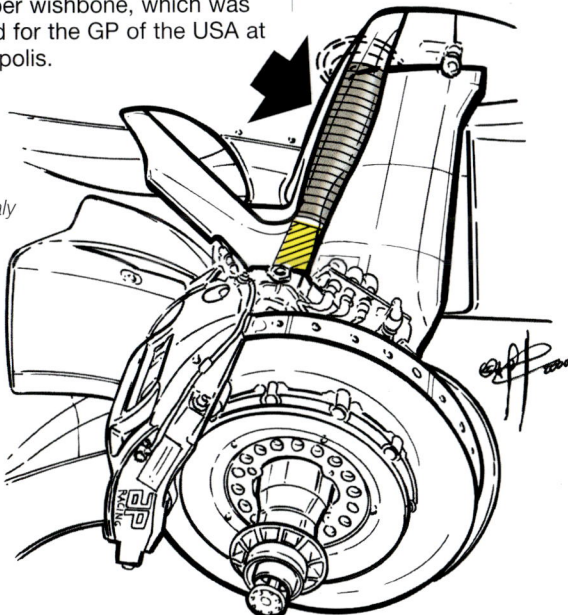

Asymmetric mirrors

GP OF FRANCE EXTRACTOR

Numerous important new developments were introduced at the GP of France. The above drawing shows the new diffuser (on the right of the drawing) with a concave area (1) towards the inside of the lower area of the central channel, instead of completely straight, as with the old unit. The new diffuser also had a knife-edge area down low (2) and a small lateral Gurney flap inside the wheel (3).

GP OF ITALY

After testing for the GP of Italy, the rear suspension was strengthened to cure the breakage experienced by Coulthard. A carbon fibre skin was applied to the upper wishbone, which was retained for the GP of the USA at Indianapolis.

ASYMMETRIC MIRRORS

McLaren's attention to detail can be seen in the modifications carried out on the mirrors, introduced at the GP of France: they were asymmetric, with the right mirror moved about 20 cm further forward to improve visibility in the French circuit's long right-hand bend before the finish line straight.

POWER STEERING

Electronically controlled power steering applied to the traditional lay-out (1) was also introduced at the GP of France, with the steering linkage at the height of the upper wishbone. The torsion (2) and anti-roll (3) bars can also be seen (3).

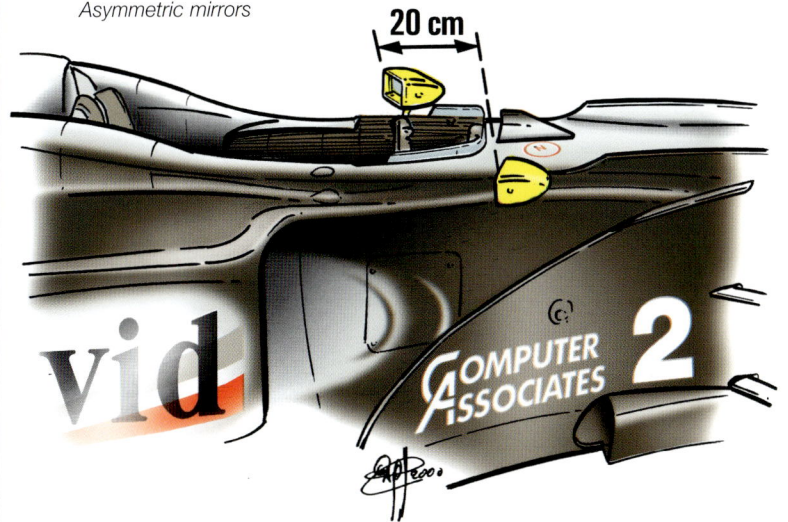

Power steering

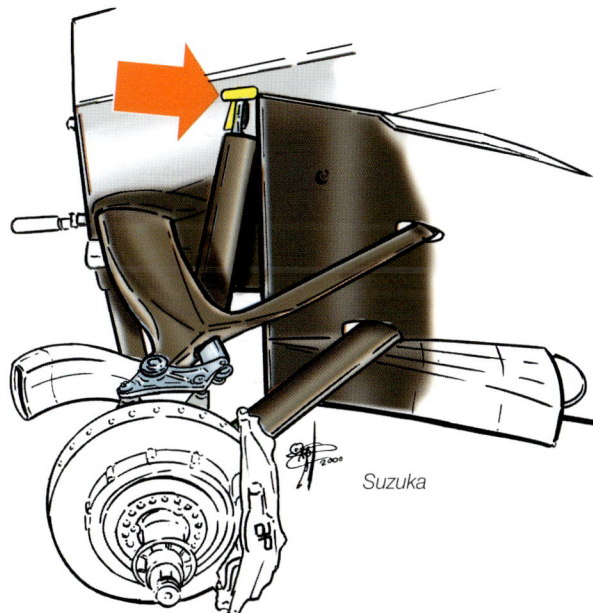

GP of Italy

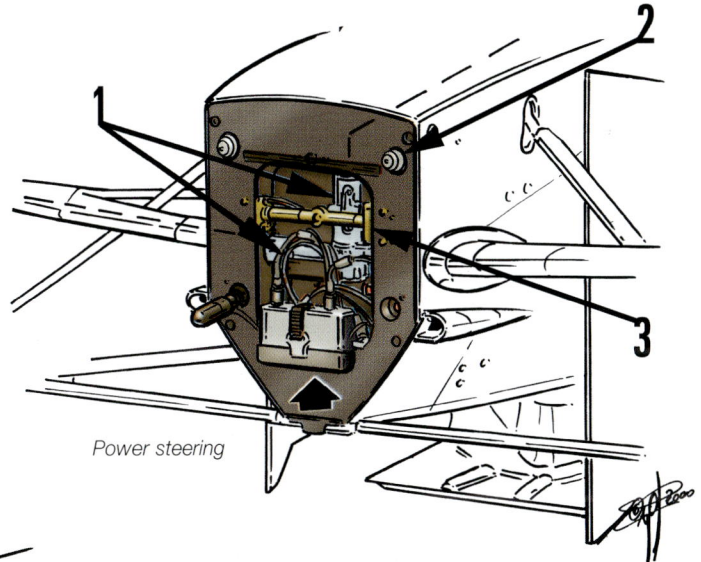

Suzuka

SUZUKA

In the race that decided the drivers' championship, Adrian Newey took care of the smallest detail, even closing off the damper rocker chassis hole with self-adhesive tape.

WILLIAMS

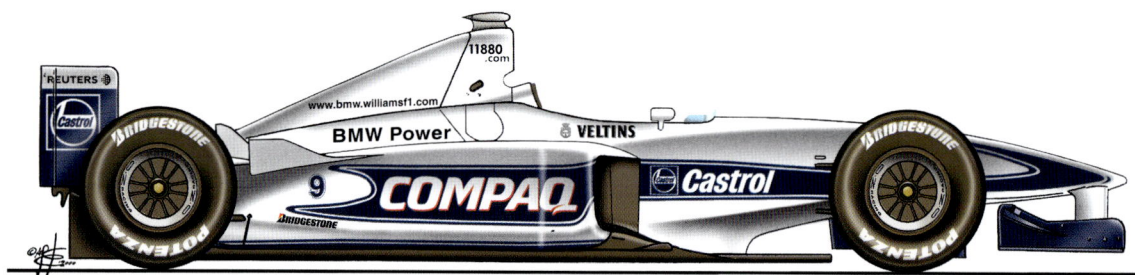

Even though 116 points behind second-placed McLaren, the BMW-powered Williams became the revelation of the season by coming third in the Formula One world constructors' championship. An important result, both because the team from Grove, England, had dropped to fifth place in '99 and that the engine by BMW, who had been out of Formula One since 1987, made its debut in 2000. The result of perfect planning by both companies, which were able to focus their efforts on what should actually have been a running-in season. Objectives started to become reality from the opening race of the season in Melbourne, with Ralf Schumacher's unexpected but much deserved third place. By the end of the season, the team had won its way to the podium three times, with the addition of the GPs of Belgium and Italy, scoring a total of 36 points. If BMW had put their trust in a completely traditional but fairly reliable 72° V10 that broke only six times in 34 races, Williams' Patrick Head and his two young designers, Gavin Fisher and Geoff Willis, the latter the aerodynamicist, did likewise and put together a car that was a direct evolution of the Renault-powered FW21, revised and cleansed of previous errors: they included the chronic understeer when entering a corner, which gave Alessandro Zanardi so much trouble in '99 and made the car difficult to set up for some tracks, along them Montreal, Zeltweg and Sepang. The FW22 was far removed from

the lay-outs that had become the trend: it was characterised by rather low sidepods and a decidedly long wheelbase, the longest of the 2000 season cars - 3140 mm against an average 3060 mm. The reasons for this choice are linked to three key factors: the generous dimensions of the BMW 10-cylinder, the need to produce a longitudinal gearbox with seven speeds instead of 1999's six and the capacity of the fuel tank, penalised by the new central position of the oil reservoir. The choice of gearbox dimensions was also conditioned by the need to find the right anchorage points for the rear suspension, in which the unhappy position of the lower wishbone that exited mid-way along the lateral diffuser was eliminated. Exhaust pipes that blew in the lower area of the central channel were dropped from the '99 GP of Great Britain and were

not brought back, although they did appear in 2000 on the McLarens, after having been revised and corrected. Regardless, it was the rear end of the FW22 and, more specifically, the underbody area that was the most innovative and one in which a considerable amount of refinement work had been invested, as described in the "Underbodies" chapter of this book. Williams should be credited with one of the few really new developments of the season, the extension of the window at the side of the gearbox faring, which made the diffusers' aerodynamics more efficient. Another strongpoint of the FW22 was its uprights, made of cast titanium and an extremely compact, miniaturised gearbox in aluminium.

COMPARISON

By comparing the 2000 (opposite page) and '99 cars as they were presented at the start of their respective seasons, it is possible to detect a certain family resemblance in the determination of the height of the nose (1) and sidepods. For the first time, Williams reduced the maximum width of the front wing to be able to adopt externally concave end plates (2). The team had already substituted the large barge boards behind the front wheels with smaller units inside the front suspension (3), combined with small horizontal fins in front of the sidepods (5), introduced for the '99 GP of Belgium, exploiting a feature first adopted by Jordan.

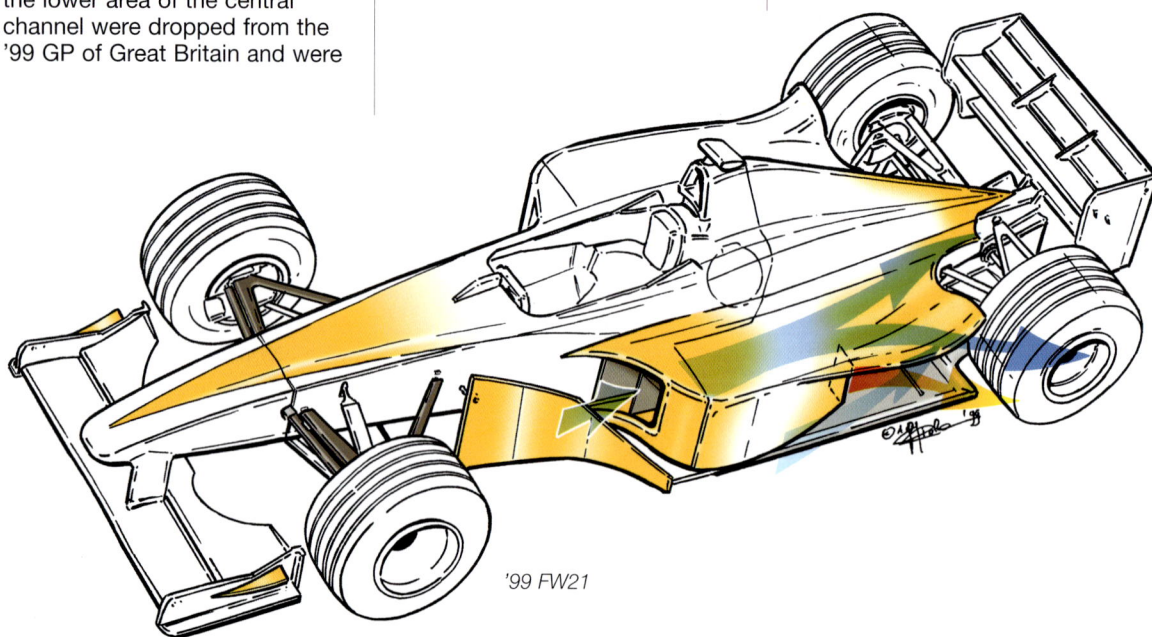

'99 FW21

88

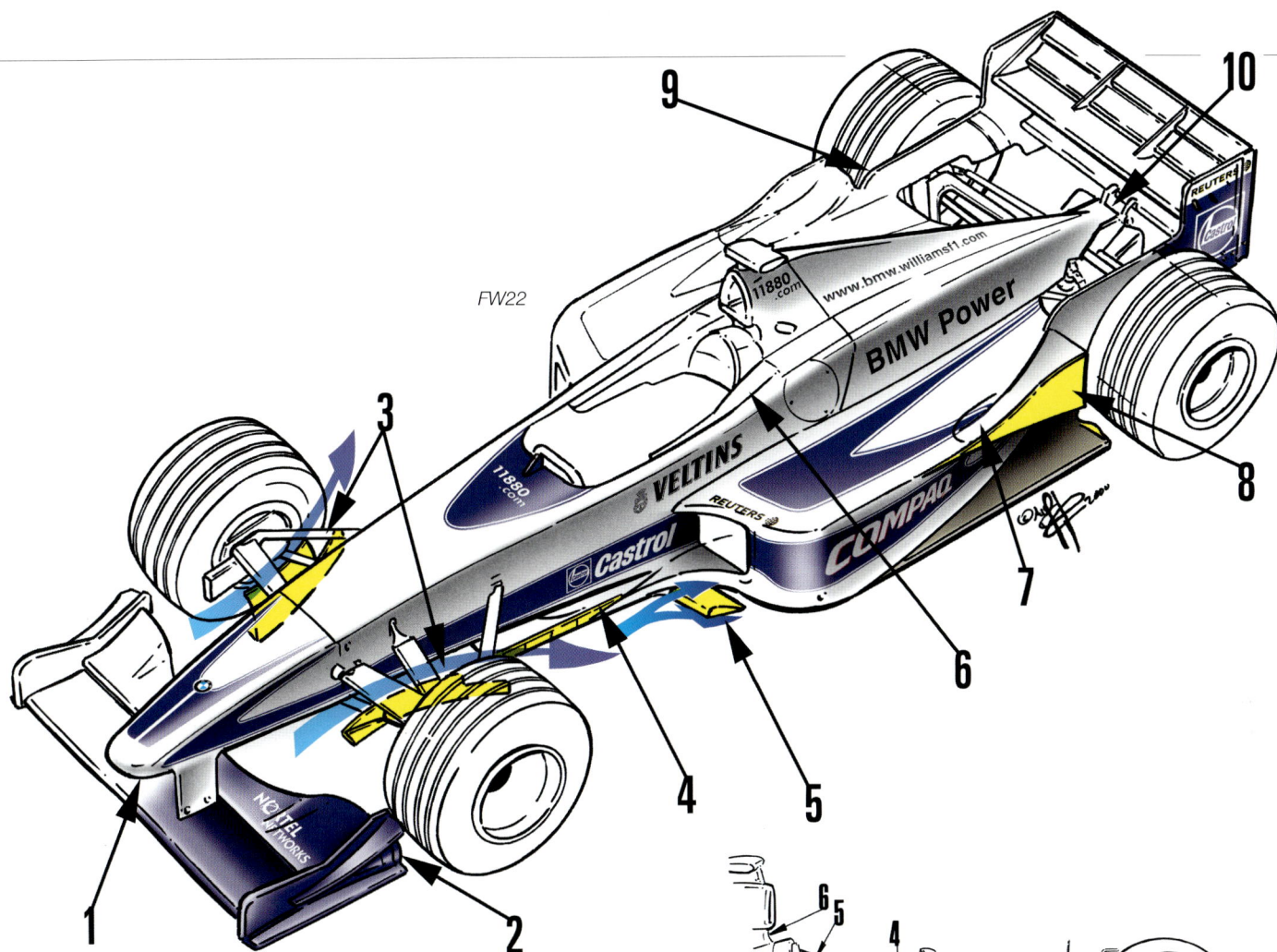

FW22

9

10

3

1

2

4

5

6

7

8

6 5

4

1

3

2

2

1

BMW Power

COM

The large vertical Gurney flaps (4) were retained at the sides of the knife edge zone, under the chassis. There were no more fins at the sides of the FW22's cockpit, which was slightly higher (6) to include regulation protection. The introduction of chimneys (7) or small planes in front of the rear wheels had been planned since the car's presentation. The use of fins (8) in front of the wheels was new. Williams and Sauber were the only teams to use connection extensions (9) between the fins in front of the wheels and the end-plates of the rear wing. The rear suspension was new, with the body covering only the central area of the gearbox (10).

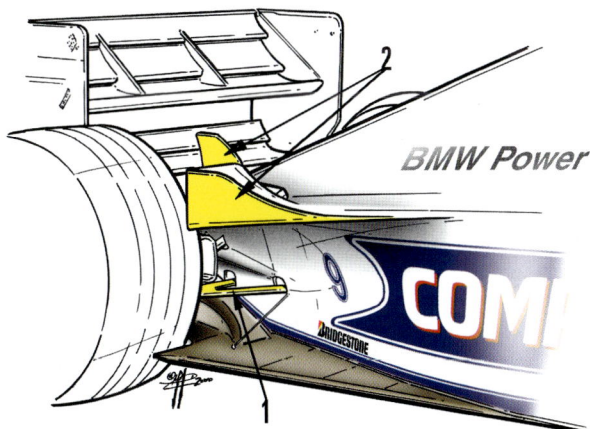

SIDE VIEW

(1) The central part of the FW22's high nose was of perfectly symmetrical progression, with two long supports for the front wing. 2) The vertical Gurney flaps introduced at the '99 GP of Japan were retained, as were the (3) small fins in front of the sidepods, first seen at the previous season's GP of Belgium. 4) The air intakes of the sidepods were raised in

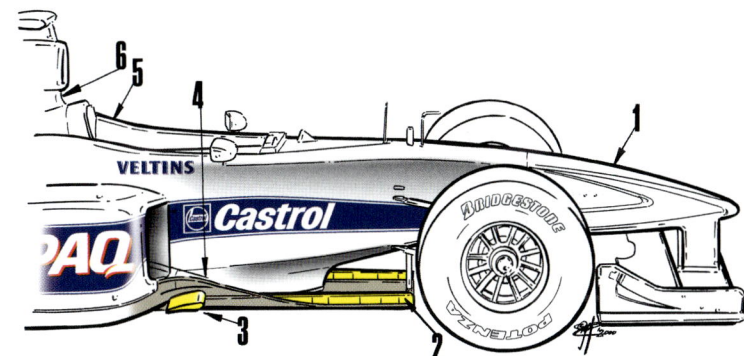

respect of the knife edge area. 5) The cockpit was higher in the area of the driver's head and there was no imitation fin-

shaped protection of the '99 car. 6) The engine's air box was moved a little further back and separated by a long headrest.

REAR VIEW

The FW22's rear suspension had a lower wishbone (1) that passed over the lateral channels of the diffuser, different to the previous Williams. One of the characteristics of the 2000 car was the presence of large fins (2) in front of the rear wheels, which were connected vertically with the very low sidepods.

UPRIGHTS

Williams adopted uprights made of cast titanium by the Belgian company Don Caster-Settas, a feature that had already been introduced by Minardi in '99. The rear titanium uprights were used from the first race of the season, but the fronts, which appeared for the first time during testing for the GP of San Marino, made their racing debut at the GP of Great Britain. It was a feature that permitted a notable reduction in unsprung weight.

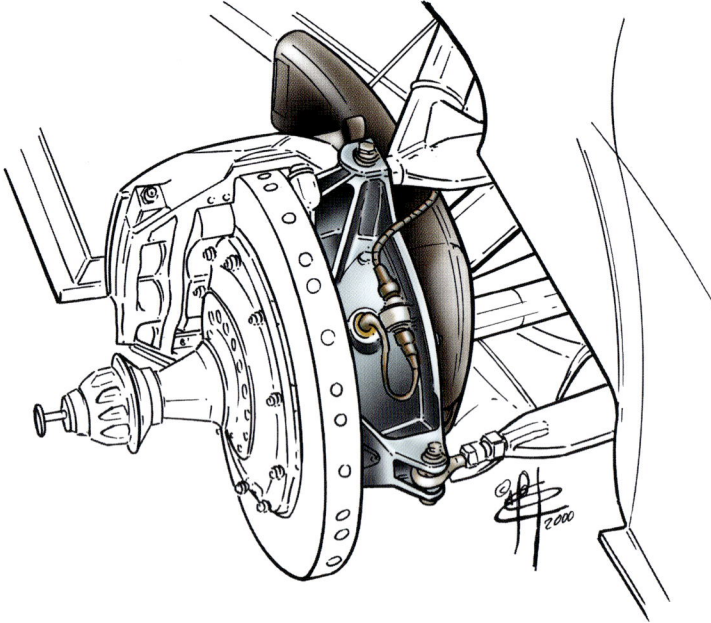

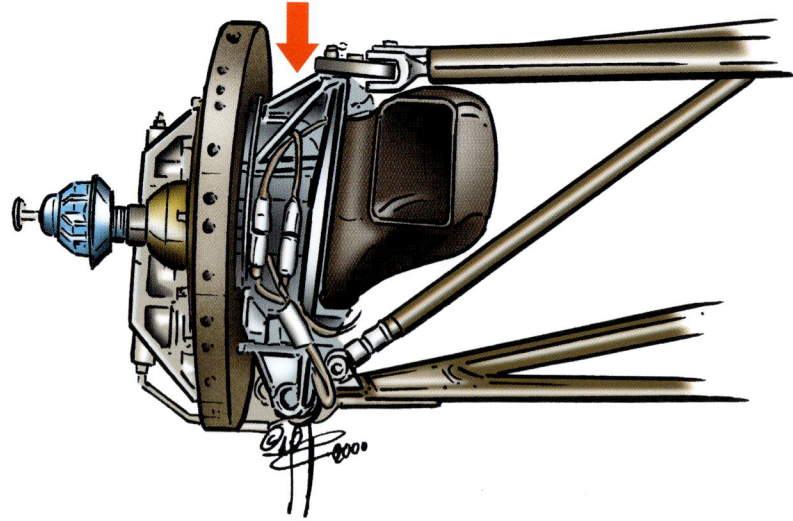

TURNING VANES

As of the previous season, Williams used low turning vanes inside the front wheels: note below the obligatory horizontal area in the view from underneath the car, to stop the upper part from twisting.

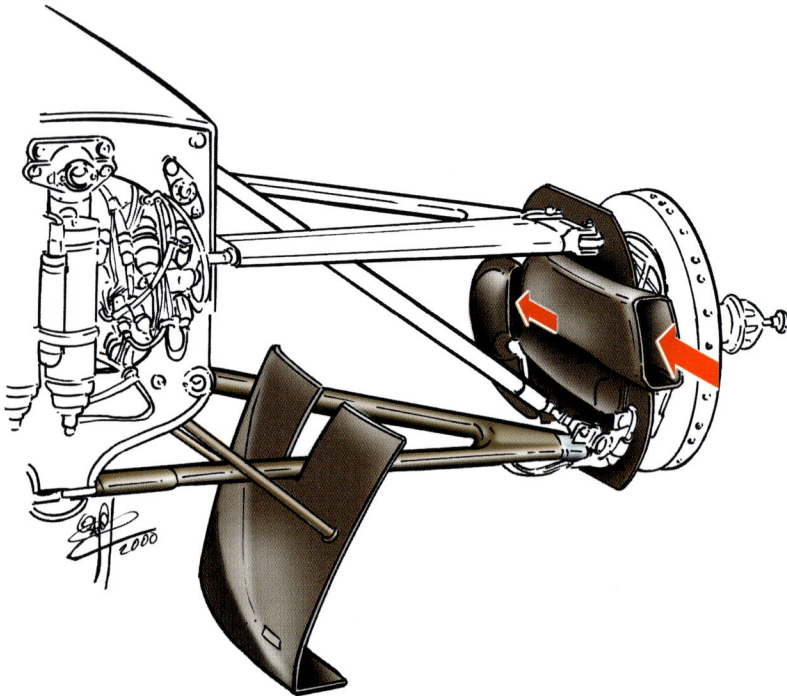

FINS IN FRONT OF THE SIDEPODS

Introduced at the previous season's GP of Belgium, the small wings in front of the sidepods were modified for the 2000 GP of Hungary. Note how the new units are longer than those of '99, visible in the rim: in addition they have an external semi-flat area.

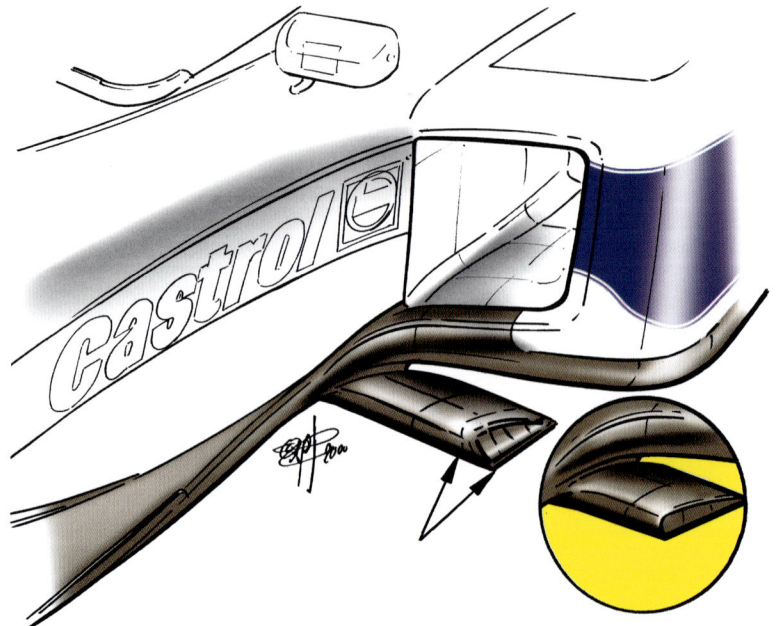

JORDAN 99

60 cm

Monaco

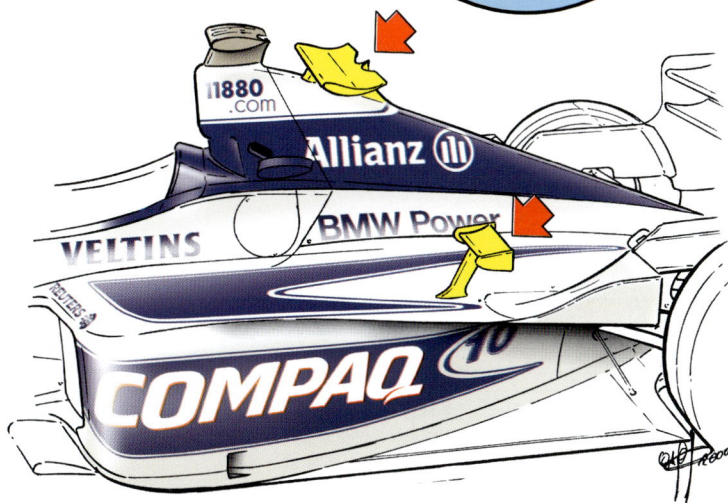

MONACO

Williams was the only team to bring back the third advanced wing, adopted the previous year by Jordan for the GP of Monaco and visible in comparative detail. It was about 60 cm wide, and had a chord of approximately 20 cm. The Williams version also had two small planes on the sides. Note, in the detailed drawing, the whale tail shape of the third wing, situated behind the roll bar.

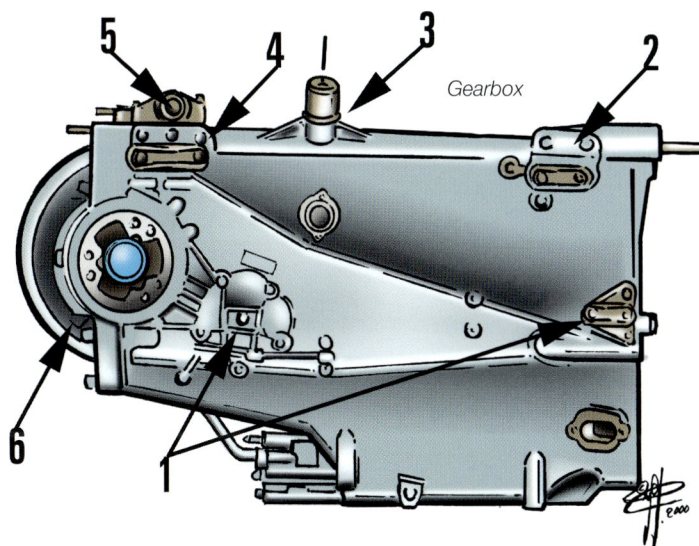

Gearbox

END PLATES

Williams used two types of similarly shaped end plates. The only difference between them was the greater height of the maximum downforce version (separated in the drawing) compared to the standard unit used for most races.

GEARBOX

The seven-speed longitudinal gearbox was of very clean design and made of cast aluminium. 1) The suspension's lower wishbone mounts. 2-4) Upper wishbone mounts. 3) Attachment points for the suspension's rockers, which used coaxial springs in the shock absorbers. 5) Roll-bar mount. 6) Differential box.

REAR SUSPENSION

The V-shape accentuated by the rear bodywork enables us to see the rear suspension mounts. 1) The toe-in link was fixed to the deformable structure behind the gearbox itself, a structure that also acted as a wing support. 2) Rear mount of the upper wishbone, closely combined with the rear wheel's retention cable mount (4), shown in yellow. 3) The pushrod mount to the suspension rocker.

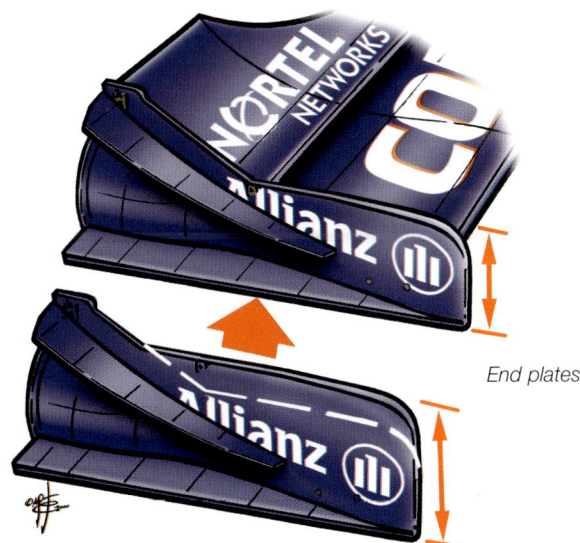

End plates

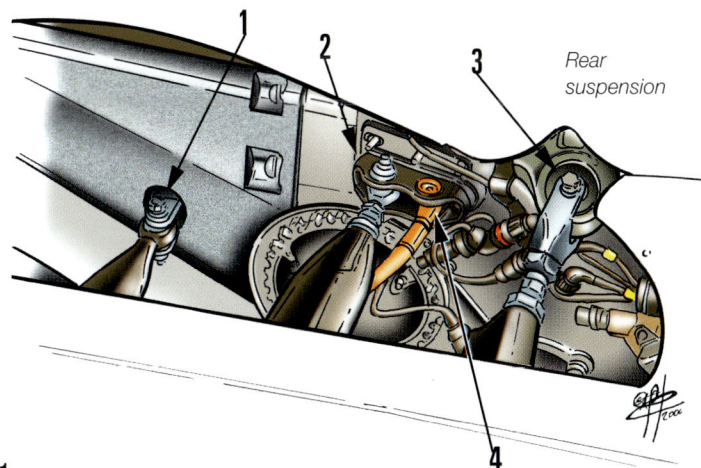

Rear suspension

Hungary

Malaysia

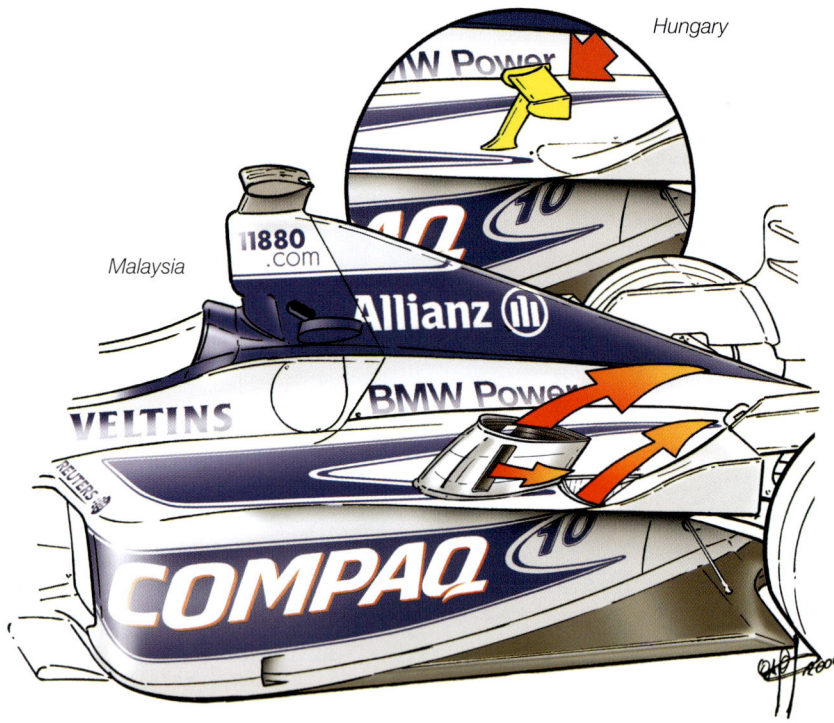

GPs OF HUNGARY AND MALAYSIA

At the GP of Hungary, Williams used two different configurations: for qualifying, they fitted small wings on the sidepods, introduced at Monaco but without the middle wing. Chimneys similar those of McLaren and Ferrari were used for the race, but more voluminous with vertical apertures on the outside to improve heat dissipation. The same alternation of solutions was used in Malaysia to help combat the Sepang track's excessive heat.

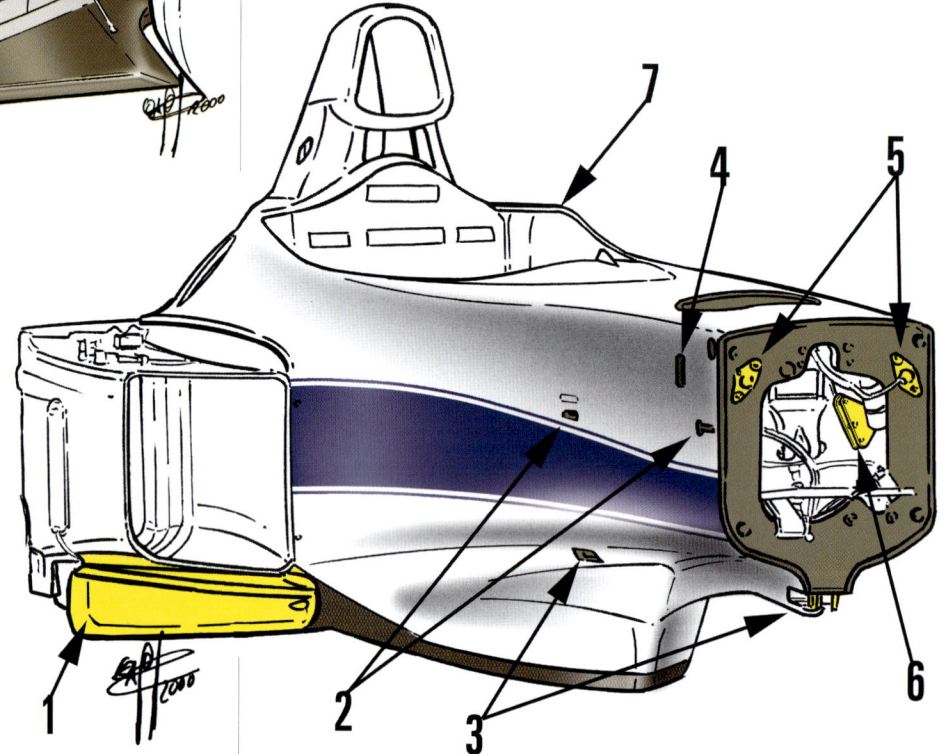

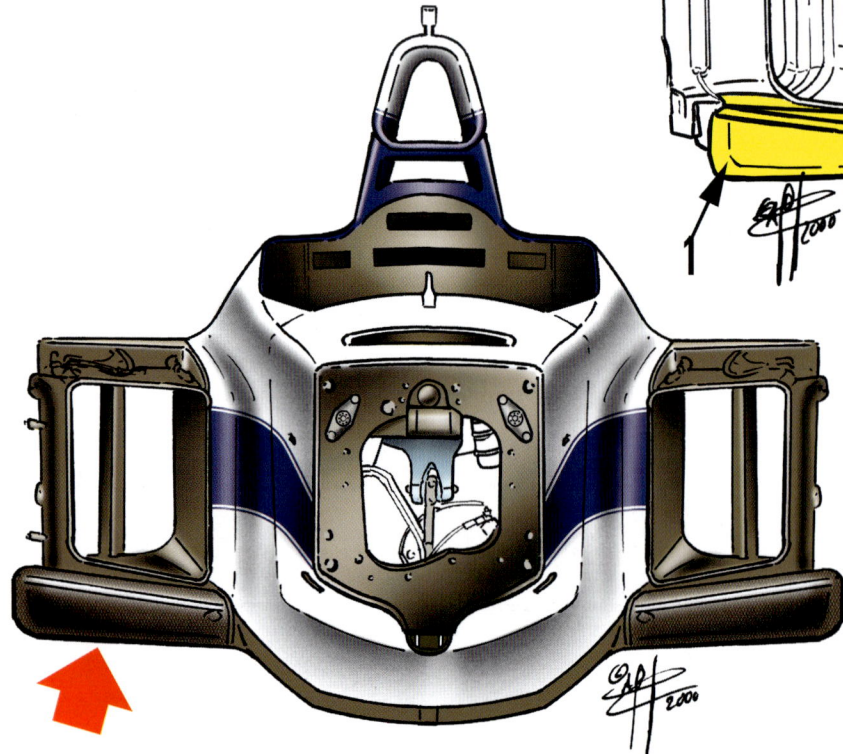

MONOCOQUE

These two drawings reveal the shape of the FW22's chassis. It can clearly be seen from the front just how much the sidepods were lower than those of other cars. The arrow indicates the deformable structure that had to withstand the lateral crash test, as stipulated by the Federation. This structure is shown in the side view of number 1. Also note the lower wishbone mounts (3) with central anchorage, while the upper wishbone is directly attached at points (2). In (4) the push rod hole connected to the suspension rocker, which can be seen at (6), in yellow. The FW22 also adopted horizontal torsion bars (5) like those of the '99 car. Note the ample dimensions of the cockpit cradle (7) at the height of the driver's shoulders.

BAR

BAR achieved its objective in its second season of F1 motor racing: and that was to design and build a reliable car. It failed to do so for its debut in '99, when its cars retired 18 times and finished eight times out of 32 starts and left Villeneuve without a single point at the end of the season. The PR02 not only took fourth place in the constructors' championship (in '99 it came 11th and last) with four fourth places by the Canadian in Australia, France, Austria and the United States, it also came third, behind McLaren and Ferrari, in the number of race laps it completed. With an abundant wheelbase of 3120 mm and a 132 litre fuel tank, the second F1 BAR was a logical evolution of the first, from which it retained its principal characteristics without great inventiveness on the part of the designers. From the height of the nose, the rather square sidepods, rounded air intake for the 10-cylinder Honda, the suspension lay-out with its torsion bars also for the rear end, there remained the cast titanium uprights made by CRP of Modena with the push rod mount of the front end incorporated in the lower wishbone instead of the traditional anchorage point. A technique that was already used by BAR in '99 and copied, even if with profound differences, by Ferrari, as illustrated in the "Suspension" chapter. BAR is one of the few teams to have its exhaust blow above the diffuser's lateral channels.
Right from the first race of the season, a Prost-style doubling of the fins appeared on the car in

front of the rear wheels, while between the GP of France and the subsequent Austrian GP the team debuted a completely revised aerodynamic system for all components. It was the body's turn at Magny Cours, the nose and diffuser at Zeltweg, the

FRONT SUSPENSION
The PR02's front suspension wishbones were in carbon fibre with ample faring and had a characteristic shape indicated by the arrow in the view from overhead. The steering linkage was lowered.

HONDA ENGINE
A larger, different shaped oil reservoir for the 10-cylinder Honda that powered the BAR. It had lost its characteristic amphora shape and had become squarer.

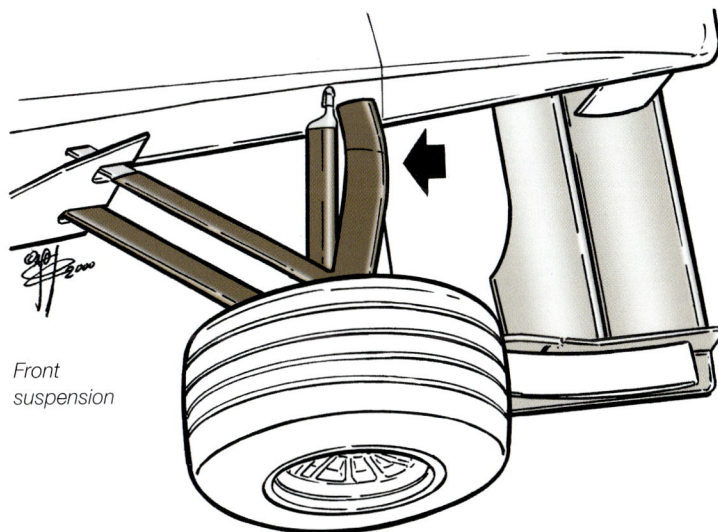

Front suspension

Honda engine

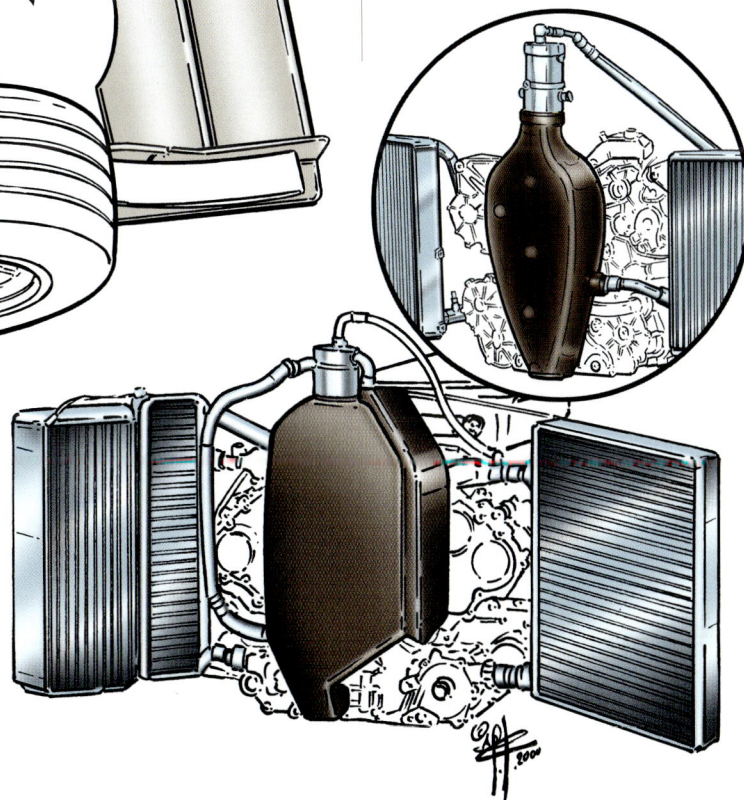

latter of which retained a three channel division, with two close vertical end plates in the area at the sides of the central channel. Additional aerodynamic refinements appeared in Germany, while power steering made its debut at the GP of Hungary, first on Villeneuve's car and, from the GP of Italy, on Zonta's.

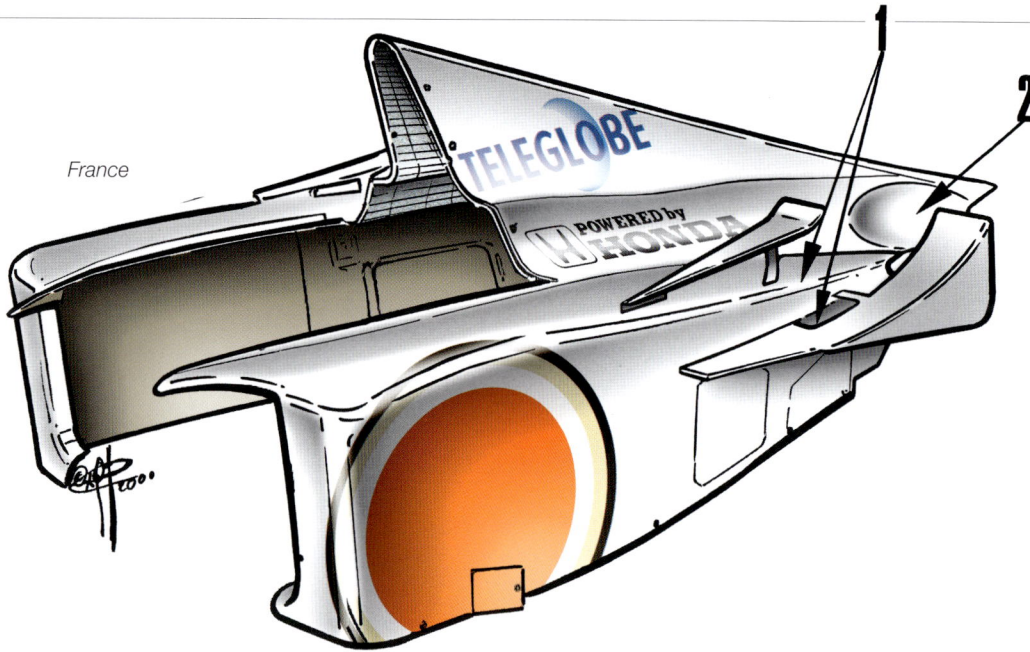

France

GP OF FRANCE

New aerodynamics including somewhat modified sidepods were introduced from the GP of France. The double fins in front of the rear wheels were further evolved, with the part that links with the perforated body (1). The whole engine cover was further lowered, as indicated by the faring (2) that covered the suspension.

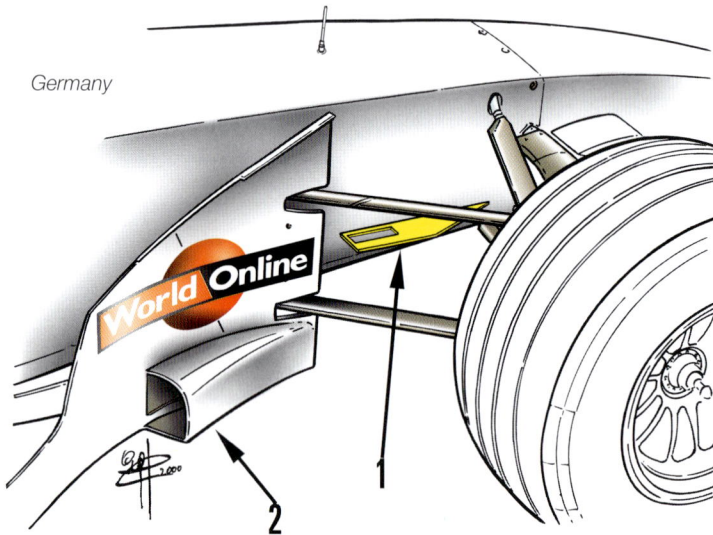

POWER STEERING

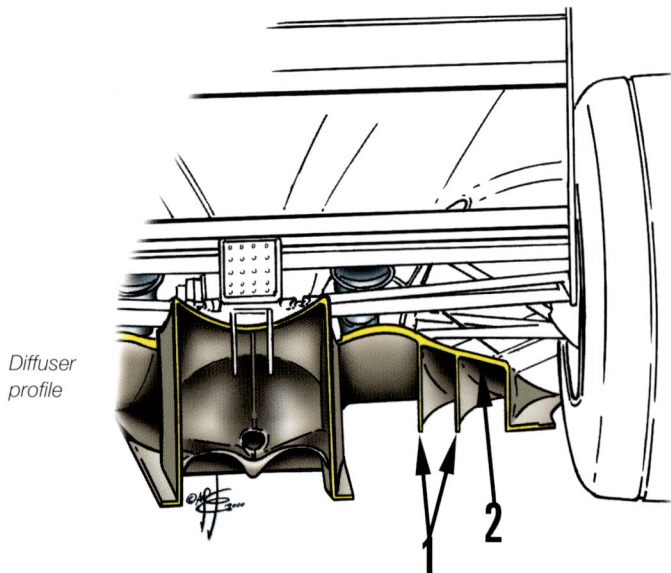

Electronically controlled hydraulic power steering was fitted to Villeneuve's car from the GP of Hungary, confirmed by a large central sphere: Zonta's car was not fitted with the system until two races later.

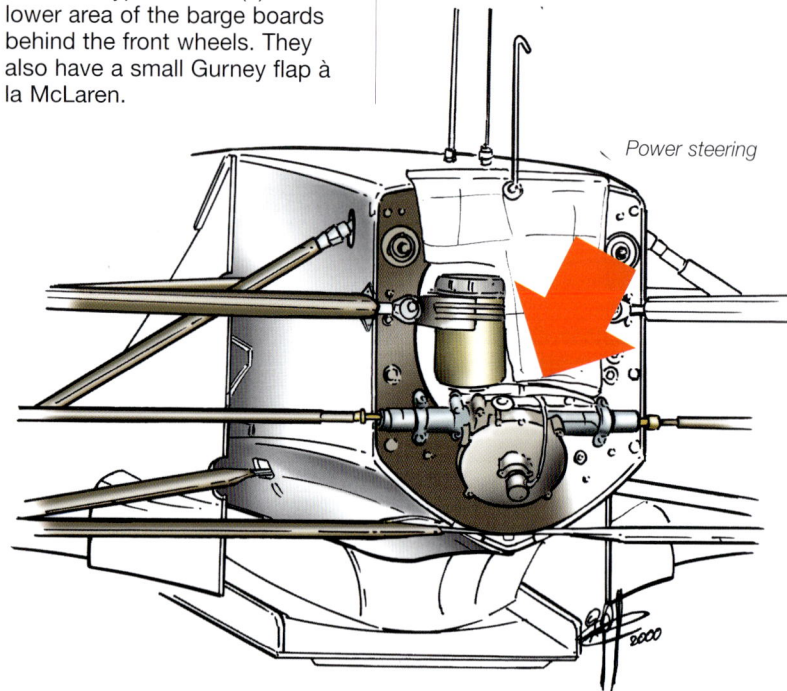

Germany

GP OF GERMANY

These small horizontal fins (1) were introduced at the GP of Germany to improve the quality of the air flow towards the rear end of the car. Note the McLaren-type air vent (2) in the lower area of the barge boards behind the front wheels. They also have a small Gurney flap à la McLaren.

Power steering

Diffuser profile

DIFFUSER PROFILE

BAR used diffusers characterised by lateral channels with two middle plates (1) and a much inclined upper area (2).

BENETTON

Benetton owes its fifth place in the world constructors' championship to a sudden inversion of trend in the design of its car. Having lost Nick Wirth, technical management returned to Pat Symons and Tim Densham, who produced a car that was, perhaps, too simple but decidedly more reliable, after producing an ambitious '99 season car full of new developments introduced at all costs which, in the end, severely compromised its performance and dropped the team to sixth place in the constructors championship. To Giancarlo Fisichella, that reliability was worth a second place in Brazil and two thirds in Monaco and Canada: there were only two

retirements due to engine problems. The car had no FTT system, which, with its 10 kg of additional weight and management difficulty, had previously obliged the team to build a car with an oversize wheelbase of about 328 cm, 18 cm more than the B 200. It should be said that this solution was dropped at mid-season, first by Wurz and then Fisichella, as was the double clutch, the source of many problems even in spite of its hypothetical advantages, but which needed to be developed far from the chaos of Grand Prix motor racing. The B 200 had much more traditional, slightly longer sidepods and the suspension lay-out remained more or less unchanged. Although simple,

the B 200 still had a number of interesting features, like the low nose that was mid-way between those of the old cars and McLarens'. The upper part of the chassis had been slimmed down, which was highlighted by the presence of two small McLaren-style fins to keep it within regulation dimensions. There was a new development in the lower area of the chassis, where the link between the monocoque and the reference plane is, generally, V-shaped and fairly angular. On the B 200 it had a much more rounded shape, the generally flat knife edge part, in particular, becoming more concave, compared to the experimental units tried during the second half of the '99 season.

SIDE VIEWS
1) In spite of an 18 cm shorter wheelbase, the difference shown in yellow (2), the B 200 was almost as long as the old B 199, due to its extended nose, as can be seen from the inclination of the central supports. 3) The knife edge zone was new, showing a bulge in the central area.
4) The B 200 had large barge boards behind the front wheels in place of small turning vanes fitted to the lateral protection (6), present on the more recent Enstone cars. 5) The upper part of the chassis was very low and had small fins to stay within the rules. 7) The sidepods were longer than those of the B 199. 8) There were also small winglets on the cockpit, either side of the driver's head. 9) The sidepods descended considerably to the rear, where there were small fins (10). 11) The diffuser plane was new, longer than that of the B 199. 12) The narrower, so-called Coca Cola zone started much earlier (see outline).

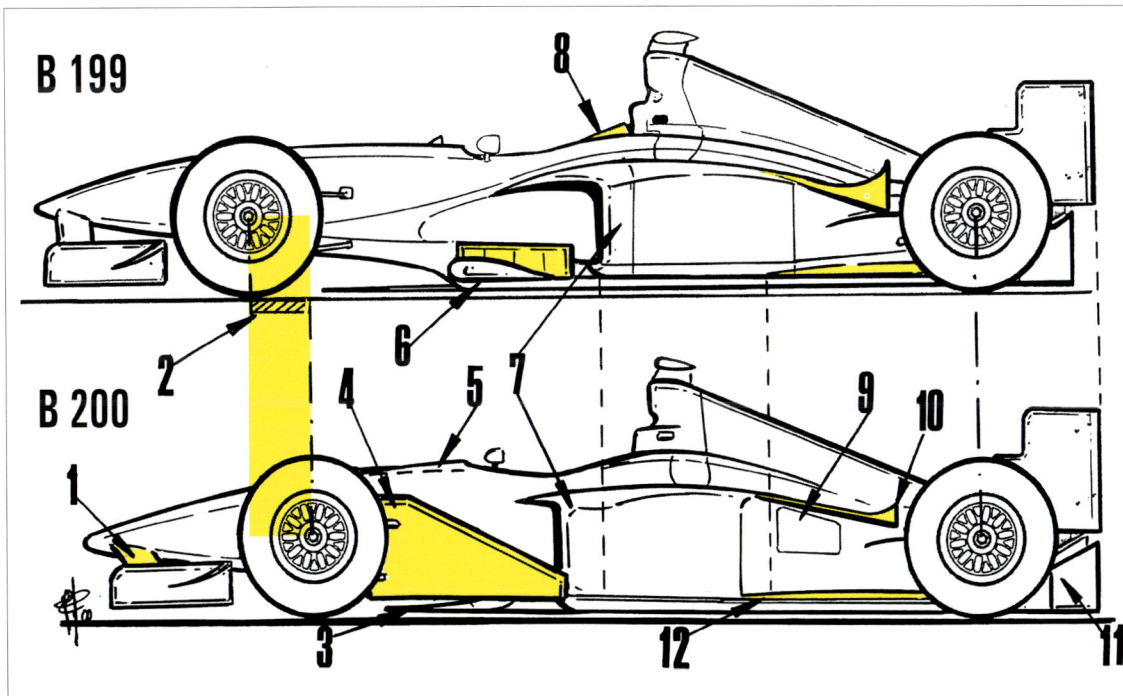

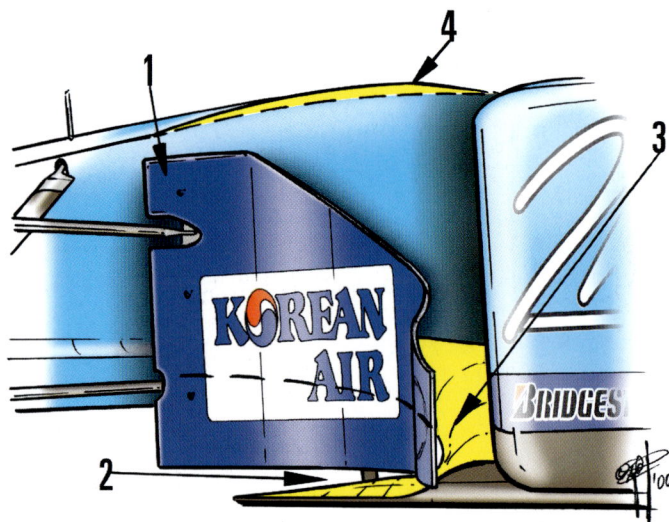

SIDEPODS

The low turning vanes applied to the lateral protection of the B 200 disappeared and were substituted by large McLaren-type, more traditional barge boards (1). 2) The knife edge zone under the chassis was a new idea. It was no longer flat, but concave up towards the centre and linked with a much rounded feature to the central part of the monocoque, where there were no more deviants or angles (3). Small fins appeared in the upper part of the chassis, to reduce dimensions.

FRONT END

The nose of the B 200 was extremely long, so as to easily withstand the most severe frontal crash test. Note the inclination of the supports (1). 2) Behind the front wheels were large barge boards à la McLaren, substituted from the GP of Austria by new units that were highly concave in the lower area (separate in the drawing). The small fins (3) that permitted the lowering of the upper part of the chassis can be easily seen. 4) The steering link was at the same height as the upper wishbone.

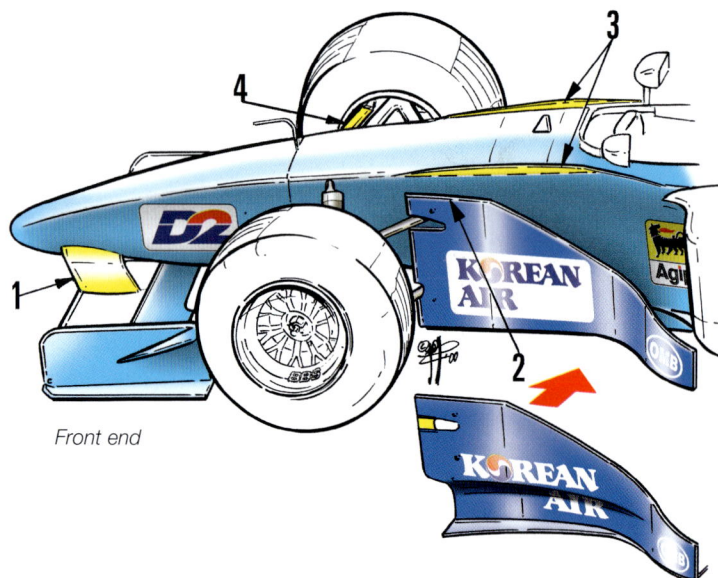

Front end

REAR VIEW

The B 200 retained exhausts that blew over the lateral channels. The only difference from the other cars was that the terminals were divided (3). A small vertical Gurney flap (1) was retained near the wheels, while the middle plate was heavily inclined to present a small horizontal knife edge zone (2).

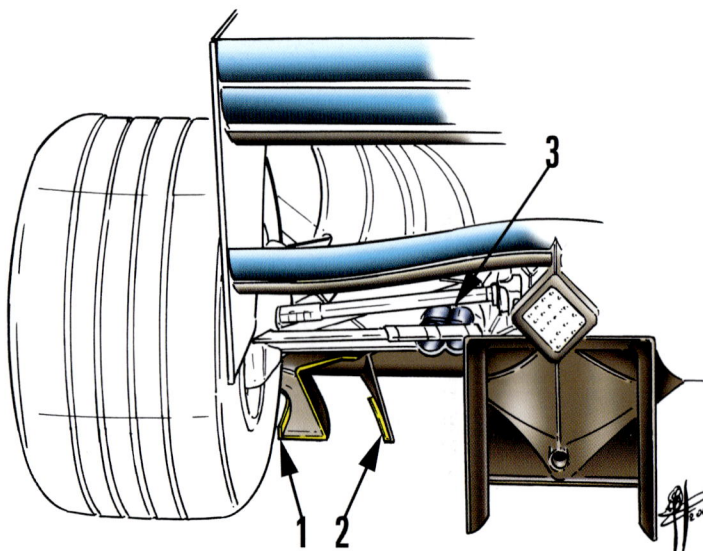

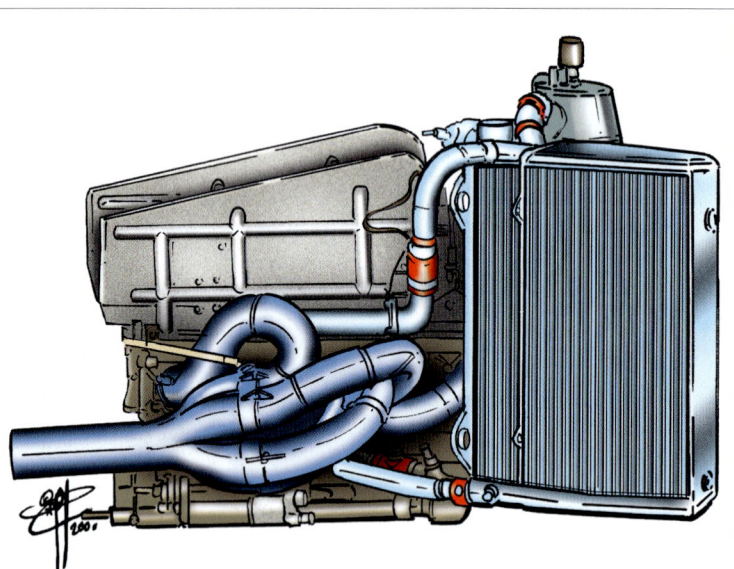

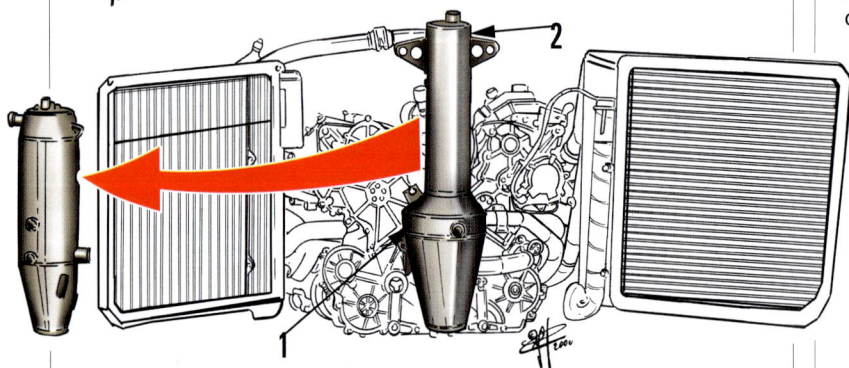

ENGINE

Compared to the previous year's version, the installation of the engine had been changed: the radiators were no longer inclined backwards, but forwards to narrow the so-called Coca-Cola zone. The capacity of the oil reservoir, which obviously remained in its central position, was increased during the season. Note how the unit mounted on the engine was taller and more bulbous down below.

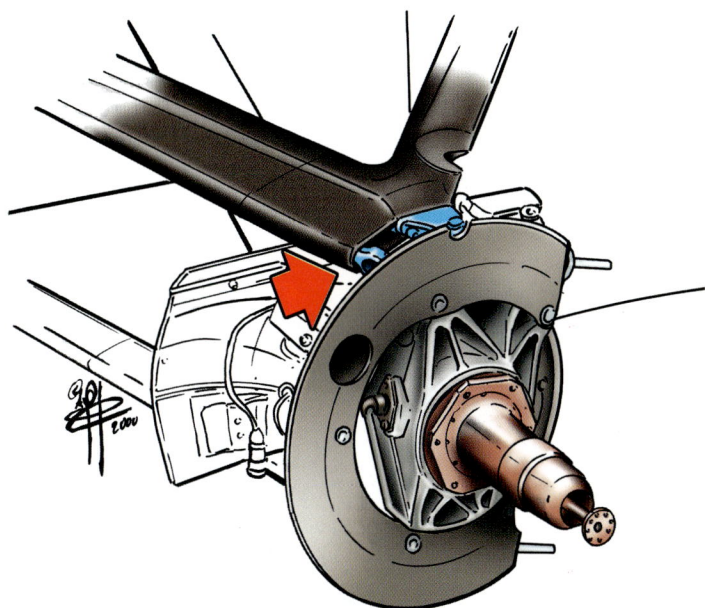

FRONT UPRIGHT

The system by which the uprights were constructed remained unchanged: but they were made from solid pieces of titanium. The only difference, compared to those of the B 199, was the mounting position of the steering link, which was no longer at mid-height but encased in the ample faring of the upper wishbone.

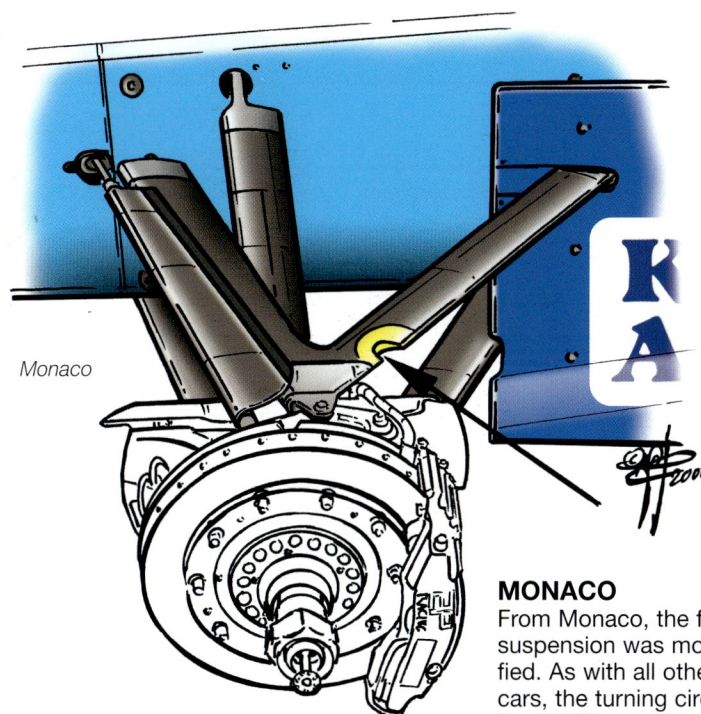

Monaco

MONACO

From Monaco, the front suspension was modified. As with all other cars, the turning circle of the B 200 was also changed, to become about 22°. The upper wishbone was slightly cut, as shown in yellow, to avoid it being fouled by the rim.

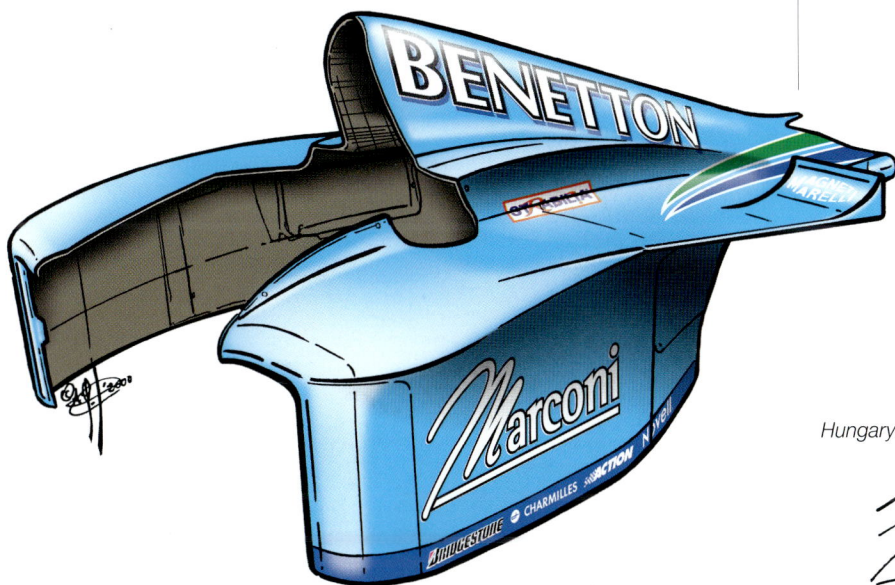

GP OF HUNGARY

A new body was introduced at the GP of Hungary with a much more accentuated descending progression in the area in front of the rear wheels, and apparent from the larger dimensions of the fins (1). The lower engine cover is shown by points (3-4). The Coca Cola bottle narrowing of the lower flat area (2) was increased. The purpose of that modification was to reduce the aerodynamic blockage in this delicate area of the car, to be able to improve efficiency.

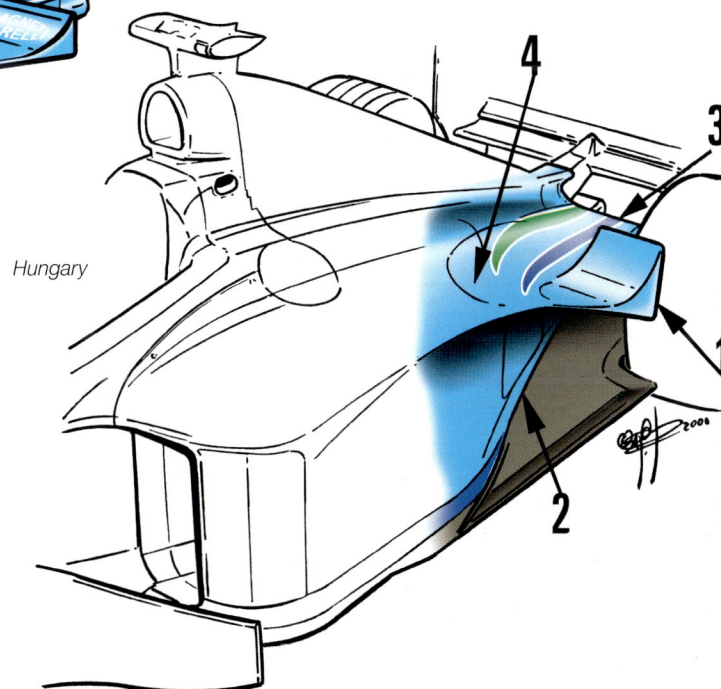

Hungary

JORDAN

To all effects and purposes, Jordan was expected to become the third force in 2000 Formula One season, able to oppose the exclusive battle for victory between the McLaren-Ferrari duo, after the Irish team's splendid third place in the '99 constructors' championship, which included two wins by Heinz Harald Frentzen in the GPs of France and Italy. Instead, Eddie Jordan's team dropped to sixth place in the 2000 table, with just two third places by Frentzen in the GPs of Brazil and the United States, plus a series of disturbing retirements, culminating in only 15 finishes during the whole year. Engines and gearboxes failed three times each, giving Jordan third place in the negative 'most retirements' table. A result that disappointed general expectations, because the EJ10 was one of the season's most interesting cars, full of advanced technical content, with an aerodynamic lay-out that was on the limit and sorted down to the last details. A fine example of the care with which the car was developed was seen in the front wing, which had its principal planes closer to the ground than any other competitor, but had end-plates that were raised towards the rear, to reduce the car's pitch sensitivity. At the opening race in Australia, the car immediately became controversial for its notable reduction of bulk in the cockpit area: that was to get around the regulations introduced by the Federation specifically to avoid the excesses Jordan had introduced the previous season, with enormous fins that replaced the drivers' head protection at the sides of the cockpit. The cockpit area of the EJ10 had been the subject of in-depth development and the drastic reduction in unwanted 'clutter' was achieved by moving the driver's head forward in respect of the engine air intake to reduce the protective area, as explained in the "Controversy" chapter on page 26. The triangular shape of the roll bar and, therefore, the engine's air intake, introduced to align with the new and more severe crash test regulations, created engine fuel feed problems with the high section of the intake, which in practice was unable to guarantee a satisfactory air flow. The EJ10 retained the same wheelbase of 305 cm, even though it had a bigger 152 litre fuel tank, and the general philosophy of the previous model, from which, however, the new car's aerodynamics and, above all, its front suspension were far removed, the latter with the first-time adoption of a torsion bar with a fairly interesting lay-out. The rear suspension concept was unchanged, retaining its coaxial springs for the shock absorbers, fitted above the new gearbox and characterised by the shafts mounted one on top of the other, to reduce transverse bulk. The Jordan was the only car to fit calipers with just four pistons instead of the standard six on the rear axle because of bulk problems, the upright-suspension grouping having arms that passed above the lateral channels of the diffuser. Jordan also maintained the unique technique of fixing the engine to the monocoque in such a way that it was not completely load bearing.

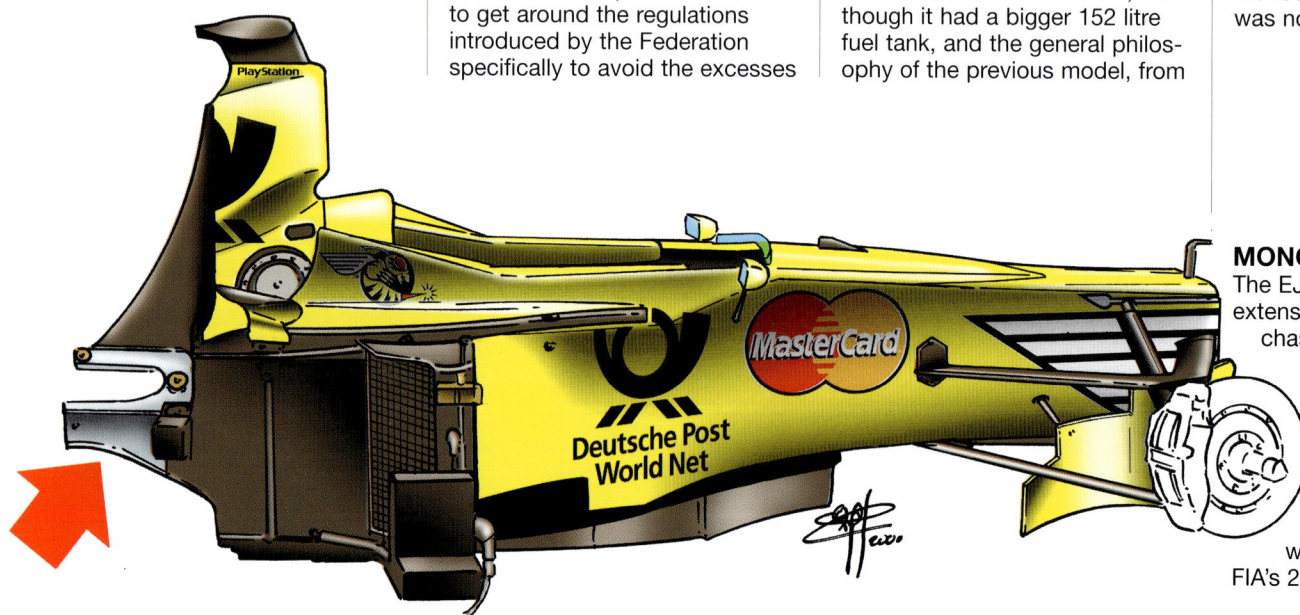

MONOCOQUE
The EJ10 retained the EJ9's two extensions at the sides of the chassis to improve the torsional rigidity of the monocoque-engine group, as was the case in '99. Last season, the two extensions were an integral part of the generous roll bar structure, which had already met the FIA's 2001 regulations.

END-PLATES

To reduce the susceptibility of the EJ10's aerodynamic load to pitch sensitivity, the end-plates were slightly raised towards the rear, which reduced the seal with the ground. The Jordan was also the car that used a principal plain closest to the ground.

GP OF BRAZIL

The first EJ10 modification was introduced at the GP of Brazil, the season's second Grand prix: it concerned the fin in front of the sidepods, which first appeared at the '99 GP of Spain. In practice, it was the terminal area that was modified: it was no longer rounded, but had a small vertical end-plate.

GP of Brazil

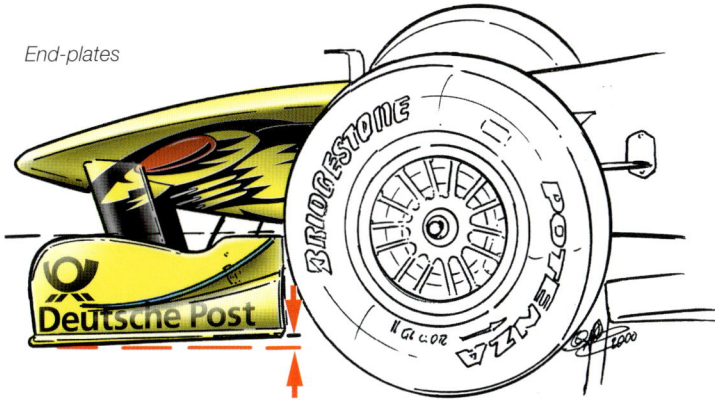

End-plates

OIL RESERVOIR

The engine layout was unchanged, with the oil reservoir fitted to the front. The tank's shape was almost the same, except that its capacity was greater due to its increased height and was all in carbon fibre, while the upper part of the EJ9's reservoir was in titanium.

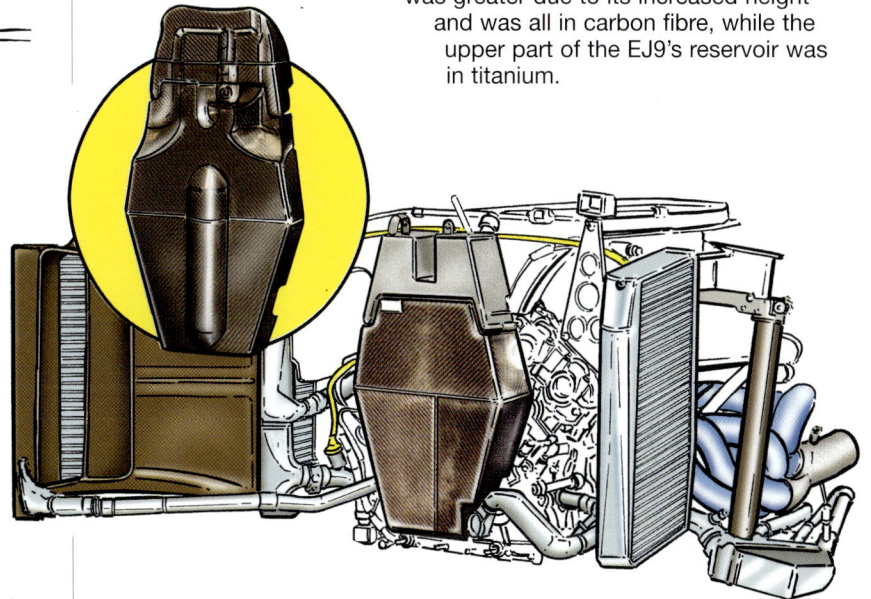

Germany

GP OF GERMANY

The new shape of the car's sidepods introduced at the GP of Germany was much different: they were more rounded and had a concave lower area, as indicated by the arrow, to create a sort of seal for the passage of air towards the rear of the car. The rear end was also new, with a more accentuated Coca Cola area.

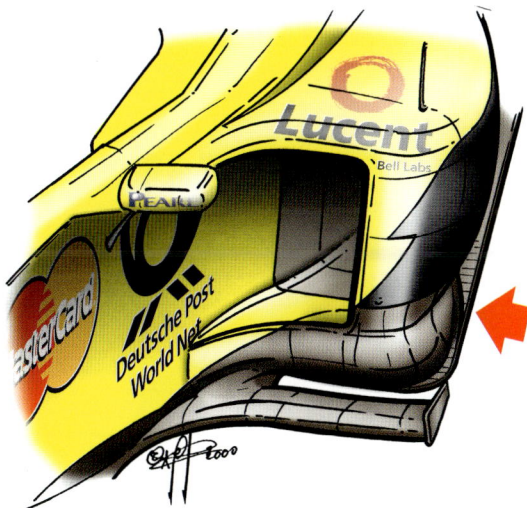

FRONT SUSPENSION

Jordan used knife-edge mounts (1) to connect the push rod link with the lower wishbone. 2) Wheel retention cable. 3) Steering linkage mount at mid-height of the upright.

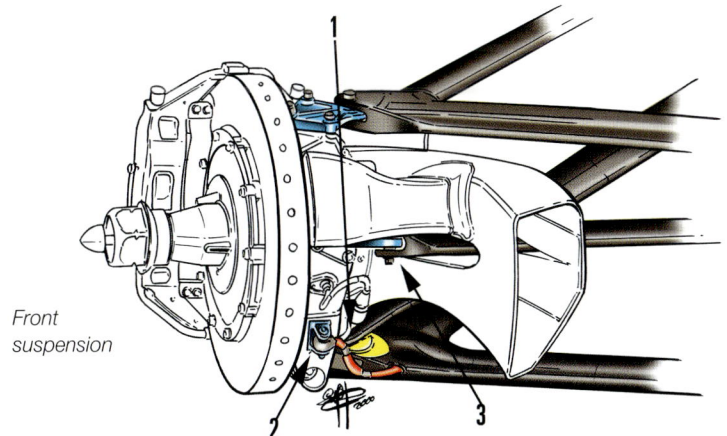

Front suspension

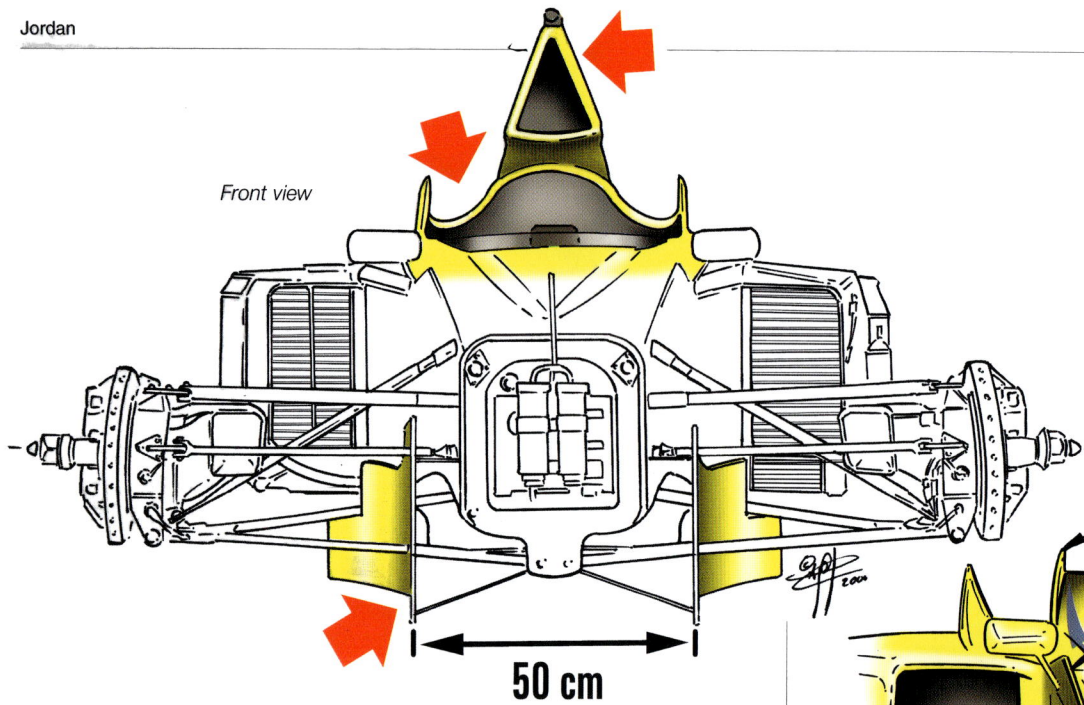

Front view

50 cm

Cockpit

FRONT VIEW AND ENGINE AIR INTAKE

A considerable amount of development work was done to reduce the cockpit mass, with the concave area at the sides of the driver's head and the two large lateral fins. Note the triangular section of the engine air box, which created a fuel feed problem or two. Detail in the box shows how the upper area was divided. In the frontal area, the EJ10 retained its turning vanes, which were lowered 50 cm in the central area up to the reference plane level.

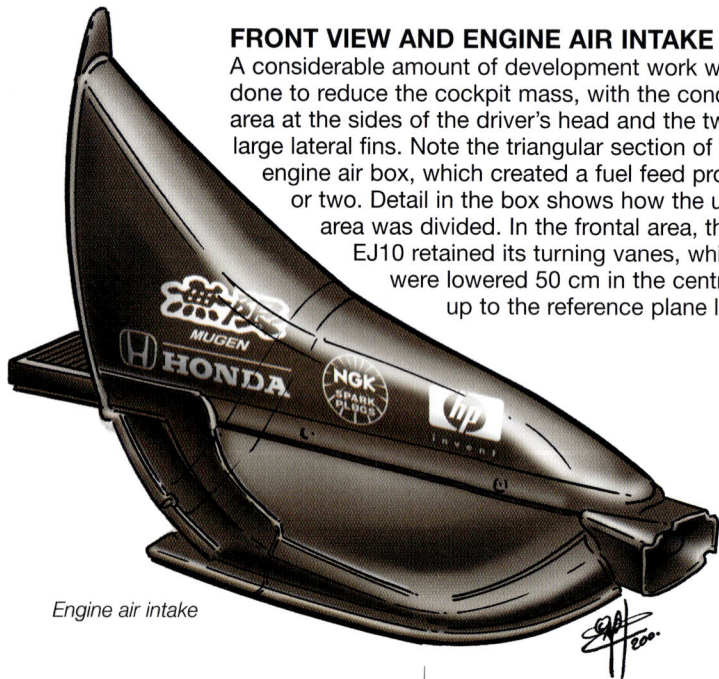

Engine air intake

COCKPIT

Much controversy was created at the opening race by the presence of the fins (1) at the sides of the cockpit: they were later banned by the Federation with a more precise regulation, as described in the New Regulations chapter. Note the presence of fins (2) also in the frontal area of the chassis, which was very low in the central zone, with a kind of faring for the cockpit.

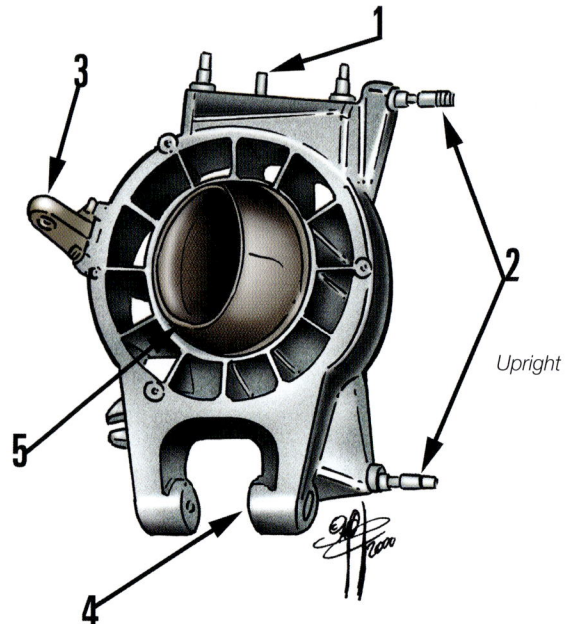

UPRIGHTS

The uprights of the EJ10 were cast. 1) Upper wishbone mounts through a plate that was also used to modify the camber.
2) Brake caliper mounts.
3) Steering linkage anchorage.
4) Lower wishbone mount.
5) As from the GP of Belgium, Jordan eliminated the brake cooling vents for qualifying, cutting out the sphere usually located at the centre of the upright.

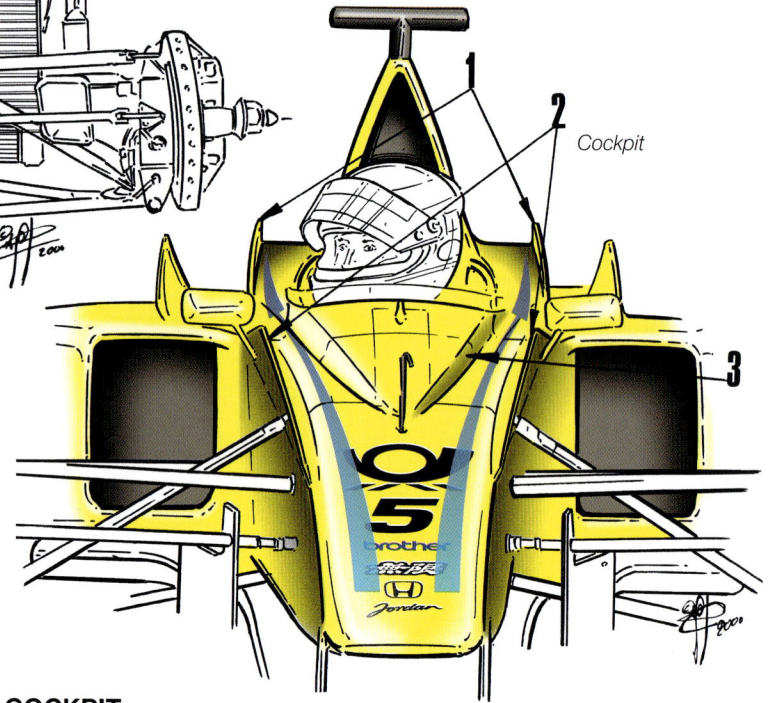

Upright

ARROWS

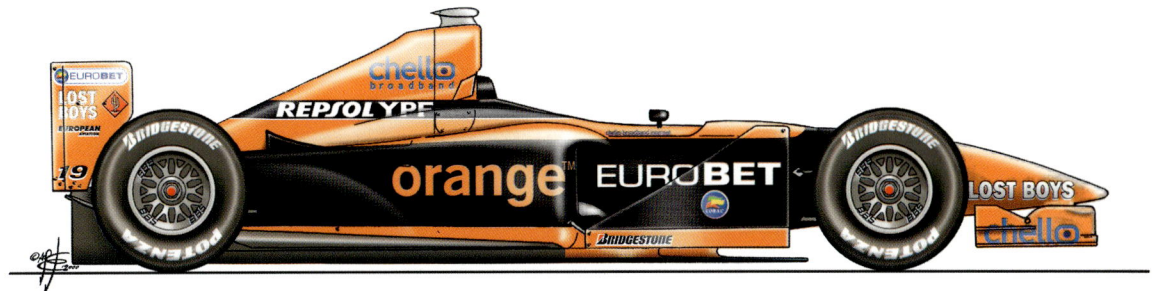

To Arrows as well as Minardi goes the credit for having enlivened the technical panorama of the 2000 season, which was almost devoid of new developments. The team's A21 car was decidedly against the trend, starting with bringing back a pull-rod lay-out for the front suspension, which was last fitted to a Formula One car, the Lotus 102 B, back in 1992. Designed by Mike Caughlan with aerodynamics by Eghbal Hamidy, the A21 revealed itself to be very fast, but not so reliable, having finished just 13 times in 34 starts, due to technical problems concentrated primarily on the gearbox, which still used the carbon fibre box designed two years earlier by John Barnard. The shortest wheelbase car in F1 – 3010 mm – the Arrows was penalised by the limited size of its fuel tank, which only held 122 litres, particularly in races like the GP of Canada, where fuel consumption determines race strategy. At the first event of the season in Australia, the A21 was considered irregular in the dimensions of the driver's head protection zone at the sides of the cockpit, which was immediately raised by the adoption of an interim solution in time for qualifying and later modified for the second race in the calendar, in Brazil. The car was one of the most unreliable of the season – beaten only by Prost. The gearbox broke no less than 6 times.

PULL-ROD SUSPENSION

The Arrows A21 brought back to Formula One the pull-rod lay-out for the front suspension. The last time that was seen was in 1992 on the front end of the Lotus 102 B, as mentioned in the "Suspension" chapter. The system's links were made in steel.

GP OF BRAZIL

The steering linkage was modified for the GP of Brazil, it having broken in Australia. In practice, the titanium content was increased to keep the carbon fibre element away from the heat of the disc brakes. Note the slightly low position of the mount of the upright linkage.

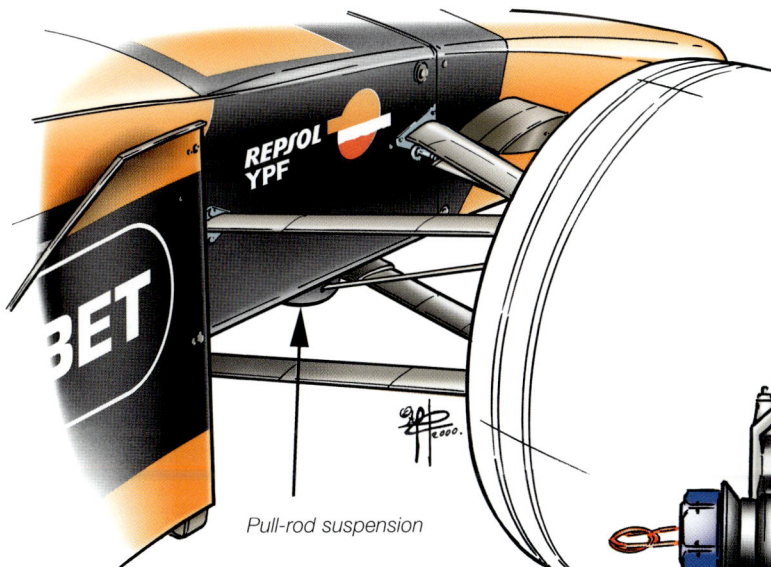

Pull-rod suspension

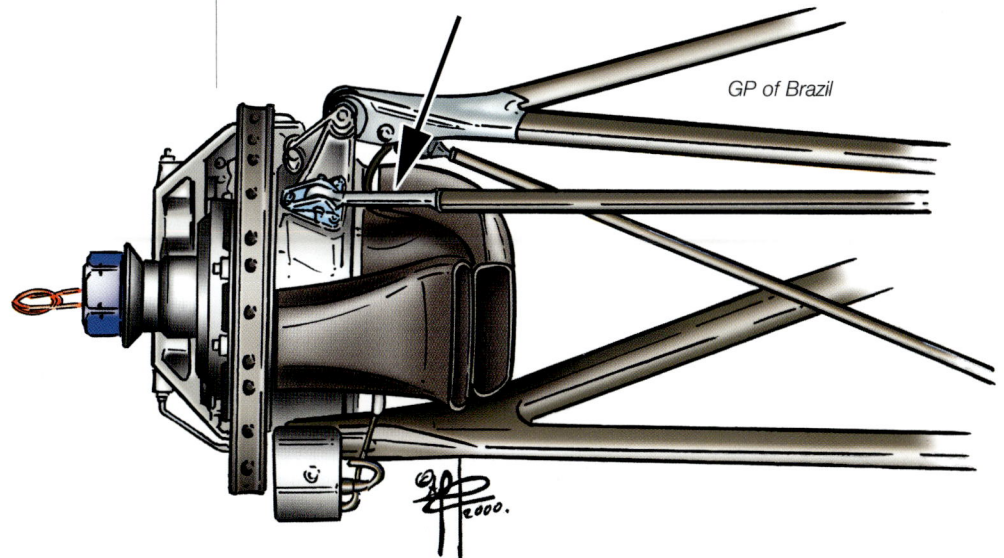

GP of Brazil

REAR BRAKE CALIPERS

Together with Minardi and Ferrari, Arrows was one of the three teams to use the semi-prone position for the rear brake calipers, with the clear intention of reducing the centre of gravity.

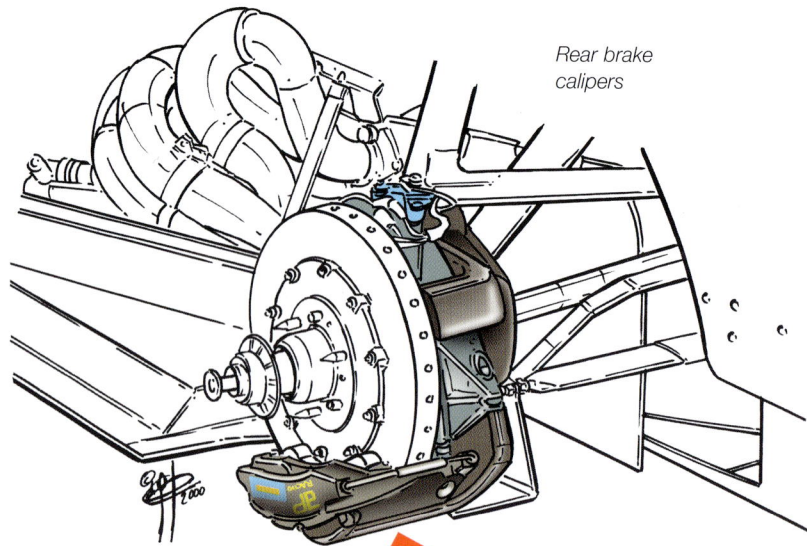

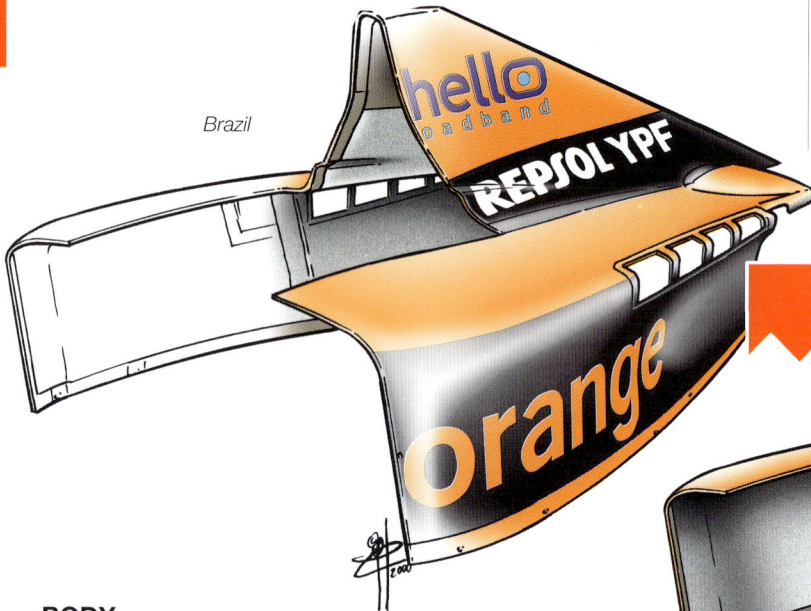

Rear brake calipers

Brazil

BODY

Different bodies were used during the season that comprised different solutions by which to improve heat dissipation. The drawings show the standard version with small, semi-horizontal fins and one with many vents with which to increase the radiators' hot air dispersal area: the latter was used in Brazil, Hungary and Malaysia.

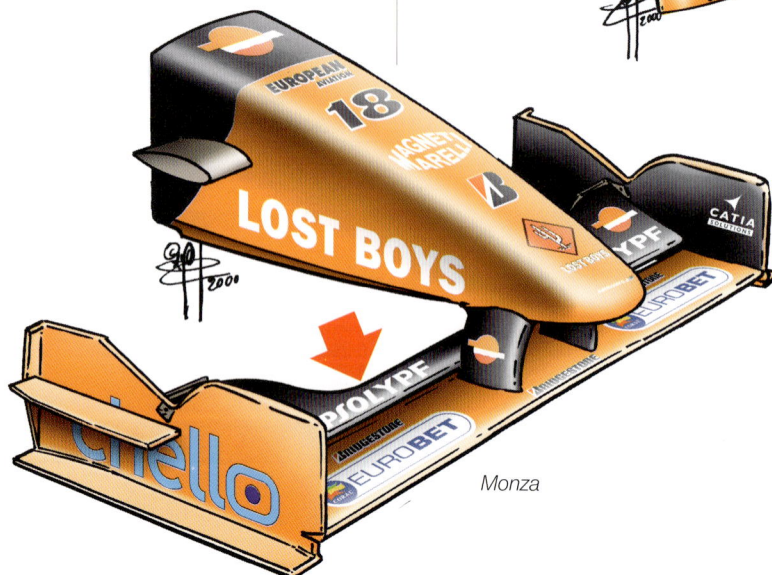

Standard

MONZA

The Arrows was the car with the smallest front wing for ultra-fast tracks like Hockenheim and Monza. The drawings show the reduced dimensions of the flap's chord, comparing it with the length of the end plates.

Monza

SAUBER

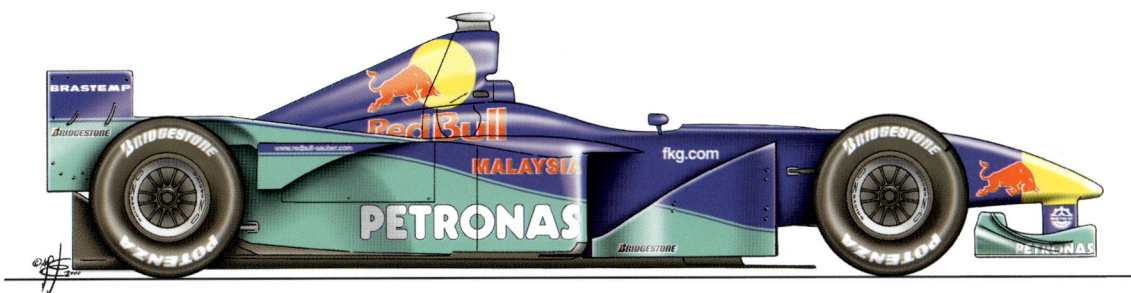

Something more than eighth in the constructors' championship was expected of Sauber, if for no other reasons than the C 19 was the fourth car to have been designed by the Swiss team, powered by the same type of engine, the 10-cylinder Ferrari, and could rely on a certain continuity of development. The C19 was a simple evolution of the

was the only car of the 2000 season without its oil reservoir in front of the engine, due to the fact that it used the Ferrari 049 power unit that was without this feature. The 2000 season immediately started badly for Sauber, with two consecutive "slip-ups" in the first two races. In Australia, Salo's car was disqualified because the end plates of its

front wing were two centimetres closer than they should have been to the front wheels, and in Brazil the team withdrew its cars before the start, because of the umpteenth rear wing support breakage, a problem that plunged the development of the car into crisis to privilege the structural aspect. The C19 included an aerodynamics packaged with three different front wings and, from the GP of Great Britain, modified diffusers that were further changed for the GPs of Germany and Belgium; new sidepods with bigger air intakes appeared at the GP of France. In the second half of the season, Sauber used a 10 kg lighter car for qualifying, four kg being saved on the rear end alone by

titanium-boxed uprights, suspension arms in carbon fibre, the pedals and body lightened. In the last two races, Sauber was able to field its cars with 35 kg of ballast.

FRONT SUSPENSION
Sauber introduced a new split anchorage point for the front arm of the suspension's lower wishbone. In place of the central fin, which interfered with the airflow in the lower area of the car, there were two lateral protrusions (1). 2) Faring of the push rod mount on the chassis. 3) From the GP of France, a 10 kg lighter version of the C19 was used for qualifying: it had suspension arms (3) in carbon fibre and uprights in titanium.

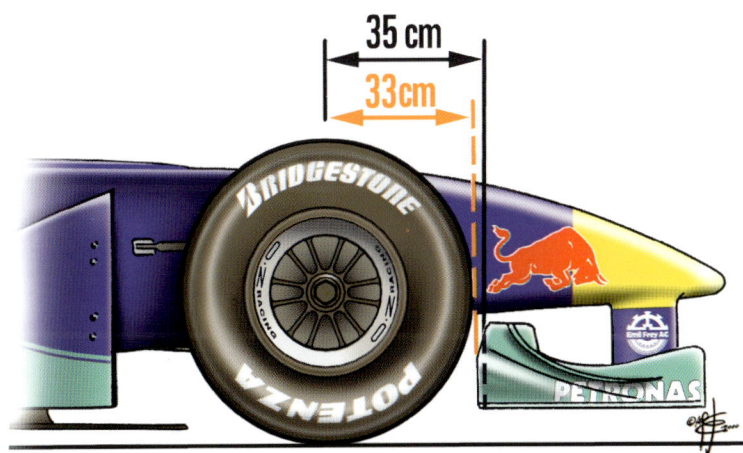

previous year's car, with the single new feature of a different shaped chassis in the lower area, with split mounts for the front suspension's wishbones. A development that improved the air flow quality in the lower area, no longer disturbed by the central fin that contains the unified mounting point of the lower wishbones of the other cars. The longitudinal, tipped gearbox with seven speeds was new. The C19

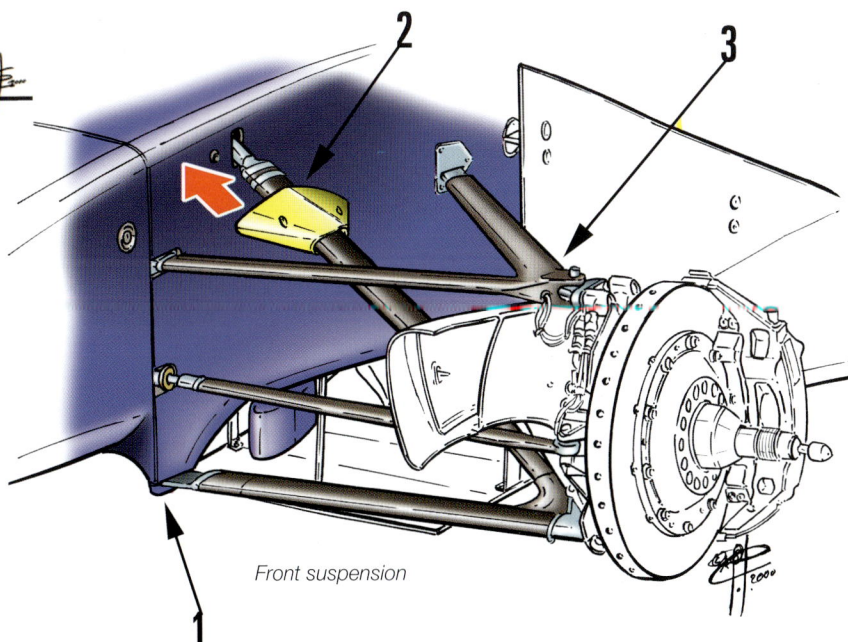

Front suspension

FERRARI ENGINE

Sauber used the 048 version of the 10-cylinder Ferrari engine, which meant they could not adopt a central oil reservoir between the engine and the monocoque. The Swiss team was the only one with its reservoir still between the gearbox and engine.

SIDEPODS

A comparison between the old sidepod air intake, which was narrower than the new, the latter being larger, particularly in the upper area: the new intake was introduced for the GP of France and permitted partial derivation, depending on track necessity.

France

Standard

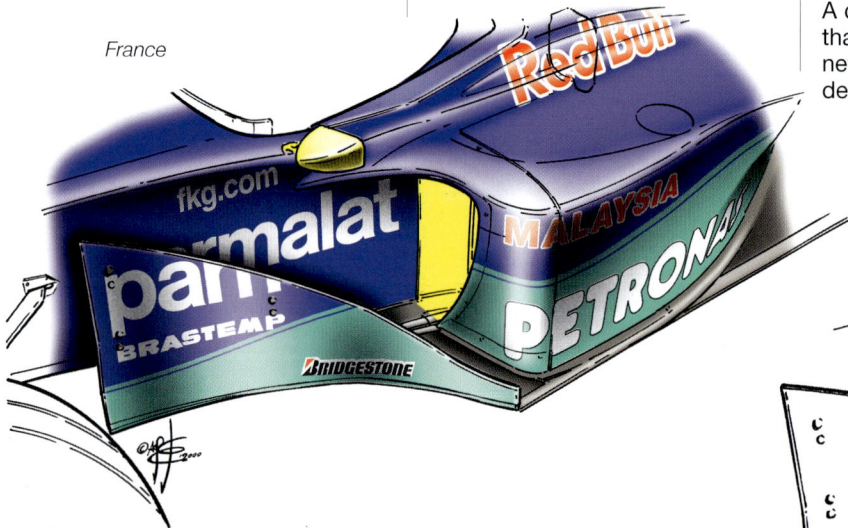

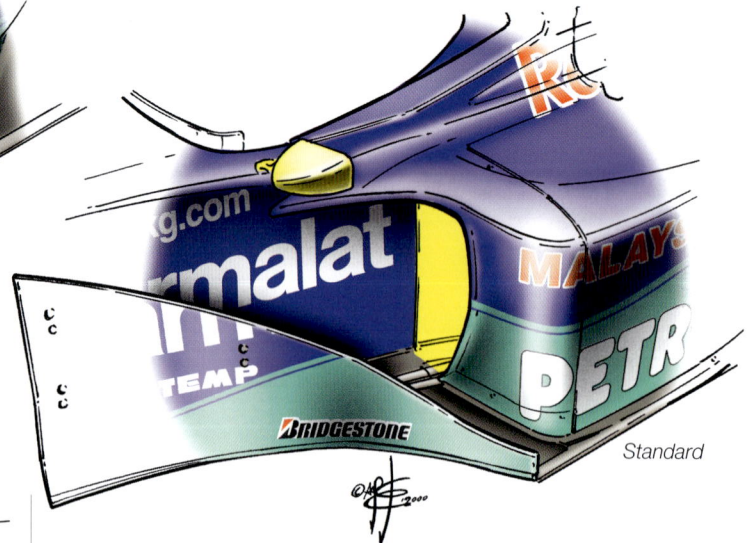

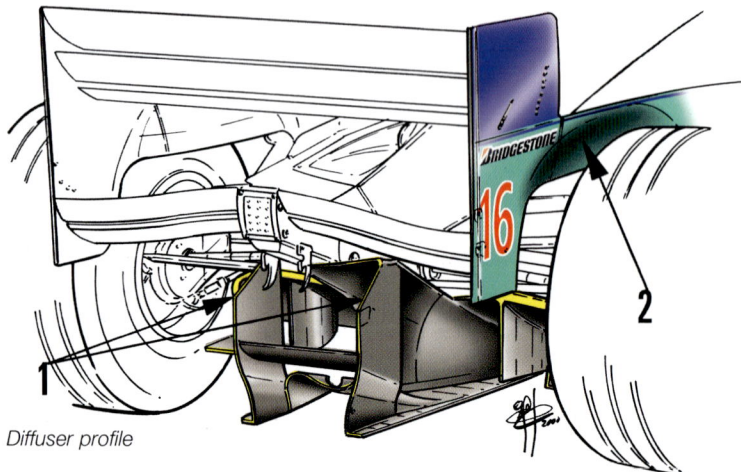

Diffuser profile

DIFFUSER PROFILE

The first modification for the GP of Great Britain was made to the central section of the diffuser profile, which was cut (1) up high. Note the long extensions (2) of connection between the fins in front of the wheels and the rear wing. More modifications for the GP of Belgium: the lateral channels were given a small Stewart-Arrows type flap, as mentioned in the "Underbodies" chapter.

JAGUAR

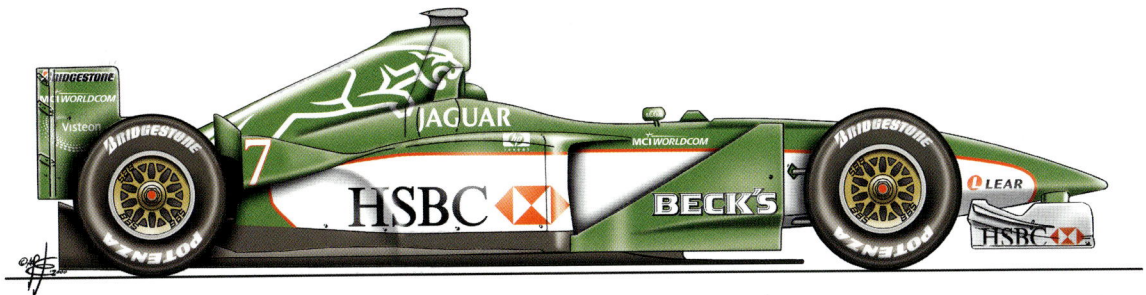

After having acquired Stewart, a team that rose to fourth in the '99 constructors championship and won its first race - the Grand Prix of Europe – the previous year with Johnny Herbert, Jaguar certainly did not make a grand entrance in Formula One motor racing. The R1, the first F1 Jaguar, was only able to come a miserable ninth in the table, with just four points by the end of a disappointing season. The only result of any importance was Irvine's fourth place at Monaco. The British team competed with a splendidly prepared car in its immaculate, brightly coloured livery, but one that was a failure from a technical point of view. In practice, the car was a little changed copy of the previous year's McLaren: it reiterated the Woking car's low nose lay-out, the shape of the sidepods and engine air intake. The only

new developments were concentrated on the rear axle and comprised a new and too complicated lay-out of the rear suspension, plus a unified system for the engine and gearbox lubricating circuit, which was the cause of the mechanical breakdown of those two major components. Jaguar suffered eight retirements, divided equally between the failure of the engine and gearbox, before it returned to the old system of separate oil system. Of the '99 Stewart, the Jaguar retained the central position of the oil reservoir which, it should be remembered, was introduced by the Scottish team in '98. The engine, a further evolution of the revolutionary 10-cylinder used in '99, blunted expectations to the point that it obliged the heads of Ford to backtrack on performance in an effort to find greater reliability. Fuel tank capacity was

increased beyond that of the '99 car from 118 to 135 litres to provide greater tactical freedom in races and avoid additional refuelling, which had penalised Stewart at the Grand Prix of Canada. The high blow in the

upper area of the engine cover was retained: it is a system first used by Ferrari at the '98 GP of Spain and subsequently taken up first by Stewart at that year's GP of Austria and then Prost at the following GP of Belgium.

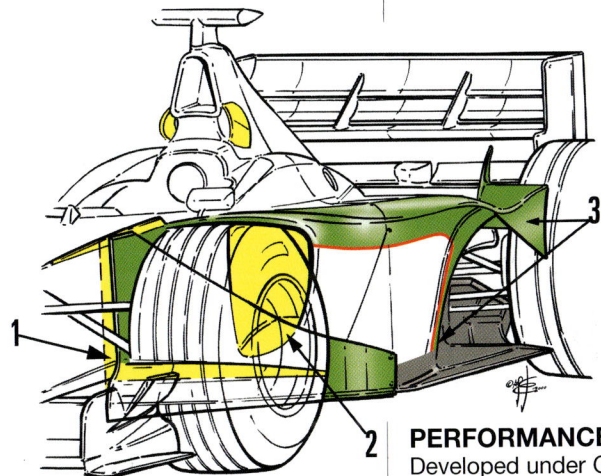

PERFORMANCE

Developed under Gary Anderson, the R1 was an evolution of the '99 McLaren, with large barge boards (1) behind the front wheels, combined with a markedly raised air intake (2) at the sides, characterised in front of the rear wheels by large fins (3) and a deeply concave zone down low.

GP OF GERMANY

Instead of barge boards, at the GP of Germany small fins appeared in front of the sidepods, which were combined with turning vanes inside the front wheels that were clearly from the Jordan school of thought. As well as being used at Hockenheim, this configuration was also adopted for the GPs of Hungary and Belgium.

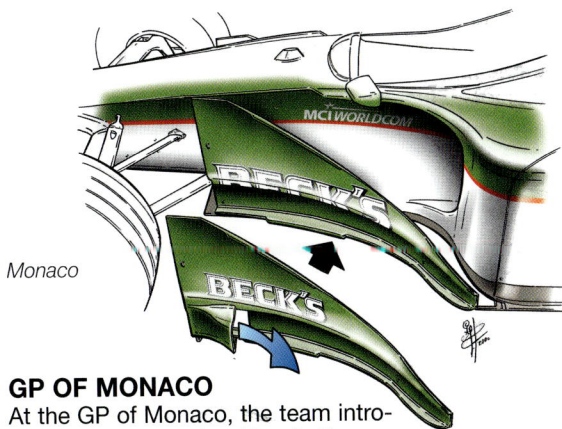

Monaco

GP OF MONACO

At the GP of Monaco, the team introduced barge boards with a further vent in the lower area (separated in the drawing) adopted by McLaren and later BAR and Minardi; those barge boards were used at Monaco, Canada, Austria, Monza, the USA, Japan and Malaysia.

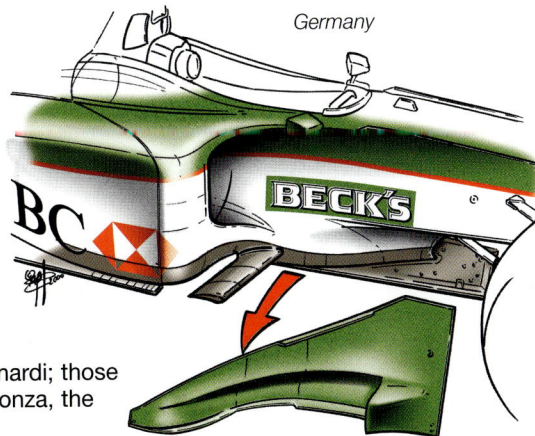

Germany

DOUBLE FINS

A new engine cover with Prost-like double fins made its debut on the Jaguar at the GP of Monaco. The first (1) was highly advanced and mounted above the sidepods; the second (2) started down low and ended right in front of the rear wheels, and had a notably curved plane.

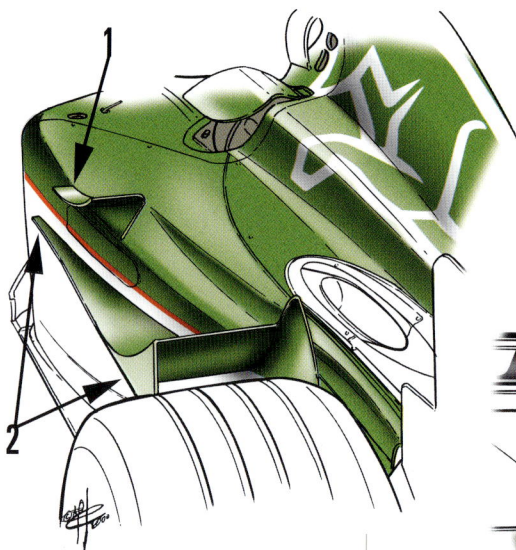

Double fins

GP OF BELGIUM

A new diffuser was introduced at the GP of Belgium: it had much inclined lateral channels and a large horizontal section in the lower area of the vertical end plates (shown in yellow) near the wheels.

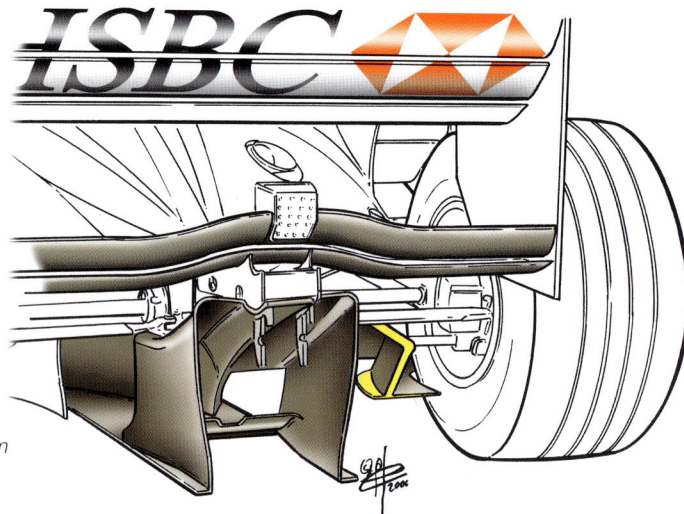

Belgium

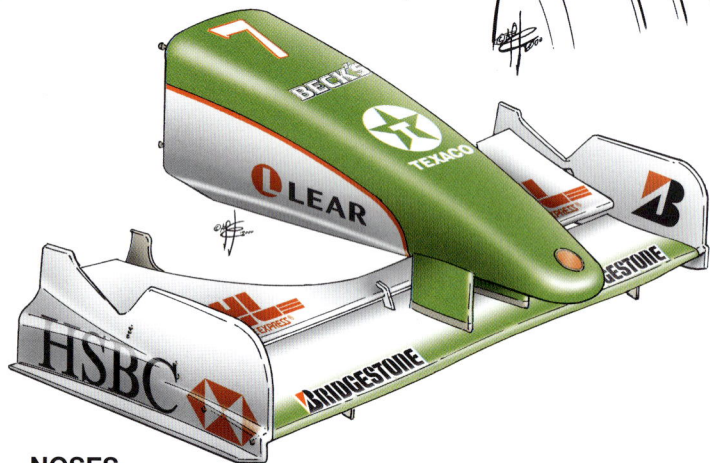

NOSES

The team tried different types of noses, both with and without fins on the outer parts of the end-plates, depending on the width of the planes. In Brazil, Herbert used a nose with arrow-shaped planes, which was later dropped in favour of the standard unit. The drawing on the right shows a nose without lateral fins but with middle plates.

GEARBOX

The rear suspension was new and the only system with shock absorbers (1) placed down low in a gearbox niche and connected to the suspension rocker by another (2). The torsion bars (3) were directly attached up high near the first rocker, to which was connected a knife edge push rod. 4) All suspension arm mounts were knife edge. 5) Jaguar retained the multi-link system, instead of adopting a lower wishbone.

Brazil

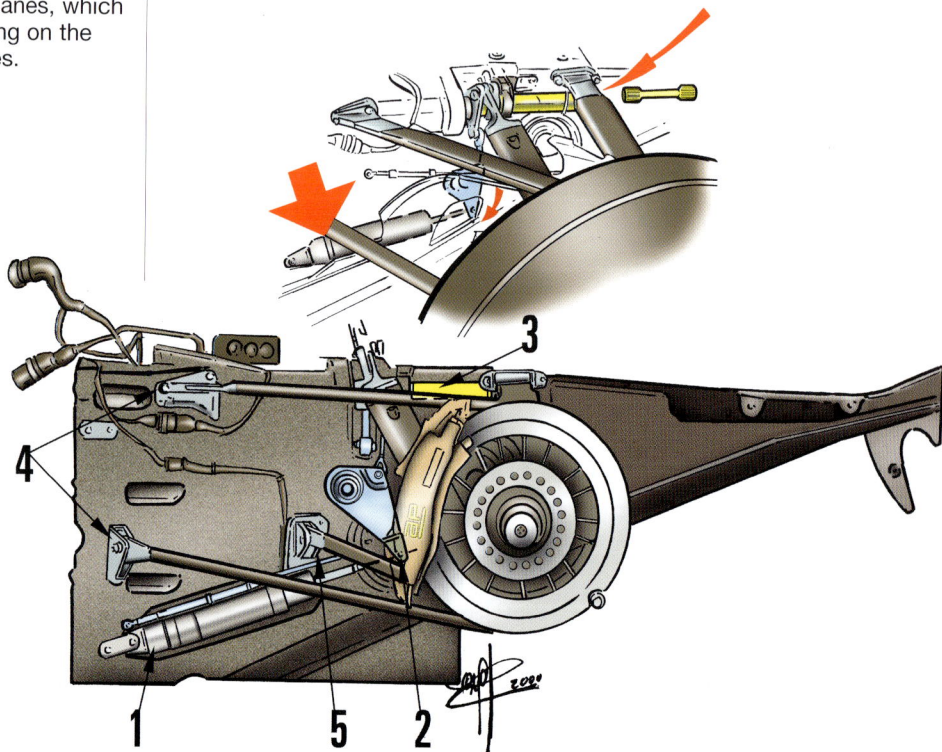

MINARDI

The Minardi M02 was one of the most interesting cars of the 2000 season, a real concentration of new developments, sufficient to justify the presence of details of the car in almost every chapter of this analysis. To Minardi goes the credit for introducing one of the few innovations of the season: a gearbox made for the first time in cast titanium by CRP of Modena, a company that had already produced titanium uprights for the '99 season using the same technique. With a wheelbase of just 3020 mm, the M02 was the second shortest car of the year after the Arrows, but it had a 142 litre capacity fuel tank compared with Arrows' 122. The aerodynamic set-up was refined in every detail, from the highly tapered square nose, squared sidepods with their elaborate end plates in front of the rear wheels, where there was the exit for the radiator's hot air, the concave protective areas of the cockpit at the sides of the driver's head – a technique adopted by Ferrari, Jordan and, in a less accentuated way, McLaren – and new features of the car's rear aerodynamics, which are described in the "Underbodies" chapter. The new means of enabling the driver to more easily enter and exit the cockpit was imaginative: two concave apertures scooped in two sections out of the frontal area of the cockpit for the easy passage of the driver's knees (see the "Cockpits" chapter). The suspension system was derived from that of the previous year's car, retaining unchanged the then innovative lay-out, especially at the rear. The low position of the brake calipers was also used again at the rear of the M02, a system that was also adopted by Ferrari and Arrows for 2000.

PRESENTATION

One of the most obvious differences between the 2000 and '99 cars were the exhausts (1), which exited in the upper area. The hot air vents (2) were placed in the upper area, inside sophisticated fins. The engine cover was so low that there were two ample pieces of faring (3) to cover the suspension, the rear (4) of which was from the '99 car.

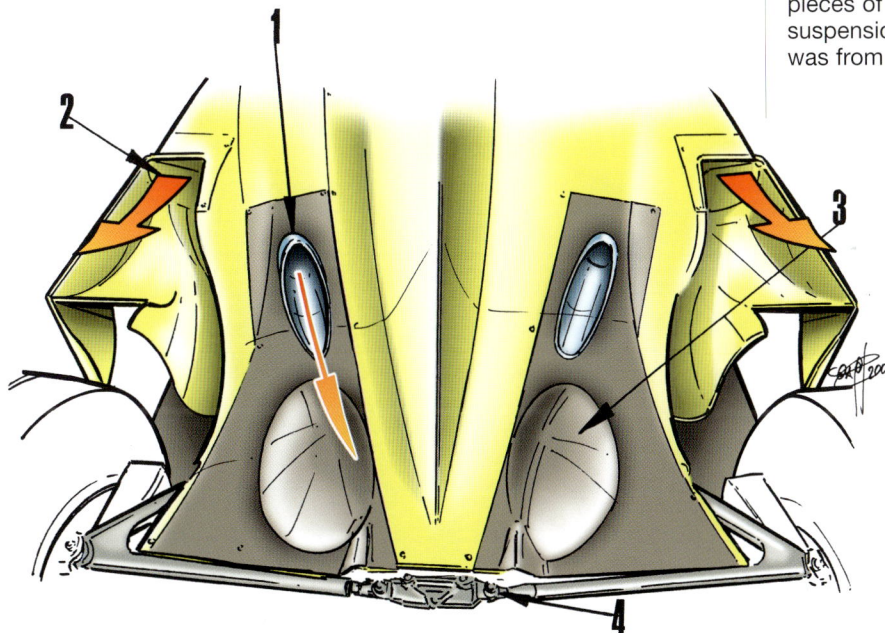

UPRIGHT

Minardi was the first team to adopt cast titanium uprights, made by the Modena company CRP, which produced a notable weight saving. They were single units, apart from the steering linkage, indicated by the arrow.

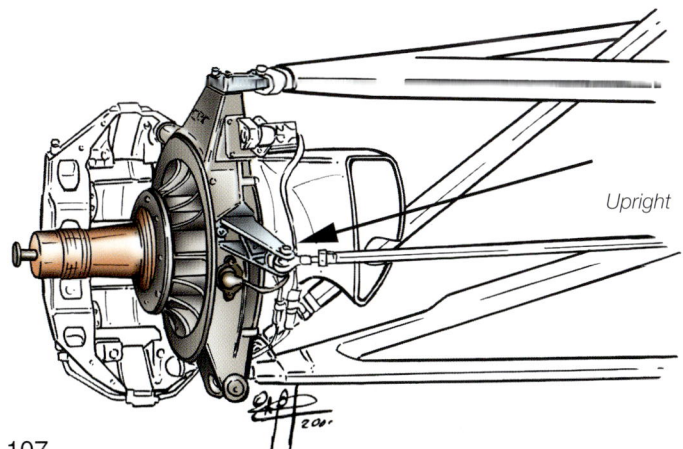

Upright

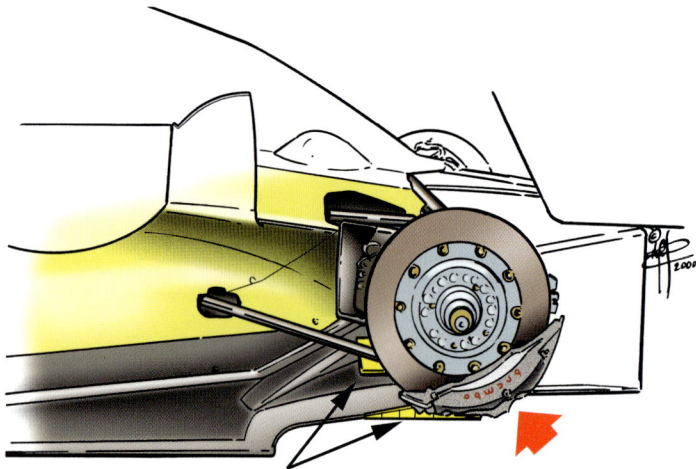

BRAKE CALIPERS

Minardi was also first to introduce the low down position for the rear brake calipers on the '99 car. Obviously, the development was retained for the M02, a feature that was copied by Ferrari and Arrows.

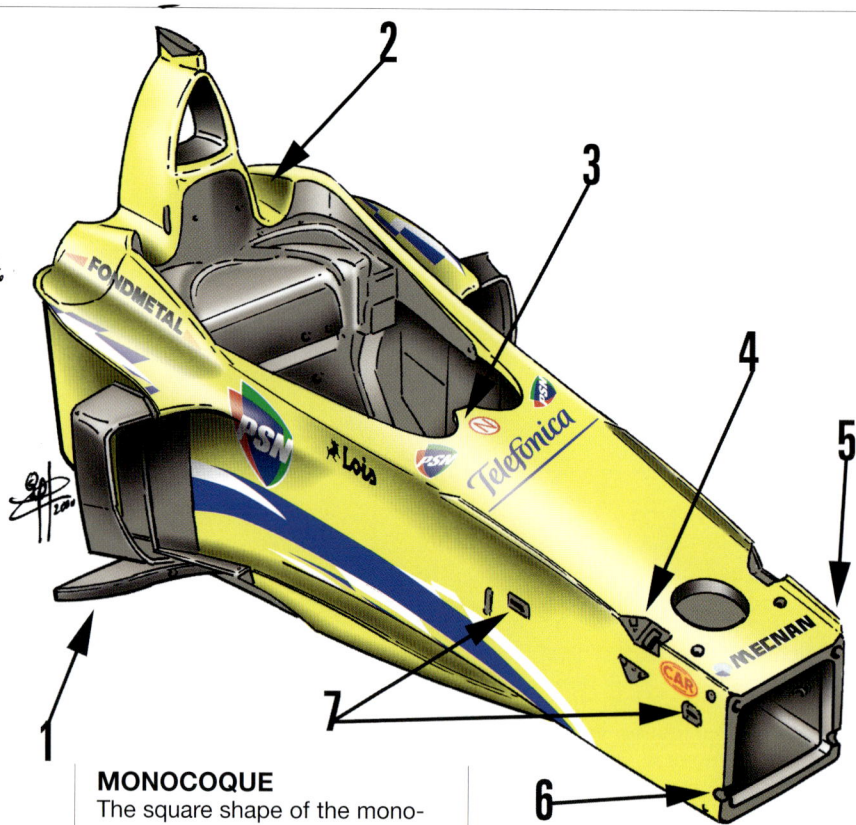

MONOCOQUE

The square shape of the monocoque was very interesting as it contained many new ideas. 1) The protection at the sides of the chassis was extremely low. 2) Unusually, Ferrari, Jordan, McLaren and Minardi all made the same decision: to make the inside of the protection area on both sides of the driver's head concave to recoup part of the flow towards the rear wing. 3) The idea of scooping out the front of the cockpit opening to enable the driver's knees to slip into the car more easily was unique. 4) Aperture for the front suspension rocker. 5) Fins to reduce chassis dimensions. 6) The steering column mount. 7) Mounts for the suspension wishbones.

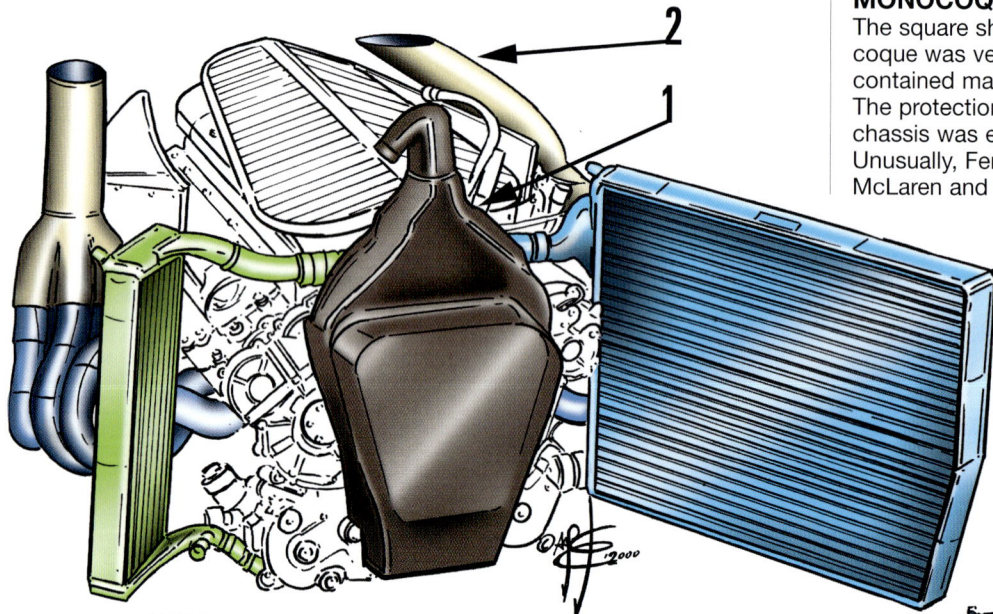

Engine installation

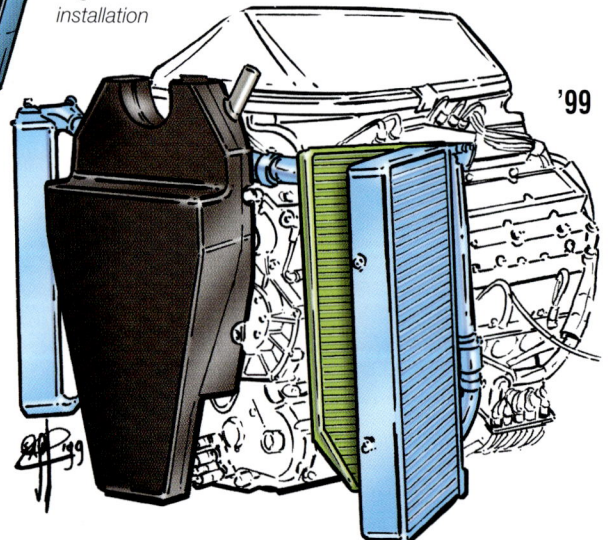

'2000

'99

ENGINE INSTALLATION

Minardi had to retain the heavy yet not very powerful Ford engine, as supplied to Stewart in '98. Note the difference in installation, with the oil reservoir (1) bigger, the radiators placed differently, with the one for oil on the right and the exhausts (2) that blew high.

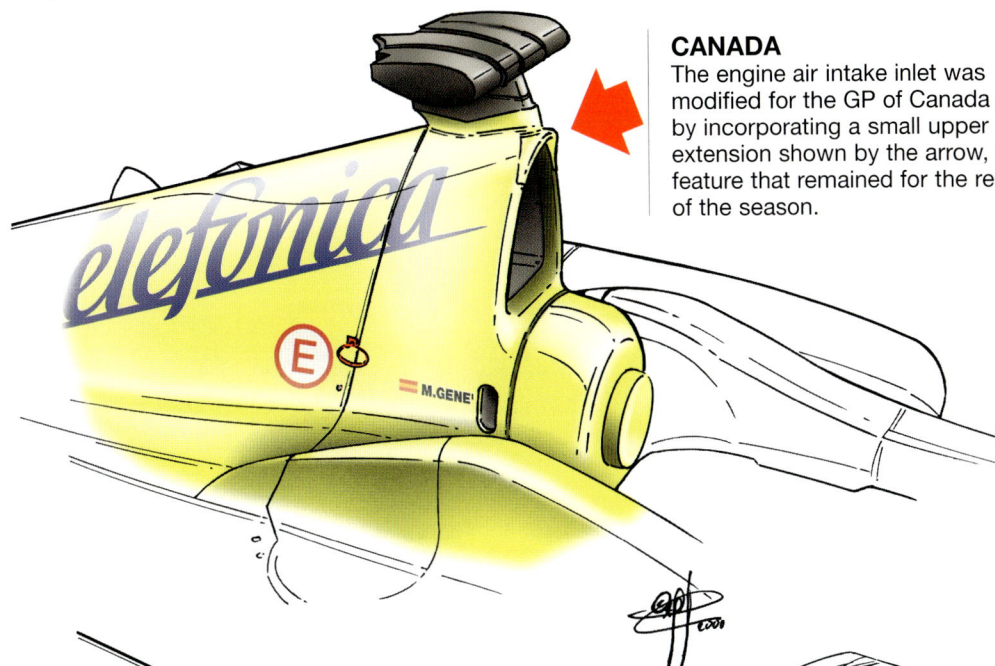

CANADA

The engine air intake inlet was modified for the GP of Canada by incorporating a small upper extension shown by the arrow, a feature that remained for the rest of the season.

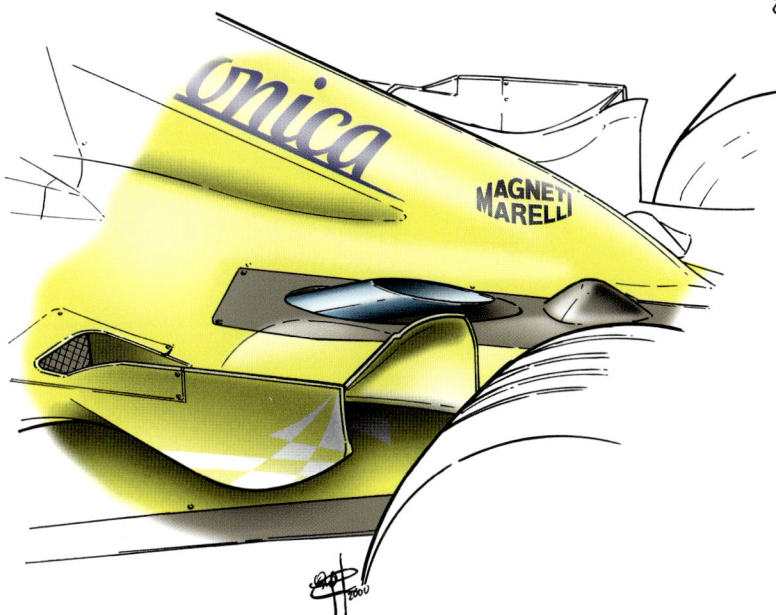

BARGE BOARD LAY-OUT

At the GP of Europe, the barge boards behind the front wheels were modified. They provided a McLaren-style low down blowing effect, were longer (2) and they had a small horizontal Gurney flap (1) of the McLaren school in the upper area.

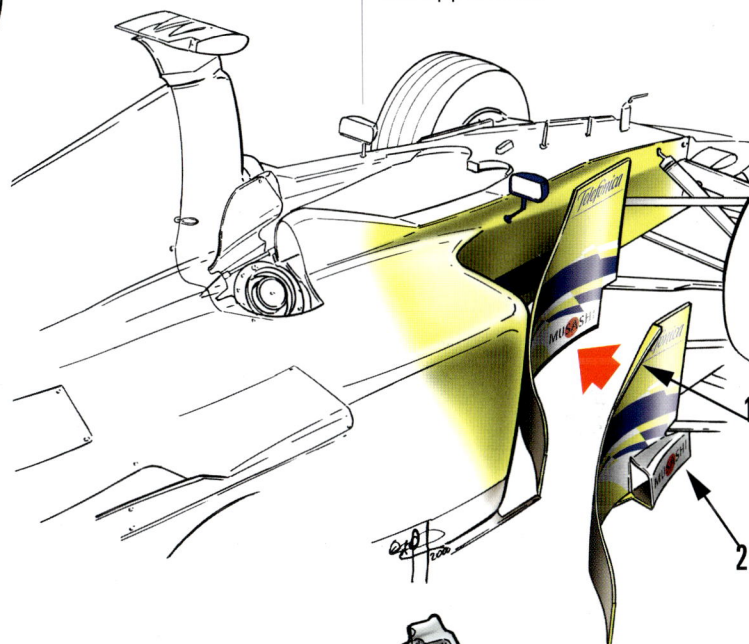

LONG EXHAUSTS

The exhaust terminals low on the sluggish 10-cylinder Ford engine were elongated for tracks that demanded more power curve and exited from the upper body.

GEARBOX

The merit of introducing a cast titanium gearbox went to Minardi, thanks to CRP of Modena, a company that also supplied BAR with uprights made by the same technique. The new gearbox made its debut at the GP of Spain on Gené's car after only 340 miles of testing and saved over 5 kg in weight, as explained in the "New Features and Trends" chapter.

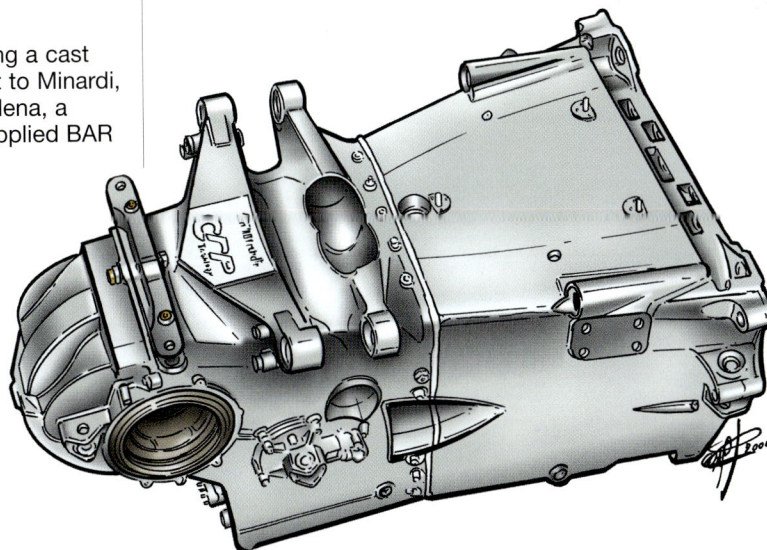

109

PROST

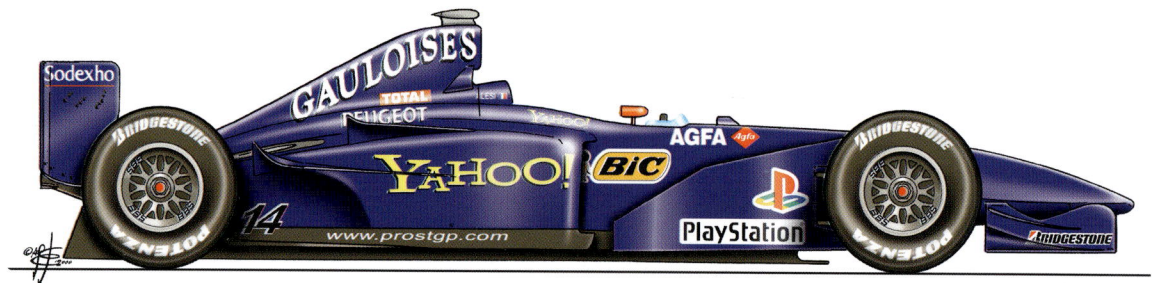

It would have been difficult to have done worse than the first two Prost cars which, as well as being uncompetitive, were uselessly unconventional. Yet the AP03, once again designed under the direction of Loic Bigois, was able to take the team down to the last place in the constructors' championship table, in spite of adopting more traditional technical features. In '99, the voluminous and long AP02, with a 3240 mm wheelbase against 3095 mm of the AP03, scraped into seventh

place regardless of a multitude of faults. Prost also took top place in the negative table as the team that covered the least race laps. Its cars finished just 10 times from 33 starts and suffered no less than 17 retirements for technical reasons: seven of them were due to its unreliable Peugeot engine which, among other things, had the lowest revolutions per minute of all the 2000 season power plants. The AP03 was the only car to have a rear suspension element – the rear arm - that interfered with the air flow of the

diffuser's lateral channels. Another unique feature, one for which the team cannot be blamed, was Alesi being the only driver to have a third pedal for the clutch, after having competed in the first two races with the control on the steering wheel. The disappointing lack of progress during the season, peppered with many arguments between the team's management, the drivers and the Peugeot bosses, exploded at the GP of France with a clamorous protest by the Peugeot managers (delay in the start-up of the

engine before testing) that led to an early announcement before the end of the season of the French car manufacturer's retirement from F1. Not long before the turning point at the GP of Monaco, another divorce took place: this time from Alan Jenkins, ex-Stewart designer. In spite of that, though, a number of aerodynamic modifications introduced by Prost were clearly of Stewart origin, among them the front wing brought in at Monaco and the rear that debuted in Canada.

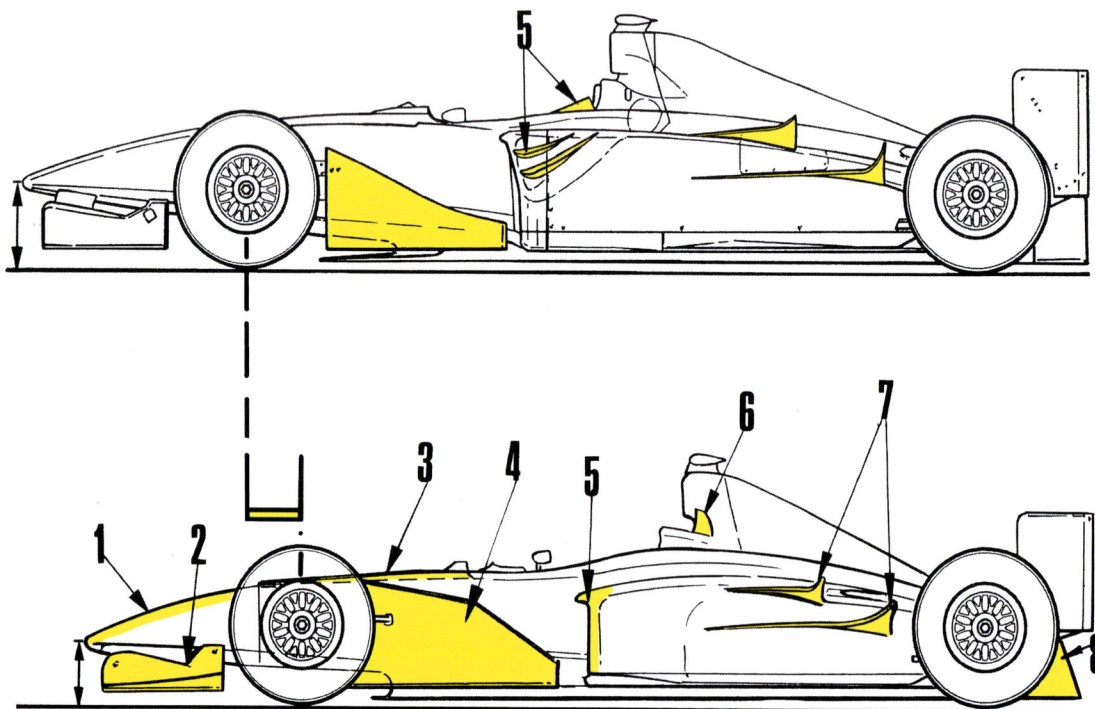

SIDE VIEWS

Compared to the AP02's above, the planes of the new AP03 2000 car below had notably reduced dimensions: 145 mm smaller. 1) The nose was lower and more tapered. 2) New end plates of the front wing were significantly developed during the course of the season. 3) The upper part of the chassis had imitation fins to reduce the section. 4) Behind the front wheels there were McLaren-type barge boards. 5) The sidepods were shorter, decidedly lower and, in particular, without the strange fins of the '99 car. 6) Small fins were applied to the sides of the engine air intake to comply with regulations. 7) The double fins remained in front of the rear wheels. 8) The diffuser was shorter and squarer.